TALK AND TEXTUAL PRODUCTION
IN MEDIEVAL ENGLAND

INTERVENTIONS: NEW STUDIES
IN MEDIEVAL CULTURE
Ethan Knapp, Series Editor

TALK AND TEXTUAL PRODUCTION IN MEDIEVAL ENGLAND

∽

Marisa Libbon

THE OHIO STATE UNIVERSITY PRESS
COLUMBUS

Copyright © 2021 by The Ohio State University.
All rights reserved.

Library of Congress Cataloging-in-Publication Data
Names: Libbon, Marisa, author.
Title: Talk and textual production in medieval England / Marisa Libbon.
Other titles: Interventions: new studies in medieval culture.
Description: Columbus : The Ohio State University Press, [2021] | Series: Interventions: new studies in medieval culture | Includes bibliographical references and index. | Summary: "Using the medieval accounts of Richard the Lionheart's life and stories of Charlemagne, Roland, John de Warenne, and other figures, Libbon argues that public talk was a collaborative mechanism that produced texts and that it was a fundamental context for those texts' transmission and reception"—Provided by publisher.
Identifiers: LCCN 2020048202 | ISBN 9780814214701 (cloth) | ISBN 0814214703 (cloth) | ISBN 9780814281147 (ebook) | ISBN 0814281141 (ebook)
Subjects: LCSH: English literature—Middle English, 1100–1500—History and criticism. | English literature—Middle English, 1100–1500—Criticism, Textual. | Public speaking. | Conversation—History. | Manuscripts, Medieval.
Classification: LCC PR260 .L53 2021 | DDC 820.9/001—dc23
LC record available at https://lccn.loc.gov/2020048202

Other identifiers: ISBN 9780814257883 (paper) | ISBN 0814257887 (paper)

Cover design by Susan Zucker
Text design by Juliet Williams
Type set in Junicode

For Mom

CONTENTS

Acknowledgments		ix
Abbreviations		xv
Note on Translations and Transcriptions		xvii
INTRODUCTION	Tuning Our Ears	1
ONE	Local Talk and the Retrospective Text	15
TWO	Public Talk and Legal Fictions	61
THREE	Talking Pictures in Fourteenth-Century London	107
FOUR	The Conversant Codex	139
FIVE	English Rumor and the Modular Manuscript	175
EPILOGUE	Turning Up the Archive	211
Bibliography		215
Index		237

ACKNOWLEDGMENTS

THIS BOOK is in part about what people say about the past: their recollections of who and what shaped them, and the documentation of that rich inheritance. I have looked forward to recalling and documenting the same here for a long time.

Without access to the manuscripts, the work of a medievalist would not be possible. I am therefore enormously grateful to those institutions that preserve our textual archive and welcomed me during the many years I was at work on this book. In particular, I wish to thank the staffs of the Advocates Library, especially Andrea Longson; the Bodleian Library, Oxford, with extremely belated and heartfelt thanks to Jean-Pierre Maillon; the British Library; Cambridge University Library; Christ Church, Oxford; the College of Arms; Gloucestershire Archives; Gonville and Caius College, Cambridge, especially Mark Statham, for his patience and generosity; the Huntington Library; the Morgan Library; the National Archives; the National Library of Scotland; the Parker Library of Corpus Christi College, Cambridge, with particular thanks to Anne McLaughlin; and the Wren Library of Trinity College, Cambridge.

I would also like to thank the Governing Body of Christ Church, Oxford, the city of Carpentras, the Bibliothèque-musée Inguimbertine, and the Institut de recherche et d'histoire des textes for permission to reproduce images in their collections. Portions of chapter 4 appeared in a different form in *The*

Auchinleck Manuscript: New Perspectives, ed. Susanna Fein (York, 2016). I am grateful to Boydell and Brewer for permission to use that work here. Research for the book in its earliest stage was supported by the Schallek Fellowship from the Medieval Academy of America and the Richard III Society, American Branch. The invitation to be a visiting scholar at Trinity College, Cambridge, made some final work at libraries possible in the summer of 2019. I am grateful to Micha Lazarus for the invitation to Trinity, and to the Medieval Academy, the Richard III Society, and Trinity College, Cambridge, for their generous support.

I have had the great fortune to be trained by pathbreaking scholars and remarkable teachers at the University of California, Berkeley, and at Oxford. As I advance in this profession, my admiration for them only grows. Berkeley's English Department fundamentally shaped me as a person, scholar, and teacher. I owe a great intellectual debt to, especially, Elizabeth Abel, John Bishop, Stephen Booth, Kathleen Donegan, Marcial González, Kevis Goodman (in whose class I first read Chaucer), Geoffrey G. O'Brien, and John Shoptaw. I have owed Lyn Hejinian my thanks for years and years. Studying poetry with her influenced how I think about form and language, both in my scholarship and in the classroom, in ways that I am still discovering. Steven Justice encouraged my earliest interests in memory and medieval literature, and asked me, when I was still a very young scholar, what I wanted to sound like on the page. That question stayed with me. Answering it has become lifelong work. I treasure Maura Nolan's counsel and friendship. Her clearsightedness on an early draft of my book prospectus sharpened not just the prospectus but the book itself.

That I arrived at Oxford to study medieval English literature when I did is proof that the universe was taking care of me. I am profoundly grateful to Helen Cooper, Vincent Gillespie, Anne Hudson, and Tony Hunt for how rigorously they trained me and for how seriously they took my ideas and ambitions. This book is meager repayment for everything they gave me. The questions that Ralph Hanna taught me to ask about books and their contents, or, rather, the methods he taught me for arriving at those questions and pursuing answers to them, are with me every time I sit down to work. His guidance over the years has been a real gift to me, as have his patience, honesty, and humor. It is a tremendous pleasure to thank him here.

Jennifer Miller, Joseph Duggan, and Jeffrey Knapp guided and supported this project in its earliest stages. They responded to my imperfect ideas with precision and incisiveness, and they saw what I was trying to do long before I myself saw it. Jeff Knapp made my ideas better without making them his own. That is a rare talent. The comments he gave me on the earliest draft of the manuscript remained essential to me through its final revision. I had hoped Joe Duggan would see this book; he told me that I could write it, and I believed him. His faith in me buoyed me continuously—more than he knew. He was a superb teacher and a formidable scholar, and I miss him. More than anyone else, Jennifer Miller has influenced the way that I think and work and teach. Her belief in my intellectual potential, and her insistence that I work to fulfill it, altered the course of my life. For over two decades she has been my teacher, mentor, and friend. Her intellectual curiosity, creativity, and daring continue to inspire me. I am proud to have been her student.

Many colleagues and friends supported the writing of this book and sustained its author. Thanks especially to Arthur Bahr, Chris Bertholf, Nicholas Bertholf, Katharine Breen, Seeta Chaganti, Chris Chism, Betsy Chunko-Dominguez, Rebecca Davis, Jamie DeAngelis, Dietmar Farkas, Susanna Fein, Shannon Gayk, Sharon Goetz, Claire Harman, Chris Jensen, Sjoerd Levelt, Marcelle Maese-Cohen, Ingrid Nelson, Sarah Elliott Novacich, Annalee Rejhon, Tim Sayer, Ian Schneider, Jennifer Sisk, Chris Springer, Jared Stanley, Michael Staunton, Danny Vincent, and Erik Vincent. Paul Strohm's friendship has been one of the great joys of living in New York. His counsel on the process of placing the manuscript and his belief in the project steadied and fortified me at several crucial moments. His generosity is unfailing. Eleanor Johnson's advice has never steered me wrong, and I thank her for supporting this project so vociferously. Swati Rana has taken this long journey from idea to book with me, while writing her own. I could not have asked for a more kindred spirit as my traveling companion. One of the many magical things about Sean Curran is that he always appears when I need him most. I thank him for the willingness with which he puts his brilliant mind to work on my work, and for seeing all of the ghosts. I am indebted to Matthew Fisher for all of the conversations about old and new books, and for always reading "just one more thing." He read most of the book manuscript, and some parts more than once, and it is better for having been under his astute eye. I also wish to thank Bard College's medievalists for their camaraderie and generosity, especially Katherine Boivin, Maria Sachiko Cecire, Karen Sullivan, and David Ungvary.

My colleagues at Bard are remarkable people and scholars. They have supported and inspired this project with their friendship and the example of their own scholarship. I am especially grateful to Alex Benson, Mary Caponegro, Nicole Caso, Omar Cheta, Odile Chilton, Deirdre d'Albertis, Adhaar Noor Desai, Michèle Dominy, Elizabeth Frank, Cole Heinowitz, Michael Ives, Pete L'Official, Ann Lauterbach, Matthew Mutter, Melanie Nicholson, Dina Ramadan, Julia Rosenbaum, Nate Shockey, Erika Switzer, Dominique

Townsend, Olga Voronina, and Thomas Wild. Rob Cioffi, Lauren Curtis, and Miriam Felton-Dansky each read parts of the manuscript, gave me insightful feedback, and more than once restored my sanity. I thank them for taking such good care of me. Christian Crouch has been a sounding board, a sage counselor, and a lifeline. She is a remarkable scholar, colleague, and friend. Her comments on two chapters clarified both prose and argument, and her belief in the value of the project from beginning to end was instrumental in its completion. The friendship and collegiality of Éric Trudel and Marina van Zuylen enriched this book in ways that are nearly impossible to articulate. It is rare in life to encounter one person who sees you clearly and completely. Imagine my surprise when I found two such people in the same place. Éric has never once made me feel indebted for his support and patience, though I am, in innumerable ways. It is entirely accurate to say that Marina has changed my life, several times over. Without either of them, for different reasons, this book would not exist.

Ethan Knapp believed in this project, and I will always be grateful. It has been a pleasure to work with him. Ana Jimenez-Moreno has been a generous and responsive editor. She shepherded me and my manuscript through the publication process with care and transparency. The book is better for her incisive work on it. I would also like to thank the anonymous readers for The Ohio State University Press. Their comments on the manuscript were perceptive and stimulating. I cannot thank them enough for the time and attention they gave to it. They took the work on its own terms and helped me to realize its strengths and improve its weaknesses. Jack McKeon helped me to prepare the final version of the manuscript. I am grateful for his support in the last stages of the process, and for his excitement about the project, which reminded me, amidst the deadlines, that I should be excited, too. Any errors are, of course, my own.

Finally, and most importantly, I want to thank my family. I first heard about Richard I from my father, George Libbon. His love of history and popular culture is everywhere in this book. My grandfather, Frank Distaso, was the son of Italian immigrants who came to the US to escape fascism. A proud Angeleno, he was quick to cry with joy at his granddaughter's smallest accomplishments. He made so many of them possible without realizing it. My grandmother, Naomi Distaso, believed long before it was a thing people thought, let alone said, that a well-educated woman could live a life of her own choosing, a life that didn't need to look like anyone else's. She was instrumental in my opportunity to have such an education, and I hope that she would be proud of the life that has been possible because of it.

This book is dedicated to my mother, Rosemary Distaso, my best friend and most brilliant teacher. I could write a whole other book about her grace, humanity, style, eloquence, intellect, ability to make the mundane special, courage, and strength. The way she moves through the world amazes and inspires me, and her love has made everything possible.

ABBREVIATIONS

ANTS   Anglo-Norman Text Society

Burnley-Wiggins   *The Auchinleck Manuscript.* Edited by David Burnley and Alison Wiggins. Edinburgh: 2003. http://auchinleck.nls.uk.

DIMEV   *Digital Index of Middle English Verse.* Edited by Linne R. Mooney et al. https://www.dimev.net.

DMLBS   *Dictionary of Medieval Latin from British Sources.* Edited by Richard Ashdowne, David Howlett, and Ronald Latham. Oxford: British Academy, 2018.

EETS   Early English Text Society (OS, Original Series; ES, Extra Series; SS, Supplementary Series)

Hanna-Rundle   Hanna, Ralph, and David Rundle. *A Descriptive Catalogue of the Western Manuscripts, to c. 1600, in Christ Church, Oxford.* Using materials collected by Jeremy J. Griffiths. Oxford Bibliographical Society Publications, Special Series: Manuscript Catalogues 2. Oxford: Oxford Bibliographical Society, 2017.

Klm   *Karlamagnús saga*

LALME McIntosh, Angus, M. L. Samuels, and M. Benskin, with the assistance of M. Laing and K. Williams. *A Linguistic Atlas of Late Medieval English*. 4 vols. Aberdeen: Aberdeen University Press, 1986.

MED *Middle English Dictionary*. Edited by H. Kurath, S. M. Kuhn, and R. E. Lewis. Ann Arbor: University of Michigan Press, 1954–2001.

MGH Monumenta Germaniae Historica (DC, Deutsche Chroniken; SS, Scriptores [in Folio]; SRG NS, Scriptores rerum Germanicarum, Nova series)

NIMEV *A New Index of Middle English Verse*. Edited by Julia Boffey and A. S. G. Edwards. London: British Library, 2005.

OED *Oxford English Dictionary Online*. http://www.oed.com.

OMT Oxford Medieval Texts

ONP *Dictionary of Old Norse Prose*. Edited by Aldís Sigurðardóttir et al. https://onp.ku.dk/onp/onp.php.

Pearsall-Cunningham *The Auchinleck Manuscript: National Library of Scotland, Advocates' MS 19.2.1*. Introduction by Derek Pearsall and I. C. Cunningham. London: Scolar Press, 1977.

PQW *Placita de quo warranto*. Edited by William Illingworth. London: Record Commission, 1818.

Richard I Gillingham, John. *Richard I*. New Haven: Yale University Press, 2002.

Richard Löwenherz Brunner, Karl, ed. *Der mittelenglische Versroman über Richard Löwenherz*. Wiener Beiträge zur englischen Philologie 42. Vienna: Wilhelm Braumüller, 1913.

RS Rolls Series (Chronicles and Memorials of Great Britain and Ireland during the Middle Ages)

SEL *The South English Legendary*

STC Pollard, A. W., and G. R. Redgrave, rev. Katherine E. Panzer. *A Short-Title Catalogue of Books Printed 1475–1640*. 2nd ed. 3 vols. London: Bibliographical Society, 1976–1991.

NOTE ON TRANSLATIONS AND TRANSCRIPTIONS

UNLESS OTHERWISE noted, translations are my own. Where I supply someone else's translation, I reproduce the language of the primary source as provided by the translator in his or her edition. Transcriptions from medieval manuscripts and other primary sources are my own unless otherwise specified. In transcriptions of vernacular texts, I regularize spacing according to modern conventions, preserve *u/v* distinction, and use italics to indicate expanded scribal abbreviation. Quotations from editions of medieval texts retain the conventions of their editions, including marks of abbreviation, *i/j* or *u/v* spelling, italics indicating editorial expansion of scribal abbreviation, and modern punctuation.

INTRODUCTION

∽

Tuning Our Ears

But our King did well at Acre.
—T. S. ELIOT, "CHORUSES FROM 'THE ROCK'" VIII

PEOPLE IN medieval England talked. This may seem a fact too obvious for words, but we ourselves seldom talk or write about their talk. What they might have said not in the literary texts that preserve representations of the medieval world, but in the actual world that existed outside of those texts: the ongoing conversations among people about the matters of the day, conversations to which anyone could have access and over which no single institution had control. The absence of such talk from our record of the medieval English past is strange. Its absence from our formulation of medieval literary history, and thus the way in which we do not account for the presence of talk or the pressures it might have exerted, is stranger still. The idea that medieval textual production could have occurred without talk is utterly contradicted by a facet of our own lived experience, about which nothing is uniquely modern. Before and after texts are written, they are embedded in a surround of conversations essential to their making. Talking prompts writing and rewriting, and discussion and debate follow reading.

This book advances a theory of how talk circulates history, identity, and cultural memory over time. Circulating talk, then, becomes central and generative, a crucial context for the making and reading of medieval England's literature. Moreover, talk was understood to be so *in* medieval England. In this book, I offer a literary history that accounts for the spaces between and around extant texts: spaces that scholars of medieval literature, especially, have tended to assume either silent or impossible to excavate, but which in fact can be made to speak, made to disclose information about the processes of writing and reading, and about the intangible daily life in which textual production occurred.

As the contents of these textless and seemingly empty spaces are recovered and made to mean, surviving texts are not necessarily prioritized as the sole or even the central bearers of evidence for literature's inception, transmission, and reception. That mythical creature of medieval manuscript catalogues and medievalists' thinking, the "now lost" copy of a text, is a response that we too often project upon the presumed silence of the past. We conjecture either generations that preceded the earliest extant manuscript copy of a text or a loss that we assume obscures our understanding of the surviving copies. Yet these conventional and familiar narratives we deploy to explain the seemingly abrupt presence of a "new" text on the medieval scene or the apparently nonsensical discrepancies among a text's surviving manuscript copies preemptively foreclose our access to the past. To include talk in our project of cultural recovery is fundamentally disruptive, both to our methods, which call for precision and which we use to plot the spectrum of plausible ways things might have happened, and to our imaginations, with which we fashion the always in-progress picture of the past we as scholars produce.

To include talk in our rendering of the past is to make visible the contributions of the broader public to medieval England's literature. People in medieval England, whatever their literacy or proximity to books, had access to talk. They could spread or suppress certain strands of it, and therefore were integral to text-making, both the kinds of texts that were made and what those texts were made to say. Talk is democratizing. The systematic exclusion of talk as essentially formative to literary texts has yielded a literary and cultural history that insists upon the silence of the past. In truth, that silence is predicated on our own perceived inability or habituated disinclination to listen.

Talk permeates the real and imagined boundaries that cultures have always constructed, and traces of medieval talk, however distorted over time, are everywhere around us. They are distorted not because they have grown fainter, but because, like a message passed between participants and over some distance in a game of telephone, old talk is misheard and misreported, excerpted and edited, in and according to new locations and times. It is distorted by ears that are tuned to a local frequency, that hear and interpret and attend relative to their specific times, places, and situated exigencies. A more destabilizing ramification of old talk's circuitous movement in and around new times and places is that chronological periodization becomes more bizarre than usual as a way of understanding historical facts as events. Periodization obscures the wending reality of talk.

So too, the relationships among text-maker, text, reader, and history are reconstituted through the process of recovering talk and charting its circulation. This book thus also intervenes, radically, I hope, in the way we "do" literary history, medieval and otherwise. It develops and models methodologies for the recovery of talk and for the conceptualization of talk's form and function, past and present. I will describe my key methodologies in this introduction, as well as the object on which I practice them and the logic that underpins its choice, and that logic's implications. But I want to begin with an example of the type of talk to which this book is attuned, and with a brief overview of the sonic landscape within and stretching beyond medieval studies.

An example of the basic interplay of talk and text warrants a place in the pantheon of Geoffrey Chaucer's self-reflexive meditations on his contemporary manuscript culture. In Book V of Chaucer's *Troilus and Criseyde,* Criseyde, newly lodged in the Greek encampment beyond Troy's wall, replies to a letter Troilus has sent from within them imploring her to return to him. Even there, she is surrounded by talk, and the poem's narrator professes to reproduce her letter, as she reproduces that talk. I cannot yet do as you wish, Criseyde writes, "But whi, lest that this lettre founden were, / No mencioun ne make I now, for feere." She then alights this train of thought for the length of a stanza in which she acknowledges Troilus's distress at their separation (his letter, she notes with no especial pleasure, arrived tear-stained) and then re-embarks: "But beth nat wroth, and that I yow biseche," she continues. "For that I tarie is al for wikked speche. / For I have herd wel moore than I wende, / Touchyng us two, how thynges han ystonde."[1] Criseyde is surrounded by speculative local talk about how things supposedly stand between them ("touchyng us two"), and knowledge of this talk has made her "tarie."

It has also made her do another thing no doubt less obvious to Troilus, who proves over the course of the poem to be a terrible close reader of Criseyde's letters and of her body (prior to this scene, he mistakes a cart in the distance for his beloved).[2] The talk she hears all around her has made her think twice about what she writes down in her letter: "But whi, lest that

---

1. Geoffrey Chaucer, *Troilus and Criseyde,* in *The Riverside Chaucer,* ed. Larry D. Benson (New York: Houghton Mifflin Co., 1987), bk. 5, lines 1602–03, 1609–12. All subsequent citations of Chaucer's works refer to this edition.

2. Chaucer, *Troilus and Criseyde,* bk. 5, lines 1158–59; and Pandarus's deflating reply: "That I se yond nys but a fare-carte" (bk. 5, line 1162).

this lettre founden were, / No mencioun ne make I now." Though Criseyde's characterization of this talk as "wikked speche" has drawn limited scholarly attention,[3] it is the presence and function of this talk that compels my own. Criseyde recognizes that the talk around her is a fundamental part of the system of textual production and reception. She is at this moment a text-maker attuned to her immediate context and able to imagine the ways in which her text will be received by a variety of potential readers. The "Criseyde model," if you will, stands in sharp contrast to the ways in which we have for so long imagined the relationship between talk and textual production in medieval England. What is being said influences what she writes, and she knows that what she writes will inform future talk.

The Criseyde model does not straightforwardly fit into our catalogue of Chaucer's frequent tinkering with sound on the page. Sound may be "but eyr ybroken,"[4] but the meaning that might emerge from sound constantly fascinates Chaucer. From the "jangling" of the *Manciple's Tale* to the *House of Fame* in its entirety, Chaucer represents sound as an essential component in the building up and tearing down of the monuments of memory around which society is structured.[5] But talk should not be rendered indistinguishable from "sound." Talk exerts different pressures on texts and their makers, and occupies spaces in the world outside of texts. Talk circulates information and goes places, and can be repeated and recovered in ways that sound does not and cannot.

Criseyde's letter preserves evidence of such talk in the world beyond her text. She gestures in her text to a site of talk, the Greek encampment, and articulates its exigencies vis-à-vis her choice of subject, language, and timing. Her letter, we know, will also become a vehicle that carries the apparent talk of the encampment across Troy's wall and into that city, where the letter itself, talk of it, or the talk it contains could be suppressed or act as a catalyst for further talking and text-making. Chaucer's ongoing preoccupation with sound, and with human speech, is less a function of his singular brilliance than of the literary inheritance passed down by his predecessors. Since Chaucer was a boy, and long before that, England's text-makers had grappled with,

---

3. See, for example, Joseph S. Graydon, "Defense of Criseyde," *PMLA* 44 (1929): 171–72. On letter-writing women and the tension between public and private space in Chaucer, see Sarah Stanbury, "Women's Letters and Private Space in Chaucer," *Exemplaria* 6 (1994): 271–85.

4. Chaucer, *The House of Fame*, bk. 2, line 765.

5. On the former, see Susan E. Phillips, *Transforming Talk: The Problem with Gossip in Late Medieval England* (University Park: Pennsylvania State University Press, 2007); and Phillips's "Gossip and (Un)official Writing," in *Middle English: Oxford Twenty-First Century Approaches to Literature,* ed. Paul Strohm (Oxford: Oxford University Press, 2007), 476–90.

harnessed, and responded to talk as a type of orality essential to all aspects of medieval England's literary production.

Throughout this book, "orality" is understood as an engine of making that is integral to literary production. Whereas orality has traditionally been known as literacy's opposite or literature's handmaiden, several important pieces of work by scholars of medieval literature have refined that reductive binary and inaugurated medieval "talk studies."[6] That work, on representations of human speech, has turned its attention mainly to "good" and "bad" speech, a binary in which "gossip" or "idle speech," at once powerful and pejorative, is theorized against institutionally sanctioned speech, such as confession.[7] Following early and important work on music and song by medieval musicologists,[8] medieval studies has more recently joined other scholarly fields in taking the "sonic turn." The richness of "sound in text," or "what texts sound like," is suggested by the 2016 special issue of *Speculum*, in which medievalists from a range of specialties compass the study of sound, "bring[ing] out the ethical, philosophical, and theological significance of sound in texts that foreground sound itself, whether as an invocation of nonhuman noise, of surreal speech, or of divine song."[9]

My work moves beyond "what texts sound like" to what the world around texts sounded like. In popular culture and in scholarship, the traditional binary of "orality" and "literacy" remains potent and has given rise to a series of other binaries that broadly structure our notions of cultural evolution: unlearned and learned, illiterate and literate, primitive and sophisticated. To bridge "orality" and "literacy" is to cross "the Great Divide."[10] My work thus

---

6. See the editors' insightful discussion in the introduction to Thelma S. Fenster and Daniel Lord Small, eds., *Fama: The Politics of Talk and Reputation in Medieval Europe* (Ithaca, NY: Cornell University Press, 2003), esp. 9–10.

7. On gossip generally, see Patricia Meyer Spacks, *Gossip* (Chicago: University of Chicago Press, 1986). Some of the earliest and most important scholarly work, focused on late medieval literature, includes Edwin D. Craun, *Lies, Slander, and Obscenity in Medieval English Literature: Pastoral Rhetoric and the Deviant Speaker* (Cambridge: Cambridge University Press, 1997); Karma Lochrie, *Covert Operations: The Medieval Uses of Secrecy* (Philadelphia: University of Pennsylvania Press, 1999); Sandy Bardsley, *Venomous Tongues: Speech and Gender in Late Medieval England* (Philadelphia: University of Pennsylvania Press, 2006); and Phillips, *Transforming Talk*.

8. Musicologists have been in the vanguard of medieval sound studies: See, for example, Emma Dillon, *The Sense of Sound: Musical Meaning in France, 1260–1330* (Oxford: Oxford University Press, 2012), esp. 51–91.

9. See Susan Boynton's introduction in "Sound Matters," by Susan Boynton, Sarah Kay, Alison Cornish, and Andrew Albin, *Speculum* 91 (2016): 1002.

10. The phrase is Walter J. Ong's; see his influential *Orality and Literacy: The Technologizing of the World* (London: Metheun, 1982); as well as Brian V. Street, *Social Literacies: Critical Approaches to Literacy in Development, Ethnography and Education* (1995; reprint,

expands upon the foundational premises of scholars of literature, especially early literature, who have theorized orality's functional relationship to texts in a limited number of scenarios: how and when the oral composition of a text occurred; how and when oral performance occurred and was received; how and when oral culture, comprised of ephemeral speech and memory, gave way to a literate society and its written record. In medieval studies, the theoretically groundbreaking scholarship I most admire, and without which my own work would not be possible, nevertheless posits the oral or unwritten as either preceding or opposing written texts.¹¹ As a mode of literary composition and transmission, the unwritten has been construed in relation to written texts in fruitful yet narrow terms: "orality," the oral delivery of texts, and, more recently, "aurality," the shared hearing of them.¹²

Two interventions about unwritten discourse underpin this book. First, that talk, itself partly constitutive of orality, is inextricable from textual production in medieval England. Second, that talk was not then and is not now wholly ephemeral. It shaped and continues to shape the medieval archive as we know it. In offering these fundamental reconceptions of talk and its temporalities, I propose a formulation of orality and literacy that differs from past formulations. Brian Stock innovatively asserts in his magisterial book of the early 1980s, *The Implications of Literacy,* that "the type of orality for which the Middle Ages furnishes the most abundant evidence is verbal discourse which exists in interdependence with texts, as for instance, do the normal spoken and recorded forms of language, which impinge upon each other in complex ways but remain mutually exclusive." Yet, he continues, "the medievals did not understand, as indeed we do not, how the spoken and written

---

London: Routledge, 2013), 53–63; and Jack Goody and Ian Watt, "The Consequences of Literacy," *Comparative Studies in Society and History* 5 (1963): 304–45.

11. For example, M. T. Clanchy, *From Memory to Written Record: England 1066–1307,* 2nd ed. (Oxford: Blackwell, 1993); and D. H. Green, *Medieval Listening and Reading: The Primary Reception of German Literature 800–1300* (Cambridge: Cambridge University Press, 1994). See also Green's Festschrift, Mark Chinca and Christopher Young, eds., *Orality and Literacy in the Middle Ages: Essays on a Conjunction and Its Consequences in Honour of D. H. Green* (Turnhout: Brepols, 2005). For an overview and survey of approaches to "oral literature," see Karl Reichl, ed., *Medieval Oral Literature* (Berlin: De Gruyter, 2012). The perennial concept of "oral performance" also places the "oral" and the "written" in opposition.

12. Joyce Coleman, "Aurality," in Strohm, *Middle English,* 68–85. See also Coleman's important contribution to the study of medieval sound and the ramifications of reading practices: *Public Reading and the Reading Public in Late Medieval England and France* (Cambridge: Cambridge University Press, 1996). On "orality" in medieval studies up to Coleman, see D. H. Green, "Orality and Reading: The State of Research in Medieval Studies," *Speculum* 65 (1990): 267–80.

styles of interchange influence each other."[13] When we do imagine the kind of mutually influential relationship between written and unwritten discourse that Stock posits and to which others have gestured,[14] the seeming ephemerality of unwritten discourse and the problem of its recovery stops us short.[15] In exposing that ephemerality as a critical convenience,[16] not something innate to talk itself, this book rejects a divide between talk and text.

I look and listen in this book for several kinds of talk, "local talk" chief among them. "Local" is a designation that situates my work among that of scholars who have long influenced my approach to medieval literature with the argument, made both outright and by example, that medieval England's literary history cannot be understood or formulated in terms of canonicity, since medieval manuscript culture could not and did not yield a contemporary "canon." These scholars have taken a different angle of approach, giving name and shape to the study of "local literature."[17] Local talk reflects and preserves

---

13. Brian Stock, *The Implications of Literacy: Written Language and Models of Interpretation in the Eleventh and Twelfth Centuries* (Princeton: Princeton University Press, 1983), 8.

14. For example, Joseph J. Duggan, "Performance and Transmission, Aural and Ocular Reception in the Twelfth- and Thirteenth-Century Vernacular Literature of France," *Romance Philology* 43 (1989): 49–58; and Paul Zumthor and Marilyn C. Engelhardt, "The Text and the Voice," *New Literary History* 16 (1984): 67–92.

15. The difficulties inherent in recovering various kinds of unwritten discourse are well documented. See, for example, Reichl, *Medieval Oral Literature*, 8: "For the study of medieval oral literature, no direct investigation is possible. All we have is the reflection of oral tradition in writing."

16. Beyond medieval studies, the assumed ephemerality of a range of voices and perspectives is being challenged. The resulting scholarship is productively disruptive and develops important new archival and analytical methods of cultural recovery. See, for example, Leah S. Marcus, *Unediting the Renaissance: Shakespeare, Marlowe, Milton* (New York: Routledge, 1996); Lisa Brooks, *The Common Pot: The Recovery of Native Space in the Northeast* (Minneapolis: University of Minnesota Press, 2008); Christian Ayne Crouch, *Nobility Lost: French and Canadian Martial Cultures, Indians, and the End of New France* (Ithaca, NY: Cornell University Press, 2014); Kathleen Donegan, *Seasons of Misery: Catastrophe and Colonial Settlement in Early America* (Philadelphia: University of Pennsylvania Press, 2014); Tabetha Leigh Ewing, *Rumor, Diplomacy, and War in Enlightenment Paris*, Oxford University Studies in the Enlightenment 7 (Oxford: Voltaire Foundation, 2014); and Marisa J. Fuentes, *Dispossessed Lives: Enslaved Women, Violence, and the Archive* (Philadelphia: University of Pennsylvania Press, 2016).

17. For example, Thorlac Turville-Petre, "Some Medieval English Manuscripts in the North-East Midlands," in *Manuscripts and Readers in Fifteenth-Century England: The Literary Implications of Manuscript Study*, ed. Derek Pearsall (Cambridge: D. S. Brewer, 1983), 125–41; Richard Beadle, "Prolegomena to a Literary Geography of Later Medieval Norfolk," in *Regionalism in Late Medieval Manuscripts and Texts: Essays Celebrating the Publication of "A Linguistic Atlas of Late Medieval English,"* ed. Felicity Riddy (Cambridge: D. S. Brewer, 1991), 89–108; Steven Justice, *Writing and Rebellion: England in 1381* (Berkeley: University of California Press, 1994); Vincent Gillespie, "Syon and the New Learning," in *The Religious Orders*

the exigencies of specific times and places, and thus shapes and is shaped by local common knowledge and local cultural memory.

Medieval people were not blank slates when they encountered texts. They took up texts as what I call "knowing readers,"[18] already bearing in mind some combination of local common knowledge and cultural memory in circulation. My work goes beyond recovering this talk and thinking through its implications for text-making and for the making of cultural memory. Fundamentally, I argue that texts embody an awareness that they will encounter talk in the world, and exhibit an instinct about how they might shape it. The addition of texts' awareness of such talk to the models of literary criticism, historical studies, and book history shifts our understanding of the dynamics among text, text-maker, and reader. In some cases, sites of talk were provoked into existence by political or social events. The subject of talk, and often the talk itself and its speakers, can be recovered, identified, and contextualized, and the range of the ramifications of its circulation traced across time and geography. In other cases, the circulation of local talk and that circulation's consequences illuminate the intricate processes of textual production.

Local talk travels not only on people's lips, but by way of books, images, letters, statutes, and other legal documents. This book thus locates within a text its maker's expectations for what a reader would have known: what she would have read, heard, and seen. These expectations, built variously into the texts themselves, are directly related to the ways in which a text's contents can mean for a knowing reader. To put this in textual terms, local talk was construed by text-makers as a kind of exemplar, and by readers as extratextual gloss. In this scenario, "how the spoken and written styles of interchange influence each other" is not only evident to text-makers and readers, but makes anyone who talked—who helped to make and circulate an airy exemplar or gloss—integral to the text-making process, even if they never opened a book.

Local talk that was "in the air" can be recovered by cross-reading different media in simultaneous circulation in a particular time and place. This might include the books a person certainly or probably had access to, for instance, and the milieux in which those manuscripts were made. Also "in the air" were the images and architecture our reader might have seen, not to mention the social and historical particularities of her specific time and place. From the

---

in *Pre-Reformation England*, ed. James G. Clark (Woodbridge: Boydell and Brewer, 2002), 75–95; and Ralph Hanna, *London Literature, 1300–1380* (Cambridge: Cambridge University Press, 2005).

18. For this terminology, and for the method of conceptualizing readers in terms of knowledge acquisition, I am indebted to Jennifer Miller.

dialogue among extant objects, circulating talk can be perceived or, better, heard. The ways in which talk was influenced by and influenced those objects, including texts, thus makes that which was unrecoverable into an essential part of how we understand literature.

Medieval text-makers understood talk's possibilities and pressures, and indeed relied upon them as part of the instability of manuscript culture. The practices dismissed by traditional book history as errors or evidence of failure—narrative discrepancies among copies, excision, and material fragmentation—comprise a set of tools deployed by scribes, bookmakers, and readers to make each copy of a text flexible: relevant to time and place, and amendable to the addition and excision of local and imported talk. Extant manuscripts preserve the ways in which their makers grappled with local talk and negotiated imported talk that interrupted or even drowned out what was circulating locally. Traditional approaches to textual editing champion the creation of a stable text that is, by necessity, a placeholder—what I call a "representative text"—fashioned from the distinct manuscript copies that together constitute a textual tradition. To produce a representative text for study and teaching, narrative and material differences are elided. It is precisely these differences among copies that, I argue, are the suggestive and indicative textual variations that register local difference, audience interest, and talk itself. Each manuscript copy in a textual tradition is a product of choice and relativism that preserves and responds to local talk and common knowledge or cultural memory.

My work also exposes, then, how local talk was a catalyst for widespread cultural memory and literature. Local talk and cultural memory give way to the "national" or widespread, in that the parts of talk routinely "copied" (to use the terminology of manuscript culture) and adopted in multiple places embed within themselves a common cultural memory. At the same time as the local persists, something of a core knowledge, widely known and widely held, emerges in the shape of a cultural memory. This ongoing conversation between the local and the national, the past and present, took place over decades and centuries.

Ongoing talk on a single subject, whether that talk is situated in a particular locality or across wide geographic expanses with no regard for our demarcations of age and era, constitutes a period of text-making. That period can, and indeed in this book must, include our own. Talk, in its medieval and modern scholarly incarnations, as well as medieval scribal copies and modern scholarly editions, exists on a single continuum of literary history. Our own scholarship—editions, articles, presentations, conversations—are, like medieval productions, made relative to time, place, and scholarly common knowledge. Everyone makes texts informed by the talk circulating around them; no one looks back with as much objectivity as time and distance imply, and thus no one's rendering of the past is not inflected by the present, broadly construed, moment. Talk thus anchors this book's overarching structure, which does not adhere to the chronological progression that periodization instantiates and that configures our thinking about inheritance.

This book's subject is talk, but the exemplary subject of that talk is Richard I or Richard Coeur de Lion, England's king from 1189 to 1199. The period of text-making about him, of which talk is expressly constitutive, begins in the late thirteenth century and continues until the twenty-first. I have chosen to focus on talk about Richard I—to use him as an object to be turned and examined from all angles—for several reasons. The first of these is that the long-standing purchase of Richard I in popular culture—his function as a watchword for medieval England—far outstrips the length and nature of his reign and his physical presence in England. Crowned at Westminster in late 1189, Richard departed for the Third Crusade early in 1190, returned to England four years later, and remained on the island for a mere month before leaving for his French ancestral lands, where he died in 1199. On Richard's orders, the parts of his body were deposited throughout France; none were returned to England. While not England's only king to spend time abroad, Richard remains unique for how far away he went and for how long he remained there. He was not routinely across the Channel as his predecessors and successors often were, but was, at times, wholly inaccessible: out on the open sea, over in the Holy Land, captured in Austria and held prisoner in Germany.

Richard's absence was a catalyst for talk. This is an argument stated here as fact, and it will be argued over the course of this book. During his reign, to know about Richard was to hear rumor, to write about Richard was to write rumor, and to talk about Richard was to spread rumor. I use "rumor" here and throughout as a subcategory of talk distinct from, say, "gossip." While "rumor" implies speculation, unlike "gossip" it does not necessarily connote secrecy, nor does it carry gossip's theoretical associations with marginalized discourse.[19] "Rumor," so closely tied to the idea of *fama* or long-term repute and widespread reputation, is characterized by its propensity to traverse time and geography in a way that gossip does not.[20]

---

19. See Phillips, *Transforming Talk*, 4–6.
20. In their foundational study, Gordon W. Allport and Leo Postman posit the "two basic conditions for rumor": "First, the theme of the story must have some *importance* to speaker and listener; second, the true facts must be shrouded in some kind of *ambiguity*." See Allport and Postman, *The Psychology of Rumor* (New York: Henry Holt and Co., 1947), 33. The present book implicitly confirms that these conditions pertain to rumors about the past

After his death, speculative talk or rumor about Richard and his reign intensified. This talk centered on how Richard should be individually and collectively remembered, and to what end. A century after his death, Richard's reign was legally and permanently enshrined as the start of England's living memory. While all of the eleventh- and most of the twelfth-century past was designated by the Crown and understood by the public to be time immemorial or "time out of mind," the "time of King Richard" was to be kept in mind in perpetuity, and woven into individuals' claims to their own inheritance. These claims took the form of narratives told publicly in law courts. To reconstruct a relationship between Richard and one's right to inheritance was more easily dictated than done. What, precisely, late medieval England's public should "remember" about Richard and his reign in absentia became a pressing matter and the subject of plurilingual, class-crossing, urgent conversation that began in late thirteenth-century law courts. Just as our contemporary current events provoke widespread discussion about what is or is not historically unprecedented, and what in the past has given rise to the present moment, medieval England's public talked about the past, the present, the relationship of the past to the present, and the bearing of both on the future.

Richard also offers a compelling disjunction between the absence from England of his physical body in life and death and the presence there of a significant, if unwieldy, cultural corpus. With no readily recognizable analogues or precedents that survive, and without obvious cultural, political, or textual provocation, the earliest extant copy of a Middle English romance about Richard was written down in Edinburgh, National Library of Scotland, MS Advocates 19.2.1. That book is better known today as the Auchinleck manuscript, probably produced between 1331 and 1340 in London.[21] After its appearance in Auchinleck, *Richard Coeur de Lion,* as we call the romance, was transmitted throughout England for another century and a half, surviving in one fragment and seven manuscript copies that date from the early fourteenth to the late fifteenth centuries. This romance about Richard serves two important pur-

---

invented and transmitted in medieval England, though in medieval England what counted as "true" is crucially different from, if not more complex than, the postwar America in which Allport and Postman researched and wrote. For a more recent study on the personification of rumor as a figure in literature, see Philip Hardie, *Rumour and Renown: Representations of Fama in Western Literature* (Cambridge: Cambridge University Press, 2012). On "truth," see Richard Firth Green, *A Crisis of Truth: Literature and Law in Ricardian England* (Philadelphia: University of Pennsylvania Press, 2002).

21. On Auchinleck's dating, see Thorlac Turville-Petre, *England the Nation: Language, Literature, and National Identity, 1290–1340* (Oxford: Clarendon Press, 1996), 111; and Helen Cooper, "Lancelot, Roger Mortimer, and the Date of the Auchinleck Manuscript," in *Studies in Late Medieval and Early Renaissance Texts in Honour of John Scattergood,* ed. Anne Marie D'Arcy and Alan J. Fletcher (Dublin: Four Courts, 2005), 95. On other aspects of Auchinleck, see esp. chapter 4.

poses in this book. First, its extant copies attest to the continued relevance of Richard in late medieval England and the enduring project to reconstruct his reign. Second, *Richard Coeur de Lion* exemplifies other texts and textual traditions that respond to, shape, and intervene in cultural memory—texts and textual traditions around which talk can be recovered and analyzed.

Such texts have never been considered under a single rubric, despite their common interests and approaches. I call this supra-genre "retrospective texts." Ubiquitous in all of England's vernaculars as romances, saints' lives, political songs, and *chansons de geste,* retrospective texts profess to be about England's past. They therefore demand participatory retrospection from writers and readers: the active speculation about the past and its bearing on the present that is a prominent feature of talk. These texts share an interest in reconstructing the past on the page, making talk about "what happened" vital to their inception and transmission. Talk can prompt a text's making or dispute its memory. Often, retrospective texts perform their retrospection through narrators who do not emerge from the past of the narrative, but belong instead to the present of the reader. These texts also raise a series of unfolding questions. They demonstrate an interest in the past: What motivated that interest? And why interest in that particular past? What effects were such texts meant to achieve through retrospection? That is, why look to the past instead of to the present or the future? Did their makers mean for them to convey knowledge to an "unknowing reader"? Or were retrospective texts made with a knowing reader in mind? If the latter, could a text's maker have anticipated the knowledge a reader already possessed?

Retrospection never happens in a vacuum. Something in the past always precipitates the act, whether individual or collective, of looking back to a specific time and place. The making of a retrospective text, then, requires a discussion about the past it depicts, a discussion that has already occurred or remains ongoing. This talk about what happened is necessarily rooted in rumor, and is often intimately related to the political or social concerns of the present moment. Medieval England's texts were likewise mutable to "new" rumors about the old days, and they often preserve a theoretical and mechanical interest in how talk about the past circulated and how it could be harnessed amidst situated exigencies of the present moment.

Richard I is an exemplary figure for this book's theorization of talk's circulation, not a fundamentally unique one. I aim for this book's approaches to be practiced upon other figures and their associated retrospective texts. To that end, each chapter of this book presents a facet of my methodology for the recovery of talk and situates those practices among our present approaches to the study of medieval literary and manuscript culture. I combine the methods of historical literary analysis with analytical models from history in a traditionally archival sense, as well as from book history.

Much like orality and literacy, the binary of book history (manuscript studies, paleography, and codicology) and literary criticism has persisted in medieval studies, partly because of the historically greater access to manuscripts and training in what to do with them available outside of the US, and partly born of the need for medievalists, dispersed across the world, to have representative texts. Over the past dozen years, the study of medieval literature has taken a material turn, occasioned in part by the wider access to manuscripts that digital technology facilitates. My approach to cultural recovery reflects my training as part of a uniquely situated generation of scholars who were trained in both the empirical foundations of book history and radical literary criticism well before that material turn. Writing this book, I have striven to make its investigations, discoveries, methodologies, and interventions useful, legible, and compelling for a wide range of scholars who practice cultural recovery in a diverse range of ways. In my simultaneous practice of literary criticism and book history, I hope to show why engaging with each manuscript copy of a text is essential to the praxis of close reading, historical studies, and manuscript studies, and how we might better synthesize book history with the readings of social urgencies that propel literary production.

This introduction begins with an epigraph from the twentieth century: a line that, even when read in its poetic context, feels as if T. S. Eliot disinterestedly snatched verse from an ongoing conversation in the air.[22] The "king" is Richard, and "Acre" the city he most famously laid siege to amidst the Third Crusade. The poem's speaker assumes that its audience will know both of these facts. Indeed, the poem's speaker, I would submit, assumes that its audience will know *more* than these facts. The king is "our" king, a determiner that presumes shared cultural memory and implies collective nostalgic possession. Not only this precise subject of talk—Richard, Acre—but the retrospective posture that it provokes, is shared by the medieval public, Eliot and his readers, and us. To track and listen at length to this conversation, this book follows our scholarly talk about Richard, the exigencies of places and scholarly praxis that drive it, and the older conversations—of the thirteenth, fourteenth, fifteenth, nineteenth, and early twentieth centuries—still circulating, potently if quietly, within our own.

---

22. Eliot wrote the text of *The Rock,* a pageant play whose earliest performance occurred on May 28, 1934, at Sadler's Wells, London. So, in fact, the line was in one real sense removed from its larger context when "Choruses from 'The Rock'" was published in T. S. Eliot, *Collected Poems, 1909–1962* (New York: Harcourt Brace, 1991), 166.

ONE

Local Talk and the Retrospective Text

SOMETIME IN the thirteenth century, a romance about the life of Richard I or Richard the Lionheart, England's late twelfth-century crusader-king, was written down in Anglo-Norman French. That original Anglo-Norman romance is now lost. Lost, too, are the first redactions and subsequent Middle English translations it inspired. What does survive as one moment from this evolving tradition is a fantastical Middle English romance about Richard. The earliest of its seven extant manuscript copies dates from the fourteenth century. It is a mere fragment. But, as a group, these extant copies reveal a process of accretion in which romance episodes, longer and ever more fanciful, were added to the narrative over time. Or so talk would have it.

The copy said to represent the fullest version of the romance survives in a fifteenth-century manuscript-book, now Cambridge, Gonville and Caius College, MS 175/96. The Caius copy takes us from Richard's birth in England to his death in France, and between those points it preserves the romance's most infamous episodes. Here Richard's mother is a demon-princess from Antioch who shoots up through the church roof at the Eucharist's elevation, never to be heard from again. Here Richard kills a lion while in a German prison and then salts and eats its heart in front of the German king, whose daughter Richard has slept with and whose son he has beaten to death. And here, in two lengthy scenes, Richard twice cannibalizes Saracens while on crusade. The first time he does so unknowingly. Having fallen ill at the siege of Acre,

Richard requests pork. None can be procured. His distraught cook follows the advice of an old anonymous knight who urges him to prepare Saracen flesh for the king. Richard recovers, and when he again requests pork, his cook, newly distressed, brings Richard the head of the Saracen he has eaten. Instead of being horrified by what he has done, Richard organizes a feast at which the heads of several Saracen prisoners—shaven, cooked, and carefully labeled with their names and high-ranking lineages—are served to his guests, messengers sent in good faith by the sultan. They do not eat. Richard does.[1]

This is the scholarly rumor of the Middle English romance we call *Richard Coeur de Lion*.[2] Or, rather, rumors, since there are two tightly woven strands of story here, one about the romance's development and transmission, and the other about what it contains. The romance and word of it do not circulate in our contemporary popular culture, but if you are a medievalist, some of this probably sounds familiar, resembles something whole or in part you have already heard, read, or, perhaps, repeated in casual talk or written work. I first heard about *Richard Coeur de Lion* (by which I mean I heard about its cannibalism) long before I read the romance. In the years since that first reading, I have listened closely to what medievalists say about it, casually and formally. Our talk and our texts are nearly identical. It is from these sources, our talk and our texts, that I have registered this chapter's first two paragraphs—the brief, as it were—on *Richard Coeur de Lion*: the ways in which we talk and write about the romance, the details we repeat and reproduce with almost no deviation.[3] The closed-circuit nature of our talk and texts

---

1. I use "Saracen" above because the term has historically been used by scholars of medieval literature when talking about the Middle English romance *Richard Coeur de Lion*. The first two paragraphs of this chapter mean to capture and replicate the language and content of that scholarly talk. Yet this way in which we have talked about Muslim figures in Middle English literature, including in *Richard Coeur de Lion*, demands, like much of the language I reproduce above, scrutiny and fundamental revision. In the balance of this book, unless quoting directly from a text, I use the word "Muslim" in place of "Saracen." I hope the former becomes part of the standard lexicon of *Richard Coeur de Lion*, and of medieval literary studies more broadly, by way of our informal talk and our scholarship.

2. *NIMEV* 1979; *DIMEV* 3231. The romance survives in seven manuscript copies of the fourteenth and fifteenth centuries and one independent fragment dated to the first quarter of the fifteenth century. Wynkyn de Worde printed two editions of the romance in roughly the first quarter of the sixteenth century. For manuscript shelfmarks and the dates of manuscripts and editions, see below in this chapter. The number of extant manuscript copies is sometimes given as nine rather than seven; in these instances, two fragments, which belong to the copy extant in Edinburgh, National Library of Scotland, MS Advocates 19.2.1 but are now held in other libraries, have been counted as individual witnesses.

3. An extensive collection of books and articles aided me in producing the brief of *Richard Coeur de Lion*. These include Susan Conklin Akbari, "The Hunger for National Identity in *Richard Coer de Lion*," in *Reading Medieval Culture: Essays in Honor of Rob-*

is predictable. The more a rumor is repeated among assiduous scholars who cite their sources, the more it is codified as common knowledge and the less it looks and sounds like a rumor.

I use "rumor" in the case of *Richard Coeur de Lion* for two reasons. First, because the text that we hold in our collective consciousness and circulate among ourselves does not exist in any of the romance's extant manuscript copies, nor is it borne out by the external evidence to which those copies gesture. Second, for the past one hundred years, the only physical copy of the romance

---

ert W. Hanning, ed. R. M. Stein and S. Pierson Prior (Notre Dame: University of Notre Dame Press, 2005), 198–227; Alan S. Ambrisco, "Cannibalism and Cultural Encounters in *Richard Coeur de Lion*," *Journal of Medieval and Modern Studies,* 29 (1999): 499–528; W. R. J. Barron, *English Medieval Romance* (New York: Longman, 1987); A. J. Bliss, "Notes on the Auchinleck Manuscript," *Speculum* 26 (1951): 652–58; Heather Blurton, *Cannibalism in High Medieval English Literature* (New York: Palgrave Macmillan, 2007); Siobhain Bly Calkin, *Saracens and the Making of English Identity: The Auchinleck Manuscript* (New York: Routledge, 2005); Jeffrey Jerome Cohen, "On Saracen Enjoyment: Some Fantasies of Race in Late Medieval France and England," *Journal of Medieval and Early Modern Studies* 31 (2001): 113–46; Helen Cooper, "The Elizabethan Havelok: William Warner's First of the English," in *Medieval Insular Romance: Translation and Innovation,* ed. Judith Weiss, Jennifer Fellows, and Morgan Dickson (Cambridge: D. S. Brewer, 2000), 169–83; Helen Cooper, "Romance after 1400," in *The Cambridge History of Medieval English Literature,* ed. David Wallace (Cambridge: Cambridge University Press, 1999), 690–719; Susan Crane, *Insular Romance: Politics, Faith, and Culture in Anglo-Norman and Middle English Literature* (Berkeley: University of California Press, 1986); Rosalind Field, "Romance in England," in Wallace, *Cambridge History,* 152–76; Rosalind Field, "Waldef and the Matter of/with England," in Weiss, Fellows, and Dickson, *Medieval Insular Romance,* 25–39; John Finlayson, "Legendary Ancestors and the Expansion of Romance in *Richard, Coer de Lyon*," *English Studies* 79 (1998): 299–308; John Finlayson, "*Richard Coer de Lyon*: Romance, History, or Something in Between?" *Studies in Philology* 87 (1990): 156–80; John Gillingham, *Richard I* (New Haven: Yale University Press, 2002); Geraldine Heng, *Empire of Magic: Medieval Romance and the Politics of Cultural Fantasy* (New York: Columbia University Press, 2003); Michael Johnston, *Romance and the Gentry in Late Medieval England* (Oxford: Oxford University Press, 2014); Peter Larkin, "The Coeur-de-Lyon Romances," in *Christian-Muslim Relations: A Bibliographical History,* ed. Alex Mallett and David Thomas, vol. 5, *1350–1500*, ed. Jason R. Dean (Leiden: Brill, 2013), 268–77; Laura Hibbard Loomis, *Medieval Romance in England: A Study of the Sources and Analogues of the Non-Cyclic Metrical Romances* (New York: Burt Franklin, 1960); Lee Manion, *Narrating the Crusades: Loss and Recovery in Medieval and Early Modern English Literature* (Cambridge: Cambridge University Press, 2014); Nicola McDonald, "Eating People and the Alimentary Logic of *Richard Coeur de Lion*," in *Pulp Fictions of Medieval England: Essays in Popular Romance,* ed. Nicola McDonald (Manchester: Manchester University Press, 2004), 124–50; Dieter Mehl, *The Middle English Romances of the Thirteenth and Fourteenth Centuries* (London: Routledge & K. Paul, 1968); Elizabeth Salter, *Fourteenth-Century English Poetry: Contexts and Readings* (Oxford: Clarendon Press, 1983); Rachel Snell, "The Undercover King," in Weiss, Fellows, and Dickson, *Medieval Insular Romance,* 133–54; Andrew Taylor, "The Myth of the Minstrel Manuscript," *Speculum* 66 (1991): 43–73; Sarah Beth Torpey, "Of Cannibals and Kings: The (Monstrous) Nature of Crusading in *Richard Coer de Lyon*," *Medieval Perspectives* 23 (2008 [2011]): 105–18.

available outside of its manuscripts has been a critical edition that fell out of print in 1913, the year of its publication.[4] In the absence of an easily accessible edition, the rumor of *Richard Coeur de Lion* has circulated among us as a remarkably stable placeholder, an authoritative if intangible "representative text" of later medieval England's cultural memory of Richard I. Essential to this rumored representative text are both certain contents—Richard's mysterious mother and the scenes of Richard's cannibalism, for instance—and the way in which we come by them. Our rumor of the making of *Richard Coeur de Lion* construes the text as a product of agglomeration, a fairly uncomplicated process of narrative growth and progress over time: from history to romance, fragmentation to completeness, the primitive to the sophisticated. Yet precisely because *Richard Coeur de Lion* is a "retrospective text," its extant copies are necessarily the opposite of all of this. Each copy is a product of choice and relativism that preserves and responds to the local knowledge and situated exigencies of the time and place in which it was made. Local knowledge about the past and the specific needs of a present moment inflect what one writes down, how one reads, what one reads for, and how people in a specific community talk about the past before a retrospective text appears, and after, in its wake.

This chapter asks how medievalists came to learn and to repeat the rumor of *Richard Coeur de Lion*. It asks how that rumor came to circulate a text that does not now, and probably never exactly did, exist. When followed to their logical conclusions, these specific lines of inquiry lead to one further, disquieting because pervasive, site of investigation: the role talk plays in our reconstruction of the past, a process that includes the editions—whether actualized or imagined in community—we produce to access that past collectively. Manuscript copies survive and from them we produce representative texts. When we turn to those texts as literary critics, we have already begun to reconstruct the past: The production of a representative text on which literary criticism can be practiced precedes that practice. As medievalists, and especially as scholars of medieval literature, we therefore not only construct literary histories of medieval textual traditions and medieval literary history writ large, we are subjects in those histories. This book's study of talk's circulation begins unconventionally, yet necessarily, not with medieval texts and text-makers, but with us, in order to clear static from the line. I use the term "text-maker" because it is capacious enough to contain those responsible for

---

4. Two editions, neither critical, of *Richard Coeur de Lion* were very recently published: Katherine H. Terrell, ed. and trans., *Richard Coeur de Lion* (Peterborough, Ontario: Broadview Press, 2019); and Peter Larkin, ed., *Richard Coer de Lyon,* Middle English Texts (Kalamazoo, MI: Medieval Institute Publications), 2015.

medieval textual and manuscript production—through composition, exemplar acquisition, copying, compiling, organizing—while not forcing me to make reductive choices about which and how many of those tasks were embodied in a single person. I use it, too, because it simultaneously accommodates the work of modern scholars. As text-makers ourselves, we are on a continuum with medieval England's text-makers. And their talk about the past is on a continuum with our own. So too, then, is the intervening talk. Until we understand the circuitous paths of and pressures exerted by old and new talk on modern text-making, we will not be able to distinguish medieval talk and comprehend its power in the production of retrospective texts, and thus in the production of memory and history, in medieval England.

Medieval text-makers understood this interplay between talk and text. A scene that does not constitute an essential part of our rumor of *Richard Coeur de Lion,* although it survives with almost no variation in each of the romance's extant manuscript copies, embodies an awareness among medieval text-makers that a text about Richard, for instance, could generate talk.[5] The scene is set in the Norman kingdom of Sicily. With the French and English crusading armies docked at Messina en route to the East, the king of France, Philip Augustus, commits "a tresoun" against Richard.[6] Philip sends a letter to Puglia's king,[7] Tancred, that "turned him seþþen to litel witt / Þat king Richard wiþ strengþe of hond / Wald him driue out of his lond."[8] Distraught ("for þat writt he seyd, 'allas!'"),[9] Tancred sends for his son, Roger, and for his barons. When they arrive, "þe king anon þe letter vndede / & seyd hou þe king of Fraunce / Him hadde ywarned of a destaunce."[10] Roger, whose voice emerges from the discussion among those assembled, says that he has heard Richard is only a pilgrim. At Roger's behest, Tancred sends for Richard so that he might say before the council whether the letter speaks falsely.[11]

---

5. It survives in all manuscripts save London, British Library, MS Egerton 2862, where water damage has made most of the copy's first thousand lines illegible; see chapter 5.

6. *King Richard,* line 95. I quote here from the earliest extant copy of *Richard Coeur de Lion,* preserved in Edinburgh, National Library of Scotland, MS Advocates 19.2.1 ("Auchinleck"), where the romance is titled *King Richard.* Hereafter, when a line or scene survives in all extant copies of *Richard Coeur de Lion,* I quote, when possible, from Auchinleck's *King Richard.* Here and elsewhere, unless otherwise noted, all citations of *King Richard* refer to *The Auchinleck Manuscript,* ed. David Burnley and Alison Wiggins (Edinburgh: National Library of Scotland, July 5, 2003), version 1.1, http://auchinleck.nls.uk/.

7. On Tancred and Roger, see Christopher Tyerman, *God's War: A New History of the Crusades* (Cambridge, MA: The Belknap Press, 2006), 394.

8. *King Richard,* lines 98–100.

9. *King Richard,* line 102.

10. *King Richard,* lines 110–13.

11. *King Richard,* line 125.

Richard assures Tancred that "no wil y duelle bot a day" in his lands,[12] and the romance's narrator casts no doubt on Richard's characterization of himself and his plans. The drama of the scene, which turns on the questions of who Richard is and what he will do, seems overblown.

Yet, as I see it, the scene's tension crests at an earlier point: after Tancred has read the letter and before Richard appears. Tancred becomes sorrowful, then angry, then perplexed. He first distrusts the letter, then his own instincts. He turns to his advisors, essentially other readers. In Richard's absence, the letter causes talk among them, and its possible meanings are inferred or conferred based on the knowledge each advisor brings to it. Tancred's son has heard that Richard is a pilgrim, but others have heard differently; the council reaches an impasse. Tancred's interpretive difficulties mirror those of the romance's fourteenth- and fifteenth-century readers, similarly holding a text about an absent and enigmatic Richard. Unlike Tancred, they could not summon Richard for answers. Tancred's attempts to construct Richard from talk and text resemble our own, as we confer about the past and its many possibilities in the absence of our subjects. Texts with absence at their centers, the scene demonstrates, do not always quiet talk. Often, they provoke it. And textual evidence is inert until infused with the perception the reader brings to a text, informed by the particularities of time and place, and the reader's knowledge. To understand how medieval England's people talked about the past, and how that talk sustained and was sustained by the retrospective texts they made—the versions and visions of the past they put down on parchment and paper—we must first make sense of our own talk about them.

Fundamental to this endeavor is our terminology, including the title *Richard Coeur de Lion* and my use of it. My opening assertion, that what we have assumed to be, or to have been, a text is in fact a rumor sustained by our ongoing talk, raises the problem logicians and rhetoricians call "mention-use": whether we deploy a word or phrase to talk about a thing ("use") or to talk about the word itself ("mention"). A standard title for this romance about Richard has never been queried, let alone resolved. Variant scholarly spellings of *Richard Coeur de Lion,* some of which appear in manuscript copies and none of which claim any particular medieval or modern authority, include "Richard Coer de Lion," "Richard Coer de Lyon," and in one recent case, though no medieval attestation exists, "Richard Coer de Leon." The earliest title that resembles something official comes from the London Stationers' Register, which reports the license transfer of "kynge Richard Cur

---

12. *King Richard,* line 151.

de Lyon" to one Thomas Purfoote in 1568/9.[13] In the earliest extant copy of the romance, which survives in Edinburgh, National Library of Scotland, MS Advocates 19.2.1, a book better known as the Auchinleck manuscript, the rubricated running title *King Richard* appears in the copy's scribal hand. I use this title when referring to Auchinleck's copy. To distinguish among the forms and texts of other extant manuscript copies, I use their individual shelfmarks.

My "use" of *Richard Coeur de Lion* is simultaneously a "mention," for with it, I mean to leverage all that we have said: to call to the reader's mind the rumor, to foreground existing collective understanding, to let *Richard Coeur de Lion* be at the outset whatever a reader might bear in mind when coming to this book. Writers (and readers), especially scholarly ones, proceed similarly all the time, often without explicit acknowledgment that the text under discussion is a theoretical one.[14] Indeed, the practice of talking and writing about a theoretical text has become second nature. When scholars discuss single copies, medieval or modern, "the text" refers to a common understanding for utility's sake as often as it does to words on a tangible page. I aim for our current scholarly common knowledge to become fluid and to transform, probably multiple times, in the course of what follows so that *Richard Coeur de Lion* comes to signify our changing idea of it and its constituent parts. For a reader to whom *Richard Coeur de Lion* means nothing beyond the name at present, it will come to mean anew.

The "modern" literary history of *Richard Coeur de Lion* with which this chapter is interested extends from nineteenth-century England and Scotland to the present day, by way of fin-de-siècle Vienna. At each of these times and places, the production of texts about Richard I was either suppressed or driven by high-stakes talk about Richard himself and the politics of the modern day. Local talk about Richard threatened to disrupt England's national narrative in the nineteenth century, for instance, and it buoyed Vienna's regeneration in the early twentieth. British antiquarians, George Ellis and Walter Scott foremost among them, inaugurated the English tradition of *Richard Coeur de Lion* in the early nineteenth century. Their research and publications were

---

13. *A Transcript of the Registers of the Company of Stationers of London, 1554–1640 A. D.*, ed. Edward Arber and Charles Rivington, vol. 1 (London: Company of Stationers, 1875), 179.

14. A notable exception occurs more than halfway through Ralph Hanna, "The Matter of Fulk: Romance and History in the Marches," *Journal of English and Germanic Philology* 110 (2011): 354: "At this point, I want to back off from considering narrative method in *Fouke le Fitz Waryn* to complicate matters slightly. I've pretended that there is a text of this name, recorded at some point in the 1320s. In fact, that is not quite the case; there are three *Fouke le Fitz Waryns*, of which the 1320s rendition happens to be the only one actually available for scrutiny."

available to and necessarily informed the work of Karl Brunner, the Austrian philologist responsible for our sole critical edition of *Richard Coeur de Lion*, published in 1913. Brunner fashioned the romance's twentieth-century iteration in part from the findings of his insular predecessors. But he also added a Continental set of rumors to the extant English ones, and his scholarship was significantly influenced, like the writings of Ellis and Scott before him, by the local talk and contemporary politics that surrounded him. The modern literary history of *Richard Coeur de Lion* is one in which the romance's unexplained absence from certain historical sites and unexpected presence at others is evidently not arbitrary when the spaces between and around the making of modern texts are attended to. Those spaces preserve not only medieval talk contemporary with Richard, but that talk's presence within and influence on modern, local talk. All of this talk, in turn, signifies the wide range of voices, and thus people, essential to textual production. *Richard Coeur de Lion* has recently been called "the most medieval of romances."[15] But, the rumor of *Richard Coeur de Lion* that we circulate in our talk and texts is not medieval, not even mostly medieval. It is the result of a series of modern readers turned text-makers whose encounters with and responses to the manuscript copies of *Richard Coeur de Lion* were shaped by the times and places in which they lived and the local talk circulating around them. On a modern scholar's best day, she is not omniscient or objective; she, like a medieval text-maker, reads and writes amidst a local milieu that influences how she interprets a text or makes an edition, and thus how she reconstructs the past. A recently published noncritical edition of *Richard Coeur de Lion* exemplifies this process.[16] In its introduction, its editor attributes the edition—both its existence and its particulars—to the absence of an in-print edition ("a new edition is long overdue") and to our scholarly talk: "In part, the extent of recent critical interest in *a*'s fabulous interpolations justifies editing this version."[17] The "*a*" version of the romance, constructed in Brunner's edition, repeats the rumor of *Richard Coeur de Lion,* including its "fabulous interpolations." Retrospective texts provoke talk among us, and the texts we as scholars make—versions of retrospective texts, whether articles or editions—are also informed by circulating talk.

The absence of urgency around answering that most basic of questions about the romance—what we should call it—instantiates *Richard Coeur de Lion*'s persistent marginal status vis-à-vis our modern Middle English canon, and the degree to which the romance about Richard has always existed as a text more in theory than on record. Brunner fashioned the first and to date

---

15. Heng, *Empire of Magic,* 67.
16. See Larkin, *Richard Coer de Lyon.*
17. Larkin, *Richard Coer de Lyon,* 21.

the only critical edition of the romance, *Der mittelenglische Versroman über Richard Löwenherz*, which was published by a Viennese academic press in 1913.[18] At the time of its publication, Brunner's edition filled a vacuum, certainly of work and possibly of interest, in its material. The Master(s) of the Rolls, under whose auspices the official *Chronicles and Memorials of Great Britain and Ireland* was determined, edited, and published between 1858 and 1911, did not include *Richard Coeur de Lion* among its number, even as the collection's "memorials" category became increasingly wide-ranging, containing, for instance, insular hagiography and what some have called folklore.[19] Omitted from that official corpus of documents that formed national identity out of the past's constituent parts, *Richard Coeur de Lion* was not—and still has not been—included in the canon of England's earliest literature, an archive unofficially overseen by the Early English Text Society (EETS). Founded in 1864, EETS had issued almost two hundred and fifty editions under its imprimatur by the end of 1913.[20] As EETS's online home page states today, "Without EETS editions, study of medieval English texts would hardly be possible"—a fact that makes *Richard Coeur de Lion*'s absence from EETS's catalogue all the more consequential and perplexing.[21] Prior to Brunner, the romance about Richard was brought to national attention by the influential insular antiquar-

---

18. Karl Brunner, ed. *Der mittelenglische Versroman über Richard Löwenherz*, Wiener Beiträge zur englischen Philologie 42 (Vienna: Wilhelm Braumüller, 1913). (Hereafter *Richard Löwenherz*.)

19. Medieval genre boundaries are porous and parts of many volumes in the Rolls Series fit this description, but, for example, T. O. Cockayne, ed., *Leechdoms, Wortcunning, and Starcraft of Early England*, 3 vols., RS 35 (London: Longman and Green, 1864–1866). Roughly contemporary precedent for the national embrace of an artifact such as *Richard Coeur de Lion* did exist. When rediscovered in Oxford's Bodleian Library in the nineteenth century, the early twelfth-century poem *La Chanson de Roland* was claimed by France as its oldest national epic, despite the poem's insular provenance. See Joseph J. Duggan, "Franco-German Conflict and the History of French Scholarship on the *Song of Roland*," in *Hermeneutics and Medieval Culture*, ed. Patrick J. Gallacher and Helen Damico (Albany: State University of New York, 1989), 98. On Xavier Marmier and the Oxford *Roland*'s identification and 1837 publication by Francisque Michel, see Andrew Taylor, *Textual Situations: Three Medieval Manuscripts and Their Readers* (Philadelphia: University of Pennsylvania Press, 2002), 26–31. See also chapter 4.

20. F. J. Furnivall founded EETS with the stated goals of, "on the one hand, to print all that is most valuable of the yet unprinted MSS in English, and, on the other, to re-edit and reprint all that is most valuable in printed English books, which from their scarcity or price are not within the reach of the student of moderate means." See Antony Singleton, "The Early English Text Society in the Nineteenth Century: An Organizational History," *Review of English Studies* 56 (2005): 91–92.

21. Anne Hudson, "The Early English Text Society, Present, Past, and Future," http://users.ox.ac.uk/-eets/index.html.

ians of the early nineteenth century, men who had access to England's literary inheritance and their hands on the ropes of cultural dissemination.

George Ellis, heir to Jamaican sugar plantations and friend of Sir Walter Scott,[22] transcribed the early fifteenth-century copy of *Richard Coeur de Lion* preserved in Cambridge, Gonville and Caius College, MS 175/96.[23] Described by Ellis as the "most perfect copy extant" of the romance among the six copies he knew,[24] Caius was the longest surviving copy and contained the most sensational material. Walter Scott himself had studied other copies of the romance, especially the Auchinleck manuscript's forty-third extant item, *King Richard,* which consisted of a single bifolium: the first and the last leaves of

---

22. On George Ellis II, see Humphrey Gawthrop, "George Ellis of Ellis Caymanas: A Caribbean Link to Scott and the Brontë Sisters," *Electronic British Library Journal* (2005): 2–5. Correspondence between Ellis and Scott dates to 1801, and upon Ellis's death in 1815, Scott inherited four quarto volumes containing Ellis's transcriptions of medieval manuscripts. One of the first volume's endpapers has been inscribed in part: "Presented by John and Charles Ellis [Ellis's cousins], executors to George Ellis, as a token of his friendship." "Richard Coer de Lion" is written in Ellis's hand above his transcription of the romance from the Caius manuscript. Scott's library at Abbotsford is now in trust to the Advocates Library, Edinburgh, and the volumes are catalogued as "Collection of English and French metrical romances." I am grateful to Andrea Longson, senior librarian at the Advocates Library, for her help in locating these volumes, assessing their provenance, and taking photographs for me. On Scott's personal library, see J. G. Cochrane, ed., *Catalogue of the Library at Abbotsford* (Edinburgh: Maitland Club, 1838), 103–5. The four volumes—essentially Ellis's field notebooks for *Specimens*—contain more than a dozen romances in English and insular French, transcribed from at least eight manuscripts that are now recognized as essential repositories of Middle English romance, but were mostly unstudied when Ellis encountered them. On Ellis's researches, see Arthur Johnston, *Enchanted Ground: The Study of Medieval Romance in the Eighteenth Century* (London: Athlone Press, 1964), 161. In addition to *Richard Coeur de Lion,* Ellis transcribed copies of *Bevis of Hampton, Tristran l'Amoureux,* the lais of Marie de France, *Sir Degaré, Robert of Cysille, The Sodowne of Babylon, Amis and Amiloun, Of Arthour and of Merlin, Sir Ysumbras, Roswal and Lilian,* and *Sir Otuel.* On the friendship of Ellis and Scott, inextricable from Ellis's private researches and published writings, see John Buchan, *Sir Walter Scott* (New York: Coward-McCann, 1932), 59; A. Johnston, *Enchanted Ground,* 148–76; and Jerome Mitchell, *Scott, Chaucer, and Medieval Romance: A Study in Sir Walter Scott's Indebtedness to the Literature of the Middle Ages* (Lexington: University of Kentucky Press, 1987), 6–10.

23. M. R. James, *A Descriptive Catalogue of the Manuscripts of the Library of Gonville and Caius College,* vol. 1 (Cambridge: Cambridge University Press, 1907), 199–200.

24. George Ellis, ed., *Specimens of Early English Metrical Romances, Chiefly Written during the Early Part of the Fourteenth Century,* 2nd ed., 3 vols. (London: Longman, Hurst, Rees, and Orme, 1811), 2:178. Of the Caius copy, Ellis noted that "several leaves are wanting." In addition to that copy, Ellis knew two editions printed in 1509 and 1528 by Wynkyn de Worde; a "Harleian MS," which he deemed scrappy; a longer copy in the collection of his friend and fellow antiquarian Francis Douce; and a "fragment" of "only two leaves" in the Auchinleck manuscript. For Ellis's published impressions of these manuscripts, see Ellis, *Specimens,* 2:177–78.

a quire whose beginning coincided with that of the romance. Scott's detailed description of the *King Richard* "fragment," as he called it, survives in a letter he sent to Ellis at the start of their private correspondence.²⁵ In their subsequent letters, they discussed the significant differences between *King Richard* and the Caius copy. *King Richard,* they agreed, shared Caius's whimsy, but lacked its salaciousness. While Caius begins with a prologue of sorts and Richard's birth and youth, *King Richard* begins with a different prologue, about the romance itself, and moves directly into Richard's decision to take the cross after the fall of Jerusalem. While Caius repeatedly defers Richard's participation in crusade with long descriptions of a tournament he organizes, a prefatory trip to the East that Richard makes with two friends, and his imprisonment in Germany on his return from that trip to England, *King Richard* includes none of these episodes. It sets Richard aboard a ship to Acre almost immediately. The scenes that follow the siege of Acre in Caius, including the cannibalism scenes, are not present in *King Richard.* Whether those scenes did not survive or never existed in Auchinleck at all was an issue never resolved between Ellis and Scott in their private correspondence.²⁶ Instead, Ellis deemed Caius the romance's central witness and published a version of it.

Using his transcription of Caius, Ellis made what he called an "abstract," a mixture of quotations he selected from Caius and his own summaries of various episodes, which he published under the title "Richard Coer de Lion" in his multivolume *Specimens of Early English Metrical Romances.*²⁷ Ellis's "Richard Coer de Lion" circulated widely. The first two editions of *Specimens* were published in 1805 and 1811 as three octavo volumes, and a single-volume edition was issued in 1848. In 1810, Henry Weber, Walter Scott's amanuensis, published *Metrical Romances of the Thirteenth, Fourteenth, and Fifteenth Centuries.* In it, Weber included his own rendering of "Richard Coer de Lion" based on Ellis's transcription of Caius.²⁸ Some fifteen years later, Ellis's transcription was again printed (though mistakenly attributed to Weber) in Thomas

---

25. For Scott's correspondence with Ellis, partially published, see *The Letters of Sir Walter Scott,* ed. Herbert Grierson, vol. 12 (London: Constable, 1937), 219–24. Grierson omits Scott's transcription and analysis that follows the quotation above; the full letter is now New York, Morgan Library, MA 426.16 (1–3); for its text, see chapter 4.
26. The majority of Ellis's concerns about this appear in his letter to Scott of October 12, 1802, now Edinburgh, National Library of Scotland, MS 873, 40r–41r.
27. Ellis, *Specimens,* 2:186. Ellis used Francis Douce's copy, now Oxford, Bodleian Library, MS Douce 228, to supplement lacunae in the Caius manuscript.
28. Henry Weber, ed. *Metrical Romances of the Thirteenth, Fourteenth, and Fifteenth Centuries,* 2 vols. (Edinburgh: George Ramsay and Co., 1810). On Weber, see Kurt Gamerschlag, "Henry Weber: Medieval Scholar, Poet, and Secretary to Walter Scott," *Studies in Scottish Literature* 25 (1990): 202–17.

Warton's *The History of English Poetry*.²⁹ It was Ellis's published abstract of the romance to which Scott referred and from which he borrowed material for his historical novels. They carried the most astonishing pieces of "Richard Coer de Lion" around the world and into popular culture.

A scene in Scott's *Montrose* (1819) is an analog to the second cannibalism episode printed by Ellis; in *The Monastery* (1820), Richard "ate up the head of a Moor carbonadoed"; for *Anne of Geierstein* (1829), Scott appears to have drawn on the episode involving Richard's mother.³⁰ When in *Ivanhoe* (1819) Richard strikes the friar following a test of strength, Scott himself notes that he drew inspiration for the scene from the German-prison episode.³¹ And among the many details from "Richard Coer de Lion" included in *The Talisman* (1825), one of Scott's most popular novels, is a description of the cure for Richard's illness on crusade: the roasted head of a Muslim he mistook for pork. *The Talisman* spread word of Richard's cannibalism among and beyond English-speaking audiences. Some sixty years after the novel's initial publication, it became one of the first English-language novels to be translated into Arabic. It appeared under the title *Qalb al-Asad*, that is, "Lionheart."³²

With Ellis's "Richard Coer de Lion" having circulated widely for roughly thirty years in various vessels, Scott apparently felt impelled to regain control of what he then called the "rumor" of Richard's cannibalism. In an appendix to *The Talisman*'s introduction in its 1832 edition, both cannibalism passages are reproduced and Ellis's *Specimens* is cited as Scott's own immediate source. Through the conceit of revealing a truth to his clamorous readers, Scott explains that although the cannibalism "imputed" to "the King of England" had "found its way into history" (surely a euphemism for Scott's own role in said wending), it was most certainly a "rumor" whose "invention" could be traced back, first, to Ellis's abstract, and even further to "an ignorant minstrel" who "ascribed" to Richard a Norman story about a "cannibalizing band

---

29. Thomas Warton, *The History of English Poetry, from the Close of the Eleventh Century to the Commencement of the Eighteenth Century*, 2nd ed., 3 vols. (London: Thomas Tegg, 1840).

30. Ellis initially raises the episode in his letter to Scott dated October 12, 1802 (see above), and again on November 1, 1802 (MS 873, 42v), in response to Scott's reply. Scott's letter is dated October 17, 1802, now Morgan Library, MA 426.16 (1–3).

31. Mitchell, *Scott, Chaucer, and Medieval Romance*, 20, 125, 130–31, 140, 177–78, 200, 202.

32. Walter Scott, *Qalb al-Asad*, ed. and trans. Ya'qub Sarruf and Faris Nimr (Cairo: Matba'at al-Muqtataf, 1886). A translator's note on the final page of the first edition states that certain details were changed from Scott's text "to suit the taste of the readers in these lands." I am grateful to Omar Y. Cheta for calling my attention to this edition and its publication history, and for translating the above note.

of Saracen warriors."[33] What apparently bothered Scott was not the rumor of cannibalism, which he baldly ascribes to "Saracen warriors," but the calcification of the rumor of Richard's cannibalism as history. The supposed running of a rumor to ground can sometimes rob it of its intrigue, but Scott's intervention itself confirms he was too late.

Upon his discovery of the romance thirty years earlier, Ellis had also worried about how "Richard Coer de Lion" might intervene in England's historical narrative. The text had the potential to cast England's kings or those who wrote about them, or both, in an unflattering light. He shared his misgivings with Scott in an unpublished letter of October 12, 1802. With the fieldwork for *Specimens* newly complete, Ellis explained to Scott that his literary etymology had turned up one sample that, to borrow a twentieth-century description of another perplexing fifteenth-century text, resembled a "chocolate-covered tarantula."[34] Ellis did not know what the Caius copy of the romance about Richard was or whether it should be admitted into the early English canon. "The story is, in many respects, so very ridiculous," he confides to his friend, "that I cannot conceive its having been written within a short time after Richard's death, or indeed at any time, in *England*; and yet it cannot have been composed in France, because the French are abused in it most abominably. Can it be of Scottish or border origin?"[35] While Scott tried to locate the rumor's "invention" to "an ignorant minstrel," Ellis hoped to deport it altogether. The romance's very existence appears to have discomfited him, to have made him uneasy about the taste and nature of medieval English writers and readers—his forebears ("I cannot conceive its having been written . . . in *England*"). Similar concern over a story's origin does not appear elsewhere in Ellis's private musings about his discoveries and transcriptions of other romances. Nor are "rumor" and "history" so expressly positioned

---

33. Sir Walter Scott, *The Talisman: A Tale of the Crusades, and Chronicles of the Canongate* (1825; reprint, London: George Routledge and Sons, 1876), 7, 9–14.

34. Ralph Hanna, "Contextualizing the *Siege of Jerusalem*," *Yearbook of Langland Studies* 6 (1992): 108. It is uncertain whether copies of the *Siege of Jerusalem* and *Richard Coeur de Lion* traveled in concert, but copies of both came into the possession of Robert Thornton, the prolific Yorkshire copyist. He included both texts in one of the collections he assembled and copied, now London, British Library, MS Additional 31042 (the London Thornton). See John J. Thompson, *Robert Thornton and the London Thornton Manuscript: British Library MS Additional 31042* (Cambridge: D. S. Brewer, 1987), 35–55; Ralph Hanna, "The London Thornton Manuscript: A Corrected Collation," *Studies in Bibliography* 37 (1984): 127–30; Susanna Fein, "The Contents of Thornton's Manuscripts," in *Robert Thornton and His Books: Essays on the Lincoln and London Thornton Manuscripts*, ed. Susanna Fein and Michael Johnston (York: York Medieval Press, 2014), 13–65; and M. Johnston, *Romance and the Gentry*, 104–5, 176–83.

35. MS 873, 40v.

by Scott as binary terms elsewhere in his published work. Few Middle English romances depict historical figures, and no other Middle English romance the men encountered could so easily have been mistaken for English history. Ellis's reluctance to accept the Caius copy as his literary inheritance, and Scott's apparent dismay at the ease with which its rumor became indistinguishable from England's history, illustrate some of the difficulties retrospective texts raise. They can intervene in cultural memory and structure the past's relationship to the present moment.

The present moment that Ellis inhabited was filled with pointed discussions among his fellow antiquarians about the past's cultural production and the national literature, and thus the national identity, that could be shaped from it.[36] Yet in *Specimens,* Ellis asserts the romance's importance as a retrospective text regardless of its risks. Ellis explains in the prefatory material to "Richard Coer de Lion" that his episodic summaries of Caius are interspersed with "such passages of the originals as appeared to me worth preserving, either from their poetical merit—from their representing correct pictures of antient manners—or from their being characteristic of the author's feelings, or of those of our nation."[37] Here Ellis ultimately characterizes the romance as an important archive, albeit one he reconstructed. To make "Richard Coer de Lion," he selected the manners, characteristics, and feelings "of our nation" "worth preserving." That is, Ellis's choices about what constituted the romance's text were not made in the service of the medieval memory of Richard, but to burnish, as far as was possible, Ellis's own time and place. The inclusion of "Richard Coer de Lion" in *Specimens* is an acknowledgment that rumor and history cannot be fully disentangled. For others, that entanglement was perhaps precisely the problem. By the late nineteenth century, Ellis's "Richard Coer de Lion" had come to represent—and thus to misrepresent— the medieval textual tradition of the romance about Richard as an unpalatable inheritance: fit for rumor, not for the national record.

The next major site of the romance's study and dissemination was, then, not England but Vienna, where *Richard Löwenherz,* Karl Brunner's critical edition of *Richard Coeur de Lion,* was published in 1913. The romance's presence in Vienna and in the hands of an Austrian scholar of early English literature is fundamental to the edition Brunner produced and to the rumor

---

36. In addition to the networks of friends and connections often described in the prefatory material to the volumes published by Ellis and his colleagues, there is also private gossip, sometimes backbiting in nature, about literary discovery and publication status. For example, MS 873, 40r: Ellis writes to Scott on October 12, 1802, "[Joseph] Ritson has not yet *published* his romances (I beg his pardon Romanceës)."

37. Ellis, *Specimens,* 1:iv.

of *Richard Coeur de Lion* that we circulate. In Brunner, we have a radically different reader than Scott or Ellis, or the Anglo-American scholars of Brunner's own era. Born in the Karlin district of Prague in 1887 to a Linzer father and a Viennese mother, the former an academic and the latter descended from one, Brunner began his training as a philologist in 1905 at the University of Innsbruck. He studied there under the university's first "Anglicist," Rudolf Fischer, before moving among Berlin, England, and Vienna, where he studied the history of the English language.[38] As a scholar with significant specialized training, Brunner came to the manuscript copies of *Richard Coeur de Lion*, indeed to the very idea of a retrospective text about Richard and his late twelfth-century reign, distinctly equipped. He was a reader in possession of the common knowledge and cultural memory that had circulated during his youth in the Austro-Hungarian Empire and his subsequent studies on the Continent.[39] He was a scholar who had access to the local talk of fin-de-siècle Vienna as he read and worked. And he was a text-maker amidst the social exigencies that shaped and were shaped by not the nation of Richard's origin, but local Viennese talk. While Ellis and Scott read *Richard Coeur de Lion* as a retrospective text about "our nation" and edited it accordingly, the terms of Brunner's relationship to the matter of Richard were entirely different.

Brunner's cultural and historical context bore crucially on how he read and what he read for, and thus on his editorial decisions, the version of the romance that he put into circulation, and the version of Richard that we have come to circulate. Like Ellis, Brunner privileged the Caius copy, but by the time of Brunner's researches more witnesses of *Richard Coeur de Lion* had been recovered. Ellis was aware of four extant medieval manuscript copies of the romance, and two early-modern editions (with a third he had heard of, but not seen), printed by Wynkyn de Worde in 1509 and 1528.[40] In addition to these two early sixteenth-century editions, Brunner knew of three additional medieval copies, bringing the number of extant manuscript copies to seven. Roughly chronologically, these are now the Auchinleck manuscript, probably produced in London between 1331 and 1340, and its fragment, Edinburgh, Edinburgh University Library, 218, whose discovery was announced in

---

38. Herbert Koziol, "Karl Brunner," in *Almanach: Österreichische Akademie der Wissenschaften* (Vienna: Hermann Böhlaus, 1965 [1966]), 260–61. For Brunner's publications, Koziol, "Brunner," 267–72; and Kurt Lumpi, "Bibliographie der Veröffentlichungen," in *Studies in English Language and Literature, Presented to Professor Dr. Karl Brunner on the Occasion of His Seventieth Birthday*, ed. Siegfried Korninger (Vienna: Wilhelm Braumüller, 1957), 284–90.

39. Koziol, "Brunner," 261. After receiving his doctorate at Innsbruck in 1910, Brunner returned to England, presumably to work on his *Habilitationsschrift*. When he was not in England during this period, he appears to have been in Berlin and Vienna.

40. Ellis, *Specimens*, 2:177–78.

1857;[41] London, British Library, MS Egerton 2862 (*olim* Sutherland), dated to the last quarter of the fourteenth century; Ellis's "most perfect" manuscript, Cambridge, Gonville and Caius College, 175/96, dated to the early fifteenth century; London, British Library, MS Additional 31042, or the "London Thornton," a large collection in the hand of prolific Yorkshire copyist (and reader) Robert Thornton, and dated to the second quarter of the fifteenth century; London, College of Arms, MS Arundel 58, a mid-fifteenth-century prose and verse copy of Robert of Gloucester's Middle English metrical chronicle into which *Richard Coeur de Lion* was copied at the point of Richard's reign;[42] London, British Library, MS Harley 4690, which has also been dated to the middle of the fifteenth century and contains a copy of the prose *Brut*; and Oxford, Bodleian Library, MS Douce 228,[43] which consists solely of a late fifteenth-century copy of *Richard Coeur de Lion*.[44]

On the basis of similar narratives and shared variants,[45] Brunner distributed these manuscripts into two main branches of transmission, descending from a hypothetical *ur*-text, which he—like Ellis, Weber, and Gaston Paris before him—speculated had itself descended from a lost thirteenth-century Anglo-Norman source.[46] This stemma's first branch, Brunner's group *a*, contains

---

41. The fragment was acquired by David Laing before 1837. See G. V. Smithers, "Two Newly-Discovered Fragments from the Auchinleck MS," *Medium Ævum* 18 (1949): 1–3; *The Auchinleck Manuscript: National Library of Scotland, Advocates' MS 19.2.1*, intro. Derek Pearsall and I. C. Cunningham (London: Scolar Press, 1977), vii (hereafter Pearsall-Cunningham); and Eugen Kölbing, "Kleine publicationen aus der Auchinleck-hs. III," *Englische Studien* 8 (1885): 115–19, for transcriptions of the fragments.

42. For some time, scholars have referred to the College of Arms manuscript as either "HDN 58" or "Arundel 58." I am grateful to James Lloyd, archivist at the College of Arms, for confirming in personal communication that the correct reference number is Arundel 58.

43. Larkin, *Richard Coer de Lyon*, 3, gives "MS Oxford, Bodleian 21802" as the shelfmark for Oxford, Bodleian Library, MS Douce 228. In fact, "21802" is Douce 228's number in the library's *Summary Catalogue*, not its shelfmark. See *A Summary Catalogue of Western Manuscripts in the Bodleian Library at Oxford*, ed. R. W. Hunt, Falconer Madan, and P. D. Record, vol. 4 (Oxford: Clarendon Press, 1897), 562.

44. For extended discussions of extant manuscript copies, see chapters 4 and 5. See *Richard Löwenherz*, 1–11, for Brunner's descriptions. For overviews and descriptions of all of these manuscripts, see Gisela Guddat-Figge, *Catalogue of Manuscripts Containing Middle English Romances* (Munich: Wilhelm Fink, 1976); and see, more recently, Philida M. T. A. Schellekens, "An Edition of the Middle English Romance: *Richard Coeur de Lion*," 2 vols. (unpublished PhD diss., Durham University, 1989), 2:6–24. Wynkyn de Worde's 1509 and 1528 editions are *STC* 21007 and *STC* 21008.

45. *Richard Löwenherz*, 14–17.

46. *Richard Löwenherz*, 11; Ellis, *Specimens*, 2:178: "The English version of this romance (for it is professedly a translation)" and "indeed, there are strong reasons for believing that the first French original, and even the earliest English version, contained an authentic history of Richard's reign." See also Gaston Paris, "Le Roman de Richard Coeur de Lion," *Romania*

the Caius and London Thornton manuscripts, both from the chronological middle of the extant textual tradition, as well as Wynkyn de Worde's editions. The second branch, Brunner's group *b*, comprises the balance of manuscripts, dating from the early fourteenth to late fifteenth centuries. Brunner formed these groups on the basis of those copies he judged narratively, not chronologically, "earlier." Narratively earlier meant, for Brunner, copies that appeared to contain more historical material.[47] He posited that the copies containing more—and more fantastical—episodes (his group *a*) were at a greater narrative remove from the *ur*-text.[48] The copies in his group *b* were, he felt, more historical in nature and thus closer to the *ur*-text.[49]

Central to understanding Brunner's editorial methodology, but never discussed in relation to it, is the fact that this stemma correlates very little with the edition he himself produced. Despite codicological study of each of these manuscripts and their texts, work thorough enough to yield textual variants for each copy, Brunner's edition is neither diplomatic nor collated. It is instead a composite of the Caius copy, whose not insignificant lacunae—a mix of self-evident gaps and projected loss—Brunner supplemented with Wynkyn de Worde's 1509 edition. Brunner's rationale for this editorial choice in part resembles that of Ellis. He selected the Caius copy because it "contains the least error" (*Es enthält am wenigsten Fehler*), because his *a* recension "offers the better text" overall (*den besseren Text bietet*), and because of Caius's extensiveness.[50] The longest extant copy of *Richard Coeur de Lion*, Caius begins with Richard's birth and ends with his death, a symmetry that suggests completeness.[51] It includes the cannibalism episodes, a jousting tournament, a pre-crusade reconnaissance mission to the East that culminates with Richard's temporary imprisonment in Germany, and the narration of many other sieges in the East after the fall of Acre. Brunner's *Richard Löwenherz* is a romance of 7,200 lines,[52] far longer than what survives in any extant manuscript copy.

---

26 (1897): 353–93; and Roger Sherman Loomis, "*Richard Coeur de Lion* and the *Pas Saladin* in Medieval Art," *PMLA* 30 (1915), 510: "Since in three places the Middle English text makes acknowledgment to a French authority, it is clear that the closely historical portions represent an Anglo-Norman poem." Similar arguments have been made since, including in L. H. Loomis, *Medieval Romance*, 147. On an Anglo-Norman source as such, see chapter 4.

47. *Richard Löwenherz*, 20–21.

48. *Richard Löwenherz*, 11–24.

49. For a more recent argument positing an Anglo-Norman history as source, see Finlayson, "*Richard Coer de Lyon*," 161ff.

50. *Richard Löwenherz*, 23. In part because their meters differ, Caius's lacunae could not be supplemented with London Thornton's copy; see *Richard Löwenherz*, 24.

51. The only other copy to begin and end perfectly—that is, without material fragmentation—is London Thornton.

52. The 1509 edition adds roughly two thousand lines to the Caius copy.

Despite the peculiarities of Brunner's composite edition and the widely acknowledged problems its critical apparatus presents,[53] Brunner's editorial decisions align with Ellis's proclivities, and with our own—proclivities for a "complete" narrative and a "perfect" copy, to borrow the language of codicology. "Completeness" is a pervasive and usually ill-defined goal of textual critics and modern readers. In the case of *Richard Coeur de Lion,* however, the narrative fullness of Brunner's *Richard Löwenherz* seems to have given the impression that it contains everything. Having everything, it has been construed as valuable: "the fullest, the most 'contaminated' and most romance-like version of the poem."[54] Textual abundance is here and elsewhere confusingly cited as at once useful to, and a product of, our project of cultural recovery. Thus, when we write or say *"Richard Coeur de Lion,"* what we almost always cite and mean is Brunner's *Richard Löwenherz.*[55] There are two immediate problems with this conflation. First, we are instantaneously mired in the debate over whether a diplomatic or a collated edition is preferable—that is, whether we want to study a text that we know at least one medieval reader read, or to construct the text an author may have first composed. Though such debate is not new among medievalists,[56] Brunner's edition, because neither collated nor diplomatic, in fact stands outside of this debate. If we are to continue circulating *Richard Löwenherz* in our talk and text as if it were an object that would have once been in the hands of a medieval person, whether a reader or a textmaker, we need to justify that choice (and envision its consequences). Second, Brunner may well have been a maximalist,[57] but he was also a person making

---

53. These include that the edition's introduction, notes, and back matter are written in an Austrian dialect; the flawed transcription; and the outdated stemma. That *Richard Löwenherz* remains both necessary and insufficient is articulated in Ambrisco, "Cannibalism and Cultural Encounters," 524 n. 3: "In general, I agree with Davis's argument about both the problems inherent with Brunner's theory of the romance's transmission and, hence, the arbitrariness of Brunner's designations. I will nonetheless continue (as do all the poem's critics) to use Brunner's designations of *a* and *b* to distinguish between the two main renderings of the romance."

54. McDonald, "Eating People," 130.

55. On this conflation, see chapter 4. See also Larkin, *Richard Coer de Lyon.* Larkin is more conservative with emendations than Brunner, but replicates Brunner's choice of exemplars because group *a* offers the most "complete" text, and, Larkin notes, the TEAMS edition "in many respects" "brings Brunner's 1913 work up to date" (21).

56. On the terms and stakes of this debate, see chapters 4 and 5.

57. For Brunner, volume functioned as a signifier of value or, at least, superiority. He applies a similar rationale in other venues. See Karl Brunner, "Middle English Metrical Romances and Their Audience," in *Studies in Medieval Literature, in Honour of Professor Albert Croll Baugh,* ed. MacEdward Leach (Philadelphia: University of Pennsylvania Press, 1961), 219: "Fragments of MSS. are left out of consideration, since they do not reveal anything for our purpose."

a text. His choice to produce an edition, and, more pressingly for his readers, many of the choices that constitute that edition, arose from the concerns of the time and place in which it was produced.

For Brunner, the copies of *Richard Coeur de Lion* would have registered, like they did for Ellis and Scott, as a textual tradition whose retrospectivity was germane to his own history and identity. But unlike Ellis and Scott, Brunner would have recognized certain episodes in the romance as old, local rumor. The peculiarities of *Richard Löwenherz,* including its apparatus, Brunner's choice of exemplars, and the parts of their contents he decided to copy, reflect and respond to the place of the edition's publication: the Vienna of Brunner's present, and the medieval Vienna embedded in Viennese cultural memory. Vienna, and Austria and Germany more broadly, had their own long preoccupations with Richard. Returning from crusade, he had been captured just beyond Vienna's city limit by the duke of Austria, Leopold V, in 1192, and imprisoned in Dürnstein in Austria's Wachau Valley, whence he was handed over to Henry VI, the Holy Roman emperor, and eventually freed in 1194.[58] Rumors of Richard's clashes with and capture by Austrian and German crusaders have been in continuous circulation on the Continent since the late twelfth century.[59] Brunner would have heard these rumors, if not as a child from his Viennese mother, then as an adult in Vienna at the turn of the twentieth century, when medieval rumors about Richard's capture circulated there around Brunner in local talk.[60]

The copies of *Richard Coeur de Lion* that depict Richard's capture as he returns to England overland from the East set that event in "Almayne," or Germany.[61] Scholars frequently analyze *Richard Coeur de Lion* in terms of its historical fidelity or lack thereof, a line of inquiry that is often an end in itself. I am interested in the romance's fast and loose play with historical facts because of the effects those moments of historical imprecision potentially have on readers. As a retrospective text, *Richard Coeur de Lion*'s historical inaccuracies produce in certain kinds of readers—knowing readers—the impulse to correct. Brunner would have known the local history, and as a reader encountering *Richard Coeur de Lion* with such local common knowledge, he no

---

58. H. E. Mayer, "A Ghost Ship Called Frankenef: King Richard's German Itinerary," *English Historical Review* 115 (2000): 137–38.

59. Persistent knowledge of Richard's capture is evinced by, for instance, the Austrian castle at Dürnstein, where Richard was initially imprisoned and which now holds the Hotel Richard Löwenherz. For other examples, see below in this chapter.

60. On this twentieth-century talk and its origins in twelfth- and thirteenth-century Vienna, see below in this chapter.

61. All but the copies in Auchinleck and Egerton 2862 contain some version of these episodes.

doubt mentally substituted "Austria" or "Vienna" for "Almayne" when reading.[62] To make this substitution, whether consciously or subconsciously, he would have triangulated the text before him with this local knowledge about the past, and with the present talk about old times that circulated in his local milieu(x): Austria, Germany, England. This is in fact the way in which any knowing reader reads a retrospective text: by triangulating the text with codified common knowledge, including historical rumor, and with the particularities of one's contemporary milieu, including local talk. That when we read we bring our state of knowledge about a subject and our present contexts to bear, and that those elements illuminate, or cause us to edit mentally, aspects of a text, is not a controversial point. But it is a crucial and rarely acknowledged one, and its ramifications for the interplay between talk and textual production are vast. Our knowledge and immediate contexts can influence how we choose objects for study and the grounds upon which our approaches to that study are made. This is not a time-bound process, but one that places us as readers, writers, and makers of editions on a continuum with past readers and text-makers.

Brunner's editorial treatment of the Almayne episodes in *Richard Löwenherz* suggests that his response to them fell somewhere between simple recognition and intense preoccupation. His most perplexing editorial choices involve the Almayne episodes, which, Brunner asserts in his edition's introductory material, are "original" to the romance.[63] This claim has always puzzled his edition's readers. The medievalists who first wrote about Brunner's edition in the early twentieth century were baffled by his editorial decisions, and especially by his treatment of the Almayne episodes. Shortly after *Richard Löwenherz* was published in 1913, Roger Sherman Loomis, then, like Brunner, just beginning his scholarly career, reviewed it for the *Journal of English and Germanic Philology*.[64] Loomis begins:

> In this volume we have a long needed critical edition of the romance *Richard Coeur de Lion,* first printed by Weber in his *Metrical Romances,* vol. II, in the year 1803 [sic]. It has on the whole been strangely neglected by scholars,

---

62. The Middle English word for the duchy of Austria existed by at least the time of the romance's copying into the Caius manuscript, since "Ostrych" appears there in the same line as "Alemayn." See Gonville and Caius 175/96, p. 65a, line 1 (I reproduce the library's page numbers here and throughout). The *MED* entry for "Ostrich(e" n. (2) gives the earliest usage as a 1387 copy of Trevisa's translation of Higden's *Polychronicon*, where the proper noun is used in the story of the Duke of Austria's banner at Acre, on which see below.

63. *Richard Löwenherz,* 17–19, 21–22.

64. On R. S. Loomis, see Albert C. Baugh's foreword to R. S. Loomis, *Studies in Medieval Literature: A Memorial Collection of Essays* (New York: B. Franklin, 1970), v–vi.

and the edition by Professor Hausknecht, long promised by the E. E. T. S., is not yet forthcoming.[65]

A ringing endorsement it is not. After Ellis and his fellow antiquarians circulated the romance, cycles of fleeting interest in the surviving copies of *Richard Coeur de Lion* alternated with the "strange neglect" that Loomis attributes to the absence of a textual monument around which scholarship could organize itself.[66] Within that sparse critical landscape, Loomis characterizes Brunner's edition as a way station whose value lies partly—or even wholly, if we grant that Loomis planned his opening gambit as fastidiously as the point-by-point critique that follows it—in the simple fact of its existence.

Loomis was not alone among his contemporaries in feeling ambivalent about Brunner's edition. Johannes Koch's review of *Richard Löwenherz*, for *Englische Studien*, appeared a year earlier than Loomis's, in 1915.[67] "The list of my objections and corrections is, as one can see, quite long" (*Die liste meiner einwendungen und korrekturen ist, wie man sieht, ziemlich lang*), Koch explains, before suggesting both kindly and rather too late that the list of nearly seventeen pages should not deter his reader from thanking Brunner for his archival and editorial labors.[68] Loomis provided a list of his own,[69] and together they contain fewer items in common than Brunner might have hoped. Most items are related directly, or through a subsequent distrust in Brunner's judgment, to a single editorial decision: *Richard Löwenherz* begins with a series of episodes that run from lines 35 to 1268 in the edition, episodes that Brunner claims in his introduction are original.[70] Brunner could have attributed the inclusion of these episodes to his guiding editorial principle that the longest surviving copy of a text is, by virtue of its volume, also the most valuable.[71] He does not.

---

65. R. S. Loomis, "*Der mittelenglische Versroman über Richard Löwenherz*, edited by Karl Brunner," *Journal of English and German Philology* 15 (1916): 455; Weber's *Metrical Romances* was published in 1810.

66. The most prominent late nineteenth-century exceptions include Eugen Kölbing, ed., *Arthour and Merlin, nach der Auchinleck-hs,* (Leipzig: O. R. Reisland, 1890), lx–cv; Paris, "Le Roman de Richard," 353–93; and H. L. D. Ward and J. A. Herbert, *Catalogue of the Romances in the Department of Manuscripts in the British Museum*, vol. 1 (London: British Museum, 1883), 944–50. R. S. Loomis, "*Der mittelenglische*," 455, summarizes recent work on the romance.

67. Johannes Koch, "Brunner, *Der mittelenglische versroman von Richard Löwenherz*," *Englische Studien* 49 (1915): 126–42.

68. Koch, "Brunner," 142.

69. See Koch, "Brunner," 126, 142; and R. S. Loomis, "*Der mittelenglische*," 455, 465.

70. *Richard Löwenherz*, 17–19.

71. *Richard Löwenherz*, 22–24.

In his edition Brunner insists on, seemingly at the price of his own editorial credibility, the episodes' original presence in and thus fundamental value to the romance. The episodes within lines 35 to 1268 include, first, the oddly propitious arrival aboard ship of an Antiochian princess, Cassodorien. She marries Henry II and bears him two sons, Richard and John, as well as a daughter, Topyas, before fleeing the narrative as mysteriously as she entered it. Forced to remain at Mass one day, Cassodorien shoots up through the church roof at the moment of transubstantiation, taking Topyas with her and knocking John to the ground. (Henry, *Richard Löwenherz* tells us, "wondred of that thynge / That she made such an endynge.")[72] Second, there is a tournament organized by a youthful Richard, now king, at which he jousts in disguise against his favorite knights, Thomas de Multon and Fulk Doilly,[73] characters who figure repeatedly in the remainder of *Richard Löwenherz* and who, immediately after the tournament, join Richard as self-described pilgrims on a reconnaissance mission to the East. And third, there is a lengthy sequence of events set in "Almayne," the land through which Richard and his men attempt to pass on their return to England. This sequence begins with a minstrel's discovery of Richard, Thomas, and Fulk in a tavern and their subsequent capture by the "King of Almayne"; culminates with Richard's imprisonment, murder of the king's son, and eating of a lion's heart (salted); and concludes when England pays Richard's ransom.[74] Loomis and Koch were perplexed by Brunner's claim that these episodes were present not only early in the romance's life but at its inception, and dumbstruck by his rickety defense of this position against not only the internal and external textual and material evidence but also the likes of Gaston Paris,[75] who, several years earlier, had contended the opposite.[76]

In *Richard Löwenherz,* lines 35 to 1268 are preceded by a prologue to the romance and followed by the arrival in England of news from the East. Through French treason Jerusalem has been lost. In Auchinleck's earliest extant copy of the romance, a unique version of the prologue directly precedes a briefer description of the French treachery and call for crusade.[77] Though

---

72. *Richard Löwenherz,* lines 235–36.
73. On their historicity and appearances in the romance, see Schellekens, "An Edition," 2:36 n. 183–85, 60.
74. Richard and his companions stop a second time in Germany, while on crusade (*Richard Löwenherz,* lines 1437–666). Brunner refers to the sequence as "Richard's Revenge" (*Richards Rachezug*) and asserts that it, unlike the first German episode, is a later addition. See *Richard Löwenherz,* 19, 21.
75. R. S. Loomis, "*Der mittelenglische,*" 458–63; and Koch, "Brunner," 129ff.
76. Paris, "Le Roman de Richard," 385–86; R. S. Loomis, "*Richard Coeur de Lion,*" 509.
77. *King Richard,* line 33, lines 1–66.

no evidence supports his contention, Brunner characterizes lines 35 to 1286 in *Richard Löwenherz* as "missing" in Auchinleck.[78] In their reviews, his colleagues dispute this claim on multiple fronts, most convincingly with dialectal evidence. A substantial number of episodes that survive in some later manuscripts, including those between lines 35 to 1268, are the work of a northern "interpolator," possibly from Lincolnshire, and not of the earlier or initial "translator" or author, located dialectally to England's southeast.[79] Beyond this, they note that Brunner's claim is self-contradictory. One of his stated criteria for discerning the romance's supposedly original parts is their "general conformity to the facts of history."[80] The story of Cassodorien, Loomis presses, certainly does not conform.[81]

Brunner's insistence on the originary importance of these episodes, and the essentialness of the Almayne episodes in particular since they constitute the largest portion of lines 35 to 1268 and consequently demand the greatest share of Brunner's argumentative attention, is more confounding when one realizes that the lines' current or one-time presence cannot be confirmed in any extant manuscript predating Caius. Nor are the lines fully extant in Caius itself. Cassodorien's story is only partially present there, and the moment at which she shoots up through the church roof is absent altogether.[82] To produce an edition containing lines 35 to 1268, Brunner filled what he perceived to be lacunae. The beginning of the Almayne sequence in *Richard Löwenherz* comes from Caius. Richard and his men stop at a tavern on their way home from their initial trip to the East:

A goos þey dyʒte to here dynere
In a tauerne in þere þey were.
Kyng Rychard þe ffyr bet,
And Thomas to þe spyte hym set,

---

78. *Richard Löwenherz*, 17: "Die in *L* [Auchinleck], fehlenden vv. 35–1286."

79. R. S. Loomis, in *"Der mittelenglische,"* describes what he considers to be various tells, including but not limited to the "criterion of historicity" (458), poetic form (458–59), and personal names that might suggest a *terminus post quem* for certain episodes (460–62). See also Schellekens, "An Edition," 2:32–33.

80. R. S. Loomis, *"Der mittelenglische,"* 458; *Richard Löwenherz*, 20–21.

81. R. S. Loomis, *"Der mittelenglische,"* 458. Moreover, Paris asserts that the scenes of Richard's captivity are not grounded in history; Brunner disagrees. See Paris, "Le Roman de Richard," 356; and *Richard Löwenherz*, 17–19.

82. Gonville and Caius, MS 175/96, p. 4b, line 30; Cassodorien's final action in the Caius copy is to take "her douʒtyr *in* her hond." Here Brunner changes exemplars, moving from Caius to copy over two hundred lines from the 1509 edition; see *Richard Löwenherz*, lines 228–448. For Brunner's explanation, see *Richard Löwenherz*, 11. On the episode as it survives in the Caius manuscript, see chapter 5.

> Ffouk Doyly tempryd þe woos:
> Dere abou3te þey þat goos!
> Whenne þey had drunken wel, afyn,
> A mynstralle come þer in,
> And saide: "Goode men, wyttyrly,
> Wole 3e haue ony mynstralsy?"
> Rychard bad þat he scholde goo;
> Þat turnyd hym to mekel woo.[83]

The minstrel recognizes Richard and his companions for he himself is English and can distinguish Englishmen "be speche, *and* sy3te, hyde *and* hewe" from those of "Almayne."[84] At this point in *Richard Löwenherz*, Caius's clear material loss of nearly 120 lines in which Richard is captured in Almayne is supplemented with the 1509 edition.[85] Affronted by Richard's rejection:

> Forthe he [the minstrel] wente in that tyde
> To a castell there besyde,
> And tolde the kynge all and some,
> That thre men were to the cyte come;
> Stronge men, bolde and fere,
> In the worlde is not theyr pere.
> Kynge Rycharde of Englonde was the one man,
> Fouke Doly was that other than,
> The thyrde Thomas of Multon,
> Noble knyghtes of renowne.
> In palmers wede they be dyght,
> That no man sholde knowe them ryght.
> To hym sayd the kynge: "Iwys,
> That thou haste tolde yf it sothe is,
> Thou shalte haue thy warysowne,
> And chose thyselfe a ryche towne."
> The kynge comaunded his knyghtes,
> To arme them in all myghtes:

---

83. *Richard Löwenherz*, lines 657–68.
84. *Richard Löwenherz*, line 678.
85. *Richard Löwenherz*, lines 679–796. Material loss is evident at this point in Caius. In addition to narrative disjunction across the opening of pages 8 and 9, the manuscript's second quire, which now begins with page 9, appears to want its first leaf. The bottom margin of page 8 contains the catchword "Forþe," which does not begin page 9, but rather matches the place in Wynkyn de Worde's edition that Brunner substitutes at this point. See also James, *A Descriptive Catalogue*, 1:199, and chapter 5.

"And go and take them all thre,
And swithe brynge them to me!"[86]

This account of Richard's capture, which Brunner reconstructed from Caius and the 1509 edition, can be traced to the late twelfth century, when the rumor that Richard was captured in a tavern or kitchen or hut while roasting a goose or some other bird began to circulate. Despite the episode's presence in some copies of *Richard Coeur de Lion*, it was not an insular rumor. The earliest extant evidence that it circulated widely in England is its partial inscription in Caius itself.[87] Rather, this rumor emanated from and was cultivated in German-speaking lands shortly after Richard was captured there.

To understand how twelfth-century talk about Richard's capture came to surround Brunner, and to grasp the spectrum of local historical knowledge that Brunner brought with him to his reading of *Richard Coeur de Lion*, we must become knowing readers proximate to Brunner. We must learn or recall the version of Richard's capture that circulated in Austria from the twelfth through the early twentieth centuries. The constituent parts of this common knowledge are preserved not in England's accounts of Richard's crusading or capture, but in local twelfth- and thirteenth-century texts about Richard and Vienna. From these texts and other evidence, it is possible to discern the talk that was in the air, and to know how and where it traveled.[88]

It was well known in medieval Vienna that Richard and Leopold V, Duke of Austria, had encountered each other during the Third Crusade, prior to Richard's capture. Upon his arrival at the crusader camp outside Acre's city wall, Leopold became the highest-ranking German noble present, and consequently, the central character in German chronicle renderings of the Third Crusade and its outcomes.[89] Leopold's contingent was small and poorly pro-

---

86. *Richard Löwenherz*, lines 679–98.

87. There is evidence that a version of the rumor circulated among England's monastic communities, on which see further in this chapter. The Austro-German version of Richard's capture is also present in the London Thornton manuscript, which is, like Caius, a fifteenth-century northern production; for their relationship, see chapter 5.

88. When assembling local common knowledge here and elsewhere in this book, I rely on a range of sources contemporary with the historical events as well as on modern histories. This modern scholarship, expert and assiduous, is necessarily grounded in the sources that circulated in, for example, medieval Austria, and thus exists on a single continuum with those older sources more proximate to the events in question. All history writing is partial and selective, and my theorization of local common knowledge acknowledges those characteristics and strives to make them, and their ramifications, more explicit.

89. On Leopold, see Alexander W. Leeper, *A History of Medieval Austria*, ed. R. W. Seton-Watson and C. A. Macartney (Oxford: Oxford University Press, 1941), 267–75. The emperor Frederick Barbarossa drowned on his way to the East in 1190; Frederick's son died

visioned, and his lofty status did not mean much on the ground.[90] He waged war as well as he could and waited for reinforcements. Philip Augustus of France and Richard of England arrived, one after the other, with their armies and siege machines in early June 1191; by early July, Acre had capitulated and Richard was settling the conditions of the city's surrender through go-betweens with the Muslim leader, Saladin.[91] Some chronicles say Leopold carried his banner in victory; others describe it flying above a tower that his contingent had captured. Whatever Leopold's ultimate contribution to the conquest of Acre (assessments differ in unsurprising ways depending on writers' geographical associations), and wherever the banner was raised, the crusade's chroniclers—Austrian, German, French, and, eventually, English—agree it was thrown down either with Richard's tacit approval or at his direct order, and that its removal, however that happened, certainly spurred Leopold's precipitous return home.[92]

German chroniclers immediately recounted the disgrace of Leopold, and by extension, Austria, as evidence of Richard's ignoble character. By the time the English king embarked upon his own journey home in 1192, he had made a handful of powerful, allied, and gossipy enemies who blocked his path. Because Richard could not take an expected route, medieval and modern historians alike periodically lose physical track of him until he reaches the outskirts of Vienna. This temporary historiographical absence of Richard's body has, since the twelfth century, given rise to multiple narratives about his possible physical movements and, by way of determining those, speculation about his mental whereabouts: if he planned, how he improvised, why he might have preferred possible routes and rivals over others.[93] In contemporary

---

shortly after reaching Acre in 1191 with his father's bones in tow. See Otto of St. Blasien, *The Chronicle of Otto of St. Blasien*, in G. A. Loud, ed. and trans., *The Crusade of Frederick Barbarossa: The History of the Expedition of the Emperor Frederick and Related Texts*, Crusade Texts in Translation 19 (Farnham, Surrey: Ashgate, 2010), 180–81.

90. Contemporary Austrian chroniclers record Leopold's challenges. See, for example, Ansbert, *Historia de Expeditione Friderici Imperatoris*, in Loud, *Crusade of Frederick Barbarossa*, 120–21.

91. On the siege of Acre, see Tyerman, *God's War*, 431–74; and *Richard I*, 123–221.

92. For example, see Otto of St. Blasien, *Chronicle*, 182–83; Richard of Devizes, *The Chronicle of Richard of Devizes of the Time of King Richard the First*, ed. and trans. John T. Appleby (London: Thomas Nelson and Sons Ltd., 1963), 46–47; and Rigord, *Histoire de Philippe Auguste*, ed. and trans. Élisabeth Carpentier, Georges Pon, and Yves Chauvin, Sources d'histoire médiévale 33 (Paris: CNRS Éditions, 2006), 308, 314–16. See also *Richard I*, 224, where Gillingham suggests that only after Leopold's capture of Richard did the banner dispute appear regularly in English accounts of the siege as, in retrospect, an event directly related to Richard's capture.

93. *Richard I*, 231–32, summarizes the possibilities. See also Lionel Landon, ed., *The Itinerary of Richard I* (London: Pipe Roll Society, 1934); Kate Norgate, *Richard the Lion Heart* (London: Macmillan and Co. Ltd., 1924), 265; and Mayer, "Ghost Ship," 134–37.

German accounts, the narrative route from Acre's harbor to Vienna's suburbs usually continues this way: Richard was shipwrecked on the Istrian coast amid the inhospitable lands of Meinhard of Görz. After escaping an attack by local nobles, Richard and his surviving men continued overland until they entered the duke of Austria's lands.[94] Leopold's men found the English king there, just beyond Vienna's city limits, hiding and absent his dignity, in, depending on the source, "a contemptible house" (*in domo despecta*), a "little hut," a "poor man's shack" (*in tugurio cuiusdam pauperis*), "cheap lodgings" (*in vili hospitio*).[95]

These last two descriptions come from Austrian versions of the story inscribed shortly after Richard's capture in the winter of 1192. The first occurs in the *Historia de Expeditione Frederici Imperatoris,* a composite chronicle probably completed no later than 1200 by an Austrian cleric called Ansbert.[96] It survives in two manuscripts copied within the first quarter of the thirteenth century, as well as one eighteenth-century copy made from a third, now lost, exemplar.[97] As the so-called Ansbert tells it, after Richard's covert arrival in the "neighborhood of Vienna" and the subsequent discovery by spies of the king and his two companions in "cheap lodgings," the Austrian duke's arrest of the English king was more than justified.[98] It was poetically just: divine payback for Richard's abuse of Leopold at Acre and his suspected engineering

---

94. On Richard's itinerary as reported in the Continental sources, see, for example, Roger of Howden, *Chronica Magistri Rogeri de Houedene,* ed. William Stubbs, RS 51, vol. 3 (London: Eyre and Spottiswoode, 1870), 195; Anton Chroust, ed. *Quellen zur Geschichte des Kreuzzuges Kaiser Friedrichs I,* MGH SRG NS 5 (Berlin: Weidmannsche, 1928), 101–3; and Otto of St. Blasien, *Chronicle,* 184.

95. Roger of Howden, *Chronica,* 3:195–96; Franz-Josef Schmale, ed., *Die Chronik Ottos von Blasien und die Marbacher Annalen* (Darmstadt: WBG, 1998), 186; Magnus of Reichersberg, *Chronicon Magni Presbiteri,* ed. Wilhelm Wattenbach, MGH SS 17 (Hanover: Hahn, 1861), 519.

96. Chroust, *Kaiser Friedrichs I,* ix, calls him the "so-called Ansbert" (*der sogenannte Ansbert*). On the chronicle's provenance, see also Loud, *Crusade of Frederick,* 1–7; and see John Gillingham, "The Kidnapped King: Richard I in Germany, 1192–1194," *Bulletin of the German Historical Institute, London* 30 (2008): 11. Since the early thirteenth century, it has been called the work of an Austrian because the manuscript copy held by the Premonstratensian monastery of Mühlhausen in Bohemia preserves this identification in the late twelfth-century hand of the abbot, Gerlach. The manuscript is now Prague, Strahov Monastery Library, MS DF III ¼. The author's affection for Leopold has been interpreted as evidence of his local affiliations; see Loud, *Crusade of Frederick,* 3, 130; and Gillingham, "Kidnapped King," 11.

97. Both Chroust and Loud, who prints a portion of the chronicle in translation (it is unclear from which manuscript[s]), assert the presence of at least two authors: the first an eyewitness writing from around 1189 to 1190 who himself had access to the eyewitness account kept by Tageno, and the second, probably an Austrian cleric, given his knowledge of and interest in Leopold's actions and legacy, who extends the narrative to 1197. Both editors offer extensive discussions in their introductions. See Chroust, *Kaiser Friedrichs I,* ixff.; and Loud, *Crusade of Frederick,* 1–8.

98. Ansbert, *Historia,* 123–24.

of the death of Conrad of Montferrat, Leopold's cousin. Perhaps more problematically, Richard had conquered Cyprus en route to Acre and captured Cyprus's ruler, Isaac Comnenos, another of Leopold's cousins, whom Richard still held at the time of his own capture.[99]

The second local and contemporaneously circulating version of Richard's capture is preserved in the prose chronicle of the canon Magnus of Reichersberg, whose Augustinian house fell under the control of the Salzburg diocese.[100] Whereas Ansbert's telling recasts the episode's stakes by weaving together Richard's narrative with that of the Austrian duchy and its history, Magnus's version embroiders the English king's capture. He was found in Vienna, Magnus tells us, "hiding himself in a poor man's shack, preparing food for himself and his few companions in the provincial kitchen and with his own hands" (*occultans se in tugurio cuiusdam pauperis, et cibos propriis manibus sibi et sociis suis paucissimis in officina rustica preparans*).[101] John Gillingham, Richard's foremost modern biographer, characterizes Richard's capture as a story "widely known."[102] "Widely known" implies widely told. According to Ansbert, even as the English king sat fifty miles from Vienna at Dürnstein, "rumor rapidly flew into neighboring kingdoms and to the princes of those realms" (*fama velox vicina regna et regnorum principes penetravit*).[103] Ansbert describes the rumor of Richard's capture in terms of its present geographic transmission, and the mutability inherent in that movement, from place to place, person to person.

The rumor of Richard's capture traversed both geographical and temporal distances in Austria, and became embedded, by way of thirteenth-century talk and texts, in Vienna's self-narrative. The late twelfth-century rumor of Richard's capture was still circulating in Vienna roughly one hundred years later. In the late thirteenth century, the Viennese writer Jans Enikel began work on his *Fürstenbuch* (*Book of Princes*), a vernacular verse account of Aus-

---

99. Chroust, *Kaiser Friedrichs I*, 102. On the Comneni line, see *Itinerarium Peregrinorum et Gesta Regis Ricardi*, in *Chronicles and Memorials of the Reign of Richard the First*, ed. William Stubbs, RS 38, vol. 1 (London: Longman and Green, 1864), xii n. On Conrad's death and the rumor of Richard's participation, see *Richard I*, 197–202.

100. See Magnus of Reichersberg, *Chronicon*, 476–523, where the record of Magnus's death occurs at 523. On his biography, see Max Manitius and Paul Lehmann, *Geschichte der lateinischen Literatur des Mittelalters: Vom Ausbruch des Kirchenstreites bis zum Ende des zwölften Jahrhunderts* (Munich: Beck, 1931), 565–66; Loud, *Crusade of Frederick*, 4–5. The chronicle survives in three witnesses: one autograph, one partial autograph (both now Graz, Steiermärkisches Landesarchiv, cod. 894), and one seventeenth-century print of a lost manuscript.

101. Magnus of Reichersberg, *Chronicon*, 519.

102. Gillingham, "Kidnapped King," 12.

103. Chroust, *Kaiser Friedrichs I*, 105.

tria and Styria from the founding of Vienna to 1246.[104] Although Jans lived in the city until at least 1302,[105] his *Fürstenbuch* depicts a Vienna he could only have known by hearing or reading old stories. The *Fürstenbuch* focuses on the Vienna of Jans's father and grandfather, and thus preserves and circulates accounts of the past that Jans inherited from them through talk and other sources. The Vienna of Jans's grandfather was, strictly speaking, that of Leopold V,[106] but given Jans's account of the period it either already was or would soon be remembered also as the Vienna of Richard I.

Jans's life, sources, and the popularity of his work evince the long and wide circulation of the rumor of Richard's capture, as well as the development of the English king's legacy in and around Vienna. The *Fürstenbuch* is roughly four thousand lines in its longest iterations and Jans spends more than four hundred of those lines intricately entangling the narrative of Vienna with that of Richard. He tells of the fight between the Austrian duke and the English king at Acre (here Richard personally throws Leopold's banner into the mud), Leopold's complaint to Frederick Barbarossa (an anachronism) and the subsequent explicit agreement among the assembled princes to bar England's king from their lands, Richard's attempt to slink secretly and guilt-ridden alone through Austria, and his capture.[107] Rather than have Richard hide in the crude kitchen of a rundown shack, Jans reports that he was discovered in one of Leopold's own kitchens in the Viennese suburbs. There, as Richard roasts a goose,[108] the royal cook recognizes him and informs Leopold.[109] The cook then mocks Richard, who denies his identity before he is taken to Vienna proper as Leopold's prisoner.[110] A version of the capture story with Richard in the duke's kitchen cooking, as in Jans's rendering and in *Richard Löwenherz*, a goose, had been circulating in Latin on the Continent from

104. On Jans's biography, and for the standard edition of his works, see Philipp Strauch, ed., *Jansen Enikels Werke: Weltchronik, Fürstenbuch*, MGH DC 3 (Hanover: Hahnsche, 1900). The *Fürstenbuch*, written in rhyming couplets, survives in seven manuscripts dating from the fourteenth to the sixteenth centuries, though no copy extends past 1246; see Strauch, *Jansen Enikels Werke*, xl–xlvii. On Jans's earlier work, see also Estelle Morgan, "Two Notes on the 'Fürstenbuch,'" *The Modern Language Review* 60 (1965): 395.

105. See Graeme Dunphy, "Jans [der] Enikel," in *Encyclopedia of the Medieval Chronicle*, ed. Graeme Dunphy, vol. 2 (Leiden: Brill, 2010), 905. Jans's name occurs in city documents for the final time in 1302. It is probably the same Jans Enikel referred to as "Jan der Schreiber" or Jans the Scrivener in a 1275 document.

106. Morgan, "Two Notes," 395.

107. For an overview of the *Fürstenbuch*'s contents, see Strauch, *Jansen Enikels Werke*, 815. The episodes involving Richard occur at lines 1152–1506.

108. Strauch, *Jansen Enikels Werke*, line 1436.

109. Strauch, *Jansen Enikels Werke*, lines 1439–48.

110. Strauch, *Jansen Enikels Werke*, lines 1483–88.

the late twelfth century.¹¹¹ Any expressly constitutive sources for the episodes that Jans inscribed about Richard—indeed for most of what he wrote in the *Fürstenbuch*—remain lost, if they ever existed in written form. The material's indebtedness to late twelfth-century rumor is apparent.

That Jans often wrote down things that he heard instead of copying information from books that he read is the scholarly consensus.¹¹² If we cannot know precisely what Jans heard or read, we do have some idea of the milieux in which he traveled: where he heard what he heard, and where he and that talk then circulated. Internal evidence suggests Jans's access to a copy of the *Continuatio Praedicatorum Vindobonensium,* which tells of Richard disguised as a "stranger" in Vienna,¹¹³ and at several points in the *Fürstenbuch,* though none directly related to Richard, Jans mentions a "book" belonging to Vienna's Schottenkloster, now Schottenstift, the Benedictine monastery founded in the mid-twelfth century and initially populated with Irish monks.¹¹⁴ Through his father, Jans was a patrician of Vienna.¹¹⁵ He owned a house within the city wall, on Wipplingerstraße,¹¹⁶ which neighbored the Jewish quarter. Jans's direct contact with his neighbors may have informed alternate perspectives included in the *Fürstenbuch*.¹¹⁷ It is probable that he had some connection to the Schottenkloster, and perhaps even to its abbot.¹¹⁸ The mix of high and low

---

111. In Peter of Eboli's *Liber ad honorem augusti*: See Gillingham, "Kidnapped King," 12. In some versions, Richard cooks "a bird" or "a fowl"; see Morgan, "Two Notes," 399.

112. Siegfried Haider, "Jans Enikel," *Neue deutsche Biographie,* ed. Otto Stolberg-Wernigerode, 10 (Berlin: Duncker and Humboldt, 1974), 338, for instance, dwells on Jans's interest in and reliance on "oral tradition" (*der mündlichen Tradition*); see Morgan, "Two Notes," 395.

113. Morgan, "Two Notes," 395; and Strauch, *Jansen Enikels Werke,* 626 n. 1.

114. For instance, see Strauch, *Jansen Enikels Werke,* lines 115ff. The monks arrived in Vienna by way of the Schottenkloster St. Jakob in Regensburg. The monastery offers its own public account of its history, which includes the consecration of its church and monastery in 1200; see https://www.schotten.wien/stift/. Jans marks the foundation in his *Weltchronik*; see Strauch, *Jansen Enikels Werke,* 545.

115. Morgan, "Two Notes," 395.

116. The street is now located within Vienna's first district. Jans's access to Jewish material (a term I use broadly here to encompass seemingly anecdotal points of view and theological teachings) is evinced in the *Fürstenbuch*; Dunphy, "Jans," 905, suggests his knowledge and perspective reflects "urban contacts."

117. Morgan, "Two Notes," 395; Henry Garland and Mary Garland, *The Oxford Companion to German Literature* (Oxford: Oxford University Press, 1997), 424; and Haider, "Jans Enikel," 338.

118. Haider, "Jans Enikel," 339.

stories to which Jans apparently had access has prompted scholarly speculation that he was, at some point, a merchant.[119]

More certain is Jans's reliance on local talk in his text. The *Fürstenbuch*'s final episode about Richard contains documented facts mixed with heavily augmented twelfth-century rumor. With the ransom Leopold received in exchange for Richard, Jans explains, Leopold built Wiener-Neustadt, a town to the south of Vienna (true); enlarged Vienna (in fact, he used the money to build the city's wall); and around the city constructed a moat, the labor for which was supplied by Englishmen, who carried earth in loads on their backs (unlikely).[120] The late twelfth-century city that Jans fashioned from talk and text is neither the Vienna of Leopold V, nor that of his own grandfather: It is a Vienna shaped by the legacy of Richard I.

"Fashioned" because Jans seems to have discriminated among what he heard in order to make a past that was locally desirable. Notably absent from his account is another, less flattering and more verifiable outcome of Richard's capture that Jans surely knew: the excommunication of Leopold V by Pope Celestine III, and the responsibility of expiation that Leopold's son and heir took on after his father's death.[121] Jans may have invented accounts, archived local talk circulating in late thirteenth-century Vienna, or thrown old rumors into new circulation. These are all ways of imagining his work's intended and unintended causes and effects that are not mutually exclusive. The *Fürstenbuch* not only remained in circulation but became, in addition to the earliest account of the city's founding, foundational to Vienna's identity. As a rare "history" in the Austrian dialect, and thus legible to a broad local audience,[122] the *Fürstenbuch* was enshrined as part of the city's official narrative. Portions of it were incorporated with attribution into the municipal *Handbook of Vienna* (*Handbuch der Stadt Wien*).[123] The anniversaries of Richard's capture and imprisonment continued to be marked in the German and

---

119. Haider, "Jans Enikel," 339.
120. Strauch, *Jansen Enikels Werke*, lines 1489–98.
121. Frank Shaw, "The Good Old Days of the Babenberg Dukes," in *Bristol Austrian Studies*, ed. Brian Keith-Smith (Bristol: University of Bristol Press, 1990), 12–13.
122. Haider, "Jans Enikel," 338–39.
123. *Handbuch der Stadt Wien* (Vienna: Jugend & Volk Gesellschaft m. b. H.). Jans is mentioned, for example, in volumes 87 (1973): 4, 8, 10; 88 (1974): 22; and 112 (1998): 17.

Austro-Hungarian Empires of the nineteenth and twentieth centuries[124]—that is, in Brunner's express milieu.[125]

The Almayne episodes have drawn the attention of almost no Anglo-American scholars.[126] Such disinterest can be partially explained by the fact that a different rumor of Richard's capture was circulated insularly. The Continental rumor of Richard's capture was imported to England, but was apparently suppressed there. Remarkably, English chronicles do not repeat the German and Austrian version, despite its wide circulation and rapid inscription across the Channel. Less surprisingly, no insular versions of Richard's capture depict him as disgraced.[127] To contradict directly the unbecoming version of Richard's capture that circulated on the Continent, English chroniclers would have had to repeat it. Instead, they implicitly rebutted it with an alternate account, relentlessly inscribed. While the earliest Austro-German versions outfit the king in the clothes of a pauper and place him in a hut, English sources from the end of the twelfth century and the first few years of the thirteenth say that Richard and his men were either dressed as pilgrims—thus externalizing the presumed internal state of the king, who had taken the cross in 1189—or disguised as Templars.[128] The latter is a more complicated portrayal, but it nevertheless accuses Leopold of illegal action.[129] Richard surrendered honorably, according to English chroniclers, after his servant (or servants), whom Leopold's men caught and tortured, betrayed his hiding place.[130] Only the English told this version of events with traceable regularity.

---

124. See Gillingham, "Kidnapped King," 7–10: For example, in the first three decades of the twentieth century, it was not an uncommon opinion that the era of Henry VI, and particularly Richard's imprisonment in Germany and homage sworn to the Holy Roman emperor, marked the height of German power. Three German scholarly studies were timed to coincide with the seven hundredth anniversary of Richard's capture. More recently, in 1993, Annweiler commemorated the eight hundredth anniversary of Richard's imprisonment: The event's figurative heart was the English king's literal one, borrowed from Rouen for the occasion.

125. See Koziol, "Brunner," 267–72. While at work on *Richard Löwenherz,* Brunner lived in Berlin and Vienna.

126. *Richard I,* 263, is a notable exception: Gillingham summarizes the scenes of Richard's imprisonment and reads them as the romance's implicit argument for Richard's heterosexuality.

127. On the story's absence from English chronicles and the texts that demonstrate its circulation in Sicily and France, see Gillingham, "Kidnapped King," 12–14.

128. For example, Gervase of Canterbury, *The Historical Works of Gervase of Canterbury,* ed. William Stubbs, RS 73, vol. 1 (London: Longman and Co., 1879), 513.

129. And they were not wrong on the moral and actual law: Celestine III excommunicated Leopold after Richard's release in 1194 for having arrested and held the pilgrim king; see Leeper, *Medieval Austria,* 281–82.

130. Roger of Howden, *Chronica,* 3:185–86; Ralph of Coggeshall, *Chronicon Anglicanum,* ed. J. Stevenson, RS 66 (London: Longman, 1875), 54–55; William of Newburgh, *Historia*

The inhabitants of insular religious houses, who talked and wrote about current events, unquestionably had access to the Austro-German account of Richard's arrest. However else it may have reached England, it traveled there in a copy of a letter that Henry VI, who took physical charge of Richard in early 1193,[131] sent to the French king Philip Augustus. Richard was captured, as Henry puts it, in a "despicable house."[132] The letter survives to us only in Roger of Howden's chronicle, where he contextualizes it either as the source or only one bearer of—it is impossible to tell from his description—"these rumors being spread through England as to the capture of its king" (*His itaque per Angliam publicatis de captione regis Angliae rumoribus*).[133] That Roger at once registers and dismisses as "rumors" the contents of a document he claims to have copied verbatim and, moreover, a document we know not to have been an English forgery,[134] complicates our reconstruction of medieval documentary culture. Roger cites no explicit source for his own version of Richard's capture and calls the version contained in the letter from Henry VI to Philip a rumor. This construal raises the question of what, in Roger's mind and in the minds of his readers as Roger imagined them, validated the first as *not* rumor and invalidated the second as rumor, or, according to Roger, as multiple rumors. Like Walter Scott, he attempts in his writing to bar the door against imported talk.

More apparent is Roger's tactic to muddy the waters by using the imported rumor's terms to fashion a local rumor. He has by this point already told his readers "the truth" about Richard's capture: the incongruousness of his pilgrim's aspect (which the king came by naturally) and apparent wealth that raised local suspicion in unfriendly lands. When Richard became aware of the weakness of his position, he, along with only one man, left his companions in the hope of misdirecting his enemies and rode until they reached the outskirts of Vienna. There his attendant was recognized while buying food as Richard

---

Rerum Anglicarum in *Chronicles of the Reigns of Stephen, Henry II and Richard I*, ed. Richard Howlett, RS 82, vol. 1 (London: Longman, 1884), 387; Gervase of Canterbury, *Historical Works*, 1:513. Richard of Devizes's chronicle does not include events after Richard leaves the outskirts of Jerusalem. On the problem of Richard's dress, see Martin H. Jones, "Richard the Lionheart in German Literature of the Middle Ages," in *Richard Coeur de Lion in History and Myth*, ed. Janet L. Nelson (London: King's College London Centre for Late Antique and Medieval Studies, 1992), 72.

131. *Richard I*, 234–35.

132. Roger of Howden, *Chronica*, 3:195–96.

133. Roger of Howden, *Chronica*, 3:196. A copy of a copy of the letter was probably sent to Walter of Coutances, archbishop of Rouen and Richard's justice, who had copies of his copy made to distribute among his brethren.

134. Gillingham, "Kidnapped King," 11 n. 22: "It is not, however, an English forgery since it was drawn upon by Philip's 'official historian,' Rigord of St. Denis."

slept, was brought to the duke of Austria, and was made to succumb under duress.[135] Matthew Paris's mid-thirteenth-century *Chronica majora* repeats a nearly identical copy of this persistently insular rumor of Richard's capture.[136] Neither the late thirteenth-century chronicle by Peter Langtoft nor the early fourteenth-century chronicle by Robert Mannying tells the imported version of Richard's capture, though both men very possibly knew it. Langtoft claims rather too studiously that he does not:

> I know not how afterwards, and for what reason,
> The king left all his people and in disguise,
> Went towards Austria to his confusion,
> Spying wrongfully the possession of another;
> Nor how in Austria by procuration
> He was suddenly taken, and kept in prison;
> What money was given for his redemption;
> How the pope pronounced his curse
> On all who took him, or by consent
> Were in counsel for his capture.
> But well I will tell you by what devotion
> He came by St. Thomas in procession.[137]

The rumors and silences about Richard's capture that circulated on the Continent and in England complicate our instinct for the complete rather than the fragmented picture of the past. There is no authoritative contemporary account of Richard's capture, only versions of it, relative to time, place, access, and political expediency. Brunner's *Richard Löwenherz* functions similarly. It does not offer an authoritative account of *Richard Coeur de Lion*. Rather, the text that Brunner made was relevant to the time and place of its produc-

---

135. Roger of Howden, *Chronica*, 3:185–86.
136. Matthew Paris, *Chronica majora*, ed. H. R. Luard, RS 57, vol. 2 (London: Longman and Co., 1874), 394–95.
137. Robert Mannyng, *The Chronicle*, ed. Idelle Sullens (Binghamton: Center for Medieval and Renaissance Studies, State University of New York at Binghamton, 1996). Peter Langtoft, *The Chronicle of Pierre de Langtoft, in French Verse, from the Earliest Period to the Death of King Edward I*, ed. and trans. Thomas Wright, RS 47, vol. 2 (London: Longmans, Green, Reader, and Dyer, 1868), 114–15: "Ne say coment après, ne par quel resoun, / Le ray laissa ses genz tuz, [et] en tapisoun / Ala devers Austrice à sa confusioun, / Espyaunt à tort autry possessioun; / Ne coment en Austrice par procuration / Fu pris sodaynement, et tenuz en prisoun; / Quel avoyr fu doné pur sa redemcioun; / Coment l'apstoyle dona sa maliçoun / Sur tuz ke ly pristrent, ou par consensioun / Furent al counsail de sa capcioun; / Mès ben ws dirray par quel devocioun / Il vynt par saint Thomas en processioun."

tion and to the local talk of the day in the German and Austro-Hungarian Empires.

Brunner foregrounds the Almayne episodes in *Richard Löwenherz* and thus the shared aspects of Richard's and Vienna's history. Brunner's own account of his edition's production confirms the pointedness of this choice. He expected different readers of his edition than the ones we have posited: readers who shared Brunner's local common knowledge and readers who would not be entirely reliant on *Richard Löwenherz*. In his prefatory material, Brunner describes *Richard Löwenherz* not as a singular edition, but as a book situated between two other volumes. The first of these, Weber's *Romances,* existed. The second was only rumored: "a new edition, announced many years ago, from the Early English Text Society," which, Brunner concludes, "seems to have been abandoned" (*Die von der Early English Text Society seit vielen Jahren angekündigte Neuausgabe scheint aufgegeben worden zu sein*).[138] Brunner might have heard about this other edition as early as 1910 when he was examining the manuscripts and printed copies of *Richard Coeur de Lion* held in London, Oxford, and Cambridge collections.[139] Regardless, he almost certainly readied *Richard Löwenherz* with word of an EETS edition in the air.

R. S. Loomis had heard the same rumor. He repeats a version of it in his review: "the edition by Professor Hausknecht, long promised by the E. E. T. S. [but] not yet forthcoming." It is against this absent presence of an authoritative volume anticipated but "not *yet* forthcoming,"[140] as Loomis expectantly frames it, that he evaluates Brunner's edition:

> It is much to be regretted that instead of a complete glossary which would have been a permanent service to Middle English scholars of every country the editor has seen fit to supply a list of words which are said to be lacking in Strattmann-Bradley [*sic*], most of which, however, are to be found there differently spelt, and a German translation of the poem, which at most is only a convenience for a limited group of scholars. With this notable exception, however, this edition provides adequate critical material and in general shows wide, laborious, and accurate research.[141]

---

138. *Richard Löwenherz*, "Vorwort."
139. Koziol, "Brunner," 267–72.
140. Emphasis mine.
141. R. S. Loomis, "*Der mittelenglische*," 455. He refers to Henry Francis Stratmann, ed., *A Middle English Dictionary Containing Words Used by English Writers from the Twelfth to the Fifteenth Century,* rearranged, revised, and enlarged by Henry Bradley (Oxford: Clarendon Press, 1891).

Loomis carves out in negative space the primary audience he imagines for Brunner's edition. His normative scholar has a copy of Stratmann-Bradley to hand and unlike Brunner wields it expertly; the German prose translation of the poem that appears at the end of Brunner's volume serves no purpose. After reading the edition, Loomis's scholar sets that "adequate" volume to one side with a sigh and the overwhelming sense that it has not served him as conveniently, efficiently, or elegantly as it might have done. Loomis expresses in his review an unhappy realization that *Richard Löwenherz*—a title Loomis never once utters in ten pages, instead referring to it as "the volume" or "this edition"—was not made with scholars like him in mind. At least, not primarily. I recognize Loomis's disenchantment because I have experienced something like it as a critical reader of *Richard Löwenherz,* with its odd appendices, strange editorial decisions, and apparatus in "Brunner's bad German," as I once heard a colleague describe it. I have also long suspected that Brunner's edition is in fact equally ambivalent about me: I am not its intended audience, only that audience's bystander.

To attribute our reception of Brunner's edition to editorial skill or lack thereof is to regard it from the viewpoint of only one kind of local reader, an Anglo-American one. Brunner's imagined audience for *Richard Löwenherz* is precisely, not accidentally, a "limited group of scholars," to borrow Loomis's characterization, of non-English speakers or nonspecialists. It was for such an audience that Brunner included a German prose translation of the poem at the back of his edition—a local, and likely local scholarly, audience. Those German-speaking scholars were in the still-burgeoning field of English studies, of which Brunner's own teachers had been in the vanguard.[142] The German rendering of the poem at the end of *Richard Löwenherz* is essentially Brunner's own "abstract." While that translation does include line numbers that correspond to the Middle English verse, it is in prose, and thus unrhymed and unmetered. One might assume that for Brunner, a philologist by training, these formal aspects of the romance would be entirely fundamental to reading, experiencing, and deciphering it. While he certainly does not withhold these elements from his readers, for those readers he explicitly projects in his foreword—readers with little or no expertise as yet in the language's

---

142. Koziol, "Brunner," 260. Brunner's training in English studies coincided with its codification as a field in German-speaking countries and its subsequent growth, thanks in large part to Brunner's mentors. See Manfred Markus, preface in *Historical English: On the Occasion of Karl Brunner's 100th Birthday,* ed. Manfred Markus (Innsbruck: Institut für Anglistik, University of Innsbruck, 1988), viii: "In 1891, the first Austrian *Seminar für englische Philologie* was opened (in Vienna). Innsbruck followed six years later (with Brunner's predecessor, Rudolf Fischer, as the first professor): At Gratz university, Luick became *Extraordinarius* in 1893."

technicalities, orthography, or historical iterations—the prose summary acts as a guide, a primer, a point of access to the story. Brunner's expectation that *Richard Coeur de Lion* would be a compelling training ground for German-speaking scholars of Middle English literature and philology offers a radical shift in perspective on the romance's appeal and Brunner's editorial choices. It demonstrates not only Brunner's affinity for *Richard Coeur de Lion,* but a supposition that the scholars who made up his local readership would find the subject matter a compelling point of entry to the field.

Brunner's stemma, while problematic, is the work of a scholar. His text, *Richard Löwenherz,* is the work of a scribe: an eighth scribal copy of *Richard Coeur de Lion* drawn from two carefully chosen exemplars. Like the scribes who preceded him, Brunner did not conceive of *Richard Löwenherz* as either the conclusion or the collation, in its least specialized sense, of *Richard Coeur de Lion*'s textual tradition. Nor could he have predicted that it would be enshrined as such. Scholarship has extrapolated Brunner's text to represent the entire textual tradition of *Richard Coeur de Lion,* but *Richard Löwenherz,* like a medieval manuscript copy, is a local and a locally retrospective text, expressly relative to its projected audience and the place and time of its production, fin-de-siècle Vienna.

Between the time of Brunner's birth in 1887 and the publication of *Richard Löwenherz* in 1913, the rumor of Richard's capture and ransom took on new urgency and relevance, especially in Vienna. On November 28, 1928, an article entitled "King Richard's Ransom" appeared in London's *Times.* The paper's man on the ground in Vienna ("our own correspondent") began his account by noting the oddness of what he was about to do: report to his twentieth-century readership "news" dating from 1194. "But," he persisted:

> The question as to whether the Austrian Government is legally entitled to the yields from the ransom of the English King [Richard I] is periodically the subject of hot disputes here.
>
> It appears that the money paid to Duke Leopold of Austria furnished funds with which the formidable wall which defended the inner city of Vienna until the year 1857 was built. When the wall was demolished the Viennese Municipality, as trustee for all public lands in the city, laid claim to the strip of ground on which the wall had stood. But the right of possession was disputed by the Imperial Government, and the latter carried the day.[143]

---

143. "King Richard's Ransom (From Our Own Correspondent)," *The Times* (London), November 28, 1928, p. 15, issue 45062.

Franz Joseph, Austria's emperor, decreed on December 20, 1857, that Vienna's medieval wall should be demolished. The decree was publicized five days later and the work begun in 1858.[144] The thorough revitalization of Vienna, which the wall's demolishment preceded, counterintuitively revitalized discussion of Richard's time in Austria and its ramifications. Writing some seventy years after the wall's demolishment, the *Times* correspondent could still bear witness to, or, better, hear this talk about the twelfth-century firsthand.

Franz Joseph ordered not only the "abolition of the enclosure and fortifications of the inner city, together with the ditches thereof,"[145] but also what should occur next, using "proceeds of the sale of this valuable land" on which Richard's wall once stood: "improvement and adornment of my residential and capital city,"[146] as well as Vienna's expansion beyond its present medieval enclosures. The land on the other side of Vienna's wall and ditches had been inhabitable since 1683, when the Turks were finally repelled, but it had not been incorporated into the city proper.[147] However long in coming, a potent mix of necessity and desire among the public fueled a reimagining of Vienna that included everything from its borders to its infrastructure,[148] and that coincided with the political upheaval needed to act on many of those ideas prior to the First World War.[149] Portions of the city were destroyed, built up,

---

144. For a translation of Franz Joseph's decree, see Frederic R. Farrow and Thomas Blashill, "The Recent Development of Vienna," in *Transactions of the Royal Institute of British Architects*, vol. 4, New Series (London: Royal Institute of British Architects, 1888), 28–29. The German version of the decree, dated December 20, 1857, appeared in the newspaper *Wiener Zeitung* on December 25, 1857.

145. Farrow and Blashill, "Recent Development," 28.

146. "King Richard's Ransom"; Farrow and Blashill, "Recent Development," 28.

147. Donald J. Olsen, *The City as a Work of Art: London, Paris, Vienna* (New Haven: Yale University Press, 1986), 58.

148. For example, Vienna's aqueduct and Stadtbahn; see Carl E. Schorske, *Fin-de-Siècle Vienna: Politics and Culture* (New York: Vintage Books, 1981), 44–55; and Olsen, *The City*, 79–80. On the local political situation that made concentrated efforts on infrastructure possible, see Eve Blau, "'A Capital without a Nation': Red Vienna, Architecture, and Spatial Politics between the World Wars," in *Power and Architecture: The Construction of Capitals and the Politics of Space*, ed. Michael Minkenberg (New York: Berghahn Books, 2014), 180–81; but see also Schorske, *Fin-de-Siècle*, 25–26.

149. Here I only gesture at the intricate and radical political changes that underpinned this long moment in Vienna's social, political, and aesthetic development. Contextualizing Vienna's own frenetic municipal politics and steadily increasing population, for instance, was the Compromise of 1867 and the establishment of the Dual Monarchy, which codified the Austro-Hungarian Empire with Franz Joseph as king in Hungary and emperor elsewhere. He ruled from Vienna as a "quasi-constitutional monarch." For an overview of this period—that is, 1860 to 1914 and the start of World War I—see Steven Beller, *A Concise History of Austria* (Cambridge: Cambridge University Press, 2006), 141–84. See also Schorske, *Fin-de-Siècle*, 31; and Blau, "A Capital," 178–83.

and expanded at a rapid pace. Between 1840 and 1870, Vienna's population and its productivity doubled.[150] In 1858 demolition commenced and in 1859 Franz Joseph approved plans.[151] By 1865, the "Ringstrasse," or "Ring Road," had replaced Richard's wall, but ran its same circular route around the city center.

For roughly the next three decades, residential buildings, commercial properties, and major institutions were built along the new boulevard.[152] In his report on "The Recent Development of Vienna" submitted to the Royal Institute of British Architects and published as part of its transactions in 1888, Thomas Blashill, an associate of that body, describes Vienna in the year after Brunner's birth:

> In regard to latitude and altitude Vienna does not differ very materially from London, but its situation, far inland, and in the vicinity of snow mountains, makes a very material difference in its climate. Its summer glows with the heat of which we may judge from a few days that sometimes occur in an exceptionally hot English season. Its winter is what we should think steadily cold, though there are pretty sharp changes of temperature. But the clear air permits brilliant sunshine at most times, so that, to our eyes, Vienna is first of all *bright*.[153]

Blashill then leads his audience on a virtual tour of the new buildings occupying the Ringstrasse,[154] "a wide boulevard or ring round the inner city connected to the broad quay next to the Danube Canal."[155] Walking the Ring from the Danube's Aspern Bridge, Blashill guides his readers past newly built and some still not quite finished structures. They signified what the twentieth-century cultural historian Carl Schorske calls "the triumph of constitutional *Recht* over imperial *Macht,* of secular culture over religious faith."[156] Whereas palaces, churches, and garrisons were aesthetically and essentially at the heart of the old medieval city anchored by Richard's wall, institutions

---

150. Schorske, *Fin-de-Siècle,* 27.
151. Farrow and Blashill, "Recent Development," 29.
152. On this period, see Blau, "A Capital," 178; Schorske, *Fin-de-Siècle,* esp. 87–95, on the last decade of prewar design, directed largely by Otto Wagner, and construction; and Olsen, *The City,* 69, 76. Between 1868 and 1873, at least forty percent of the housing available along the Ringstrasse had been completed.
153. Farrow and Blashill, "Recent Development," 37.
154. Farrow and Blashill, "Recent Development," 29–37.
155. Farrow and Blashill, "Recent Development," 29.
156. Schorske, *Fin-de-Siècle,* 31.

open to and run by the public reflected the nineteenth-century's political and social changes.[157]

Yet, to know the new was to recall some commonly known version of the old. The general scholarly consensus is that the new Vienna could not be physically or mentally disentangled from the old, partly because of the intricate building scheme associable with the Ringstrasse,[158] and partly because of the nineteenth-century's national, and nostalgic, turn: "The ecumenical approach of Bossuet and Voltaire was abandoned by an age that was genuinely convinced of the centrality of the growth of the nation-state to an understanding of the past," as Donald J. Olsen puts it.[159] For the Viennese, as well as for Londoners and Parisians, that impulse to view the present through the lens of the past was coupled with what Olsen describes as "hard historical knowledge," newly pervasive among the more educated middle and upper classes.[160] It is difficult to say which particular details of the past Brunner, like his projected audience, knew or did not know, but the local rumors and talk about Richard are expressly constitutive of Olsen's "hard historical knowledge," which is to say, a common knowledge about the past, inflected by present-day local talk and old and new rumors.

Richard, whose relationship to Vienna, and to Austria and Germany, had been codified over hundreds of years, was monumentalized throughout the city even as his wall was demolished. Jans Enikel's local history was enshrined on July 18, 1894, when Enekelstraße was named for him in Vienna's newly apportioned sixteenth district.[161] The coinage Leopold V had adopted using part of the silver from Richard's ransom was commemorated with a plaque on Vienna's Heumarkt, the site of the Austrian Mint, founded during the first half of the nineteenth century.[162] And sometime in the second half of the nineteenth century, a building was torn down on Dietrichgasse,[163] an alley running parallel to the Danube in Vienna's then newly allocated third munici-

---

157. Schorske, *Fin-de-Siècle*, 31.

158. For example, Olsen, *The City*, 309, on Vienna's treatment of its physical past "with greater solicitude than either London or Paris" during the "Ringstrasse Era."

159. Olsen, *The City*, 298; Schorske, *Fin-de-Siècle*, 36.

160. Olsen, *The City*, 298–99.

161. A street was also named for him in Linz, though I have been unable to discover the date.

162. In the first half of the nineteenth century, the Mint's official site became the Heumarkt in central Vienna. The plaque is located at Heumarkt 4. The Austrian Mint's official website dates its foundation to Richard's ransom; see https://www.muenzeoesterreich.at/eng/about-us/our-history.

163. Leeper, *Medieval Austria*, 280 n. 1: "the traditional house of Richard's arrest" remained standing "till about 1880."

pal district. The third district, called Landstraße (literally "country road") and situated just southeast of the Ring, encompasses what in the twelfth century was known as the suburb of Erdberg, supposedly the place of Richard's capture. In his multivolume study on the "old streets and squares" (*die alten Strassen und Pläetze*) of Vienna, Wilhelm Kisch states that by the time of his work's publication in 1888, a new building had gone up on Diectrichgasse affixed with a plaque: "On this place stood the hunter's lodge in which Richard I, king of England, was captured by Leopold of Austria in 1192 and brought to Dürnstein Castle."[164]

This plaque prompted Kisch to record the spectrum of speculative talk about the circumstances of Richard's capture, talk clearly inherited from the twelfth century and still circulating among the Viennese in the last decades of the nineteenth century. People said that perhaps a child who was dispatched to buy provisions for Richard and his men aroused local suspicion when he paid with Byzantine coins and, probably under duress, betrayed the coins' origin, or perhaps a soldier who had been at the siege of Acre recognized Richard and reported his presence. Or, people said, perhaps while cooking a fowl over an open flame, a fellow Englishman identified Richard, either by sight or by voice; perhaps while cooking a fowl over an open flame, the precious ring Richard wore was revealed to those around him when he reached his hand forward to turn the spit.[165] Kisch, for his part, suspected that the initial structure on the site, whatever it may have been, was destroyed by the Ottoman Turks during their sixteenth- and seventeenth-century invasions of the city, and that at the time of Richard's capture the land itself would have been completely covered by the Danube.[166] The plaque, then, commemorates less the traditional house than it does the traditional talk: the only extant and verifiable relic of Richard's capture.

For those on the freshly cleared ground in fin-de-siècle Vienna, the considered destruction of the past's physical form also cleared mental ground on which an alternate history could be erected. A more ethereal knowledge. For the historian and journalist Heinrich Friedjung, whose life in Vienna coincided with its spatial and political changes, generations of burghers—the old and unrecognized Viennese middle class—were, over the course of the

---

164. Wilhelm Kisch, *Die alten Strassen und Pläetze von Wien's Vorstädten und ihre historisch und ihre interessanten Häeuser*, vol. 1 (Vienna: Oskar Frank, 1888), 523. The plaque reads: "An dieser Stelle stand das Jägerhaus, in welchem im Jahre 1192 Richard I König von England durch Leopold von Österreich gefangen genommen und von da nach Schloss Dürnstein A. D. D. gebracht wurde."

165. Kisch, *Die alten Strassen*, 1:524.

166. Kisch, *Die alten Strassen*, 1:524.

destruction and reconstruction that constituted the liberal-bourgeois Ringstrasse era, figuratively exhumed, "like huge coal beds lying under the earth."[167] Friedjung describes a spectrally strange process of monumentalization that was contingent on the (new, liberal) political actors and actions of Friedjung's specific milieu to be sure. But such remembrance was also provoked by the sudden absence of objects that anchored both collective and individual narratives of the past, however distant. In the absence of Richard's wall, Brunner exhumed not a Viennese burgher, but something almost as intangible: the corpus, memory, "rumor," to borrow Scott's description, of Richard, a figure foundational to Vienna, and deeply relevant to German, Prussian, and Austro-Hungarian local cultural memory and identity in the decades before World War I. *Richard Löwenherz* is a monument to Vienna's Richard, like the other commemorations necessitated by the destruction of the ultimate monument to that foundational moment in Vienna's past, its wall.

In the absence of alternative critical editions,[168] Brunner's edition has become for us the most accessible and by far the most accessed monument of *Richard Coeur de Lion*'s text and transmission. *Richard Löwenherz* has been assessed by "objective" readers according to historical accounts of Richard's life and reign: How close does the romance come to "the truth," how radically does it deviate?[169] Answers to these questions have traditionally informed our accounts of *Richard Coeur de Lion*'s transmission, its completeness, its relevance to us and to its contemporary medieval audiences. But the pressure that local talk exerts on retrospective textual production makes it incumbent upon us to approach *Richard Löwenherz* and other retrospective texts from the various subjectivities of their makers and readers. The text that Brunner produced amid local talk has informed our own talk about the past. Moreover, as a reader and a text-maker, Brunner approximates the kind(s) of subjective medieval readers and text-makers that copies of retrospective romances, saints' lives, and *chansons de geste* provoked and produced. Now that we ourselves are knowing and local readers like Brunner, let us return to the Almayne episodes in *Richard Löwenherz*.

The unique material and variants in Brunner's chosen exemplars, the Caius manuscript and the 1509 edition, tell a version of *Richard Coeur de*

---

167. Quoted in Schorske, *Fin-de-Siècle*, 45.

168. For a recent edition of the copy preserved in London, British Library, MS Additional 31042, see M. C. Figueredo, ed., *"Richard Coeur de Lion*: An Edition from the London Thornton Manuscript," 2 vols. (unpublished PhD diss., University of York, 2010); and Schellekens's unpublished PhD dissertation, cited above, which provides diplomatic editions of the copies in Auchinleck, Egerton 2862, Arundel 58, and Douce 228.

169. This line of textual interrogation relative to *Richard Coeur de Lion* can be traced from the present day back to Ellis. John Finlayson's essays are more recent and influential examples.

Lion that would have been, for Brunner, expressly local. Of the manuscripts and editions he knew and accessed, Brunner's chosen exemplars contained the longest accounts of Richard's capture and imprisonment in Almayne, as well as an episode present in only two manuscripts. In that episode, after being ransomed and freed, Richard returns to Almayne to establish peace between it and England.[170] The two manuscripts that contain Richard's return are Caius and Douce 228. Yet the king of Almayne is less thoughtful in his first encounter with Richard in Douce 228 than he is in Caius, and the reconciliation between England and Almayne is less secure. In Douce 228, the king of Almayne's actions are seemingly motivated by only a long and unexplained hatred toward Richard. In Caius, the king's distrust of Richard is justified by his worry that Richard will usurp his lands, and he holds Richard for ransom specifically because of Richard's tryst with the king's daughter, Margery. Where in Douce 228, Richard swears by Constantine's mother, Helen (and in Arundel 58 and Harley 4690 by "Gamelyn"), in *Richard Löwenherz*, he swears by a local saint who was especially meaningful in the Austro-Hungarian Empire before its fall, "Martyn" of Tours.[171]

Other local stories, too, might have been pertinent as Brunner read the extant manuscript copies of the romance and made choices about his own exemplars. An episode in which the king of Almayne's son nonsensically challenges an imprisoned Richard to a fight and is subsequently killed by a blow to the face, is not extant in the Caius copy. Here Brunner supplements Caius with the 1509 edition, which includes the fight between Richard and the king of Almayne's son, as well as a series of subsequent scenes, unessential to any aspect of the plot. In these scenes, the king and his queen hear the surprising news of their son's death, a death they (like the reader) cannot completely comprehend as a logical event, but whose aftermath nevertheless occupies considerable narrative space.[172] A knight tells the king that Richard has killed his son and the king immediately and dramatically falls to the ground in shock and sorrow; when he rises to his feet he requests details, but none are known. He then tells his queen, who,

Whenne [she] vndyrstood,
Ffor sorwe, sertys, sche wax nygh wood.
Her kerchefs she drewe, her heer also,
"Alas," she sayd, "what shall j do!"

---

170. *Richard Löwenherz*, lines 1465ff.
171. *Richard Löwenherz*, line 763.
172. *Richard Löwenherz*, lines 745–890.

> She cratched hereselff in þe vysage,
> As a wymman þat was in rage.
> þe face fomyd al on blood,
> Sche rente þe robe þat sche in stood,
> Wrong here handes þat sche was born:
> "Jn what manere is my sone jlorn?"[173]

This question hangs in the air. The king, unsure, turns to his knight, who calls Richard's jailor to "bere wytnesse off þat sawe, / In what maner þat he was slawe."[174] As the knight, king, and queen hear for the first time what happened, the reader hears of it for a second time, having been privy to the son's death as it happened. Austro-Hungarian dynastic politics also shaped Brunner's daily world and dovetailed with his editorial project. Rumor swirled around the untimely death of the crown prince Rudolf in 1889; his cousin, the ill-fated Franz Ferdinand, became Emperor Franz Joseph's living heir, and the state attempted to suppress any unauthorized talk on the matter. But rumors did not cease to circulate and continued to do so even after the monarchy's collapse in 1916 led to factual revelations about these events.[175] New truth could not replace or even be discerned from the old speculative talk.[176] Brunner, as a local resident, had access to all of this context and may well have seen synergies between this local intrigue and the episode in his exemplars.

Brunner's edition has been a useful stopgap, as R. S. Loomis foretold, but it is more fundamentally a retrospective text that responded to, and has generated, talk. By placing *Richard Löwenherz* in its proper position as the most recent locally attuned copy of *Richard Coeur de Lion,* rather than a text representative of the entire textual tradition, the surviving medieval copies and other traces of the romance are more easily perceptible. The romance's extant witnesses include the seven medieval manuscripts and two early sixteenth-century printed editions Brunner knew, and two fragments discovered and identified after *Richard Löwenherz* appeared in 1913. The first of these, now Gloucester, Gloucestershire Archives, MS D2700/V/1 No. 8, has been dated to the first quarter of the fifteenth century and is independent of any extant

---

173. *Richard Löwenherz,* lines 825–34.
174. *Richard Löwenherz,* lines 842–43.
175. For example, Gerda Butkuviene, "Book Review: Myths of Mayerling; *Crime at Mayerling. The Life and Death of Mary Vetsera,* by Georg Markus; *The Hapsburgs' Tragedy,* by Leo Belmonto," *The Vienna Review,* March 11, 2012. The publication's tagline is "Be a Local."
176. William Tuohy, "1889 Hapsburg Tragedy at Mayerling: 'Love Deaths' Remain Fascinating," *Los Angeles Times,* March 19, 1989.

manuscript.[177] The second fragment, now St. Andrews, University Library, MS PR 2065 R.4, belongs to Auchinleck's *King Richard* and runs nearly consecutively with the Auchinleck fragment discovered in the mid-nineteenth century. Together, the two Auchinleck fragments total roughly seven hundred lines that once sat within the *King Richard* bifolium still preserved between Auchinleck's boards.[178] No manuscript copy is in direct relation to any other, meaning we have a fraction of what once existed. A record of one now lost copy survives, as does a gesture at another. An inventory made between 1475 and 1479 of books belonging to John Paston II includes one "Richard Coeur de Lyon," though the specifics of its narrative and earlier provenance remain unknown.[179] In the longer recension of his late thirteenth-century Middle English chronicle, Robert of Gloucester makes oblique reference to a "romance" about Richard.[180] And Robert Mannyng's Middle English chronicle, which Mannyng himself dates in its closing lines to 1338,[181] also mentions in passing what "þe romance sais" about Richard.[182] Mannyng's account of Richard's reign at times resembles manuscript copies of *Richard Coeur de Lion* so closely that Neil Ker uncharacteristically mistook a pastedown of Mannyng's chronicle for a fragment of the romance.[183] For all of our scholarly talk, the scene in which Richard's mother shoots through the church roof survives in only one manuscript; the scenes of Richard's cannibalism survive in two manuscripts, but not completely in both.[184]

---

177. Norman Davis, "Another Fragment of 'Richard Coer de Lyon,'" *Notes and Queries* 16 (1969): 447–52. When Davis examined the fragment, its shelfmark was Badminton, Duke of Beaufort, MS 704.1.16, and it is still listed as such in *NIMEV* and *DIMEV*. However, the fragment is now on deposit in the Gloucestershire Archives with the above shelfmark.

178. See Smithers, "Two Newly-Discovered Fragments," 1–11; Pearsall-Cunningham, vii; and chapter 4.

179. Norman Davis, ed., *Paston Letters and Papers of the Fifteenth Century*, vol. 1 (Oxford: Oxford University Press, 1971), 516–18.

180. Robert of Gloucester, *The Metrical Chronicle of Robert of Gloucester*, ed. William Aldis Wright, 2 vols., RS 86 (London: Eyre and Spottiswoode, 1887), vol. 2, line 9987. The chronicle survives in two recensions, which largely agree until Stephen's reign. Wright and others have argued for a date of 1300. See also Matthew Fisher, *Scribal Authorship and the Writing of History in Medieval England* (Columbus: The Ohio State University Press, 2012), 12, 97–98; and see chapter 3.

181. Mannyng, *The Chronicle*, pt. 2, lines 8356–58.

182. Mannyng, *The Chronicle*, pt. 2, lines 3870–71; and see chapter 4.

183. N. R. Ker, *Fragments of Medieval Manuscripts Used as Pastedowns in Oxford Bindings with a Survey of Oxford Binding c. 1515–1620* (Oxford: Oxford Bibliographical Society, 2000 [2004]), 87, no. 919. The fragment is Oxford, Merton College, 23.b.6. Davis corrected Ker's misidentification in "Another Fragment," 451–52.

184. On the states in which these episodes survive, see chapter 5.

No longer drowned out by the talk of fin-de-siècle Vienna, these textual relics raise countless open questions. For instance, what constituted *Richard Coeur de Lion*? And what constituted medieval England's cultural memory of Richard? Chief among such questions is that which I posed at the start of this chapter, about the role talk plays in our modern scholarly practices of cultural recovery and textual production. The medieval talk and rumor examined in this chapter has for the most part been talk and rumor contemporary with Richard. But because the extant insular textual corpus of Richard was fleshed out after his death—indeed, for a long time after—we must ask the same question of medieval practices of cultural recovery and textual production. What role did talk play in medieval England's reconstruction of the past? Answers to that question must be pursued in medieval England's archive of talk and text.

TWO

Public Talk and Legal Fictions

AFTER NEARLY TWO decades of investigating local administrations, taking formal stock of his lands, and attempting to legislate soundly the rights and properties of the Crown, in May of 1290 Edward I aimed to codify his efforts with the "statute of *quo warranto*," which affirmed that the king could bring writs of *quo warranto* to determine whether or not franchises and liberties, including ecclesiastical advowsons, were held by proper warrants.[1] If not, the king could (re)claim his property. Such writs put the burden of proof squarely on the defendants, who then needed to produce documentation showing continuous ancestral use of lands and privileges within a temporal limitation: since "before the time of king Richard our cousin, or in all his time" (*ante tempus Regis Ricardi consanguinei sui aut toto tempe suo*).[2] Edward had in fact

---

1. *Quo warranto* means here "by what warrant." Franchises were royal privileges held by a subject, and liberties were those privileges in aggregate or the geographical area over which the lord held administrative, not lawmaking, authority. On these terms, see M. T. Clanchy, "The Franchise of Return of Writs," *Transactions of the Royal Historical Society* 17 (1967): 59 n. 1. On *quo warranto* legislation as a "campaign" and the other legal undertakings of Edward's reign, see Donald W. Sutherland, *Quo Warranto Proceedings in the Reign of Edward I, 1278–1294* (Oxford: Clarendon Press, 1963), 2, 16–32; and F. W. Maitland, *The Constitutional History of England*, ed. H. A. L. Fisher (1908; reprint, Cambridge: Cambridge University Press, 1974), 18–23.

2. Here and elsewhere I quote from the 1290 statute as it appears in *Statutes of the Realm*, ed. and trans. A. Luders et al., vol. 1 (London: Record Commission, 1810), 107. Luders

been pursuing an informal but rigorous campaign of *quo warranto* for twelve years prior to 1290, and by that campaign's end in 1294, over 1,600 *quo warranto* writs had been issued.[3] These writs were concerned chiefly with the uppermost social class's unique types of privileged holdings and were meant to paper over the long-standing theoretical conflict at the heart of the matter: whether the lands and privileges of the lay lords were irrevocably earned through ancestral participation in conquest, or were innately the king's to take away.[4]

The most famous defendant in the *quo warranto* campaign has become John de Warenne, sixth earl of Surrey, a baron whose successes during the reigns of Henry III and Edward I were as public as his failures.[5] According to the chronicle attributed to Walter of Guisborough, an Augustinian canon regular of the late thirteenth century, when legally compelled in 1278 to show by what warrant he held a portion of his lands, John de Warenne waved a rusty old sword in front of the king's justices and announced:

> Here my lords, here is my warrant! My ancestors came with William the Bastard and conquered their lands with the sword, and I shall defend them with the sword against anyone who tries to usurp them. The king did not

---

takes the name "Statutum de Quo Warranto" from "Old Printed Copies," by which he means no earlier than the beginning of the sixteenth century (1:xxv), and the text from *Rotuli de Placita ad Parliamentorum* 18 Edw. I. m.7. D. 107. This name and text are now standard. When compared, scholarly summaries of the 1290 statute present a confused picture of its demands and effects. On these differences, as well as the details and sweep of the *quo warranto* campaign, see below in this chapter. For a description of the statute that attempts to consolidate the different critical accounts, see Michael Prestwich, *Edward I*, rev. ed. (New Haven: Yale University Press, 1997), 258–61, 347.

3. Sutherland, *Quo Warranto*, 1–2. Although new inquests had been conducted at Edward's order since 1274, his *quo warranto* campaign began in earnest in 1278 with the Statutes of Gloucester; see *Statutes of the Realm*, 1:45–46.

4. On this problem, see Maurice Keen, *England in the Later Middle Ages*, 2nd ed. (New York: Routledge, 2003), 9–12. There is a critical consensus that the terms of *quo warranto* were a compromise on Edward's part between Bractonian theory, which favored the Crown, and conquest theory, which sympathized with the descendants of participants in the Norman Conquest. According to conquest theory, heirs of William I's men did not need to show a warrant if they could demonstrate seisin since 1066. On this compromise, see Prestwich, *Edward I*, 347.

5. John de Warenne had a checkered involvement in the Second Barons' War, changing sides several times and fleeing to France in 1264. He was appointed a custodian of the northern shires in 1265, and in 1296 was made warden of Scotland. He returned to England after his defeat by William Wallace at Stirling Bridge. See F. M. Powicke, *The Thirteenth Century, 1216–1307* (Oxford: Clarendon Press, 1953), esp. 153–54, 187–88, 218–19, 423–25, 612–14; and Prestwich, *Edward I*, esp. 23–34, 37–54, 471–78. See also G. Lapsley, "John de Warenne and the Quo Warranto Proceedings in 1279," *Cambridge Historical Journal* 2 (1927): 118–19.

conquer and subject the land by himself, but our forebears were partners and colleagues with him.[6]

Based on internal and external evidence, the episode's events seem more "story" than "history," though this is a troubled distinction, especially when it comes to medieval chronicles. *Quo warranto* proceedings were concerned with liberties and privileges specifically, not the all-encompassing "lands" the chronicle suggests; the king could not have simply seized or usurped a baron's holdings, though here he is accused of having done so; and since at least the start of the thirteenth century, the king's justices refused to acknowledge the legality of any symbolic object other than a seal, so the outdatedness of a sword should have come as no surprise to its owner.[7] According to the extant plea rolls, John de Warenne or his counsel did appear in front of justices to answer *quo warranto* writs for liberties in Yorkshire, Lincolnshire, Norfolk, Surrey, and Sussex, but there is no mention of an ancestral sword, only documentary and oral assertions of ancestral tenure.[8]

Initially extracted from its chronicle context and reprinted in early twentieth-century histories to illustrate the question of whether liberties were rightfully held through ancestry or should revert to the Crown,[9] the "popular legend" of John de Warenne was reintroduced to us in the late twentieth century when historian Michael Clanchy enshrined the "Earl Warenne story" in *From Memory to Written Record,* a book that has become canonical among medievalists. Clanchy argues there that the increase of England's bureaucracy and documentation, especially in the twelfth and thirteenth centuries,

---

6. Walter of Guisborough, *The Chronicle of Walter of Guisborough,* ed. Harry Rothwell, Camden Third Series 89 (London: Royal Historical Society, 1957), 216 n. d.: "Ecce domini mei ecce Warentum meum. Antecessores enim mei cum Willelmo bastardo uenientes conquesti sunt terras suas gladio et easdem gladio defendam a quocunque eas occupare volente. Non enim rex per se terram deuicit et subiecit sed progenitores nostri fuerunt cum eo participes et coadiutores." Walter's chronicle runs from 1066 to 1305, relying on earlier northern sources such as William of Newburgh, *Historia post Bedam,* and Martinus Polonius until 1290. Entries from 1290 to 1305 include a number of unique documents probably derived from the priory of St. Mary at Guisborough. On Walter's original contributions, see Walter of Guisborough, *Chronicle,* xxv–xxxi. On Walter, see John Taylor, "Guisborough [Hemingford, Hemingburgh], Walter of (fl. c. 1290–c. 1305), Chronicler and Augustinian Canon," *Oxford Dictionary of National Biography,* September 23, 2004, https://www-oxforddnb-com.ezprox.bard.edu/view/10.1093/ref:odnb/9780198614128.001.0001/odnb-9780198614128-e-12892.

7. These discrepancies are further summarized in Clanchy, *From Memory,* 35–36, 38.

8. See *Placita de quo warranto,* ed. William Illingworth (London: Record Commission, 1818), 191 and 215, 421 and 429–30, 485 and 498, 745, 750–51 (hereafter *PQW*).

9. For example, Helen M. Cam, *Liberties and Communities in Medieval England: Collected Studies in Local Administration and Topography* (Cambridge: Cambridge University Press, 1944), 174–77.

demanded and produced a functional, widespread, workaday—as opposed to a pleasurable, literary—lay literacy.¹⁰ Though his book's title conflates orality and memory into a single intangible archive and sets it in opposition to a textual one, Clanchy explicitly cautions his readers against misinterpreting his title and central claim as an argument for "a single and invariable line of progress from illiteracy to literacy, and, by implication, from barbarism to civilization."¹¹ In other words, we should reject as fallacy the paradigm that there was orality, then literacy, then us: "orality giving way to literacy as dinosaurs gave way to mammals."¹² Yet, the Earl Warenne story has come to embody precisely such an imaginary transitional moment.

Among medievalists, "Earl Warenne" has become a byword for *quo warranto,* and *quo warranto,* in turn, has become emblematic of legal bureaucracy's rise: a fulcrum in the increasing prevalence of documents, Clanchy's account of that process, and its implications. My own mention of *quo warranto* to a fellow medievalist prompted him to sit forward in his chair, wave an imaginary sword, and declare, "This is my warrant!" This was not an isolated event. The immediate association between the *quo warranto* campaign and the Earl Warenne story is paralleled in critical accounts of the legislation. Scholars have continued to reproduce the story itself, sometimes freshly translating it, but more often reprinting a translation without returning to the chronicle's text or its historical context.¹³ Our collective understanding that the Earl Warenne story and *quo warranto* exemplify a cultural shift from memory and orality to the written record has been maintained if not fortified by sheer repetition.¹⁴ I suspect that the way we now read *quo warranto* and retell the Earl Warenne story has much to do with Clanchy's self-contradicting and thus

---

10. Clanchy, *From Memory,* 3, 19.
11. Clanchy, *From Memory,* 20.
12. Coleman, "Aurality," 69.
13. Notable exceptions are Clanchy, *From Memory,* 35–41; Sutherland, *Quo Warranto,* 82 n. 2; and Cam, *Liberties,* 176–77.
14. The Earl Warenne episode is not only referred to at length, but actually reproduced in Sutherland, *Quo Warranto,* 82 n. 2; Clanchy, *From Memory* 36; and Prestwich, *Edward I,* 259, to name a few. Others do not reproduce the episode because, as they state, it has been so thoroughly internalized by scholars: see, for example, Matthew Fisher, "Genealogy Rewritten: Inheriting the Legendary in Insular Historiography," in *Broken Lines: Genealogical Literature in Late-Medieval Britain and France,* ed. Raluca L. Radulescu and Edward D. Kennedy (Turnhout: Brepols, 2008), 132. Matthew Giancarlo reproduces more of the "story," but maintains that it "is familiar as a classic exemplum of the clash between legal-documentary forms and folk traditional assertions of right"; see Matthew Giancarlo, *Parliament and Literature in Late Medieval England* (Cambridge: University of Cambridge Press, 2007), 12–13. In R. F. Green, *Crisis of Truth,* 267, the chronicle quotation is taken directly from and refers the reader back to Clanchy, *From Memory,* as a source and interpreter; this is representative of the circular trajectory the story travels within critical texts.

highly uncharacteristic framing of the scene as an "evocation of dying oral culture" and "a desperate assertion of the primacy of oral tradition over recorded history and non-literate forms of proof over Edward I's lawyers and their demands for charters."[15] Such characterizations figure the Earl Warenne story as witness to the binary of memory/orality and written record that Clanchy himself otherwise rejects. Implicit in this modern reading, too, is a hypothesis about medieval reception: that the Earl Warenne story would have produced intense nostalgia in its contemporary reader, who would have recognized the statute of *quo warranto* as silencing voices and relieving memory of its post as the past's chief gatekeeper.

This chapter argues that legal upheaval generally, and the statute of *quo warranto* particularly, in fact gave rise to talk. By placing the statute of *quo warranto* in the long legal tradition from which it emerged and in which it is rarely studied, this chapter shows the influence of England's legislation on the ways in which England's past—especially its late twelfth-century past—was reconstructed in the late thirteenth century and circulated through a process of telling and retelling. Put otherwise, England's history was fundamentally shaped by the circulation of urgent public talk about its past: talk not replaced by, but rather preserved in, the written record. Key witnesses in this argument are the official plea rolls and unofficial law reports in which survive both verbatim and officially redacted testimony about litigants' relationships to their ancestors, to their ancestral possessions, and to England. I read these records differently than have legal historians, for whom they function largely as collections of legal and historical facts. These documents have a more complex quality. They preserve thousands of narratives constructed by the English public, provide evidence that wide-ranging talk about the past locatable to a particular time and place occurred, and constitute an archive of the very talk itself. This talk reveals a pressing and widespread late thirteenth-century project among litigants like John de Warenne to reconstruct their, and therefore England's, past. A critical engagement with the interplay between litigants and this legislation reveals how parts of England's past came to be remembered, forgotten, or recognized as touchstones constitutive of, first, individual, and, then, collective identity.

The Earl Warenne story is about the persistence of orality, not about its demise. Evidence is, as the Earl Warenne story itself reminds us, complicated and attachment-forming. What we have been repeating by way of evidence is not the whole story. This is—or at least comes closer to it:

---

15. Clanchy, *From Memory*, 36–39.

Soon after, the king disturbed some of the land's magnates, desiring to know through his justices by what warrant they held their lands, and if they did not have a good warrant, he immediately seized their lands. The Earl Warenne was called among others before the king's justices and asked by what warrant he held his lands. He produced in their midst an ancient and rusty sword and said, "Here my lords, here is my warrant. My ancestors came with William the Bastard and conquered their lands with the sword, and I shall defend them with the sword against anyone who tries to usurp them. The king did not conquer and subject the land by himself, but our forebears were partners and colleagues with him." And the rest of the magnates held with him and his response, and they went away agitated and infuriated. But when the king heard this he feared for himself and kept quiet from this initial misstep. Soon after, the Welsh rose up and the king had great need of his magnates. When the king held a certain parliament and the magnates' sons stood around him in the evening, he asked them, "What do you talk about amongst yourselves when I am in council with your fathers?" One of them replied, "You would not be offended if I speak the truth?" And the king answered, "No." "Truly, my lord king, we speak in this way:

> The king he wants to get our gold,
> And the queen our handsome lands to hold,
> And the Quo warranto
> Will do us all in."

Afterwards, the archbishops and bishops began to disturb their underlings, especially the religious men, wishing to know by what right they held their churches and for what personal uses in their dioceses. And the same sense is "quo iure" as "quo varento." Although the meanings and the names are varied and diverse, nevertheless the Highest will judge both.[16]

---

16. Walter of Guisborough, *Chronicle*, 216 n. d: "Cito post inquietauit rex quosdam ex magnatibus terre per iusticiarios suos scire volens quo Waranto tenerent terras et si non haberent bonum varentum saysiuit statim terras illorum; vocatusque est inter ceteros Comes de Warenna coram justiciarios regis et interrogatus quo Warento teneret produxit in medium gladium antiquum et eruginatum et ait 'Ecce domini mei ecce Warentum meum. Antecessores enim mei cum Willelmo bastardo uenientes conquesti sunt terras suas gladio et easdem gladio defendam a quocunque eas occupare volente. Non enim rex per se terram deuicit et subiecit sed progenitores nostri fuerunt cum eo participes et coadiutores.' Adheseruntque sibi et sue responsioni ceteri magnates, et tumultuantes et inpacati recesserunt. Rex autem cum audiret talia timuit sibi et ab incepto errore conquieuit. Et cito post insurrexerunt Walenses et magnatibus suis rex multum indiguit. Cum teneret rex quoddam parliamentum et filii magnatorum

This fuller scene is a variant. It survives in one fifteenth-century copy of Walter of Guisborough's chronicle and three fourteenth-century copies of the Osney-Abingdon compilations,[17] which interpolate portions of the Guisborough chronicle without attribution. But this scene is, more particularly, what I call a "modular" variant: a self-contained variant that can be easily added to or absented from a text without disrupting that text's narrative. A modular variant can also be made or modified to accommodate whatever local talk is circulating around its copying so that its text resonates locally. For instance, the role here played by the Earl Warenne could easily be, and sometimes was, recast with another historical figure. The four manuscripts in which the Earl Warenne variant appears were produced in religious houses associable by proximity or rule: two of the Osney-Abingdon copies are locatable to the Augustinian priory at Osney, and the third to the Benedictine house at Abingdon, within easy walking distance of Osney.[18] The variant and the Earl Warenne's presence in it possibly originated among these southern houses before being interpolated into the northern manuscript, London, British Library, MS Lansdowne 239, produced at the Augustinian priory at Guisborough and now

---

starent coram eo in vesperis dixit eis 'Quid loquimini inter vos quando nos sumus in consilio cum patribus vestris?' Et respondit vnus 'Non offendamini si veritatem dicam?' Et rex 'Non.' 'Certe, domine mi rex, nos dicimus sic:

Le roy cuuayte nos deneres,
e la rayne nos beau maners,
e le Quo voranco,
sale mak wus al at do.'

Archiepiscopi et episcopi postea ceperunt inquietare subditos suos et precipue religiosos scire volentes quo iure possiderent ecclesias suas in proprios vsus in suis dyocesibus, et idem est sensus Quo iure seu quo varento licet voluntates et nomina varia sunt et diuersa vtrumque tamen iudicabit altissimus." I am grateful to Robert L. Cioffi for bringing his expert eye to Walter's idiosyncratic Latin and my translation of it.

17. These are London, British Library, MS Lansdowne 239; Cambridge, University Library, MS Dd. 2.5, which has an Abingdon provenance; and Oxford, Bodleian Library, MSS Digby 168 and Digby 170, both locatable to the Augustinian priory at Osney. On the chronicle's extant manuscripts, see Walter of Guisborough, *Chronicle*, xv, xii–xiii. Like Guisborough Priory in the north, neither southern house was untouched by Edward I's legal program, thus lending the story, whether fact or fiction, relevance well into the fourteenth century. On the houses' disputes, legal and otherwise, with Edward, see Prestwich, *Edward I*, 414–20, 423, 426, 430, 433–35; and Powicke, *Thirteenth Century*, 704–5, 717–18. The full variant's relevance to the religious houses that copied it extends beyond the Earl Warenne intrigue to the inclusion of advowsons in the *quo warranto* campaign. On Osney's participation, see *PQW*, 93 and 665; on Guisborough Priory, see *PQW*, 115, 117, and 210.

18. See William Dugdale, *Monasticon Anglicanum*, vol. 6 (London: Longman, 1830), 1, 248–56; and William Page, ed., *The Victoria History of the County of Oxford*, vol. 2 (London: Archibald Constable and Co., Ltd., 1907), 90–93.

the Guisborough chronicle's chief witness.[19] In southern England, John de Warenne, as Earl of Sussex and Surrey,[20] was the star of a series of stories, both official and unofficial, about his legal outbursts that circulated in talk and text.[21] In two northern copies of the variant,[22] Gilbert of Clare, seventh Earl of Gloucester, sixth Earl of Hereford, noted *quo warranto* objector, and known in northern England for his participation in the Scottish question, assumes the Earl Warenne role.[23] The variant's formal, modular adaptability to local talk surely facilitated its circulation, and while it might have been "well known," it was not known for the reasons scholars have posited. The variant's stable core consists of the action and noise that occurs around the Earl Warenne role, not necessarily the Earl Warenne himself.

Harry Rothwell, whose *Chronicle of Walter of Guisborough* remains the standard edition of the Guisborough chronicle and thus of the Earl Warenne variant, stipulates in his introduction that Walter's work has been "misused" as a historical touchstone. "The results when we can check [Walter] are such

---

19. Lapsley, "John de Warenne," 112–13; and Cam, *Liberties*, 176, suggest a southern provenance.

20. If we were to entertain the notion that the sword-waving episode occurred, and occurred in 1278 as Walter's chronicle suggests, the most likely location would be the *quo warranto* hearings held in Surrey, to which John de Warenne was summoned. See n. 8, above, and Cam, *Liberties*, 176. Other sites have been posited by, for example, Clanchy, "Franchise," 74–75 and *From Memory*, 38; and Giancarlo, *Parliament and Literature*, 13. The record's silence is not definitive proof of the event one way or the other.

21. The Patent Rolls of 1270 attest that John de Warenne struck (and probably killed) Alan de Zouche before the Bench at Westminster that year, and that he was fined and pardoned shortly thereafter. Their disagreement, which had its roots in the Second Barons' War, was heard over the course of a year by several different justices in the West Midlands and the South, and thus was no doubt heard *about* by the public in those locations. Accounts of the event appear in, for example, the contemporary southern chronicles *Flores Historiarum* and *Annales de Wintonia* (see Lapsley, "John de Warenne," 118–19), as well as in the longer recension of Robert of Gloucester's late thirteenth-century chronicle, where John de Warenne's courtroom violence disturbs the peace after the Second Barons' War; see Robert of Gloucester, *Metrical Chronicle*, vol. 2, lines 12014–29. While none of its extant copies derive from monastic libraries, Robert's chronicle is associable through internal and external evidence with Oxfordshire and thus with the milieu of Osney and Abingdon at the turn of the fourteenth century. See Antonia Gransden, *Historical Writing in England I, c. 550 to c. 1307* (1974; reprint, London: Routledge, 2000), 432–38.

22. Edinburgh, National Library of Scotland, MS Advocates 33.5.3 (a copy of Walter's chronicle), and London, British Library, MS Cotton Claudius D.vii (the Lanercost Chronicle), are both dated to the fourteenth century. The Augustinian priory of Lanercost was north of Guisborough Priory. On Advocates 33.5.3, see Andrew Watson, *The Manuscripts of Henry Savile of Banke* (London: Bibliographical Society, 1969), 23; on the Lanercost Chronicle, see *Chronicon de Lanercost*, ed. Joseph Stevenson (Edinburgh: Maitland Club, 1839), 174, 193.

23. Prestwich, *Edward I*, 259–61; and Sutherland, *Quo Warranto*, 146–47.

that it is impossible for us to trust him when we cannot," is a point proven, for instance, by the faulty date Walter supplies for his own priory's foundation.[24] Walter's chronicle, Rothwell presses, should be recognized and used for what it actually is: a particular local view, only authoritative insofar as it represents "the talk of the North."[25] Specifically, talk that began in 1290. From that year, the Guisborough canons, located in Yorkshire's North Riding and holding property in Annandale just across the Scottish border, found themselves in the midst of the Anglo-Scottish conflict. Thus situated, they were no doubt privy to intrigues worth talking about amongst themselves and further abroad.[26] Rothwell distinguishes between the modern notion of an encompassing, widely accepted historical narrative and that which Walter reports from his local and temporal milieu. This distinction can be applicable to most, if not all, medieval chronicles.

Much more radical is Rothwell's suggestion that we reimagine Walter's text as "talk of the North." Urging readers to recognize what appears on the page as "talk" is a textually destabilizing stance that halts the movement from oral culture to written record in its tracks. It revises where the lines between local talk and history should be drawn and, potentially, calls for the reversal of "oral to written." Rothwell stops short of theorizing an inextricable relationship between talk and text, where text preserves talk circulating in the air in much the same way ancient bones are fossilized and preserved in sedimentary rock, clear impressions of localized and time-bound moments. But that is precisely what I argue talk is: a form of history, a form often unrecognized because it is unstable, unsettled, and expressly constitutive of public contestation. In addition to the Earl Warenne variant's accommodation of the talk that circulated in the North and elsewhere depending on the milieu in which it was copied, the variant consistently depicts a relationship between talk and legal texts.

At its heart, the Earl Warenne variant is about talk produced by legal upheaval and that talk's transmission and preservation. The spectacle *quo warranto* provokes at court, where the Earl Warenne waves the rusty sword before the king's justices and narrates its (and his) descent in an actualization of the historical, in fact arouses talk: talk within the variant, talk in the four-

---

24. Walter of Guisborough, *Chronicle*, xxix. On Guisborough's founding, see William Page, ed., *The Victoria History of the County of York*, vol. 3 (London: Archibald Constable and Co., Ltd., 1913), 208–9; and Dugdale, *Monasticon Anglicanum*, 6:1, 265–76.

25. Walter of Guisborough, *Chronicle*, xxix. In his review of Rothwell's edition, John Taylor, following Rothwell, posits very little daylight between what was circulating in the air and what was written down on the page. See Taylor's "Review of *The Chronicle of Walter of Guisborough*, edited by Harry Rothwell," *Scottish Historical Review* 38 (1959): 62–63.

26. Walter of Guisborough, *Chronicle*, xxix.

teenth century whence our earliest copy of the episode survives, and modern scholarly talk. The Earl Warenne's fellow barons raise their voices in agreement and return to their homes unsettled and grumbling. We know they continue to talk amongst themselves and within their communities not because the variant reproduces their words, but because we hear that their talk reaches the king, first indirectly, and then directly, at his own prompting. The king hears of the dispute and the subsequent unrest in the shires, and when he wishes to be in the know about what is being said, he asks the barons' sons, not the barons themselves, what they and others talk about (*Quid loquimini inter vos quando nos sumus in consilio cum patribus vestris*). Their answer reveals a process of transmission by which their fathers' talk has been codified as popular—collectively made and widely circulated—rhyme.

Like the Earl Warenne's sword relic, the barons' dissatisfaction has been passed down from father to son and then disseminated by and among nonofficial and even nonbaronial voices speaking in Latin, Anglo-Norman French, and English, embodied by the variant's macaronic quatrain: "Le roy cuuayte nos deneres / e la rayne nos beau maners / e le Quo voranco / sale mak wus al at do."[27] In the representation of this process in Walter of Guisborough's chronicle, the statute of *quo warranto* provokes talk; its route in conversational and cultural diffusion crosses class and, because it is generated by the public and reaches the king last, runs counter to our expectations.[28] The macaronic quatrain the barons' sons repeat to the king comprises a small and unofficial popular history, what we might call a political poem, collectively made and known by telling and retelling. Within the Earl Warenne variant, then, the chronicle depicts the *quo warranto* campaign as, among other things, a generator of two very specific kinds of talk: First, narratives about an individual's ancestral past told in front of an audience that includes the king's justices and

---

27. *IMEV* 1844.5; *DIMEV* 3040. The quatrain survives in four manuscripts. It is noteworthy that no two copies of the quatrain are exactly alike. This dynamism parallels in text what I argue happens in this scene "off-stage" via talk, and, moreover, it demonstrates the productive nature of divergent copies. A brief discussion of the quatrain occurs in R. M. Wilson, *The Lost Literature of Medieval England* (London: Metheun & Co. Ltd., 1952), 190. Rossell Hope Robbins mentions it in passing as a "macaronic extract of 1279" and a "ballad scrap"; see "A Highly Critical Approach to the Middle English Lyric," *College English* 30 (1968): 75. It is absent from Peter Coss, ed., *Thomas Wright's Political Songs of England: From the Reign of John to that of Edward II* (Cambridge: Cambridge University Press, 1996). My thinking on linguistic and lyrical disruption has been informed by Christopher Baswell, "Multilingualism on the Page," in Strohm, *Middle English*, 38–50; and Ingrid Nelson, *Lyric Tactics: Poetry and Practice in Later Medieval England* (Philadelphia: University of Pennsylvania Press, 2016).

28. See, for example, P. R. Coss, "Aspects of Cultural Diffusion in Medieval England: The Early Romances, Local Society and Robin Hood," *Past and Present* 108 (1985): 35–79.

a cross-section of the public. And second, the popular rumor these narratives and their public articulation in turn generate: rumor about the narratives themselves, and also about the experience of witnessing such storytelling and legal spectacle.

A study of surviving plea rolls and records reveals that the Earl Warenne's narration of his ancestral history and the talk that narration generated—not his sword waving—would have been the most familiar acts to a broad English public. By the late thirteenth century, that public was practiced in recalling ancestral and local history, placing it within a longer chronology, and recounting it publicly in court. That public would also have recognized the implicit technical constraints the Earl Warenne pushes back against: the need to accord one's ancestral memory and its tokens with the requirements and restrictions prescribed by England's legislation on legal memory. This process, in which inherited or seemingly organic memories were reconstructed according to the terms of legal memory, produced what I call "legal fictions." The family of laws that limited legal memory—laws from which the statute of *quo warranto* descended—dated back to the Norman Conquest and had always generated upheaval. These laws precipitated retrospection and discussion of the past with oneself, among family members, in front of justices, and even surrounded by friends, neighbors, and strangers. Beginning with the enshrinement of *quo warranto* in 1290, such talk became preoccupied with what happened and what was said to have happened during the late twelfth-century reign of Richard I, rendering "the time of King Richard" infinitely reproducible and pervasively reproduced, and making the line between public talk and history impossible to locate. To ground my analysis of the interplay between litigants and this family of laws, I offer in the next several pages, and will return to over the course of this chapter, an account of England's legislation on legal memory.

An investigation of the documents associable with the *quo warranto* campaign leads one down a particular path of English legal history signposted with coronation dates and remnants of old royal travel itineraries, and strewn with branches of the Plantagenet family tree. In the midst of this scene, the statute of *quo warranto* comes into perspective as a singular piece of a significant picture of legislation limiting legal memory, legislation in which, for the previous two centuries, the Crown had been revising, reordering, and reprioritizing parts of England's past. Legislation enacted in 1275 laid out the revised limits on legal memory for various legal actions:

> And Forasmuch as it is long time passed since the Writs undernamed were limited; It is Provided, That in conveying a Descent (*conte de decente*) in a

Writ of Right, none shall [presume] to declare of the Seisin of his Ancestor further, or beyond the time of King Richard, Uncle to King Henry, Father to the King that now is; and that a Writ of Novel Disseisin, [of Partition,] which is called Nuper obiit, have their Limitation since the first Voyage of King Henry, Father to the King that now is, into Gascoin. And that Writs of Mortdancestor, of Cosinage, of Aiel, of Entry, and of Nativis, have their Limitation from the Coronation of the same King Henry, and not before. Nevertheless all Writs purchased now by themselves, or to be purchased between this and the Feast of St. John, for one Year complete, shall be pleaded from as long time, as heretofore they have been used to be pleaded.

(Statute of Westminster I, 3 Edw. I, c. 39.)[29]

And nearly forty years prior to that, in 1237, the statute outlines:

Touching Conveyance of Descent (*De narracione descensus*) in a Writ of Right from any Ancestor from the Time of King Henry the elder, the Year and Day, It is Provided, that from henceforth there be no mention made of so long Time, but from the Time of King Henry our Grandfather; and this Act shall take Effect at Pentecost, the one and twentieth Year [of our Reign,] and not afore, and the Writs before purchased shall proceed: Writs of Mortdauncestor, of Nativis, and Entre, shall not pass the last Return of King John from Ireland into England; [and this Act shall take effect as before is declared.] Writs of Novel disseisin shall not pass the first Voyage of our Sovereign Lord the King that now is, into Gascoine; and this Provision shall take his [*sic*] Effect from the time aforesaid, and all Writs purchased before shall proceed.

(Statute of Merton, 20 Henry III, c. 8.)[30]

---

29. *Statutes of the Realm*, 1:36: "Et pur ceo q̄ le tens est mult passe puis q̄ les briefs desuz nomeez furent aut feiz limitez; Purveu est q̄ [om] conte de decente, en le brief de dreit, q̄ nul ne seit oy por demaunder la seisine son auncestre de plus lointein seisine q̄ del tens le Rey Richard, oncle le piere le Rey q̄ ore est; e q̄ le brief de Novele deseisine, e de porpartie q̄ est appelle nup[er] obiit, eient le terme puis le primer passage le Rey Henry, piere nostre Seign' le Rey q̄ ore est, en Gascoyngne. Et le brief de Mort Dauncestre, de Cosinage, del Ael, e de Entre, e brief de Neivete eyent le t'me del Corounēmt le Rey Henri, e ne mie avaunt. Mes q̄ tuz les briefs ore [a par mesme] ou q̄ lem p'chasera entre ci e la Seint Johan en un an, seient pledez del tens q̄ avaunt soleient estre pleidez."

30. *Statutes of the Realm*, 1:3: "De narracione descensus in br̄i de recto, ab antecessore a tempore H. Reḡ senioris, anno & die. P̄visum est qd̄ de cet'o non fiat [mencio de] tam longinquo tempore, s3 a tempore H. Regis Avi nr̄i & locum habeat ista p̄visio ad Pentencosten, anno vicesimo primo & non ante, [p̄] bria prius impet'ta p̄cedant: bria mortis antecessoris, de nativis, [& de ingressu] non excedant ulimū reditum dn̄i Reḡ Johnis in Angliam. Br̄ia nove dissēie non excedant p'm transfretacoem dn̄i Reḡ qui nūc est in [Vascoñ], & locum

These are examples of legislation on limitation dates, legislation that prescribes dates beyond which plaintiffs' accounts of the past should not venture in a range of legal actions to determine proper seisin (present possession or occupation) or proprietary hold (right) of lands and other objects.[31] The 1237 legislation is the earliest of its kind to survive in documentary form, but through its language and the records of prior proceedings, legal historian Paul Brand has defined two previous periods likewise governed by limitation dates: in land disputes, "pre-1237" legislation current between about 1200 and 1237 set the limit of legal memory at the death of Henry I (December 1, 1135), and "pre-1200" legislation set the limit in land cases at the Norman Conquest of 1066.[32] To the best of our knowledge, then, prior to the enactment of *quo warranto* in 1290, legislation limiting legal memory occurred at some point after jurisdictional grants were made to Norman conquerors in 1066, limits were updated around 1200, and then updated again in 1237 and 1275. The furthest limit in the updates of 1237 and 1275 is that set for "actions of right," which determined proprietary right to freehold land.[33] To prove his claim, a plaintiff who acquired a writ of right, the document that initiated the legal action, could not go back beyond the limit of living memory, thought, opti-

---

habeat ista p̄visio a tempore p̄dicto, et br̄ia prius impetrata procedant." Three other versions of this legislation survive; they differ in wording but are consistent in the particulars. See Paul Brand, "'Time Out of Mind': The Knowledge and Use of the Eleventh- and Twelfth-Century Past in Thirteenth-Century Litigation," in *Anglo-Norman Studies 16: Proceedings of the Battle Conference, 1993*, ed. Marjorie Chibnall (Woodbridge: Boydell Press, 1994), 40 n. 15.

31. The clearest and most elegant description of England's forms of action remains F. W. Maitland's published course of lectures, *The Forms of Action at Common Law*, ed. A. H. Chaytor and W. J. Whitaker (1909; reprint Cambridge, Cambridge University Press, 1969). All subsequent uses of "forms of action" in this chapter refer to the system of Forms of Action or the Writ System of English medieval law. Actions could be "real," meaning in regard to real property, or "personal," for example, a debt, duty, or damages. To bring an action in the king's courts of common law, as Bracton stipulates, a plaintiff needed first to obtain the king's writ for the proper form of action. Each type of writ set into motion the particular procedure for the type of action that the plaintiff had judged best suited his or her case. An action could begin in a local court (e.g., shire or hundred), or in the king's court, depending on the action's type. For further description and discussion of specific forms of action, including of right, see below in this chapter.

32. Brand, "Time Out of Mind," 41–42. Claimants began using the date of Henry I's death as a new historical limit *c.* 1200; Brand points out that the 1237 legislation gives the earlier limit for actions of right: "a tempore H. Regis senioris, anno & die." My thinking in this chapter is greatly indebted to Brand's assiduous archival work and his innovative characterization of litigants as keepers of memory and unofficial record.

33. See Maitland, *Forms of Action*, 24–26; and R. C. van Caenegem, *Royal Writs in England from the Conquest to Glanvill: Studies in the Early History of the Common Law*, Publications of the Selden Society 77 (London: B. Quaritch, 1959), 207.

mistically, to be about a hundred years from any present moment.³⁴ For the actions enumerated in the legislation, evidence on the far side of that limit or any other limit set by the Crown was considered time immemorial or "time out of mind."

At first glance, the legislation reproduced above keeps time in a familiar way, as might a chronicle: according to the movements of England's rulers. In fact, legal time is kept here in a far less straightforward manner. There is no universal origin of legal memory and no single, clearly delineated path from the past to the present.³⁵ Each of the various limitation dates within a single statute keeps time according to a different point of origin, and they do so simultaneously. Within the 1237 statute, for instance, one limitation date or prescribed origin of legal memory applies to actions of right, another to actions of novel disseisin, and still another to the assize of mort d'ancestor, and these dates had been and would again be updated.³⁶ These legal boundaries of remembrance were ever-shifting, and legally circumscribed memory was studded with occasions of the Crown that were perennially moveable, replaceable. While some of these events were no doubt well-known, such as

---

34. Clanchy, *From Memory*, 152; Maitland, *Forms of Action*, 17–26. A *breve de recto tenendo* or writ of right—that is, of property—needed to be obtained by a plaintiff wishing to claim the right of inheritance or proprietary right to freehold land.

35. The plural limitation dates that occupy a single legislative gesture make them unexpectedly difficult to discuss using terms the critical field has established. Part of the problem results from a tendency to conflate the *quo warranto* statute, which sets a limitation date exclusively for liberties, franchises, and advowsons, with the limit for writs of right, while neglecting other types of disputes. For example, Clanchy, *From Memory*, 152, discusses a single "limit of legal memory" when referring to the 1275 legislation and later legislation.

36. Many forms of action and related procedures were developed in England. Here I briefly define most of the actions mentioned in the above legislation; they will reappear in this chapter. A writ of novel disseisin needed to be obtained if one had been recently disseised of freehold without just cause or judgment: That is, the assize of novel disseisin did not settle issues of proprietary right, only "seisin" or present possession or occupation. A writ of mort d'ancestor could be brought by an heir who should have been but was not seised of his or her ancestor's possession upon that ancestor's death. Both novel disseisin and mort d'ancestor are possessory assizes, unconcerned with right. Only a son, daughter, brother, sister, nephew, or niece could claim to be the seised heir in mort d'ancestor. To account for other relationships of the heir to the deceased, for example, grandfather, or great-grandfather, or cousin, the actions of aiel, besaiel, and cosinage, respectively, were established during the reign of Henry III. In this manner, the number of forms of action grew to accommodate the different permutations of disputes related to right and seisin that arose in the course of daily life. Nuper obiit or partition writs were filed for the recovery of land in the case of a common ancestor. Writs of entry (*de ingressu*) settled land disputes and involved a deciding body of twelve. The assize of darrein presentment determined who previously made the appointment to a vacant church benefice, and thus who could do so next. On these forms of action and others, see Maitland, *Forms of Action*, 16–27, 39–42.

the ascension of Henry III, others were surely less so. Would a litigant have to hand the date of John's last return from Ireland? According to the legislation, significant areas of the past, too, were wholly foreclosed to plaintiffs who in their initial claims should neither speak of ("no mention [should be] made") the time before the reign of Henry II, for instance, nor, presumably, do the work that would necessarily precede such speech: the mental or emotional traversing of whatever parts of the past lay on the far side of a limit. Defendants were not similarly limited, thus multiplying the versions of the past in circulation.[37] Barons like John de Warenne, as well as bishops and abbots, also needed to adhere to these limits except in cases involving their franchises and liberties, for which tenure could trace back to the proverbial water's edge of England's memory, 1066. The statute of *quo warranto* altered this.

In keeping with the customary scope of legal memory, the *quo warranto* statute of 1290 looks back a hundred years from its present moment to 1189, the year of Richard's coronation, but it otherwise does not entirely resemble the line of legislation on legal memory from which it descends. Rather than acquiesce to the barons' insistence that no part of the past be foreclosed to them as in all other actions, the statute splits the difference. For holders of liberties, franchises, and advowsons, it makes "the time of King Richard" a uniquely vertical marker on an otherwise flat topography,[38] not a hard and fast limit of legal memory like those dates given in the statutes of 1237 and 1275. Instead, Richard's reign, like a marcher castle with inattentive lookouts and an unarticulated mission, vaguely occupies the boundary between living memory and time out of mind. Consider the statute's core:

> That all under his Allegiance, whatsoever they be, as well Spiritual as other, which can verify by good Enquest of the Country, or otherwise, that they and their Ancestors or Predecessors have used any manner of Liberties, whereof they were impleaded by the said Writs, before the time of King Richard our Cousin, or in all his time, and have continued hitherto so that they have not misused such Liberties, that the Parties shall be adjourned further unto a certain day reasonable before the same Justices, within the which they may go to our Lord the King with the Record of the Justices,

---

37. Brand, "Time Out of Mind," 45–46.
38. The statute has generally been interpreted to mean that the limitation date is fixed at 1189, the year of Richard's coronation, making 1189 a *terminus post quem*; see, for example, Clanchy, *From Memory*, 42; and Prestwich, *Edward I*, 347. But, see also Sutherland, *Quo Warranto*, 92–93, who notes that the legislation actually allows for proof of continuous seisin from before the time of Richard and throughout his reign, thus blurring time out of mind and a limit of legal memory.

signed with their Seal, and also return; and our Lord the King, by his Letters [Patents] shall confirm their Estate. And they that cannot prove the Seisin of their Ancestors or Predecessors in such manner as is before declared, shall be ordered and judged after the Law and Custom of the Realm; and such as have the King's Charter shall be judged according to their Charters.[39]

Instead of setting 1189 as a hard limit, the statute conceptualizes both the present and the past in terms of their closeness to and distance from Richard's reign: the enshrined landmark that barons and bishops should use to gain their historical bearings, to reconceive of their ancestral pasts. Predecessors and ancestors existed either "before the time of King Richard" (*ante tempus Regis Ricardi*) or "in all his time" (*toto tempe suo*). The hundred-year distance between "his time" and the present is rhetorically elided (*& hucusq*ue *continuarunt*), thereby rendering Richard almost present and his reign nearly contiguous with that of Edward I.

In addition to this new formulation of the past relative to Richard's reign, the statute diverges from prior, related legislation in other ways. It stipulates that *quo warranto* will function according to new processes distinct from those already in existence for extant legislation on legal memory. While in all other forms of action it was the plaintiff's responsibility to obtain the appropriate writ and present proof to support his claim, after the king's writ of *quo warranto* was served, the defendant was responsible for showing confirmation of "seisin" (possession or hold) over the liberties and franchises in question.[40]

---

39. *Statutes of the Realm*, 1:107: "qd omes de regno suo quicunq̄ fuerint, tam viri religiosi q alii, qui p̄ bonam inq̄uiscīoem prīe aut alio modo [sufficienti] verificare potint, qd ip̄i & eo3 anteccessores, vel predecessores usi fuerūt libtatib3 quibuscunq̄, de quib3 per bria predca fuerūt implitati, ante tempus Reḡ Ricardi consanguinei sui aut toto tempe suo, & hucusq̄ [sine interrupc̄one] cōtinuarūt, [Et] Ita qd libtatib3 illis nō sint abusi, qd p̄tes adjornent ulterius [coram eisdem Justic̄] usq̄ certū diē & racionabilem, infra quem dn̄m Regem adire possint cum recordo Justic̄ [sub] sigillo suo [signato,] & redire; & dn̄s Rex statum eo3 affirmabit per litteras suas. Et illi qui nō poterint seisinam antecessores seu p'decessores suores verificare, eodem modo, quo predc̄m est, deducant & judicent scd̄m legem cōmunem; Et illi, qui hent cartas regales, scd̄m cartas illas [& earumd̄ plenitudiem] judicent." The issue of prescriptions was reconsidered: An apparently official summary of the statute was issued shortly after 1290, revising the process so that if quiet possession of liberties was claimed to be continuous from before the time of King Richard, the possession would be acknowledged, and only if it were subsequently challenged did the defendant need to seek its reconfirmation by the king. See Sutherland, *Quo Warranto*, 93–94.

40. On challenges to this modified process, including by Gilbert of Clare in 1279, see Sutherland, *Quo Warranto*, 8–9. Henry III similarly created the actions of aiel and cosinage c. 1237 to address inheritance disputes not covered by mort d'ancestor, but, unlike *quo warranto*, these new actions did not reverse the standard procedure in which the plaintiff was

The statute also moves all *quo warranto* proceedings, including pending cases from the unofficial campaign of the 1280s and those already underway but as yet unresolved, from Westminster, where they were typically heard by the King's Bench, to the relevant shire, where they would fall under the jurisdiction of the "justices in eyre": the king's itinerant Bench, which from time to time traveled England in circuits making "eyre visitations" to each shire and hearing local civil and crown pleas.[41]

In the summer of 1293, while traveling in two circuits, one through Kent and the other through Yorkshire, the chief justices of each circuit received letters from Edward further supplementing the present legislation on legal memory, including the statutes of 1275 and *quo warranto*. A copy of the letter received by the chief justice of the northern circuit, Hugh de Cressingham (who would be skinned alive four years later at Stirling Bridge as Edward's treasurer—or "treacherer," according to the wordsmith Scots who killed him),[42] survives:

> Edward by the grace of God king of England, lord of Ireland and duke of Aquitaine, to his dear and faithful Hugh de Cressingham and his colleagues, justices in eyre in the county of York, greeting. Because we wish that in each and every of our writs, both of *quo warranto* and also of right, which hereafter may be brought and pleaded in our name before us or any of our justices, there shall be a limitation in their narrations to the time of King Richard and after, and not earlier time, we order you that in each and every writ of this kind that may happen to come before you henceforth this to be done, and enrolled in your rolls, and you shall cause this to be firmly observed. Witness I myself at Canterbury 12 July in the 21st year of our reign [12 July 1293].[43]

---

responsible both for obtaining the appropriate writ and articulating a narration. See Maitland, *Forms of Action*, 17.

41. The practice of conducting eyre visitations was codified during the reign of Henry II and continued into the fourteenth century, but the system's heyday ran roughly from the 1170s to the late thirteenth century. See W. L. Warren, *Henry II* (Berkeley: University of California Press, 1973), 256, 286–87, 296–97. On the eyre court visitations and extant records, see the indispensable guide: David Crook, *Records of the General Eyre*, PRO Handbooks 20 (London: Her Majesty's Stationary Office, 1982).

42. Walter of Guisborough, *Chronicle*, 303: "And they called him not the king's treasurer but the king's treacherer" (*uocaueruntque eum non thesaurarium set traiturarium regis*). On Stirling Bridge, see also G. S. W. Barrow, *Robert Bruce*, 4th ed. (1965; reprint, Edinburgh: Edinburgh University Press, 2005), 92–93.

43. *PQW*, 203; however, here I quote the letter's text as it appears in Sutherland, *Quo Warranto*, 212–13: "Edwardus Dei gracia rex Anglie, dominus Hibernie, et dux Aquitanie dilecto et fideli suo Hugoni de Cressingham et sociis suis justiciariis itinerantibus in comitatu

Setting aside its royal pleasantries, the letter contains an emphatic mandate that certain pleas in front of Edward's justices should be limited "in their narrations to the time of King Richard and later time, and not earlier time" (*fiat limitacio in narracionibus eorundem de tempore regis Ricardi et de tempore subsequenti et non de tempore anteriori*). Whether this was a clarification of what was originally meant by the 1290 statute or a pure revision of it on Edward's part, the letter repositions Richard's reign as the hard limit of legal memory. All "narrations," to borrow the letter's characterization of claimants' testimonies, should begin no earlier than 1189.[44] And for whatever reason—perhaps time out of mind was not being properly enforced in such cases—the letter reasserts the limitation date in place since 1275 for actions of right, mandating that plaintiffs could not go "beyond the time of King Richard" in those narrations. This is the legislation on legal memory that the voices of the public respond to in the rest of this chapter.

By the very end of the thirteenth century, England had developed a stubborn, if puzzling, attachment to "the time of King Richard." Shortly before the turn of the fourteenth century, the limit of 1189 for *quo warranto* and actions of right was being extrapolated throughout England as a general limit of legal memory.[45] When war began with France in 1294, Edward first suspended *quo warranto* proceedings and then ordered in the Michaelmas parliament that he had "granted for the favor of his people and because of impending war in Gascony that all his writs, both those of *quo warranto* and those in pleas of land, shall at present remain without day, until he or his heirs desire to speak thereof."[46] This ended the *quo warranto* campaign, but the new general limit

---

Ebor' salutem. Quia volumus quod in omnibus et singulis brevibus nostris tam de quo waranto quam de recto que de cetero nomine nostro deferri contigerit et coram nobis seu quibuscumque justiciariis nostris placitari fiat limitacio in narracionibus eorundem de tempore Regis Ricardi et de tempore subsequenti et non de tempore anteriori, vobis mandamus quod in universis et singulis brevibus huiusmodi que coram vobis venire contigerit de cetero fieri et in rotulis vestris irrotulari et firmiter observari faciatis. Teste me ipso apud Cantuariam, xii° die Julii anno regni nostri vicesimo primo." An almost identical letter was sent to John Mutford and the justices in Kent (*PQW*, 352). On these letters, see also Sutherland, *Quo Warranto*, 107–9.

44. Sutherland, *Quo Warranto*, 100: "The effect was immediate and substantial." The degree of enforcement was left up to the individual justice.

45. Brand, "Time Out of Mind," 54. Sutherland, *Quo Warranto*, 226, reaches a similar conclusion. See also Clanchy, *From Memory*, 152. This is not to say that legal documents from the past were not in circulation and freshly copied: See, for example, the manuscript books of Andrew Horn, discussed in Hanna, *London Literature*, esp. 54–73.

46. G. O. Sayles, ed. and trans., *Select Cases in the Court of King's Bench Under Edward I*, Selden Society 58 (London: B. Quaritch, 1939), 28: "Concessit ob favorem populi sui et propter instantem gwerram Vasconie quod omnia brevia sua, tam de quo warranto quam de placito terre, sine die remanerent ad presens quousque ipse sive heredes sui inde loqui volu-

of legal memory held steady at 1189 and was never again updated.[47] For all intents and purposes, England's legal memory now began with the coronation of Richard, a *terminus post quem* that outstripped its original purpose. However ancient a terminus 1189 may seem to us, or however ancient we may think it seemed to those who found themselves in court during the last decade of the thirteenth century, more than one hundred years after the now fixed limitation date, extant documentation from court proceedings constitutes an alternate picture in which Richard's reign sits squarely in the midst of late thirteenth-century life.

The centering of Richard within the late thirteenth-century's legislation on legal memory induced a fundamental shift in his place within litigants' "narrations," to borrow the terminology of Edward's letter. This is not to say that prior to the late thirteenth century Richard had no role in insular accounts, broadly construed, of England's past; he did. From his death in 1199 to just before the statute of *quo warranto* was promulgated in 1290, medieval England's view of Richard's reign in retrospect is mainly preserved by a wide range of insular Latin and Anglo-Norman chronicles, which chiefly constituted Richard's insular textual corpus.[48] That stories sometimes wildly different from those contained in chronicles were also being told during this period is primarily evinced not by textual remnants,[49] but by images that illustrate scenes of those stories and imply their contemporaneous circulation. Of those that survive, the image most frequently repeated during this period depicts Richard's apocryphal hand-to-hand combat with Saladin.[50] This and other rumors circulating in England about what happened on the Third

---

erint." Sutherland, *Quo Warranto*, 30 n. 2, finds no evidence indicating that suspended cases were later revisited.

47. Sutherland, *Quo Warranto*, 30. The exception to the 1189 limit was the assize of novel disseisin, which required a "recent" limit; see Caenegem, *Royal Writs*, 261–62. Clanchy calls the standing limit of 1189 "a novelty" in retrospect, but also suggests that updating was no longer needed at the end of the thirteenth century because "litigation now depended primarily on documentary evidence and not on mortal memory" (*From Memory*, 152). On this claim, see below.

48. For a range of these, see chapter 1.

49. Though some did exist; see, for instance, Geoffrey of Vinsauf, *Poetria nova*, trans. Margaret F. Nims, intro. Martin Camargo, rev. ed., Medieval Sources in Translation 49 (Toronto: Pontifical Institute of Medieval Studies, 2010), lines 368–430.

50. For example, on the wall of Henry III's Antioch Chamber at Windsor, and perhaps in Winchester Castle, the Tower of London, and Nottingham Castle, as well as on the Chertsey Tiles, where captions possibly once accompanied the image. On the wall-painting, see E. W. Tristram, *English Medieval Wall Painting: The Thirteenth Century*, with a catalogue compiled in collaboration with Monica Bardswell, vol. 1 (New York: Oxford University Press, 1950), 215 and 528; and Christopher Tyerman, *England and the Crusades, 1095–1588* (Chicago: University of Chicago Press, 1988), 117. On the tiles, see R. S. Loomis, "Richard Coeur de Lion," 514–15;

Crusade may have emerged from war stories told by crusaders who returned home from Richard's campaign, an enterprise that touched nearly every family in late twelfth-century England, and therefore held meaning for most thirteenth-century families because of ancestral participation.[51] But the very construction and assertion of those stories and rumors suggests that in the era of *quo warranto* Richard became a newly relevant subject not only in litigants' narrations, but also in their minds and memories, and on their tongues.

The legislation on legal memory required England's public to remember a different Richard than had been in circulation until that point. This presented a difficult retrospective project. Litigants needed to recall not the crusader among his men, but the king among his people; not Richard's governance abroad in the lands he conquered and failed to conquer, but at home in the ones he inherited. Moreover, the conditions of the late twelfth-century crusade had significantly complicated the intricate business of governing, with effects that lasted well into the *quo warranto* era of the late thirteenth century. A flurry of charters, for instance, was issued by those preparing to go on crusade (transfers of seisin, grants to religious houses in exchange for prayer or funds), but once abroad, issuing charters was difficult.[52] Deeds issued under Richard's first great seal had been declared void during his reign if not reissued under a new seal.[53] Edward's legislation enshrined retrospection, but to understand what that process actually entailed, we must examine the legislation as experienced by the public.

In the retrospection it demanded and the ways in which the fruits of that retrospection were made public, legal memory was as influential to the broader public's conceptualization of England's past as any chronicle or written history. Legislation on legal memory played a role in mapping the individual memory of anyone in England whose identity, as constituted by their ancestry and possessions or status, needed official confirmation.[54] We usu-

---

and J. J. G. Alexander and Paul Binski, eds., *Age of Chivalry: Art in Plantagenet England, 1200–1400* (London: Royal Academy, 1987), 204, no. 16. See also chapter 3.

51. Nicholas Paul, *To Follow in Their Footsteps: The Crusades and Family Memory in the High Middle Ages* (Ithaca, NY: Cornell University Press, 2012), 11–12; and Tyerman, *England and the Crusades*, 65–70. See also Megan Cassidy-Welch, *War and Memory at the Time of the Fifth Crusade* (University Park: Pennsylvania State University Press, 2019).

52. Jane Sayers, "English Charters from the Third Crusade," in *Tradition and Change: Essays in Honor of Marjorie Chibnall, Presented by Her Friends on the Occasion of Her Seventieth Birthday*, ed. Diana Greenway, Christopher Holdsworth, and Jane Sayers (Cambridge: Cambridge University Press, 1985), 201–12.

53. On the details of Richard's first and second great seals, see Sayers, "English Charters," 196; and below, in this chapter.

54. Brand, "Time Out of Mind," 51–52: "Litigants knew or thought they knew quite a lot about the eleventh- and twelfth-century past. Much of this knowledge was connected with property that they possessed or to which they thought they had a claim."

ally discuss England's legal memory in terms of only one kind of limit: that governing "actions of right." This approach obscures and homogenizes the numbers and types of people implicated by legal memory, its limits, and its updates. The statutes of 1237 and 1275 contain limits for multiple actions used by a broad cross-section of the public, from freeholders to widows to serfs. On one end of the spectrum, a writ of right set in motion the lengthy and legally intricate action brought by a claimant who stated that he had proprietary right of the freehold in question; on the other, a writ of nativis (*de nativo habendo*) triggered an action designed to recover a very different kind of possession: a person. A writ of nativis was brought by a claimant in order to recover a serf. While the plaintiff needed to initiate the process, that process gave a voice to the purported serf. The person in question could challenge the plaintiff's claim with a competing action (*de libertate probanda*), and argue for free status by providing an alternate account of his or her ancestral narrative.[55] Long before the promulgation of *quo warranto*, then, a population far more varied than John de Warenne and barons like him had out of necessity become practiced at remembering ancestral and local history: "Remembering," writes Paul Brand, "that a particular ancestor or predecessor had been the last of their ancestors to be in possession of that property; remembering how the family had lost possession of it; remembering how it was that their family had acquired it or that their title had been confirmed in previous litigation."[56]

To "remember" the ancestral past in accordance with the legislation on legal memory was to reconstruct that past.[57] A claimant had to be dynamic, creative, and a revisionist willing to add and to excise, to forget selectively, and to recall conveniently in order to turn an individual ancestral memory into a legal memory that would fall within the legislation's limits and proceed according to its strictures. In land cases prior to 1208, the plea rolls indicate that the plaintiff, responsible for obtaining a writ and initiating the related action, needed only to state in general terms how he or she was related to

---

55. Maitland, *Forms of Action*, 29–30. The writ *de libertate probanda* forced the associated sheriff to put the case in front of the king. A writ of right of dower could be brought by a widow who claimed her dower from the heir, usually the husband's son, who held it. For a brief overview of widows as claimants and women's property rights in the thirteenth century, see M. T. Clanchy, ed., *Civil Pleas of the Wiltshire Eyre, 1249* (Devizes: Wiltshire Record Society, 1971), 16–17. For a claim to a "naif and fugitive," in which the relevant parties provide conflicting narrations of descent, see Eric James Gallagher, ed. and trans., *The Civil Pleas of the Suffolk Eyre of 1240*, Suffolk Records Society 52 (Woodbridge: The Boydell Press, 2009), 231, no. 1108. On other types of actions, see also n. 31 and n. 36, this chapter.

56. Brand, "Time Out of Mind," 52.

57. Following Brand, I use "remembering" to describe the processes preceding the telling of such accounts, but "remembering" is a shorthand that elides the physical and mental labors litigants necessarily undertook.

the ancestor on whose seisin a claim was based. After 1208, a procedural shift required that the plaintiff recount in much greater detail how the land, privileges, or other items in question had descended to him or her. Plaintiffs and defendants "needed to have detailed knowledge of the family tree which linked them with the ancestor on whose seisin they based their claim."[58] So expert were litigants that they commonly satisfied the stipulation for writs that required specific ancestors or predecessors be named.[59] One thirteenth-century defendant traced his family's seisin back seven generations to 1135 and multiple Yorkshire manors.[60]

In remembering the past and reconstructing it as a legal memory, litigants became authors and narrators of legal fictions: narratives of inheritance truncated, edited, refocused, and sometimes, it seems, invented to fit within the strictures of legal memory. The legislation's language in fact figures litigants' responsibilities in narratorial terms. Claimants were responsible for the *narracione descensus* (Statute of Merton, 1237), the *conte de decente* (Statute of Westminster, 1275), as well as to show (*monstrer*) and to verify (*verificare*) proof of familial or ecclesiastical tenure that could withstand inquest (*Quo warranto* and its summary, 1290).[61] Straightforward "inheritance" encompasses neither the process involved nor its stakes. The construction of a convincing and confirmable narration of descent (even if confirmed only by jurors who said, for instance, that they had heard corroborating accounts) necessitated that litigants act as makers and tellers of narratives. As historians and genealogists, they located the time and place when possessions or privileges came into their ancestors' hands, and traced those tangible or intangible inheritances as they moved from hand to hand and into the present moment.[62]

We think of inheritance as a passive act of reception,[63] but medieval litigants found themselves actively engaged in what I call "retrospective inheritance," an active project in which the past's bearing on an individual's present

---

58. Brand, "Time Out of Mind," 44.
59. Clanchy, *From Memory*, 36.
60. TNA: JUST 1/1050 m.8od.
61. These statutes are cited above. This language refers to procedures that chiefly concern the seisin of land or privileges, but narrations were relied upon to prove and dispute claims in most other types of cases.
62. Here I must register a distinction between originary acquisition, that is, the very first time property or rights were seised by an ancestor, and the most recent seisin, which would have been the legal basis for most thirteenth-century claims. However, "recent" belies how far back the plaintiff often needed to go to locate the ancestor most recently seised. This search could easily take a thirteenth-century plaintiff back to the eleventh or twelfth centuries. Prior to the 1275 legislation on limitation dates, it was not unusual for a thirteenth-century plaintiff to have to go back to at least 1135 for evidence of the most recent seisin.
63. Notably, most *OED* definitions for "inheritance" are in the passive voice.

could not be overlooked; indeed, it was the point. Retrospective inheritance comprised mental and physical labor, and multiple trajectories: Complex retrospection necessarily preceded moving forward in the present. To assemble the required narration of descent,[64] to understand his or her place in the present, and to justify it to the court, a litigant would move back through the archival and memorial past to reconstruct the origin of a claim, before reversing course and retracing the route of inheritance and its collected historical resonances forward into the present moment. The legislation's vocabulary recognizes the material significance of litigants' labor, binding the narrative, monetary, and historical economies at stake in retrospective inheritance and its narration. Both *conte* and *narratio* were terms directly related to those who would count money or tell tales or advocate,[65] and they interchangeably connoted a tale, a story, a narrative, or a rumor; an enumeration; a financial account; a plea in court.[66] A litigant's legally recognized and perhaps personally validated identity, rights, and possessions hinged on the litigant's ability to assemble and

---

64. Thirteenth-century narrations of descent primarily survive in two forms: as official records now held in the National Archives, written in Latin, and compiled in rolls by the clerk(s) who accompanied the justices in eyre, and as unofficial law reports written in Anglo-Norman French and, more rarely, English. Probably written by a spectator, the unofficial reports are extant in Year Books from Edward I's reign; for them, see Alfred J. Horwood, ed. and trans., *Year Books of the Reign of King Edward I*, 5 vols., RS 31 (London: Longmans, Green, Reader, et al., 1863–1879); and Paul Brand, ed., *The Earliest English Law Reports*, 4 vols. (London: Selden Society, 1996–2007). The unofficial reports, the work of someone present at court who may have been affiliated with the proceedings, were disseminated widely as tools for teaching law, and even possibly repurposed in other educational contexts, where it appears the names of the original, older sergeants and justices were replaced with those of contemporary figures. On eyre court procedure, see Constance M. Fraser, ed. *The Northumberland Eyre Roll for 1293* (Suffolk: Boydell Press for the Surtees Society, 2007), 66–67; on slightly earlier practices, see Frederick Pollock and F. W. Maitland, *The History of the English Law before the Time of Edward I*, vol. 2 (1898; reprint, Cambridge: Cambridge University Press, 1985), 644–58. On the responsibility of a justice's clerk, see Crook, *Records*, 3–4. On law languages, see Paul Brand, "The Languages of the Law in Medieval England," in *Multilingualism in Later Medieval Britain*, ed. D. A. Trotter (Cambridge: D. S. Brewer, 2000), 69–76.

65. The degree to which these meanings were entangled and that entanglement eventually formalized is exemplified by the presence in court of *narrators* and *conteurs*, professional pleaders who spoke for litigants, though their presence was not required or universal. A litigant could speak on his or her own behalf. Matthew Paris mentions the professional pleaders at the Bench at Westminster as early as 1239, and Clanchy, *Civil Pleas of Wiltshire Eyre*, 12–13, argues that there is no reason to think pleaders were not employed in eyre. Yet because the pleaders were not considered separable from the litigants, but rather their mouthpieces, little documentation exists of pleaders in eyre court records. On related procedure, see Paul Brand, "Origins of the English Legal Profession," *Law and History Review* 5 (1987): 45–46.

66. See *DMLBS s.v.* "narratio"; and *The Anglo-Norman Dictionary*, http://www.anglo-norman.net/gate/?session=S369581285714661, "conter."

articulate a narration of descent relative to the present moment—to tell a good story, either accurate or persuasive. To tell one's own story.

Donald Sutherland defines the limit of legal memory in the common law as "the most remote time of which mention might be made in narrations,"[67] but the practice of retrospective inheritance—assembling a narrative and articulating a narration of descent down to the present moment—ensured that time past was not remote to litigants. Neither, crucially, was it something in whose wake the present merely persisted. The past was a supple thing on whose expedient narrative reconstruction the present, or, more precisely, one's perception of the present, depended. Of the myriad realities preserved in the plea records, the Earl Warenne episode, to return to this chapter's opening example, reproduces the attachment a litigant could develop to his or her narration of descent and the version of history it alleged. The Earl Warenne holds close the Norman Conquest by way of both inherited narrative and artifact, asserting that his sword and the memory it evokes should be legally recognized as equal to if not better than documentation.[68] But that concern is inextricable from the larger conviction, portrayed more subtly in the scene, that the story of the sword is the accurate account of what happened. The Earl Warenne refuses to traffic in legal fictions and resists the artificiality required of him to reconstruct his familiar, rich, and specific ancestral memory in accordance with the processes, limits, and limitations of legal memory.

What the Crown and the Earl Warenne share in his story, and what the Crown's legislation and its litigants share in the records of pleadings, is an interest in the project of reconstruction, its process of addition and excision, and a keen awareness of that process's personal and collective stakes: what will and will not count as official and personal history. Besides the account of the past explicitly articulated by the litigant, a narration of descent reveals to its modern reader details of the context in which it was made and presented to the court. Tension between the individual and the institution is embedded in these narrations. A narration of descent might convey a litigant's desire to tell and thus to put on record an organic ancestral memory. But an unedited memory becomes, in the record, an alternative history when written down alongside its official revision. The plea records preserve an ongoing dispute

---

67. Sutherland, *Quo Warranto*, 226. He discusses the limit of legal memory as it applies to actions of right, though this definition can be equally applied to *quo warranto* claims post-1293, and most other forms of action post-1237.

68. On objects and images as mnemonic devices more generally, see Mary Carruthers, *The Book of Memory: A Study of Memory in Medieval Culture* (Cambridge: Cambridge University Press, 1990), 147–49.

over who makes individual memory, and therefore a struggle between the public and the Crown over who gets to make history.

Narrations of descent, which point up competing modes of identity and history-making, preserve a range of approaches to the project of retrospective inheritance and the resulting narratives. Two narrations, one from the 1270s and the other from the 1290s, exemplify the breadth of that spectrum. Baldwin Wake held lands in Lincolnshire and Northampton. He was summoned in 1279—that is, before the statute of *quo warranto* was enshrined and after the limit for actions of right had been updated in 1275 to Richard's reign—to answer the king's writ of *quo warranto* for his liberties, including his ancestral right to maintain gallows. Baldwin gives a detailed narration of his ancestral seisin in the extant plea roll.[69] He dates seisin to the time of "William the Bastard," and claims it continued through the reigns of Henry I, Richard, John, and Henry III. His narration was revised in the clerk's hand: "The jurors say upon their oath that Baldwin and all his ancestors from the time of King Richard had gallows in the manor of Cold Kirby from the time of King Richard and before."[70] More than a revision of language, this is a rigorous editing of time past by the clerk or court.

Fewer than twenty years later, during the yearlong Yorkshire eyre that began in 1293, Roger le Bigod, Earl of Norfolk, was likewise summoned to answer a writ of *quo warranto*. "The earl by his attorney comes," and

> he says that he and all his ancestors from time immemorial have always used liberties of this sort there without any break in time, except however that King Richard relative of the present king seized the manor of Settrington and afterwards gave back his seisin of the manor together with some other holdings to one Roger Bygot, great-grandfather of the earl, whose heir he is, with infangthief and all other liberties belonging to the holdings; and he says that all his ancestors before King Richard seized the holdings have always used there liberties of this sort; and similarly from the time when King Richard gave back the holding to Roger the great-grandfather.[71]

---

69. TNA: JUST 1/1076 m.85.

70. Barbara English, ed. and trans., *Yorkshire Hundred and Quo Warranto Rolls* (York: The Yorkshire Archaeological Society, 1996), 162–65. Hereafter, when this edition is cited, the translations are English's. I am indebted to those scholars who have edited, and often translated, the rolls and records of several individual eyre visitations. Their work cuts a path for scholars from many disciplines who wish to bring their expertise to bear on legal records. Throughout this chapter, when translations of rolls and records consulted are available, I print them; otherwise, translations are my own.

71. English, *Yorkshire*, 244.

While Baldwin Wake's narration follows a chronological path, Roger builds his like a fortress, laying thick its language: "he and all his ancestors"; "from time immemorial"; "always used"; "without any break." The single crack, which counterintuitively would have strengthened the narration in his day (and makes it noteworthy in ours) is "King Richard," who seised Settrington only to give it—and more—back to Roger's great-grandfather. Either this ancestral memory, precise in its fortuitousness, came down to Roger, or he and his attorney were savvy in their reconstruction of individual memory as legal fiction, for Roger's narration posits an express relationship between his family's narrative and that of Richard. Whatever the truth of the past may have been, for the purpose of this claim Roger's process of retrospective inheritance involved significant consideration of Richard that necessitated awarding him a pivotal role in the narrative Roger told about his ancestors and England. Like Baldwin, the only other king Roger names is Henry III, "father of the present king." Yet in stark contrast to Baldwin, Roger associates neither himself nor his ancestors with anyone prior to Richard, and he demurs even from associating Richard with the king's own ancestors. Instead, "King Richard" is the "relative of the present king" in Roger's narration: the earliest English king within living memory, and proximal as Edward's most immediate predecessor. Baldwin and Roger inhabit opposite ends of the legal spectrum of narrations. Across that spectrum, the language of *quo warranto* became integral to how the public reconstructed ancestral pasts to produce legal fictions.

With decentralization of *quo warranto* cases in the eyre courts came the widespread consideration and discussion of Richard's reign before and during the pleadings that occurred in each shire. After 1290, "the time of King Richard" was a phrase and an idea in widespread circulation. "An awareness of the new legislation," notes Sutherland about the statute of *quo warranto* specifically, "is shown in every roll."[72] After 1293, Richard became a popular mechanism by which to reconstruct, and sometimes to conjure, the past. Edward's letter to his justices in eyre proved technically circumscriptive and functionally generative. By explicitly putting a stop to those narrations that were set in or relied upon time before Richard's reign, Edward implicitly commissioned the invention of more set during it. In their narrations, litigants contend with how to make "his time" relative to their own. They grapple with what may have happened during "the time of King Richard," and with what it can be made to do in the present. The records of *quo warranto* cases heard in the 1293 Yorkshire eyre visitation, for instance, suggest that either Richard was

---

72. Sutherland, *Quo Warranto*, 100.

prone to taking away and giving back liberties and privileges to such an extent that his actions touched nearly every family of a certain class in England, or that late thirteenth-century litigants were finessing their narratives of descent so that Richard and his time could play a crucial role, or both. The former possibility is not out of the question: To raise money for crusade, Richard, more than any other king, sold off (sometimes after pointedly reacquiring) the Crown's offices and privileges.[73]

Litigants' answers to the question of what happened during "the time of King Richard" seem to be rooted in the late thirteenth-century narrations themselves—the collection of accounts of liberties, franchises, and various other lands, rights, and privileges awarded during Richard's reign—regardless of whether final verdicts were rendered. In some of these narrations, we can see the development of the version of Richard familiar in our modern popular culture. He is described as a king whose largesse was unmatched by his contemporaries or successors, and whose people longed for him in his absence.[74] Such depictions of Richard's munificence almost always benefit the narrating litigant. In 1293, for instance, the abbot of Thornton was summoned to court to answer by what warrant he and his men claimed to hold over twenty special privileges.[75] The plea roll notes that the abbot's attorney produced for Hugh de Cressingham a writ by the charter "of King Richard"—a charter in which, as the clerk witnesses in his record, the abbot's attorney claims:

> [King Richard] granted and confirmed various gifts and various feoffments of his various enfeoffers in the vills to a certain predecessor of that abbot, and granted that he and his successors might hold the holdings with soke and sake, toll and team and that he and his men might be free of shires and hundreds and pleas and suits and gelds and danegelds and themantale and concealments and scots and aids and assessments and gifts and scuatages and hidages and sumages and murdrum and ridings and wapentakes and aid of the sheriff and his ministers and bornewing and works and breaches of castles or walls or bridges or fishponds or enclosures or toll and passage and pontage and pedage and stallage and from all earthly service and exaction both by land and by water in every place in the king's power. He [the abbot

---

73. J. C. Holt characterizes the sum total of these sales as "massive"; see Holt, *Magna Carta*, 2nd ed. (Cambridge: Cambridge University Press, 1992), 50–51.

74. See *Richard I*, 343: "By the end of 1198—the earliest date for [Roger of] Howden's composition of this complaint—there was undoubtedly discontent in England at the weight of the king's financial demands. It is particularly strongly reflected in [Ralph of] Coggeshall's obituary notice on Richard, and his assertion that no previous king of England had ever raised so much money."

75. TNA: JUST I/1093 m.10d.

by his attorney] claims also that he and his men may not be impleaded except before the king or his chief justices by the charter of King Richard which he produces, and which shows that the king forbids canons and brethren of the abbey of Thornton or their men from any of their holdings to be put in a plea except before the king and his chief justices. King H. father of the present king by his charter given in the 52nd year of his reign confirmed all the liberties.[76]

A charitable reading would deduce that Richard had the remarkable foresight to direct the making of such a document, which ensures in its overwhelming comprehensiveness that no abbot of Thornton would be called to answer for any claim ever again. The simultaneous precision and breadth with which the current abbot's specific rights are articulated is undercut, however, by the vagueness of the original recipient, "a certain predecessor," who handed down the charter, which was confirmed by Henry III for just such an occasion as the Yorkshire eyre and the present abbot's predicament. The procurement of charters from Richard's time appears to be not uncommon across counties after 1290. Besides the attested instances of forgery—an ethically and materially complex literary act—during this period,[77] the climate itself post–*quo warranto* would have been ripe for forgery based on its resemblance to earlier moments of widespread political or legal disruption (some of which occurred in and shortly after Richard's own reign), when forgery surged.[78]

As Hugh de Cressingham's clerk records, the king's attorney in eyre, Roger Hegham, had his own suspicions. He presses the abbot, asking by which liberties exactly the abbot claims soke and sake, toll and team. The

---

76. English, *Yorkshire*, 215.

77. On forgery during the informal and formal periods of *quo warranto*, see, for example, Clanchy, "Franchise," 76–77; and Clanchy, *From Memory*, 319. The scholarship on forgery more broadly is vast. See, for example, Alfred Hiatt, *The Making of Medieval Forgeries: False Documents in Fifteenth-Century England* (Toronto: The British Library & University of Toronto Press, 2004), esp. 4–28; T. F. Tout, "Medieval Forgers and Forgeries," *Bulletin of the John Rylands Library* 5 (1919): 208–34; Giles Constable, "Forgery and Plagiarism in the Middle Ages," *Archiv für Diplomatik, Schriftgeschichte, Siegel- und Wappenkunde* 29 (1983): 1–41; and Derek Pearsall, "Forging Truth in Medieval England," in *Cultures of Forgery: Making Nations, Making Selves*, ed. Judith Ryan and Alfred Thomas (New York: Routledge, 2003), 3–13.

78. On such moments, see, for example, Marjorie Chibnall, "Dating the Charters of the Smaller Religious Houses in Suffolk in the Twelfth and Thirteenth Centuries," in *Dating Undated Medieval Charters*, ed. Michael Gervers (Woodbridge: Boydell Press, 2000), esp. 52–58; Alfred P. Smyth, *King Alfred the Great* (Oxford: Oxford University Press, 1995), 373–93; Julia Barrow, "The Chronology of Forgery Production at Worcester from c. 1000 to the Early Twelfth Century," in *St. Wulfstan and His World*, ed. Julia Barrow and Nicholas Brooks (Aldershot: Ashgate, 2005), 105–22, esp. 122; and Sayers, "English Charters," 195–97, 211–12.

abbot (or his attorney) then gives a brief narration of descent, tracing his seisin of such liberties from the time of King Richard to the present moment. Roger responds that this narration is no good because of discrepancies between what the charter covers and additional liberties and privileges that the abbot's predecessors, and the abbot himself, acquired after the charter's issue. Moreover, Roger continues, casting present suspicion upon the abbot's narrative, the abbot and his men had in fact been taxed without protest until this very moment. The abbot, after arguing for Thornton's right to tax ale since ancient times, asks for inquiry to be made around the county on these issues. The clerk's record concludes with the justice's call for further inquiry. Agreement to undertake such inquiry is not rare in the plea rolls, and neither are the terms of this particular disagreement. Roger and the abbot's attorney argue their positions in terms of Richard's time and what is or is not permissible in the present according to what did or did not happen in the late twelfth century. The account of the abbot of Thornton's pleading ends with a new beginning: Instead of closing the issues at hand, the matter is opened up for further inquiry and discussion.

Widespread public discussion about what Richard was like, and what it was like to live in England during his reign, was variously provoked by the visitations of the justices in eyre in each shire. Eyre visitations were sites of public talk: talk about local intrigue, about the past, and about the past's bearing on the present. The voices in the plea rolls emanated from bodies—thousands of them. Many eyre rolls have been edited and published with introductions that tally the numbers and types of people involved in a single visitation. Yet those people have not been reanimated in the context of the eyre and they have not been recognized as the immediate audience for the cases documented in the plea rolls. The implications of their numbers, therefore, have not been pursued. Thousands of people would wait, expectantly, for the justices' arrival at designated places in a shire. Eyre visitations were sources of public culture and cultural production: spaces in which public talk amplified some parts of the past and fell silent on others.

Civil cases, brought by the people of the county, crown cases, and, from 1290, writs of *quo warranto,* were heard by the justices in eyre, who were divided into two panels. One panel traversed the southern circuit and the other the northern. Actions could be begun, concluded, or fully carried out in a single eyre visitation; however, actions begun during one general eyre could be adjourned to the next, and an action begun in one county could be completed in another.[79] Edward I reinstated the general eyre in 1278 after a six-year

---

79. Gallagher, *Civil Pleas of Suffolk,* xxx. Actions such as novel disseisin often could not wait for an eyre court.

respite.[80] The practice of sending royal justices out into the counties began in the reign of Henry I and was codified by Henry II,[81] who increased the types of formal actions. From the 1170s onward, the eyre court handled the majority of civil litigation involving freeholders, a vast category that included, for instance, the king, his barons, and abbots and bishops on one end, and tenants and widows on the other.[82] Under Henry III, the sophistication of the eyre court and the workload borne by its justices increased in part, at least, because when conducted efficiently, the eyre was a significant revenue source for the Crown. Even as people chafed against the articles of the eyre, which stipulated that justices should attend to crown pleas—fining and amercing counties, hundreds, towns, and individuals for various infractions; collecting the chattels of outlaws and convicted criminals for the king; gathering local treatment of the king's rights[83]—they took full advantage of the justices' presence to advance their own interests in civil cases.[84] By the time of Edward's reign, eyre visitations were the central spaces in which the laws limiting legal memory intersected with the personal interests and narrations of England's public.[85]

The eyre was a political wedge,[86] but it was also a vital social space. Eyre visitations were popular, semi-regular, and anticipated events—ancestors of sorts to the mystery plays that would be mounted annually by towns such as York in the next several centuries. During an eyre visitation, a community's

---

80. See Sutherland, *Quo Warranto*, 18; and Sandra Raban, *A Second Domesday? The Hundred Rolls of 1279–80* (Oxford: Oxford University Press, 2004). During those six years, Edward amassed more cases on jurisdictional rights in the Hundred Rolls than could be settled at Westminster. Assemblage of the Hundred Rolls presaged, and in the case of the 1278 to 1280 inquiry, overlapped with the *quo warranto* campaign's start in 1278.

81. Warren, *Henry II*, 256, 286–87, 296–97. For a comprehensive history of the eyre court system, see the introduction to C. A. F. Meekings, ed. *Crown Pleas of the Wiltshire Eyre, 1249* (Devizes: Wiltshire Archaeological and Natural History Society Records Branch, 1961).

82. Clanchy, *Civil Pleas of Wiltshire*, 17–18.

83. Pollock and Maitland, *History of English Law*, 2:644–47; and Gallagher, *Civil Pleas of Suffolk*, x.

84. Warren, *Henry II*, 294–95.

85. Sutherland, *Quo Warranto*, 28–29: The years 1278 to 1294 were "the years of the Quo Warranto campaign, and [the] eyres were its setting." The general eyre was twice suspended during this period, first from 1282 to 1284, during the second Welsh war, and again from 1290 to 1292. When the eyre began again in 1292, it comprised two circuits with new justices.

86. Baronial and ecclesiastical discontent peaked in 1242, 1252, and 1256. Henry III's increasingly frequent use of the eyre visitations to raise funds, especially via the long arm of sheriffs, bailiffs, and other local personalities, buttressed objections to the king's request for grants. See J. R. Maddicott, "Magna Carta and the Local Community 1215–1259," *Past and Present* 102 (1984): 47–48; Gallagher, *Civil Pleas of Suffolk*, x–xii, lv–lx; and Paul Brand, *Kings, Barons, and Justices: The Making and Enforcement of Legislation in Thirteenth-Century England* (Cambridge: Cambridge University Press, 2003), 93.

past mysteries were excavated and its present secrets made public, so that talk among the public of the eyre's arrival was replaced by talk of its revelations. This talk occurred among staggeringly large groups of county locals and "foreign" attendees from neighboring shires. There were over six thousand people at the Suffolk eyre of 1240.[87] The population of Ipswich would have doubled or tripled on the first day of its eyre.[88] The Suffolk tally is no aberration. Attendance at the 1249 Wiltshire eyre would have been between four thousand and five thousand if we count only participants and not spectators.[89] The Northumberland eyre rolls of 1293 comprise nearly forty membranes that contain roughly 1,150 civil and crown actions, some of which could not be heard or settled and were adjourned to the Yorkshire eyre, with litigants and their narrations crossing county lines.[90] In the Yorkshire eyres of 1279 to 1281 and 1293 to 1294, 187 cases are recorded relating to *quo warranto* writs alone.[91] It seems, writes Albert Cantle about a Lancashire eyre whose records are preserved in no fewer than nine assize rolls and 402 membranes, "that almost every rank of medieval society, spiritual and secular, individual and corporate, was represented among those summoned" to Lancaster in the summer of 1292.[92]

An eyre visitation was a public spectacle and accordingly both a source and a site of public talk and rumor. Advance notice of an eyre visitation would have had to reach a shire's locals, as well as participants from other counties, in time for them to prepare:[93] technical concerns that bespeak the planning, organization, and word-spreading necessary for the eyre system to function.[94] Eric James Gallagher's exhaustive editing and analyzing of the 1240 Suffolk

---

87. See Gallagher, *Civil Pleas of Suffolk*, xiv–xvi. This total does not include officers of the court nor some directly implicated in crown pleas—for example, criminals and first finders of bodies. Gallagher finds 5,862 individuals named in civil pleas in the eyre roll, and he puts the number of attendees at 5,364. Of these, 1,383 were plaintiffs, 2,026 were defendants, and 918 were vouchers to warranty or sureties. Eliminating duplicated names, Gallagher finds roughly four thousand involved in civil pleas alone. There were also present 146 attorneys and 365 jurors, including 180 knights who could be selected as jurors for the grand assize.

88. Gallagher, *Civil Pleas of Suffolk*, ix–x, xii–xvi. The 1240 Suffolk eyre, part of the general eyre of 1239 to 1241, ran from April 29 or 30 to June 11. The justices in eyre visited Ipswich, Cattishall, and Dunwich.

89. Meekings, *Crown Pleas of Wiltshire*, 20.

90. Fraser, *Northumberland Eyre*, x–xi.

91. English, *Yorkshire*, 5.

92. Albert Cantle, ed. *The Pleas of Quo Warranto for the County of Lancaster* (Manchester: The Chetham Society, 1937), 35.

93. Cantle, *Pleas of Quo Warranto*, 110, provides the summons for the Lancaster Boroughs in advance of the justices' arrival.

94. On the publicizing of an eyre visitation, see Clanchy, *From Memory*, 166, for sheriffs as (sometimes dubious) keepers of the documentary archive; and Gallagher, *Civil Pleas of Suffolk*, xix, xxi.

pleas reveals the gender and socioeconomic diversity at the Suffolk eyre. "The first day of the eyre at Ipswich," Gallagher muses, "must have generated quite a buzz of excitement."[95] At least one justice in the 1249 Wiltshire eyre was treated to a feast upon arrival in the county; gifts or bribes for justices from local bishops, magnates, prelates, and anyone else in the county with an interest in the court's docket were not unusual.[96] A case survives in the Northumberland eyre record that was a direct result of the visitation itself: A complaint records a scrum among litigants over limited accommodation in Newcastle—the itinerant justices' single stop in the county.[97] Jurors were not always called in *quo warranto* cases, but when assembled they comprised anywhere from ten to twenty-four men, and, at least in the Yorkshire eyre of 1293 to 1294, there was no single constant jury for the eyre, exponentially increasing the number of county men and foreigners who had direct and detailed knowledge of the cases being heard. An extant report detailing a dispute between the abbot of Reading and a group of Hereford bailiffs in 1292 notes that the jury members were foreigners to a man (*tot de foreyns*).[98] In a situation that recalls the crowd, travel, and plurilingual voices of the Earl Warenne variant, any local talk prompted by the case, accounts of the hearing and stories told there and in the broader eyre, were carried with jurors back to their native counties and possibly repeated. Jurors in eyre were under no obligation to keep quiet.[99]

Extant records convey the local intrigue of an eyre visitation. The following examples from the plea rolls of the 1249 Wiltshire eyre give a sense of the types of cases brought before the court. Each of these examples, while brief, contains a mix of answered and unanswered questions, making each case ripe for local conversation and speculation among the public in attendance. It is easy to imagine the amount of talk such cases generated during an eyre visitation. For instance, the crown plea rolls tell us that in the Hundred of Cadeworth, one Adam the swineherd "fell suddenly dead" on the doorstep of Netherhampton church, and that, in another case, one Maud, whose lands were worth twenty shillings per annum and was the daughter of Roger the forester of Bereford, was given by the king in marriage to William Carenteyn. In the Dunworth Hundred, Emma, the daughter of Robert le Corb', "put herself in Anestye church, confessed to being a thief and abjured the

---

95. Gallagher, *Civil Pleas of Suffolk*, xx.
96. Meekings, *Crown Pleas of Wiltshire*, 13–14, citing Winchester manorial accounts. On the justices' itinerary, see Crook, *Records*, 172.
97. As described at Fraser, *Northumberland Eyre*, ix, and edited in the same volume as items 882 and 1041.
98. On this case, see below in this chapter.
99. English, *Yorkshire*, 8–9.

realm." In another Dunworth case, "Agnes daughter of Beatrice of Holdebyr' and Agnes her daughter were killed in Beatrice's house in Holdebyr.' The first finder has died. Agnes Bone of Aldebur' and William le Copyner, her brother, [were] accused of the death of Agnes and Beatrice [sic]. William is in gaol. . . . Agnes Bone fled." And in yet another case of Dunsworth, "Walter le Turk, Robert de la Mare of Berewyk', Hugh de Muleburn' and John Smeppe of Stoppe, accused of larceny, do not come. The jurors say that, except for Walter, they are not guilty. So let Walter be exacted and outlawed."[100] These particular crown pleas do not begin to plumb the depths of those recorded in the hundreds of Dunworth and Cadeworth, let alone in all of the hundreds of the 1249 Wiltshire eyre visitation. Agreements are reached, chattels accounted for, judgments deferred, mercy given, and chirographs are written up, split, and distributed. Though less violent, the civil pleas from the same eyre are no less compelling. They make public the private disputes among neighbors, and they announce the socioeconomic distinctions among litigants. At Wilton, the court summoned Philippa de Nevill' "to answer Robert of Esturmethorp on a plea that she render him 6 marks, which she owes him and unjustly withholds"; "Assize of mort d'ancestor to declare whether Arnulf le Muner, father of Agnes daughter of Arnulf, was seised of 1 messuage in Berghton', which Robert the smith holds. He comes and says . . . the messuage is a villeinage of the king. Agnes cannot deny this. So Robert is without day and Agnes is in mercy. She is poor."[101] Nearly six hundred pleas from the Wiltshire eyre of 1249 survive.

Jury findings throughout the records similarly reveal how unofficial local talk became official local history recorded in the clerk's roll. Scores were settled or further complicated and the dirty laundry of a county, a hundred, a town was aired in public. The qualifications "they say" or "the jurors say" are common in the records, sometimes indicating agreement of a jury with the statements of the claimant, and other times disputing the narration they have just heard. The record of a case from the 1293/4 Yorkshire eyre describes the summons of one Walter de Fauconberge to answer a *quo warranto* writ. Although Walter defended his claims to free warren at length, he failed to convince all members of his jury, who then offered their personal and collective recollections: "The jurors say upon their oath" that Walter had appropriated warren in the lands of several men named in the record, "and had denied them hunting there." Further, "as to amends of breach of the assize of bread and ale, they say that he always punishes infringements by amercements and

---

100. Meekings, *Crown Pleas of Wiltshire*, 244–47, cases 503, 505, 484, 482, and 486, respectively.

101. Clanchy, *Civil Pleas of Wiltshire*, 109–10, cases 337 and 339.

not by punishments."[102] The rolls demonstrate the degree to which voices were intermingled and narratives contested. In one case of the same Yorkshire eyre,[103] the abbot of Selby, by his attorney, answers the *quo warranto* writ, but his answers are disputed by the king's attorney. Both sides call for an inquest. Twelve jurors, whose names the clerk recorded, give under oath their knowledge on all relevant matters—knowledge that alternately supports and contradicts the abbot's narration. They recount pertinent happenings "After the time of King Richard," "in the time of King H. father of the present king," and "in the time of King Richard and after." As far as the abbot's right to wreck, they say the abbot's men had once attacked the men of one William de Anton for mortally wounding a porpoise on the shore of the River Ouse. A fight then ensued between William's men and those of the abbot over who would take the porpoise, and a sturgeon. In a somewhat unforeseeable resolution, both the porpoise and the sturgeon went to the Bishop of Durham's men. The abbot of Selby's case typifies the ways in which both Richard and local talk had come to inhabit not only the same narration, but the same conversation.

The roll that contains the abbot of Selby's case is a highly textured record of talking as much as a written record. It preserves evidence of talk in the world beyond the tangible document. From it, we know that the jurors talked among themselves and to others present. Claimants and defendants talked with their attorneys and with the justice. There was discussion among other members of the court and observers. We know that jurors could speak freely, and that they may have carried word of the case to their respective homes. When it occurred, the event in question was no doubt a source of local talk in Selby and Durham, and it was discussed again when the parties involved prepared their narrations to obtain a writ and appear at court. The roll also conveys the conceptualization of the past—distant and recent—that underpinned this talk. Time is kept by Richard's reign in the narration. Relevant aspects of the case occurred not only in the present, but "after," "after and in," and "in relation to" Richard's reign. That is, "the time of King Richard" appears engrained as a mechanism for excavating and a tool for reconstructing the past: It is the backdrop in front of which the present scene is blocked and plays out.

In the most fully developed legal fictions, litigants not only keep time by Richard's reign in their narrations, but produce narrations of Richard's reign itself. Records and reports from the eyre visitations in 1292, 1293, and 1294,

---

102. English, *Yorkshire*, 218–20.
103. TNA: JUST 1/1093 m.16d.

especially, contain narrations of descent attuned to the largesse and supposed comings and goings of Richard. At the Hereford eyre of 1292, the abbot of Reading brought a writ of attachment on behalf of himself and his men against the bailiffs of Hereford, "and said that whereas King Richard, ancestor of our lord the King who now is, did by his charter grant to the Abbat of Reading and his men" (*e dyt ke par la ou le Roy Richard, ancestre nostre seynur le Roy ke ore est, granta al Abbe de Redyngge e a ces homes, par sa chartre*) freedom from tolls, payments, and liability throughout England.[104] The bailiffs' pleader, Tilton, argues first that the complaint should not be answered on account of a technicality: Each of the abbot's men, who are free men, must bring charge individually. The abbot's pleader, Howard, counters this, saying, "You assert what you wish" (*Vus dystes vostre talent*), but none of these men could make plea without the abbot, who stands as their head.[105] John Berwick—the justice leading the justices in eyre who circuited Herefordshire from June 8 to July 28, 1292, stopping in Hereford and Leominster—concurs.[106] A lengthy dispute then follows. Tilton speaks first, on behalf of the bailiffs:

> As to the franchise, Sir, we tell you that once upon a time the town of Hereford was in the hands of King Richard (*nus vus diom ke en akun tens si fut la vile de Hereford en la mein le Roy Ricard*), who in his time was seised of the right of taking toll of the Abbat and his men, and of taking murage and pavage [toll for and expenditure on street and wall maintenance]. King Richard did by his charter grant out of his seisin the town of Hereford to the good men of the town, to be holden of him in fee farm, at a rent of £40 yearly, in as full a manner as he held it, and as freely as he held it. By virtue of his charter and his grant, the good men were thereafter seised of the right of taking toll from the Abbat and his men in the same manner as King Richard did when &c.; and no other tort have we committed, but have only continued the seisin of King Richard by virtue of the grant which he made to us; ready &c. And this is our answer to the toll. As to the murage and pavage, we answer thus,—that it is only a special grant for three years, more or less, which the King sometimes makes to the good men of this town. And thereupon, Sir, we tell you that at the time when the King granted the franchise of &c. to the good men of this town, the town was not very well

---

104. Horwood, *Year Books*, 1:90–91. This case and others heard in Herefordshire during the eyre of 1292 whose unofficial reports Horwood edits and translates correspond to official rolls once belonging to Berwick and his fellow justices: TNA: JUST I/302 and TNA: JUST I/303.

105. Horwood, *Year Books*, 1:92–93.

106. Crook, *Records*, 174–75.

walled; wherefore our lord the King, who now is, did, seven years ago, at the entreaty of the good men of the town, grant to them murage and pavage; and so, by virtue of the grant from our Lord the King, we came and distrained the Abbat and his men to give murage and pavage.[107]

Berwick, following the findings of the jury, decided in favor of the abbot and his men, declaring that their charter from Richard's reign articulated sufficient protection against murage and pavage.[108] The dispute among the Hereford bailiffs and the abbot of Reading and his men offers an intriguing story manifesting from the local knowledge of jurors: The bailiffs had bullied the abbot's men, repeatedly exacting tolls from them.

A second narrative is embedded within this account. It is a legal fiction in which the supposed happenings in Hereford during Richard's reign are inextricable from what the bailiffs argue should happen in their late thirteenth-century present. Through their pleader, the bailiffs set the scene roughly one hundred years earlier: in twelfth-century Hereford (*en akun tens si fut la vile de Hereford*), a time when the town was "not very well walled" (*e la vile ne fut pas mut ben perclose*) and was "in the hands" of King Richard (*en la mein le Roy Ricard*). They tell of Richard's relationship to the town in terms both broad ("King Richard did by his charter grant out of seisin the town") and intimate ("and no other tort have we committed, but have only continued the seisin of King Richard by virtue of the grant which he made to us"; *par le grant ke yl fit a nus*). The "us" to whom Richard granted seisin by charter ostensibly refers to the same group of bailiffs who now "answer thus" with a collective "we" the question of murage and pavage (*E qant a la murage e pavage si responum nus issy*). These first-person plural pronouns conflate the past with the present

---

107. Horwood, *Year Books,* 1:92–95: "Pur la franchise, Sire, nus vus diom ke en akun tens si fut la vile de Hereford en la mein le Roy Ricard, le quel fut seisi en son tens de prendre toune del Abbe e de ces homes, e de prendre murage e pavage. Le Roy Ricard granta par la chartre la vile de Hereford hors de sa seisine a les prodeshomes de la vile, pur tenyr de ly en fee ferme, por .xl. livres par an, en la maner ke yl la teint, e aussi franchement com yl la tint. Les prodeshomes seisi par sa chartre e par son grant tote voyz pus en sa de prendre tounuz de la Abbe e de ces homes, en la manere com le Roy Ricard feseit al oure &c.; e ke nul autre tort avum fet, fors continue la seisine le Roy Ricard par le grant ke yl fit a nus; prest &c. E issy responum nus qant a la tounu. E qant a la murage e pavage si responum nus issy, ke coe neit fors un espessiale grant ke le Roy fet a le fez a treis anz plus ou meins a les prodeshomes de cete vile: dunt, Sire, nus vus diom ke al oure ke le Roy aveit grante a les prodeshomes de cete vyle la franchise &c., e la vile ne fut pas mut ben perclose; par quey nostre seynur le Roy ke ore est, a la priere les prodeshomes de la vile, granta a eus murage e pavage, ore a .vii. anz passe; la venimes nus, par le grant nostre seynur le Roy, e feseymes destreindre le Abbe e ces houmes de doner murage e pavage."

108. For the full case, see Horwood, *Year Books,* 1:91–96.

and make Richard's reign relevant to the present moment. "Us" binds together both the present-day bailiffs and their late twelfth-century predecessors. To construct this narrative, the bailiffs had researched or projected Hereford "in Richard's hands," and mentally occupied the past so completely that past and present are indistinguishable from one another in their narration. The bailiffs' narration exposes a new narrative of England in which what happened during Richard's reign has urgent implications for what will happen during Edward's. Here was a new story about Richard, authored and put into circulation by the bailiffs and their pleader. In it, Richard's reign is the *terminus post quem* for Hereford's relevance, and Hereford, and England by extension, are located "in his hands." Twelfth-century Hereford, unlike Vienna, did not have a wall; it had Richard. That Richard was essential to medieval England—both the place and the idea of it—is a narrative for which 1290 itself is the *terminus post quem*. The eyre courts were the places in which and from which that narrative was told and retold.

Legislation on legal memory precipitated the need for such a narration, but the Hereford contingent engaged in a retrospective project that went well beyond what the law explicitly demanded: a project, the records show, in which many others along the northern and southern circuits of the eyre participated. In this legal crucible, individual memory and identity fused with collective memory and identity. There are precedents for legal memory's influence on collective memory. Nearly contemporaneous with the infamous Earl Warenne scene is the case of a man from Huntingdonshire, one William, son of Albert of Ramsey, whose claim to a manor took the court behind 1066 to Cnut's reign.[109] The justices determined that "no writ runs from so long a time" and dismissed his case entirely.[110] Legislation on legal memory made it technically illegal to overwrite the effects of 1066, to substitute life before the Conquest with life after it, or even to trace that "before and after" along a single, uninterrupted line. Legal memory was being made to do other, arguably bigger, work in William's case and others like it. A law dating from at least the first part of Henry II's reign set a unique limit making it illegal for *Anglici* to base a claim on the seisin of an ancestor prior to the death of Henry I on December 1, 1135.[111] The claim that "no writ runs from so long a time" speaks

---

109. TNA: CP 40/14 m.19.

110. Regardless of the limit, William's case would not have moved forward because of several other technicalities; see Brand, "Time Out of Mind," 37.

111. See Caenegem, *Royal Writs*, 217 n. 2. Enacted fewer than one hundred years after 1066, the law under which foreigners, that is, those born in Normandy (*alienigenae*), carried free status while native-born English (*Anglici*) held fewer rights and were of less value, reflects a colonial—to use an apt anachronism—attitude pervasive in the late thirteenth century. Nevertheless, the "Presentment of Englishry" stood until 1340. It is not clear that religious

to a real or imagined paucity of ancient documents, but it also articulates legal memory's muscular power to add, excise, and generally reconstruct England's past. The cases show a push and pull between the ways in which individuals identified with England through the processes and outcomes of retrospective inheritance and the Crown's use of legal memory as, among other things, a means of managing the idea of England by managing its past.

The language of the 1275 legislation on limitation models the past's suppleness, which was an inherent quality and, by the thirteenth century, a known quantity of legal memory. The legislation narrates the Plantagenet line of descent as running from "le Rey Richard oncle," to Henry III, "le piere," to Edward, "le Rey qe ore est."[112] The legislation exhibits a self-consciousness that Edward's kingship is contingent on his unbroken link to his ancestors. It is striking, then, that the narration elides the reign of Edward's grandfather, John. Although John's reign was more recent than Richard's, the omission of John from England's legal memory is pervasive under Edward. John's lone appearance in extant legislation on legal memory is in the legislation of 1237, when the assizes and actions of mort d'ancestor, nativis, and entry were limited to the date of John's final return to England from Ireland.[113] This elision of John and the foregrounding of Richard's reign as the site of Edward's ancestral origin exhibits in microcosm an answer to the question of why Richard's reign became the origin of England's legal memory.

Scholars have typically approached Richard's connection with legal memory by noting that in 1290, Richard's reign coincided with the hundred-year customary limit on legal memory. This is true but also insufficient as an explanation. New collective narration of descent that began with Richard overwrote the reigns of John and Henry III, which together witnessed two baronial revolts, the first leading to Magna Carta and the second to the Second Barons' War (1264–67). The challenges Edward faced after the death of his father in 1274 confirm that the Second Barons' War and the way it ended, with the death of the lead rebel-baron Simon de Montfort and the seizure of rebel lands that could be returned upon payment, were, at best, not yet the stuff of memory and, at worst, daily preoccupations for the new king and his subjects. Many of those accused who contested the charge did so in the over-

---

houses had to exclude the Anglo-Saxon past in their claims; however, in cases where religious houses claim seisin before 1066, they also typically provide evidence of much more recent seisin. On English and Norman ethnic and cultural differences, see Hugh M. Thomas, *The English and the Normans: Ethnic Hostility, Assimilation, and Identity, 1066–c. 1220* (Oxford: Oxford University Press, 2003), esp. 46–55.

112. *Statutes of the Realm*, 1:36, quoted above.
113. *Statutes of the Realm*, 1:3, quoted above.

burdened and often unruly eyre courts.[114] Some cases related to the Dictum of Kenilworth, which marked the war's official if not actual end, were still being decided in those eyre courts in the first years of Edward's reign.[115] In several instances, Edward personally reinstated former rebels to trusted status within his inner circle.[116] And with Edward's expulsion of the Jews from England in 1291, he restructured the debts of the rebel barons, since Jewish lenders had largely facilitated the reseisin of their lost lands. Many of Simon de Montfort's supporters had already been in dire financial straits before the rebellion, partially because of nearly century-old debts carried from participation in the Third Crusade with Richard. Edward, through *quo warranto* and his stricter assertion of its legal limit in 1293, required that the official memory of a very specific past be reconstructed and reinscribed. Successfully answered writs of *quo warranto* could elide Magna Carta and the Second Barons' War by putting forward on the official record new narratives that obscured ancestral participation in the First Barons' War from 1215 to 1217, personal participation in the Second Barons' War from 1264 to 1267, or both.[117] The number of families that participated in both rebellions is striking, and the vast majority who joined the cause of Simon de Montfort against Henry III were called by Edward to answer writs of *quo warranto*.[118]

Significant precedent for the legal remembering and forgetting of entire reigns existed, and Edward may well have known this. The pre-1237 limitation date had essentially excised "the Anarchy," Stephen's politically and socially vexing mid-twelfth-century reign. Litigants could go back to the 1135 death of Stephen's predecessor, Henry I, to claim seisin, but they were forbidden from

---

114. C. H. Knowles, "The Resettlement of England after the Barons' War, 1264–67," *Transactions of the Royal Historical Society* 32 (1982): 32–33.

115. Crook, *Records*, 133–42.

116. These included John de Warenne (see above in this chapter); John de Vescy (Prestwich, *Edward I*, 57); and Adam Gurdon (Powicke, *Thirteenth Century*, 130).

117. In the chaos of civil war, franchises could be more easily usurped. That the Second Barons' War precipitated the *quo warranto* campaign has been proposed by others. See Sutherland, *Quo Warranto*, 19; and Knowles, "The Resettlement," 25. On the Second Barons' War more generally, see Powicke, *Thirteenth Century*, 209–11.

118. Compare the lists of families whose members were central to Magna Carta in F. M. Powicke, "The Bull 'Miramur plurimum' and a Letter to Archbishop Stephen Langton, 5 September 1215," *English Historical Review* 44 (1929): 91–93, with those who rebelled in the Second Barons' War in C. H. Knowles, "The Disinherited, 1265–80: A Political and Social Survey of the Supporters of Simon de Montfort and the Resettlement after the Barons' War" (unpublished PhD thesis, University of Wales, Cardiff, 1959), appendix 1. A further comparison between Knowles's list and the writs issued and listed in *PQW* yields almost an exact match.

bringing an action that claimed seisin during Stephen's reign.[119] This legislation was not content with limiting an individual's memory, but strove instead to strike Stephen's reign from the collective memory altogether.[120] The extant contemporary documentation reveals no attempt to recall Stephen's reign in defiance of this pre-1237 law. No attempt, that is, until 1279, when Edward himself claimed inheritance of an advowson in Hampshire, which he brazenly asserted was seised not only during the Anarchy, but also by Stephen.[121] In the contemporary paperwork, the space for the name of the king's ancestor from whom the land had descended is blank, intimating an awareness of the claim's uniqueness, as well as perhaps some uncertainty on the clerk's part. When necessary, Edward's claims went behind limitation dates. After 1293, however, Edward's claims to lands within England's borders, like the claims of the public, no longer ventured back beyond Richard's reign.[122] If Stephen was forever "out" of memory, Richard was "in," in perpetuity.

To the question of why 1189 *remained* the origin point of legal memory and became, shortly before 1300, an unofficial universal *terminus post quem*, scholarship has replied that Edward's own demand for documentation was either confirmed or inspired by an increase in documents that occurred ten years before and ten years after the turn of the thirteenth century, a feat chiefly attributed to one man, Hubert Walter.[123] Hubert Walter's tenure as a novel record maker and keeper commenced in earnest during Richard's reign. Already Archbishop of Canterbury and one of the king's fellow crusaders to the East in 1190, Walter was appointed Richard's chief justice in 1193, and after Richard's death in 1199, John's chancellor.[124] Among his many bureaucratic and judicial innovations were the invention of the three-part chirograph; the establishment of local *archae* in which documentation of Jewish debts was kept; the making and saving of several series of plea rolls, feet of fines, and Chancery enrollments of outgoing letters; recording in quadruplicate taxable

---

119. However, litigants could claim to have been deseised during Stephen's reign; see Brand, "Time Out of Mind," 44.

120. Brand, "Time Out of Mind," 44, cites cases from 1194 where litigants claim to have lost property during the Anarchy, in one instance referred to as "wartime."

121. The archbishop of Rouen, who held a charter from Henry II, eventually resolved the problem. See Brand, "Time Out of Mind," 41.

122. Sutherland, *Quo Warranto*, 226. "Within England" is a necessary stipulation because of the nearly contemporaneous Scottish question.

123. Clanchy, *From Memory*, 68 and 152; after monastery records failed him on the Scottish question, Edward turned to the Chancery archive in 1291.

124. He had previously served under Henry II as Baron of the Exchequer. On Walter's biography, see C. R. Cheney, *Hubert Walter* (London: Nelson, 1967); and *Richard I*, esp. 238–39, 274–82. On the presumed connection between Walter's tenure and the limit(s) of legal memory, see Clanchy, *From Memory*, 152–53.

county holdings; and the establishment of local coroners and their rolls.[125] Eyre visitations occurred in the reign of Henry II, but the earliest substantial set of official eyre records survives from Richard's reign and the general eyre Hubert Walter organized and oversaw in 1194.[126] "In Edward's reign," writes Clanchy, "the era of Hubert Walter began to be recognized as a turning point in the history of keeping records."[127] In turn, the argument goes, Edward's new requirement of documentation made redundant the function of legal memory and the updating of limits was allowed to lapse.[128]

In its focus on "the era of Hubert Walter," however, this argument fails to reconcile that documentary plenty with another fundamental characteristic of the late twelfth century: acute absence. Never discussed in the context of legal memory, but germane to any account of late twelfth-century documentation, and certainly to the ability of any thirteenth-century litigant (including Edward I) to account in narrative form for his or her ancestors during that period, is the fact that Richard reigned largely in absentia. Between 1190 and 1194, he was first on crusade and then captured. Fewer than a dozen probably authentic royal charters survive from Richard's time on crusade.[129] Apparent plans for a field chancery were disrupted when the vice-chancellor drowned off Cyprus, along with the royal seal, en route to Acre in April 1191.[130] Though a second seal was devised and the lost seal recovered, it was nevertheless decided in May of 1198 that all deeds issued under the earlier seal would be considered void if not reconfirmed.[131] Richard died the following year. Moreover, warrants for jurisdictions and associated privileges issued during Richard's reign often granted lands and rights implicitly instead of explicitly, leaving questions of intention open to interpretation in the late thirteenth-century reign of Edward I, a period during which explicit warranty was required.[132]

---

125. See the previous note; and Clanchy, *From Memory*, 68–72.
126. Crook, *Records*, 2–3.
127. Clanchy, *From Memory*, 152.
128. For example, Clanchy, *From Memory*, 152; Cam, *Liberties*, 180.
129. Sayers, "English Charters," 195–96.
130. Sayers, "English Charters," 196–97.
131. Sayers, "English Charters," 196 n. 4; Sayers notes that the loss of the first seal "provided a pretext" for the required reconfirmation. Nevertheless, the "pretext" arose from the events of crusade. See also Claude Fagnen, "Essai sur quelques actes normandes de Richard Coeur de Lion," in *Positions des thèses de l'École des Chartres* (Chartres: École des Chartres, 1971).
132. On legal idiosyncrasy during Richard's reign, see S. J. Bailey, "Warranties of Land in the Reign of Richard I," *The Cambridge Law Journal* 9 (1946): 192–209, esp. 193–96. The implicit warranty often granted in the twelfth century remained a problem in the last decade of the thirteenth century. See, for example, the record of a *quo warranto* writ brought at the Hereford eyre of 1292 against one Sir Reginald de Grey and his wife, Maud, and the ensuing

As these examples indicate, Walter's late twelfth-century archive was likely not an unproblematic cache for its late thirteenth-century users, and it remains problematic now. Copies of dated charters were not regularly kept by the Crown until John's reign, and even then, recovering the appropriate document proved its own problem. The local *archae* had been seized and destroyed by Montfortians, and the Jewish debts kept therein were temporarily forgiven by Simon de Montfort himself between 1264 and 1265.[133] In locating the retrospective pull of Richard's reign in the tenure of Hubert Walter and not in the particularities, texture, and ambiguities of the reign itself, we void the Crown's articulated conditions of late thirteenth-century legal memory and overwrite the enshrined mechanism by which litigants were called on to remember and reconstruct the past: "the time of King Richard."

Edward I's stance toward the past and his use of Richard, specifically, go beyond the intrigue of documentation. Edward's nature and the workings of legal memory suggest that "the time of King Richard" was personally meaningful. The books Edward had to hand, or whose stories he otherwise knew, point up not so much a free-ranging bookishness as a focused interest on the project of retrospective inheritance and in his own narration of descent.[134] Accounts of his approaches to political problems evince a king who thought about the past, whether fact or fiction, and who was interested in the ways that past could be harnessed in and to the present moment. Geoffrey of Monmouth's account of Arthur's reign and his translation of Merlin's prophecies were both used as justification for Edward's claim to the Scottish throne.[135] Edward's successful revival of the Arthurian cult—most famously exemplified by the 1284 Roundtable near Caernarvon, and by the ceremony in 1278 during which the supposed Glastonbury tombs of Arthur and Guinevere were opened and their bones solemnly transferred to the high altar at Edward's order and in his presence—is well documented. One of this era's foremost scholarly documenters, Juliet Vale, makes an observation that has gotten lost alongside the pageantry she describes: "This spectacular event was the first in a series in which it is possible to observe Edward both entering into contem-

---

dispute because their warranty, which dated to Richard's reign, was not explicitly stated in the document they produced. In Horwood, *Year Books*, 1:98–104, esp. 101-3.

133. Clanchy, *From Memory*, 321 and 70; and J. R. Maddicott, *Simon de Montfort* (Cambridge: Cambridge University Press, 1994), 315.

134. What Edward I might have read, as opposed to the stories he might have known through hearsay or visual programs, is most thoroughly treated in Juliet Vale, *Edward III and Chivalry: Chivalric Society and Its Context 1270–1350* (Woodbridge: The Boydell Press, 1982), 19–22. On Rustichello da Pisa, see Prestwich, *Edward I*, 118–20.

135. F. M. Powicke, "Edward I in Fact and Fiction," in *Fritz Saxl, 1890–1948, A Volume of Memorial Essays from His Friends in England*, ed. D. J. Gordon (London: Nelson, 1957), 134.

porary enthusiasm for Arthurian England and at the same time manipulating this interest and binding it to the fabric of local legend."[136] In the biography we most often sketch of Edward, his historical preoccupation is Arthur. But the last decade of the twelfth century, and Richard, could never have been far from his mind or absent from his memory.

The parallels between Edward and Richard are too numerous to dismiss out of hand as coincidental. From childhood, Edward would have seen images and probably heard stories about Richard's apocryphal hand-to-hand clash with Saladin during the Third Crusade. Records survive that describe the painting of a "Combat of Richard" on the walls of Henry III's "Antioch Chamber" at Clarendon Palace.[137] Despite, or as we shall see in chapter 3, because of, Henry's interest in that subject, it was Edward who fulfilled his father's pledge to crusade, following in 1270 the route that Richard had taken only eighty years earlier through Sicily and Cyprus to Acre.[138] Edward's personal affinity for and formal support of tournaments—an attitude and policy that broke with his father's and grandfather's apparent disinterest in and official abrogation of the pastime—has traditionally been attributed to Edward's preoccupation with the Arthurian imaginary,[139] but this too marks Edward's return to Richard's very real policy. In 1194, Richard had legalized tournaments in an effort, perhaps, to channel the martial energies of those barons who had taken opposite sides, some with Richard and others with John, during the king's absence from England. Similar civil skirmishes were recorded in the wake of the Second Barons' War, as Edward ascended the throne.[140] The memory of Richard's reign must have been potent, too, amidst two current events beyond England's proper borders: Edward's entanglement with the so-called Scottish question from 1290, and the loss of Acre in 1291. One hundred years earlier, Richard had for financial expediency issued the Quit-Claim of Canterbury, which returned various castles to the Scottish king, William; acknowledged Scotland's independence; and, unexpectedly, secured Richard a

---

136. Vale, *Edward III and Chivalry*, 17.

137. Alexander and Binski, *Age of Chivalry*, 204; and *Calendar of the Liberate Rolls, Henry III, Vol. 3, A. D. 1245–1251* (London: H. M. Stationary Office, 1937), 362.

138. Prestwich, *Edward I*, 72.

139. For example, R. S. Loomis, "Edward I, Arthurian Enthusiast," *Speculum* 28 (1953): 114–27.

140. Noël Denholm-Young, "The Tournament in the Thirteenth Century," in *Studies in Medieval History, Presented to Frederick Maurice Powicke*, ed. R. W. Hunt et al. (Oxford: Clarendon Press, 1948), 244; and Vale, *Edward III and Chivalry*, 2, 16. Cam, *Liberties*, 174, also notes that the earliest known writs of *quo warranto* can be dated to Richard's reign, when clergy were asked by what warrant they held churches.

future ally against his usurping brother.[141] One hundred years earlier Richard had also laid siege to and won Acre, an adventure for which crusader families were still in debt to their Jewish lenders during Edward's reign.

The self-conscious, and naturally self-interested, gaze of England's public was fixed on "the time of King Richard": a thing ephemeral for them and for us. Legal memory had always required litigants to contest and reconstruct the past, but from his first appearance in the legislation, Richard demanded another kind of engagement. In the insular texts and images dating from the late twelfth century to just before the statute of *quo warranto,* accounts of Richard are rarely also accounts of England.[142] During his life, Richard's public identity in England—both his person and his actions—was largely constituted by rumor. In many ways, his presence in and influence on the city of Vienna was better documented and more direct, both in the moment and retrospectively, than was his presence in and influence on England. After his coronation at Westminster on September 3, 1189, England was without Richard from December 11, 1189, until March 13, 1194.[143] He spent the balance of his life in his French ancestral lands, and died in 1199 near Limoges.[144] His wishes for his remains resemble his choices for his body in life: Richard's body was buried away from England and literally scattered around France, his heart at Rouen, his brain and entrails at Charroux, his corpse at Anjou. The official narrations of descent that arose from the last decade of the thirteenth century, and the associated widespread and unofficial talk about Richard that no doubt took on a strange urgency under the strain of legal proceedings, began to fill the vacuum of Richard's absence with mutually generative legal fictions and talk.

This collective retrospective project reached beyond the eyre court to reconstruct Richard's reign as vital to England's cultural memory. For instance, a letter of indulgence supposedly issued in 1291 and preserved in the register of Robert Gilbert, bishop of London from 1436 to 1448, provides forty days' relaxation of penance for those who would go to the chapel within the burial ground of London's All Hallows, contribute to the chapel's maintenance, and "pray for the souls of Richard, once king of England, whose heart was buried under the high altar there, and of all the faithful dead resting in

---

141. Prestwich, *Edward I,* 356–75; *Richard I,* 113.

142. On these extant visual and textual remains, and those rumored to have once existed, see chapter 3.

143. I borrow this phrase from John T. Appleby, *England without Richard, 1189–1199* (Ithaca, NY: Cornell University Press, 1965). Robert Bartlett estimates that Richard was physically present in England for only six months of his ten-year reign; see Bartlett's *England Under the Norman and Angevin Kings, 1075–1225* (Oxford: Clarendon Press, 2000), 12.

144. Roger of Howden reports the king's request for burial places; see *Richard I,* 324–35.

Christ" (*pro animabus nobilis Richardi quondam Regis Anglie cujus cor in eadem capella sub summo altari requiescit humatum, et omnium fidelium defunctorum in Christo quiescentium*).[145] A recipient of the indulgence, its explanatory clause states, would follow in the footsteps of Edward I himself, who, when not yet king, had a dream in which he was told by the Virgin Mary that once he had obtained her image from a particular Jew, placed it on the north side of the chapel, and worshipped there, he could be "the subjugator of Wales and the hammer of the whole of Scotland."[146] Edward purportedly confirmed the story in 1291 at Norham, where he and magnates from England and Scotland were attempting to settle the question of Scottish succession. Richard did have at least an indirect connection to All Hallows, which was founded in the seventh century by the Abbey of Barking. Richard confirmed Barking Abbey's charter in 1198 and in the same year released Barking from its obligation to pay an annual rent of sixty shillings.[147] Word of Richard's association with All Hallows was still circulating in 1465, when Edward IV granted lands to the Earl of Worcester, John Tiptoft, master of the guild of St. Mary, for the chapel's maintenance. The grant attributes the chapel's foundation to Richard,[148] at once locating its beginnings within legal memory and codifying Richard's association with one of London's most venerable churches. F. M. Powicke, who first brought the indulgence to light, cautions that he "can see little to redeem [the indulgence's] legend."[149] Most spurious to his mind is the claim that Richard's heart resided under the chapel's altar. (Even today, All Hallows maintains a connection to the king, saying "it is thought" that its Undercroft Chapel's altar comes from the Chapel of Richard Coeur de Lion in the

---

145. Part of the indulgence is reprinted in Powicke, "Edward I," 124–25. Richard's rumored and real affiliations are briefly discussed in Rosemary Horrox, "Richard III and All Hallows Barking by the Tower," *Ricardian* 6 (1982): 38; Nigel Saul, *The Three Richards: Richard I, Richard II, and Richard III* (London: Hambledon, 2005), 106–7; and Philip Schwyzer, *Shakespeare and the Remains of Richard III* (Oxford: Oxford University Press, 2013), 168.

146. Quoted in Powicke "Edward I," 123; Powicke's translation. A detail of Edward's dream—that the Welsh occupy the Isle of Ely—connects the legend (or perhaps Edward's supposed dream) to the Barons' War. The Montfortians held the island between 1266 and 1267, much to Edward's chagrin. As Powicke notes, Edward wanted his father to be more aggressive on the matter.

147. See Powicke, "Edward I," 128; and David Lysons, *Counties of Herts., Essex, and Kent*, vol. 4 of *The Environs of London* (London: Cadwell and Davies, 1796), 60. Lysons, *Counties*, 4:65, also lists Richard's sister, Matilda, as one of Barking's abbesses.

148. Powicke, "Edward I," 127.

149. Powicke, "Edward I," 123.

Templar Church of Athlit.)[150] "King Richard's heart" Powicke says, "was well known to be in Rouen cathedral."[151]

The context of legal memory shifts the ground under the indulgence's claims. While Edward's supposed confirmation of the "legend" in 1291 loosely associates it with Scottish succession, that date also places the indulgence's conception and confirmation in the time of *quo warranto* and the talk of Richard it provoked in the shires. What seems outlandish to Powicke—that a patent fiction about Richard had entered circulation—in fact confirms several realities of the *quo warranto* period: a connection forged in the public imagination between Richard and Edward I; the prolificacy of the public's reconstructions of Richard and his reign; their instinct (likewise apparent, for instance, in the Hereford bailiffs' narration) to use that process to prove Richard's affection for England; and, intimately related, their desire to repatriate him, to create Richard's narrative corpus in the absence of his physical one. In the pseudo-narration of descent peddled in the indulgence, Richard's heart belonged to England.

---

150. See the All Hallows By the Tower web page on the Undercroft Chapel: http://www.ahbtt.org.uk/content.php?page_id=13.

151. Powicke, "Edward I," 125.

THREE

Talking Pictures in Fourteenth-Century London

BETWEEN 1326 AND 1327, years encompassing the fall and regicide of Edward II and the ascent to the throne of his young son, who on February 1, 1327, was crowned Edward III, king of England,[1] a book intimately related to current events was illuminated in London.[2] Oxford, Christ Church, MS 92 appears to have been made in two stages, begun in September 1326 when Edward II was still in power and his fate as yet undetermined, and completed by the time of

---

1. On the youth of Edward III, see W. M. Ormrod, *Edward III* (Stroud, Gloucestershire: Tempus Publishing Ltd., 2005), 16–27, 57–58. Edward's accession, with his mother, Isabella of France, acting as regent, was proclaimed earlier, on January 24, 1327.

2. Unless otherwise noted, descriptions of the manuscript are my own. On its contents and codicological makeup, see below in this chapter; and Ralph Hanna and David Rundle, *A Descriptive Catalogue of the Western Manuscripts, to c. 1600, in Christ Church, Oxford*, using materials collected by Jeremy J. Griffiths, Oxford Bibliographical Society Publications, Special Series: Manuscript Catalogues 2 (Oxford: Oxford Bibliographical Society, 2017), 190–96 (hereafter Hanna-Rundle). Christ Church 92 itself has been digitized: https://digital.bodleian.ox.ac.uk. See also its black-and-white facsimile, with extensive introductory and descriptive materials: M. R. James, ed., *The Treatise of Walter de Milemete, De nobilitatibus, sapientiis, et prudentiis regum* (Oxford: Oxford University Press for the Roxburghe Club, 1913). A monograph on the manuscript has also been published: Libby Karlinger Escobedo, *The Milemete Treatise and Companion Secretum Secretorum: Iconography, Audience, and Patronage in Fourteenth-Century England* (Lewiston: The Edwin Mellen Press, 2011). On Christ Church 92's date, see Hanna-Rundle, 195–96; and M. A. Michael, "The Iconography of Kingship in the Walter of Milemete Treatise," *Journal of the Warburg and Courtauld Institutes* 57 (1994): 35–36.

his death a year later.[3] The political tumult that constituted the book's express provenance may explain why Christ Church 92, an otherwise fully illuminated and corrected manuscript, contains at its end a series of full-page line drawings made by the manuscript's main artist and then seemingly abandoned.[4]

These drawings occupy fols. 72r through 78v of the book's eighty-one folios, and, unlike the richly finished miniatures and borders throughout the rest of the manuscript, they are not illuminated. If the drawings were meant to be illuminated, that process was halted before any details or further decoration could be added. At the center of each folio is a picture, surrounded by a plain border of double lines. The drawings' common subject is siege warfare, but the coats of arms that sometimes identify a miniature's participant(s) (often either armored or warring) in the earlier portion of Christ Church 92 are not present here. The soldiers' identities and allegiances are unknown. They are outfitted in conical helmets that leave their faces—eyes, eyebrows, nose, and downturned mouth, each made with one or two pen strokes—uncovered. They wear shoulder plates to a man, but only some wear knee guards; no chain mail or other protective gear appears under their unmarked tunics, leaving the soldiers looking vulnerable in their stocking feet, with an unarmored toe pointed every so often over the double-lined borders meant to contain the action. The question of where that action takes place is impossible to answer from the stark white background.

Roughly when it takes place is easier to discern. Enough detail exists to suggest that these may be pictures of time past rather than reflections of the manuscript's present moment. On fol. 72r, two soldiers stand guard, shields up, on city ramparts; fols. 72v and 73r comprise a single image, with soldiers on the verso pushing a manned siege tower toward the fortified city on the recto. The images on fols. 73v–74r also comprise a single scene, as soldiers on fol. 73v mine and scale city walls, while on fol. 74r two soldiers load a four-armed windmill with Greek fire aimed across the page opening. The drawings on fols. 74v and 75r (see figure 1, a and b) constitute another scene: A soldier loads the mill's arms with buzzing beehives, which are launched across the opening. Fol. 75v depicts the common siege practice of mining, where soldiers with pickaxes work to undermine the city walls. Although this picture appears

---

3. See Michael, "Iconography," 37; his assertion has been widely accepted.

4. James, *Treatise*, xxii, detects the work of four artists in the borders and miniatures, but stipulates the number is debatable (xxi). Lucy Freeman Sandler raises the count to five; see Sandler, *Gothic Manuscripts 1285–1385*, 2 vols. (Oxford: Oxford University Press, 1986), 2:92. Both James (xxi–xxiv) and Sandler (2:92) agree that a single artist (James's "Artist I," Sandler's "Hand I") was responsible for designing and executing both borders and miniatures on individual pages and in stints throughout the manuscript (e.g., fols. 1r–5v, 59v–78v), including the line drawings at its end.

self-contained, the single soldier on fol. 76r takes notice and aims a fiery arrow at it. On fol. 76v, three soldiers push a mobile scaling platform in the direction of another image of a walled city across the opening on fol. 77r. There are three final drawings. A walled city stands on fol. 77v: unmanned, perhaps, because a balloon with a hawser holding a flaming stone dangles menacingly above the city. The viewer's eye can trace this weapon to its origin by following the rope, from which the hawser hangs, across the folio opening and back to three soldiers acting as both counterweight and guide on fol. 78r. In the final line drawing on fol. 78v (see figure 2), a soldier aims a catapult at a blank recto.

An early fourteenth-century reader would have looked at these drawings and seen old-fashioned warfare. The pervasive conical helmets worn by all but two soldiers would have been out-of-date by then and replaced with a helmet that covered more of the face.[5] The two exceptions on fols. 75v and 76r wear brimmed helmets nearly as anachronistic in the early fourteenth century.[6] The weapons with which the artist has armed his forces are also mostly old things: the boxy siege tower, the scaling ladders, the bulky stone throwers, the abbreviated bows and arrows, and the windmills hurling Greek fire and beehives—the oddness of the latter signaling either archaism or otherworldliness, or both.[7] These armaments look particularly outmoded alongside other, more innovative, weaponry in the manuscript. Christ Church 92 is probably best known for its illumination of a working cannon.[8] Appearing immediately before and in the same hand as the line drawings, it is one of the earliest extant depictions of a cannon in an English manuscript.[9]

---

5. The drawings' lack of decoration makes it impossible to know precisely what further details the artist had in mind, but the helmets and, especially, the weaponry, date to roughly the late twelfth and early thirteenth centuries. After 1150, a rounded model of the conical helmet prevalent since the previous century, absent a nasal, appeared. Around 1180, a variation, cylindrical and slightly tapered, appeared; see Ian Peirce, "The Knight, His Arms and Armour, *c.* 1150–1250," in *Anglo-Norman Studies 15: Proceedings of the Battle Conference 1992*, ed. Marjorie Chibnall (Woodbridge: The Boydell Press, 1993), 259.

6. See, for example, Pamela Porter, *Medieval Warfare in Manuscripts* (London: The British Library, 2000), 23–26.

7. Malcolm Hebron, *The Medieval Siege: Theme and Image in Middle English Romance* (Oxford: Clarendon Press, 1997), 29, mentions that beehives were among the items that may have been used in siege warfare since "at least the ninth century." Yet Hebron describes beehives as defensive rather than the offensive weapons.

8. Fol. 70v.

9. The other is the cannon depicted on fol. 44v in Christ Church 92's companion manuscript, London, British Library, MS Additional 47680 (*olim* Holkham), on which, see below. See also Michael Prestwich, *Armies and Warfare in the Middle Ages: The English Experience* (New Haven: Yale University Press, 1996), 292–93.

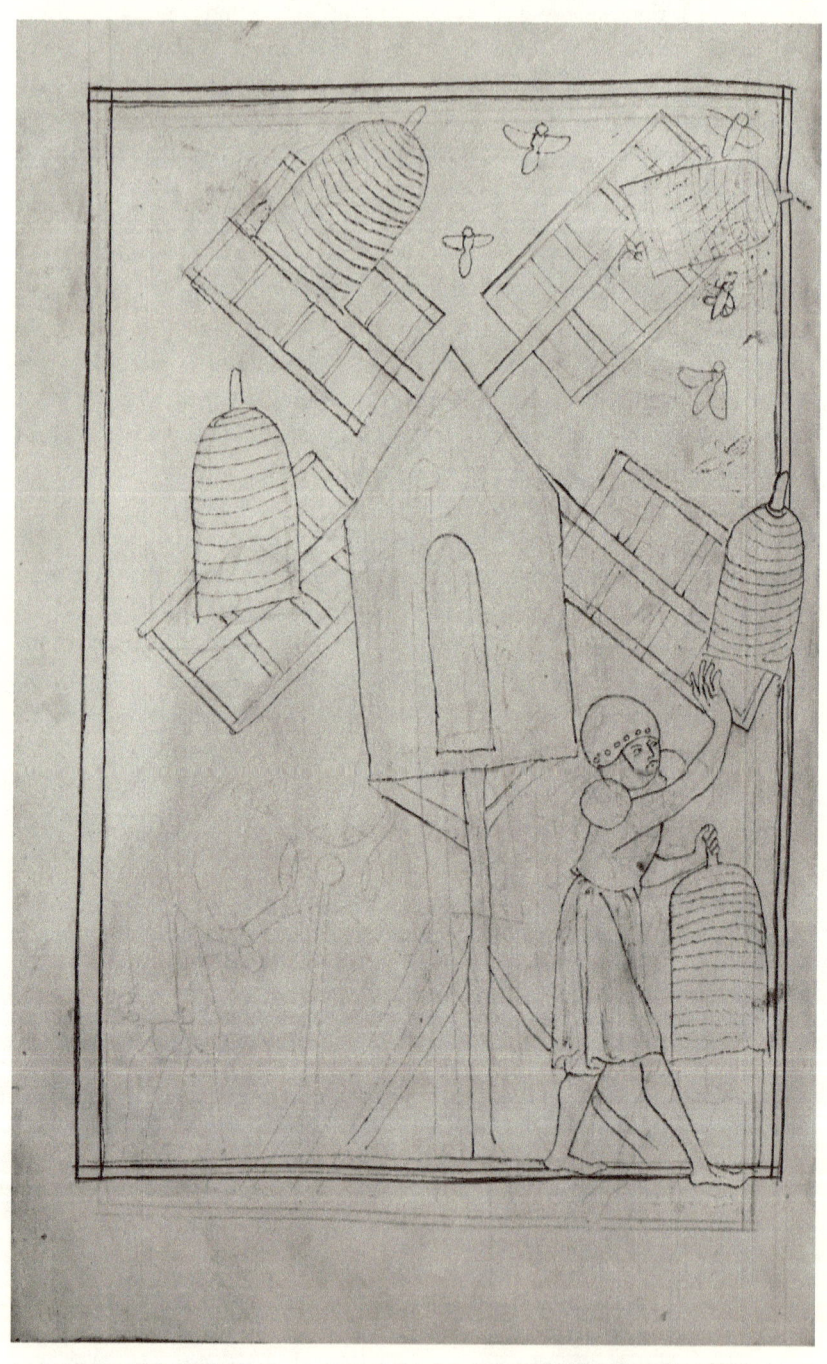

FIGURE 1a. Oxford, Christ Church, MS 92, fol. 74v. Governing Body of Christ Church, Oxford.

FIGURE 1b. Oxford, Christ Church, MS 92, fol. 75r. Governing Body of Christ Church, Oxford.

FIGURE 2. Oxford, Christ Church, MS 92, fol. 78v. Governing Body of Christ Church, Oxford.

The fourteen full-page line drawings preserved in Christ Church 92 also stand in stark contrast to the rest of the eighty-one-folio book.[10] The text block measures roughly 135 x 73/75 mm and is ruled for twenty long lines per page, as well as for wide historiated borders on each folio that contains text; alternating blue and violet paraphs with gold leaf signal textual divisions.[11] Headings are rubricated, and historiated initials mark the start of each of the book's sixteen chapters, preceded by a table of contents. In addition to the historiated and decorated borders and initials are fifteen half-page panel miniatures and six full-page miniatures. These miniatures, initials, and borders are painted in blue, violet, red, green, pink, white, yellow, and gray, and gold leaf has been used extensively throughout.

When constructing literary histories, we prioritize texts. But in the insular literary history of Richard I, the Middle English romance *Richard Coeur de Lion* does not come next, after the public talk of the eyre courts. The line drawings in Christ Church 92 do. This is less an argument of the present chapter than a point of fact. I described these drawings at length in part because there is no easy shorthand for them: No associable text exists within Christ Church 92, and no textual antecedents are extant outside of that manuscript. What the drawings might depict, how they might mean, how they might have been meant to mean, are open questions. For later readers such as us, whose knowledge includes manuscripts and printed books produced after Christ Church 92, the line drawings evoke *Richard Coeur de Lion*.[12] They have been read by scholars as glosses of that romance, a reading that posits them as evidence of the romance's textual circulation and popularity. But Christ Church 92 appeared at least a handful of years before the Auchinleck manuscript, which contains the earliest extant inscription of *Richard Coeur de Lion*. The reversal of that chronology, in which we make the image ancillary rather than primary, is a retrospective problem on our parts. It is a reconstruction of medieval cultural production that locates meaning in texts or in the convergence of image and text. Yet a textless image can indicate that its meaning was circulating elsewhere, including in the air.

This chapter asks how we can read these images without introducing later texts, and thus how they may have been read at the time of the manuscript's production. I reconstruct the early fourteenth-century milieu in which and by which the seemingly partial work of the manuscript's "Artist 1," and indeed the entirety of Christ Church 92, was made and seen. If we forgo the para-

---

10. Michael, "Iconography," 37, misstates fifteen drawings.
11. The leaves measure 246 x 160 mm.
12. Ralph Hanna rather brilliantly identified the probable romance-historical subject of these images. See Hanna, *London Literature*, 120; and below in this chapter.

digm of textual priority, the drawings in Christ Church 92 become, for us, the first traces of a "new" story, preserved apart from a literary text—a story that was, when the uncaptioned line drawings were made, already in circulation in the air in some form. By cross-reading different types of media—specifically a range of images, objects, and texts in simultaneous circulation—we can know what was in a particular milieu: what people were thinking, or thinking anew about, and what they were talking about with one another. Such cross-reading does not confirm a teleological progression from talk to image to text. Instead, it reveals that fragmented and flexible discourses drove and responded to medieval England's literary and historical text-making.

The first part of this chapter consists of a model reading of the manuscript. In this reading, the line drawings are reached by going through Christ Church 92 while cross-reading the circulating media—visual, written, and unwritten—that a contemporary knowing reader would have brought to the manuscript. This mode of reading Christ Church 92 foregrounds, especially in the chapter's second half, a line of less obvious questions about the ways in which the manuscript itself looks backward and forward, about its own interest in retrospection and posterity, and about how the picture of the past circulating in various media—a picture that Edward III partially inherited from his grandfather, Edward I—necessitated fundamental reconstruction to be of use in the fourteenth-century present, and in the future.

Oxford, Christ Church, MS 92 was made for Edward III.[13] The dedicatory letter on fol. 9r notes that the book is from the royal clerk Walter de Milemete, and the rubric on fols. 1r–1v dedicates it to the new king shortly after his coronation in February 1327.[14] Edward was then fourteen years old. The least delicate evidence that Christ Church 92 was changed during the deposition of his father, Edward II, from a book for an heir to a book for the new king appears on fol. 10r. There, "rex dux" and "nuper" were added to update the young Edward's status: now "quo*d* vos domine rex dux," and "no*st*ri Regis nup*er* anglie." The urgency of the moment appears everywhere in the manuscript, undercutting its attempts at order and erudition. The contemporary table of contents lists the first chapter as on "the supplications and divine

---

13. Christ Church 92 was identified around 1706 by Thomas Hearne as the mate to Additional 47680, and was donated to Christ Church, Oxford, in 1707 by alumnus William Carpenter. Its whereabouts between Edward III and Carpenter remain rather opaque, though its "luxury binding" suggests it continued to be highly valued. On its chain of custody, see Hanna-Rundle, 194–96.

14. Christ Church 92, fol. 1r: "Hic incipiunt rubrice capitulorum huius libri de nobilitatib*us* Sapiencijs *et* prudencijs Regum Editi ad honorem illustris domini Edwardi dei gracia Regis anglie Incipi [fol.1v] entis regnare Anno domini ab inca^r^nac*i*one Milesimo Tricentesimo vicesimo sexto."

purposes which the king ought to contemplate," but Edward no longer had time to contemplate his future kingship: In that chapter's place are images of action. Half and full-page miniatures open the manuscript, marking the prince Edward's knighting, his coronation as Edward III, and his imminent marriage to Philippa of Hainault. On fol. 1r, he sits on a throne, crowned, and holding a falcon; in a full-page miniature on fol. 3r, Saint George—in what may be the earliest extant depiction of George as the patron saint of England—dons a conical helmet and a crusader's white tunic with red cross and presents the arms of England to an armored Edward, who wears a tunic with England's heraldry of the three leopards or "lions passant guardant."[15] On fols. 3v–4r, in a full-page miniature that extends across the opening, Edward's impending marriage is symbolized by the depiction of the storming of the Castle of Love. Fol. 5r contains a half-page miniature in which the Trinity delivers the arms of England to Edward; he kneels before God in symbolic arms-giving in the full-page miniature on fol. 14v, and he is crowned by God on fol. 18v. On fol. 21v, Edward is enthroned. The final miniature, spread frieze-like across the opening of fols. 59v and 60r, is of pitched battle on horseback, bloody and graphic, with a figure dressed like a king of England (a visor covers his face) leading the charge. The book's most self-reflexive image appears on fol. 8v, where a half-page miniature depicts the presentation of a book that is presumably Christ Church 92 itself by a figure who is presumably Walter de Milemete. He kneels against the picture's plane and offers his gift to the king.[16]

Christ Church 92 is an adaptation of the Latin *Secretum secretorum*, the epistolary mirror for princes that Aristotle supposedly composed for his pupil Alexander the Great.[17] Probably by the time he ascended the throne, Edward III owned three iterations of Aristotle's treatise on kingship, including Christ Church 92. A French translation of the work, now Paris, Bibliothèque nationale, MS fr. 571, was a gift to Edward in late 1326 or early 1327 from Philippa of Hainault.[18] A copy with dense Latin text, now London, British Library,

---

15. Michael, "Iconography," 37–39.
16. On Walter de Milemete, see Michael, "Iconography," 35.
17. *Secretum secretorum* was a ubiquitous text in the middle ages. On its textual tradition, and for a discussion of the text as a generator of secrets, see Lochrie, *Covert Operations*, 98–118, and 104, respectively.
18. Papal confirmation of the marriage contract was obtained in August 1327 and they were married on January 24, 1328. Michael first identified the royal provenance of Paris, Bibliothèque nationale, MS fr. 571, and identified the book that is now Cambridge (MA), Harvard Law School Library, MS 12 as part of the original manuscript; see M. A. Michael, "A Manuscript Wedding Gift from Philippa of Hainault to Edward III," *The Burlington Magazine* 127 (1985): 582, 584–99. Today the Paris manuscript contains the *Livre du Trésor* of Brunetto

MS Additional 47680,[19] was produced under Milemete's supervision roughly contemporaneously with Christ Church 92, between 1325 and 1327.[20] M. R. James characterizes the slightly earlier manuscript as a "safe gift" for the heir apparent, with "no allusions to contemporary politics."[21] With Christ Church 92, Milemete attempted to engage Edward in the business of good kingship largely through pictures, and he addresses Edward directly at several places in the manuscript, explaining just how it should function in relation to the more verbose copy Milemete had already given him. Christ Church 92, Milemete clarifies, is a supplement: "These things are more fully contained in *De secretis secretorum et prudentiis regum,* which I have sent you" (*quo in libro de secretis secretorum et prudentiis regum plenius sunt contenta et per me uobis missa*).[22] The manuscript's contemporary table of contents advertises seventeen chapters, all but the first of which were completed. Their thinness reflects Christ Church 92's supplementary nature,[23] less full in its verbal didacticism and less textually faithful to Aristotle's original than the already completed manuscript (Additional 47680).[24] "No one who does read it," James observes of Christ Church 92, "will be much the wiser."[25] Mirrors for princes were not rare in the fourteenth century, but Edward, first as prince and then as king, was a unique case.

Latini; *Secret des secrets* (fol. 124); prayers in Latin and French; and a romance of Raoul le Petit, *Dit de Fauvain.* The Harvard portion comprises a copy of the *Statutes of England* in Anglo-Norman French.

19. See James, *Treatise,* xxxviii–lxiii.

20. Hanna, *London Literature,* 122–23: "Both Milemete's books are the product of the second of the three widely attested early fourteenth-century London collections of book-artisans." On the Milemete group, see Sandler, *Gothic Manuscripts,* 1:32, 2:91–93. At least six artists worked on both of Milemete's manuscripts. Of those six, three were involved in decorating both books. Roughly contemporaneously with the production of Christ Church 92, these illuminators worked separately and together on a significant number of extant books made for religious and secular patrons. See, for example, Sandler, 2, nos. 82, 83, 86, 87, 88, 89, and 90; and Otto Pächt and J. J. G. Alexander, *Illuminated Manuscripts in the Bodleian Library,* vol. 3 (Oxford: Clarendon Press, 1973), nos. 575, 577–80, 587, 610, and 634.

21. James, *Treatise,* xii. Additional 47680 is the earliest but also the "less finished" of the two books.

22. Christ Church 92, fol. 70r. Hanna's translation: *London Literature,* 143 n. 14.

23. The table of contents lists chapter 1 as "Of the supplication and divine purposes which the king ought to contemplate," but this chapter is missing; for discussion of the changes to the manuscript's initial program, see below.

24. Christ Church 92, folio 9v: "I have shaped two books, composing the present one from my own study, and another of the philosopher Aristotle, which contains great wisdom and human discretion" (*presentem librum propio studio duxi componendum et eciam librum philosophi Aristotelis in quo magna prudencia et discrecio humana continentur*). Hanna's translation: *London Literature,* 143 n. 14.

25. James, *Treatise,* xiii.

The contents of Christ Church 92 intimate that under no circumstances should anyone see in Edward III, nor should he see in himself, his father. It was precisely Edward II's perceived deficiencies that necessitated his son's abrupt kingship and catalyzed the rapid production of bespoke books on how to rule England correctly.[26] The coup by which Edward III ascended the throne was spearheaded by his mother Isabella and her lover Roger Mortimer, and it led, initially, to a regency until Edward III and his cohort wrested power from her in 1330. Still, the young Edward's precipitous kingship would not have been possible if Isabella's ambitions and plans had not coincided with the intense dissatisfaction her husband had engendered in his subjects, from his barons down to his contemporary biographer. Edward II had barely withstood baronial revolts in 1310 and 1312, and in 1325 Queen Isabella, in France on a diplomatic mission, kept the prince Edward from returning to England after he arrived in France as the duke of Aquitaine and count of Ponthieu to pay homage to Charles IV. Isabella vowed not to return to England until her husband had disentangled himself from the Despensers, the unpopular baronial family under whose sway he had fallen. By Easter 1325, rumor was circulating in France that Isabella had taken up with Mortimer, an English expatriate, and by that Christmas talk had reached England that they would return together to overthrow the king.[27]

Isabella engaged the young Edward to Philippa of Hainault and used the betrothal dowry to raise a mercenary army under the command of Mortimer and Philippa's uncle. In late September 1326, the party sailed to England, landing at Norfolk, where they gathered more fighting men, money, and baronial support. The bishops of Oxfordshire began preaching that an end to Edward II's misgovernment was at hand, and Isabella issued public proclamations denouncing her husband and the Despensers whom he harbored. Edward II fled toward Wales and was captured by the armies of English marcher lords who pledged Isabella their support. He was taken into custody and the Despensers caught with him were executed. A parliament on January 7, 1327, denounced the king; he resigned the throne in absentia and was formally deposed eight days later.[28] If, after all of this, Edward III needed more

---

26. Michael, "Iconography," 36–37, provides a list of probably implicit rebukes of Edward II in Christ Church 92's text; see also Hanna, *London Literature*, 121–22.

27. Michael Prestwich, *The Three Edwards: War and State in England 1272–1377*, 2nd ed. (London: Routledge, 2003), 71–101. A sense of the public sentiment toward Edward II is conveyed in his contemporary biography, although it ends prior to Isabella's return to England. See *Vita Edwardi Secundi*, ed. and trans. Wendy R. Childs, OMT (Oxford: Clarendon Press, 2005).

28. T. F. Tout, "The Captivity and Death of Edward of Caernarvon," in *Collected Papers of Thomas Frederick Tout*, vol. 3 (Manchester: Manchester University Press, 1934), 145–90;

proof that his father was not a fit model, there stood the fact that at the time of the younger Edward's coronation at Westminster in 1327, Edward II was imprisoned ninety miles outside of London in Kenilworth Castle. After a failed escape attempt, he was killed later that year in the dungeon of Berkeley Castle. Some said it was strangulation, others said suffocation, and still others told the story of a red-hot poker shoved up his backside, though the rumor that Edward II had survived and gone into hiding was equally persistent.[29]

Finding desirable models for Edward III necessitated looking to the past, but Christ Church 92 urges its reader to engage in retrospection that largely avoids Edward's familial retrospective inheritance.[30] Instead, the manuscript points its reader to legendary figures, men whom Edward seems to have known about and been interested in since his boyhood. The most obvious of these resides in the fundamental conceit of Paris, Bibliothèque nationale, MS fr. 571, Additional 47680, and Christ Church 92: all treatises on kingship written for Alexander the Great and adapted for a "new Alexander," Edward III. Milemete urges him to read Christ Church 92's text and visual program as expressly instructive. "When you have come, lord, with God's grace to manhood and to a state of greater power and dignity, as I foresee truly you will," the text insists on fol. 13r, "I believe firmly and without doubt, if you perform resolutely following the doctrine I have recently composed for king Alexander, you will be deservedly able to have various successes."[31] *Secretum secretorum* may have been chosen as a guide for the young Edward in part because of its advice on the importance of kingly judiciousness and discretion, practices at which Edward II had been judged inexpert.[32] Yet despite the number of other

---

Prestwich, *Three Edwards*, 88; and Geoffrey le Baker, *The Chronicle of Geoffrey le Baker*, trans. David Preest, with introduction and notes by Richard Barber (Woodbridge: The Boydell Press, 2012), 29–32.

29. The rumor's persistence was directly related to the execution of Edward II's half-brother in 1330, despite his sworn allegiance to Isabella and Mortimer. On the rumor, see Ian Mortimer, "The Death of Edward II in Berkeley Castle," *English Historical Review* 120 (2005): 1175–214.

30. On royal models, see below in this chapter. Hanna, *London Literature,* 117–18, suggests that Christ Church 92 recommends Edward I as a double model: for kingship and for being a "chivalric inheritor."

31. Hanna's translation: *London Literature,* 117, 143 n. 15: "Merito et uos, domine, per Dei graciam cum ad uirilem perueneritis etatem et ad statum maioris potencie et dignitatis, ut michi uerisimiliter uisum est, credoque firmiter, opinor indubitanter, si secundum doctrinam regi Alexandro nuper editam . . . firmiter operari . . . [various successes] habere poteritis."

32. In particular, chapters 9 and 10 in Christ Church 92: on the importance of a king's literate abilities, and on the king's discretion and secrecy, respectively. Chapter 9 impresses upon its reader the importance of a literate king, for a king who can read and write well can send and receive his own messages, and can also verify the authenticity of those messages by

handbooks on kingship no doubt available as exemplars, especially given Isabella's bookishness,[33] the fact that *Secretum secretorum* was repeatedly given to Edward III—in French, in Latin, and finally in Christ Church 92—implies an attachment or a presumed attachment of the young Edward to Alexander the Great. The repeated gift also exhibits some certainty on the part of Edward's guardians that this particular vehicle would profitably influence him if it could be presented in just the right manner.[34] Noting that Edward III received multiple handbooks on kingship, his foremost modern biographer dismisses them in aggregate as a collection probably of little or no importance to the young king.[35] But that Edward would acquire a collection of so many things he did not want is unlikely. What a person collects, whether he selects objects for himself or is given things by others familiar with his proclivities, rarely signifies dislike or disinterest today, and there is little reason to think it would have done so in fourteenth-century England. The collection Edward amassed, and not all at once, of this particular text tells us something about the stories he knew and liked, and the ways in which the contents of Christ Church 92 may have been assembled and for what purpose.

The fixedness of Alexander in Edward's books, both as a model of kingship and as a model receiver of instruction on kingship, evinces an earlier attachment to the stories of legendary heroes than has previously been supposed for the young king.[36] Christ Church 92's textual and visual depiction of Alexander the Great would in fact have added to a picture that Edward could have gradually been building from hearing other stories about and seeing other images of Alexander that had long been circulating in England. Some-

---

examining the hand in which they were written. In chapter 10, Milemete suggests several ways of testing a man's discretion; for example, can he easily be made to reveal others' secrets?

33. On Isabella's involvement in the insular and continental literary milieux, see below.

34. This appears to have been a sustained and organized effort among those surrounding the young Edward. Christ Church 92 and Paris, Bibliothèque nationale, MS fr. 571, have one of Milemete's illuminators in common. Isabella may have played a role in the latter manuscript's text, as Michael, "Wedding Gift," 589, notes: "Although Philippa of Hainault is represented presenting the book to Edward it does not seem likely that she would have had complete control over these subtle references found in the parts of the text written in England." Noted bibliophile Richard de Bury was among Isabella's retinue when she and her son were in France in 1326, and in his own work, the *Philobiblon*, Richard uses Aristotle's *Secretum secretorum* as the basis for his discussion on educating a prince. On Isabella and Richard de Bury, see Susan H. Cavanaugh, "Royal Books: King John to Richard II," *The Library* 10 (1988): 304–16, esp. 311–12. For an inventory of Isabella's books, see Susan H. Cavanaugh, "A Study of Books Privately Owned in England: 1300–1450" (unpublished PhD diss., University of Pennsylvania, 1980), 275–80, 456–60.

35. Ormrod, *Edward III*, 55.

36. On Edward III's character, see Ormrod, *Edward III*, 55–57.

time between 1175 and 1185 Thomas de Kent composed an Anglo-Norman romance of Alexander, *Le Roman de toute chevalrie,* which survives in manuscript copies from the thirteenth and fourteenth centuries.[37] Literally closer to home for Edward III, his great-grandfather, Henry III, had "The History of Alexander," a narrative that by the mid-thirteenth century was apparently so well known that it could be ordered by name, painted on the walls of the royal chambers at Clarendon Palace and Nottingham Castle.[38] Henry III's son, Edward I, was likewise enamored with the classical hero, and after his death in 1307 he was publicly invoked as England's own Alexander.[39] The popularity of Alexander's "history" was stable if not on the rise in the first half of the fourteenth century. Its earliest extant Middle English rendering, which survives as *Kyng Alisaunder* in the Auchinleck manuscript, was produced in London a handful of years after Edward received his various copies of *Secretum secretorum.*[40]

Edward was undoubtedly equally familiar with the second prominent model Christ Church 92 figures for the young king, Saint George. By the early fourteenth century, George was likewise storied in England as a knight in life and an equally martial saint who, according to popular tradition, was glimpsed fighting alongside the crusaders in 1098 during the First Crusade's

---

37. The Anglo-Norman *Roman de toute chevalrie* survives in five witnesses, including three manuscripts and single leaves used as pastedowns in two medieval books. The earliest of these is Cambridge, Trinity College, MS O.9.34, dated to the second quarter of the thirteenth century. The latest extant copy, Durham, Cathedral Library, MS C.IV.27B, dates from the middle of the fourteenth century. See Thomas de Kent, *Le Roman d'Alexandre ou Le Roman de toute chevalrie,* ed. Brian Foster and Ian Short, trans. Catherine Gaullier-Bougasses and Laurence Harf-Lancer (Paris: Honoré Champion, 2003), vii–xi and lxvi–lxviii. On the lives of Alexander in insular and continental circulation, see Venetia Bridges, *Medieval Narratives of Alexander the Great: Transnational Texts in England and France* (Cambridge: D. S. Brewer, 2018).

38. Tristram, *Wall Painting,* 1:18 and 1:214–15. The "Alexander Chamber" was located at Clarendon Palace, and in 1251 the "same story" of Alexander was ordered painted in the Queen's Chamber in Nottingham Castle. The custom seems to have been to decorate the top third of a wall with the stories or "histories," sometimes extending around a chamber. The lower two-thirds were then covered with painted hangings.

39. Hanna, *London Literature,* 117–18. On Edward III's preoccupation with chivalry and heroes "of old," including Arthur, see Vale, *Edward III and Chivalry,* esp. 42–56; and R. S. Loomis, "Edward I," 114–27.

40. See *Kyng Alisaunder,* ed. G. V. Smithers, 2 vols. EETS OS 227 and 237 (Oxford: Oxford University Press, 1952 and 1957); and Smithers, "Two Newly-Discovered Fragments," 1–2, on the discovery of its additional fragment. See also Venetia Bridges, "Absent Presence: Auchinleck and *Kyng Alisaunder,*" in *The Auchinleck Manuscript: New Perspectives,* ed. Susanna Fein (York: York Medieval Press, 2016), 88–107.

siege of Antioch.⁴¹ Purportedly firsthand accounts from the frontlines of the Third Crusade relate stories of England's crusaders calling out to George for intercession during difficult moments in battle.⁴² In England's Second Barons' War, the royalist armies under the future Edward I wore red crosses that evoked the image of George described in crusading stories.⁴³ It is this crusader George—a warrior, England's savior, and, conveniently, a royalist—who awards the arms of England to Edward III in Christ Church 92. The fullpage miniature's composition urges its reader to see the two figures almost inextricably: Edward and George register visually both as mirror images and a matched pair. Their helmets, armor, and tunics are identical, save that Edward's is red with the lions passant guardant in gold, while George wears the white tunic and red cross of the crusader. Their upper bodies turn toward one another, torsos out, with arms facing the picture's plane outstretched toward one another. Their upper bodies are mirror images, identical yet opposite, while their lower bodies are exact copies, with each figure's right foot pointing to the right and each figure's left foot pointing leftward and down, breaking the picture's frame. The image pictures Edward here as at once aspiring and already beginning to fit visually into the mold of George. The notion seeded in Christ Church 92—that Edward should model himself after the saint—bore fruit. Later in his reign, Edward III founded the Order of the Garter at Windsor (1348), thereby establishing George as the official patron saint of England. In the miniature of Edward III and Saint George on fol. 3r the king stands on the left, facing the future with his back to the past.

As he engaged in directed retrospection, Edward would also have been able to picture his future self as a model, and as a model for future readers. The horizontal battle scene across the opening of fols. 59v and 60r depicts a fiercely modern, or, depending on the precise relation of the miniature to current events, futuristic battle. The *bas-de-page* image is tightly packed with decapitated and lifeless bodies over which England's knights, individually identifiable by their arms, charge en masse to the right side of the frame, toward an opposing and unmarked army. The man leading the charge wears England's arms on his tunic, signifying kingship. Among his knights are those bearing the Lancastrian arms. Their inclusion in the image signals that

---

41. As reported, for instance, by William of Malmesbury in his *Gesta Regum Anglorum*, ed. and trans. R. A. B. Mynors, completed by R. M. Thomson and Michael Winterbottom, OMT (Oxford: Clarendon Press, 1998), 639. Tristram also reports that a French wall painting dated to 1249, and depicting four crusaders led by George, once existed in the church of St.-Jacques-des-Guérets (Loir-et-Cher).

42. Helen J. Nicholson, trans. and ed., *Itinerarium Peregrinorum et Gesta Regis Ricardi*; *The Chronicle of the Third Crusade* (Aldershot: Ashgate, 2001), 251–53.

43. See Tyerman, *England and the Crusades*, 148–49.

Edward III already had or soon would realign himself with that family, members of whom had led an uprising against his father in 1321.[44]

Christ Church 92 would have trained Edward, and indeed any reader of the manuscript, to read for instructive models of kingship and martial prowess. It is with this expectation, if moving through the book from beginning to end, that the reader reaches the drawings at the back of the manuscript. Like the "histories" of Alexander the Great and Saint George, the drawings should depict a man with whom the young Edward was already familiar, even enamored—not a vast army or collection of characters. The linear narrative that the drawings depict, the longest single visual sequence in the manuscript, also suggests this is not a tableau, like the miniature of Edward and George, but a story. That these are images of specifically old-fashioned siege warfare is in keeping with the retrospection the manuscript elsewhere demands of its reader, and for a fourteenth-century reader, the weapons and action would point more specifically to the siege warfare of crusade.[45] The drawings could return us to the grounds of Saint George's most famous story by illustrating the First Crusade's siege of Antioch, but their attention to the multiplicity of siege engines reflects the enumeration and fame of those engines used in another siege, Acre in 1191: by England's telling, the most successful siege of the Third Crusade and the most archetypal siege in which England had participated.

For the fourteenth-century public, and a royal reader of Christ Church 92 more specifically, Richard, crusader and conqueror, was already very much in the picture. He was the man most immediately associated in the minds of England's public with crusade generally, and with the Third Crusade specifically. The earliest part of England's official participation in the Third Crusade—Richard's travel to and conquering of Messina and Cyprus en route to Acre, and his siege of that city—had been circulating in talk and text since the late twelfth century. The events that followed that siege were often jetti-

---

44. On heraldry in general, see David Pearson, *Provenance Research in Book History: A Handbook* (London: The British Library and Oak Knoll Press, 1988). The heraldry in Christ Church 92 is meticulously treated by A. van der Put in James, *Treatise,* lxivvv–lxxii.

45. On the development of Western siege technology from the First Crusade to the Third, see Tyerman, *God's War,* esp. 142, 448–52, and 23: "Although fleeting references exist to large wooden siege machines in western Europe before the First Crusade, only during that expedition were westerners extensively exposed to such engines, the use of which they very quickly mastered, probably with Greek help." On technical details of siege engines, see Randall Rogers, *Latin Siege Warfare in the Twelfth Century* (Oxford: Clarendon Press, 1992), esp. 230–36, where he offers a detailed picture of the weaponry and tactics employed in the 1191 siege at Acre. (No bees are mentioned in his primary sources.) Prestwich, *Three Edwards,* 281–93, also describes siege weaponry used in England and by the English abroad, especially in the thirteenth and fourteenth centuries.

soned from the narrative of Messina, Cyprus, and Acre: Richard's slaughter of nearly 3,000 Muslims captured at Acre when he and Saladin could not agree on terms for their ransom. His besting of Saladin's army at Arsuf en route to Jaffa. And Richard's illness, truce negotiations with Saladin, and eventual return to England, still holding the sea coast from Tyre to Jaffa, but having never captured, or even set foot in, Jerusalem, the express goal of the entire adventure.[46]

Chief among the extant textual records are works roughly contemporary with the Third Crusade. These include the extensive Latin chronicles of Roger of Howden, who was a clerk at the court of Henry II and present on the Third Crusade until 1191 as part of the contingent from Yorkshire's East Riding.[47] Roger's works, the *Gesta Regis Henrici Secundi* and the *Chronica Magistri*, were completed by the time of his death, in 1201 or 1202.[48] The *Estoire de la Guerre Sainte*, an octosyllabic poem in Anglo-Norman probably completed before 1196 and internally ascribed to "Ambroise" (*Ambroise dit, qui fist cest livre*),[49] survives in one manuscript and a fragment, both from the second half of the thirteenth century. Ambroise describes the years 1190 to 1192 from the point of view of an eyewitness with the crusaders in the Holy Land.[50] Closely connected to Ambroise's work, and perhaps confirming a wider

---

46. This is obviously a redacted summary; see *Richard I*, 123–221, and Tyerman, *God's War*, 431–74.

47. At Acre, Roger of Howden witnessed a charter of the Yorkshireman John of Hessle; see Tyerman, *England and the Crusades*, 72. In his account of Acre, Roger includes a list of the men from Yorkshire and Lincolnshire who died during the sieges between 1190 and 1192; see his *Gesta Regis Henrici Secundi Benedicti Abbatis, The Chronicle of the Reigns of Henry II and Richard I*, ed. William Stubbs, RS 49, vol. 2 (London: Longmans, 1867), 148–50.

48. These are edited by Stubbs as multivolume works for the RS; see above. On the dates of composition for the *Chronica*, which was Roger's revised and later work, see David Corner, "The Earliest Surviving Manuscripts of Roger of Howden's 'Chronica,'" *The English Historical Review* 98 (1983): 297–310. An Anglo-Norman prose chronicle, written between 1240 and 1320 and thought to derive from Roger of Howden's work, survives in two manuscripts dated to the mid-fourteenth century: now Cambridge, Trinity College, MS O.4.32, and Oxford, Bodleian Library, MS Fairfax 10. See Ruth J. Dean, *Anglo-Norman Literature: A Guide to Texts and Manuscripts* (London: The Anglo-Norman Text Society, 1999), 38, no. 56. It has been edited as R. C. Johnston, ed., *The Crusade and Death of Richard I*, ANTS 17 (Oxford: Blackwell, 1961).

49. Ambroise, *The History of the Holy War: Ambroise's "Estoire de la Guerre Sainte,"* ed. Marianne Ailes and Malcolm Barber, trans. Marianne Ailes, 2 vols. (Woodbridge: The Boydell Press, 2003), vol. 1, line 171.

50. Dean, *Anglo-Norman Literature*, 38, no. 56.1. The text survives in the single manuscript, Vatican City, Biblioteca Apostolica Vaticana, MS Reg. lat. 1659, and as a fragment once used for binding, now Tokyo, Keio University, MS 170.X.9.11. On the leaf's discovery, see M. L. Colker, "A Newly Discovered Manuscript Leaf of Ambroise's *L'Estoire de la Guerre Sainte*," *Revue d'histoire des textes* 22 (1992): 159–62.

circulation and influence of that Anglo-Norman poem than its two extant witnesses suggest, is the so-called *Itinerarium peregrinorum,* which survives in at least twelve extant copies, dated from the twelfth through the sixteenth centuries, and three reported but now lost copies from the seventeenth century.[51]

Much of medieval England's earliest common knowledge of the siege of Acre is still in circulation today as our own. One of our finest historians of crusade, Christopher Tyerman, necessarily uses the ostensibly firsthand descriptions of Roger of Howden, Ambroise, and the *Itinerarium* to construct much of his account of the siege of Acre:

> The last weeks of the siege were dominated by the contest of the Christian siege engines, catapults, sappers, and scaling ladders against the defenders' incendiary missiles, stone-throwing machines and counter-sappers. Each Christian commander possessed his own great stone-throwers. The duke of Burgundy, the Templars, the Hospitallers and the Pisans each had one. Philip II had many, his best, called "Malvoisine" or "Bad Neighbour," constantly needing repair as it was a prime target of enemy bombardment. The count of Flanders ran two, which, after his death on 1 June, were taken over by Richard I, who built two more as well as a couple of mangonels and a siege tower. Philip also constructed a protected shooting platform and an elaborate scaling device, although both were destroyed by fire. The common fund, established in the Christian camp at least since the autumn of 1190, paid for its own stone-thrower, "God's Petrary."[52]

When Jerusalem fell to Saladin on July 4, 1187, Richard—then still only a prince but the principal heir of his father's empire of Anjou, England, and Normandy, as well as his mother's duchy of Aquitaine—was the first northern prince to take the cross.[53] After the death of Henry II in July 1189, Richard

---

51. See *Chronicles and Memorials of the Reign of Richard I,* ed. William Stubbs, RS 38, vol. 1 (London: Longman, Green, Longman, Roberts, and Green, 1864), lxxi–ii. For a fuller description of the texts' manuscript history, see Hans Eberhard Mayer, *Das Itinerarium Peregrinorum: Eine zeitgenössische englische Chronik zum dritten Kreuzzug in ursprünglicher Gestalt* (Stüttgart: Anton Hiersemann, 1962), 7–45. See also Nicholson, *Itinerarium,* 5–17. For an overview of the potential relationship between Ambroise and the *Itinerarium,* see Colker, "Newly Discovered," 159–63.

52. Tyerman, *God's War,* 449. See, for example, Nicholson, *Itinerarium,* 201–25; Ambroise, *The History,* vol. 1, lines 2295–5559; and Roger of Howden, *Gesta,* 2:169–92, 230–31.

53. On the mobilization of Western armies, especially in England and Normandy, for the Third Crusade, see Tyerman, *England and the Crusades,* 57–86. On Richard's taking of the cross and his initial involvement in preparations, see *Richard I,* 85–88.

was crowned and anointed at Westminster on September 3, 1189. By December 11, 1189, after a swift and shrewd fundraising campaign during which the new king of England apparently said (in contemporary rumor that survives down to us) that he would sell London to finance the crusade if only he could find a buyer,[54] Richard crossed from Dover to Calais on his way to the Holy Land, leaving William of Longchamp, bishop of Ely, in charge of England as its new chancellor.[55] Richard and Philip Augustus of France convened at and then departed separately from Vézelay on July 4, 1190, meeting again on September 23 at Messina, where Richard arrived in grand fashion and to great acclaim, as described in the twelfth-century *Itinerarium*:

> Then, when rumors (*fama*) spread that the nobleminded king of England was approaching, the people rushed out in crowds, wanting to see him. Pouring on to the shore they struggled to stand where they could see him coming in. Look! Far away they saw the sea covered with innumerable galleys, and from afar the sound of war-trumpets echoed in their ears, with clarions resounding clear and shrill. As the fleet came nearer, they saw galleys rowing in good order, adorned and laden throughout with various sorts of weapons, with countless standards and pennants on the tips of spear shafts fluttering in the air in beautiful array. The prows of the galleys were each painted differently, with shields glittering in the sun hung on each bow. You would have seen the sea boil as the great number of rowing oars approached. The ears of the onlookers rang with the thundering of war-trumpets—known as *trompes*—and they were thrilled with delight at the approach of this diverse uproar.
>
> Then, behold the glorious king!—with the troops of sailing galleys like an accompanying escort, he stood out on the prow which was higher and more ornate than the rest, as if to see things unknown or to be seen by the unknown. Willingly putting himself on show for all to see, he was carried towards the densely packed shore.
>
> Elegantly dressed, he came ashore, where he found the sailors whom he had sent on ahead waiting for him with others in his service. They received him joyfully and brought forward the warhorses and his noble horses which he had entrusted to them for transportation. The locals flocked in from all sides to join his own people in escorting him to his lodging. The common folk talked among themselves about his great magnificence, which had left

---

54. Richard of Devizes, *Chronicle*, 9. On Richard's aggressive, lucrative, and swift fundraising campaign, see *Richard I*, 114–18; and Tyerman, *England and the Crusades*, 75–83.

55. See William of Newburgh's account, quoted in *Richard I*, 121; on William of Longchamp, see also Appleby, *England without Richard*, 92–93.

them stunned. "This man is certainly worthy of authority! He deserves to be set over peoples and kingdoms. We had heard of his great reputation, but the reality that we see is far greater."[56]

Other contemporary and purportedly firsthand accounts of this scene agree on the spectacle of Richard's arrival to a degree that evinces its status as the common knowledge in circulation.[57]

Stories of Richard's time at Messina and travel from there to Acre were especially well known in early fourteenth-century England. Following trouble between his men and the Greeks of Messina, Richard took the island in the first week of October 1190, reaching a treaty with Tancred of Sicily within days. On April 10, Richard and his force, including roughly two hundred ships and perhaps seventeen thousand soldiers and sailors, left Messina, but some of this number were shipwrecked and captured along with their belongings by the emperor of Cyprus, who refused to return the captives and treasure to the English king. Richard attacked Cyprus. When the emperor still refused to meet Richard's terms, Richard conquered Cyprus, shackled its emperor, and taxed the island's population. Richard then set out for Acre, arriving there on June 8, 1191. Crusaders had been laying siege to the city for two years, but together the armies of Richard and Philip forced the city to capitulate and terms of surrender were reached on July 12, despite the fact that both kings had been taken ill upon their arrival. On July 31, Philip precipitously left Acre for France.[58]

The anonymous author of the *Vita Edwardi Secundi*,[59] a biography of Edward II probably composed around 1325 and thus contemporary with Christ Church 92, recounts wide transmission of this image of Richard as crusader and conqueror.[60] In his description of the year 1312, Edward II's biographer heralds the birth of the future Edward III, saying:

---

56. Nicholson, *Itinerarium*, 157. The Latin text is available in the *Chronicles and Memorials of the Reign of Richard I*, 1:156–57.

57. Nicholson, *Itinerarium*, 156–57; *Chronicles and Memorials of the Reign of Richard I*, 1:156. Other contemporary chroniclers largely agree with this account: See Roger of Howden, *Gesta*, 2:125, and his *Chronica* 3:55. See also Ambroise, *The History*, vol. 1, lines 559–604.

58. Tyerman, *God's War*, 431–74; Tyerman, *England and the Crusades*, 65–69; and *Richard I*, 123–221.

59. John Walwayn has been suggested as the biography's author; see *Vita Edwardi Secundi*, xxiv–xxv.

60. The *Vita Edwardi Secundi* survives in Oxford, Bodleian Library, MS Rawlinson B. 180, as a copy made of the now lost medieval manuscript by Thomas Hearne in the eighteenth century. The lost manuscript has been dated to c. 1348, and the text's composition to about 1325, ending abruptly as it does with a supposed transcription of a letter sent in the same year

Long live, therefore, the young Edward, and may he himself embody the virtues that enriched each of his forefathers separately. May he follow the industry of King Henry II, the well-known valour of King Richard, may he reach the age of King Henry [III], revive the wisdom of King Edward [I], and remind us of the physical strength and comelieness of his father.[61]

This passage reflects the wider public sentiment toward Edward II, and through the rhetoric of instructive retrospection, it holds Richard and Edward III's other ancestors up as models for the young king. In doing so, the passage also more subtly envisages a wider public interest in Richard than in Edward's other useful relatives. Unlike the industry of Henry II or the wisdom of Edward I, Richard's valor has the distinction of being known, and even "well known" (*notam probitatem*). The biographer repeats this characterization of Richard as a model of valor in opposition to Edward II and in conjunction with Richard's transmission through popular culture:

Behold, our King Edward [II] has now reigned six full years and up until now he has achieved nothing praiseworthy or memorable, except that he has made a splendid marriage and has produced a handsome son and heir to the kingdom. How different were the beginnings of the reign of King Richard, who, before the end of the third year of his reign, scattered far and wide the rays of his valour. In one day he courageously took Messina, a city of Sicily, and ably subjugated the land of Cyprus in a fortnight. Then, how he bore himself at Acre, and in other foreign parts history vividly relates in both the Latin and French tongues.[62]

The glorious bygone days of Richard that the biographer paints here so vividly (and has silently passed over three intervening reigns to get to) is of course not a past the biographer himself experienced, but one about which he,

---

from the English bishops to Isabella, imploring her to return to England to reconcile with her husband.

61. *Vita Edwardi Secundi*, 62–63: "Viuat igitur iuuenis Edwardus, et, auitis patribus assimilatus, quod singulos ditabat solus optineat. Regis Henrici secundi sectetur industriam, regis Ricardi notam probitatem, ad regis Henrici proueniat etatem, regis Edwardi recolat sapienciam, uiribus et specie referat cum corpore patrem."

62. *Vita Edwardi Secundi*, 68–69: "Ecce nunc rex noster Edwardus sex annis complete regnauit, nec aliquid laudabile uel dignum memoria hucusque patrauit, nisi quod regaliter nupsit et prolem elegantem regni heredem sibi suscitauit. Alia fuerunt inicia regis Ricardi, qui nondum elapso triennio regni sui probitatis sue radios longe lateque dispersit; nam Messanas ciuitatem Sisilie uno die uiriliter subiecit, et terram Cypri in quindecim diebus potenter subiugauit. Deinde apud Acon et in aliis partibus transmarinis [quomodo] se habuerit, historia Latino et Gallico sermone digesta luculenter percurrit."

writing no earlier than 1313, had only heard. Hearing is key. In his description of the transmission of Richard's "history," Edward II's biographer does not prioritize texts. The process he describes is one of a disembodied "history" that travels here and there "relating" Richard's greatness, and doing so in the appropriate language, presumably so that what is told can be heard and understood by the largest possible audience.

Images and records of images that survive from the middle of the thirteenth century confirm that stories about Richard were being invented and circulated apart from text, such as those told in the eyre courts about Richard's place in the individual pasts and memories of England's public. There were other stories, too, that told of a man on crusade and some that, like the stories of Alexander and George, would have surrounded Edward III in his youth and informed his reading of the drawings in Christ Church 92. According to the Close Rolls from 1247 to 1251, Henry III ordered the "History of Antioch" painted in the chambers of the king's chaplains in the Tower of London (*faciat historiam Antioch in camera capellanorum regis Turris Londonie*).[63] Along with the "History of Alexander," Henry III had a story that was apparently identifiable as the "Combat of King Richard" painted on the walls of the Antioch Chamber at Clarendon Palace in 1251. Leaden stars, crescents, and a masonry pattern in red and white were found in the Antioch Chamber's ruins.[64] The Liberate Rolls record the order to "wainscot the king's chamber under the chapel, to remove the wall across it, to paint therein the story of Antioch and the duel of king Richard, and to paint the wainscot green with gold spangles."[65]

The painting of the "Combat of Richard" does not survive, but another image fitting that description and probably also produced for Henry III does: painted floor tiles recovered from the site of Chertsey Abbey in Surrey and dated to around 1250. These tiles depict Richard and Saladin on horseback, in hand-to-hand combat.[66] Decorated primarily with red, yellow, and blue, the tiles' complete scene consists of two side-by-side roundels. In the roundel on the left, Richard charges to the right with his lance pointed at Saladin. Saladin, in the other roundel, is in the process of being fatally struck by

---

63. Tristram, *Wall Painting*, 1:578.
64. Tristram, *Wall Painting*, 1:17, 70, 73, 131, 215, 528.
65. *Calendar of the Liberate Rolls, Henry III*, 3:362.
66. See Alexander and Binski, *Age of Chivalry*, 204, no. 16: The Chertsey Tiles were probably intended for a royal palace, and perhaps specifically for Westminster Palace, because of the tiles' particular fineness, and also because "the subject of Richard's victory over Saladin was a favourite theme of Henry III. It was painted on the walls of the Antioch Chamber at Clarendon Palace." The tiles have also been dated slightly later, to around 1270–80, based on the armor depicted: See R. S. Loomis, "*Richard Coeur de Lion*," 514–15.

the English king's lance as he charges toward Richard. It is this lance that ingeniously connects the two scenes, extending from the left roundel to the right, its grip in Richard's hand and its point emerging from Saladin's torso and shoulder. He wears a turban-style headdress and carries a curved sword, while Richard wears a crown atop his helmet and bears the lions passant guardant on his shield. Any direct meeting, let alone hand-to-hand combat, between Richard and Saladin is, as far as we know, apocryphal rumor. The infamous siege of Antioch, which was a point of pride for the West in the long history of the Crusades and which was surely the reference point for the Antioch Chamber, predated Richard and the Third Crusade by a little more than one hundred years.[67] That the stories of Antioch and Richard's combat were wedded, at least in the royal household, suggests a new "memory" of Richard was made and circulated in mediums other than writing. These particular "histories" were some of Henry's favorite subjects, for around the same time either the story of Antioch or the combat of Richard was also the inspiration for wall paintings in his castles at Winchester and Nottingham.[68] The association of the late eleventh-century siege and the late twelfth-century king figures Richard as not only a representative of the Third Crusade, but a signifier of crusade in general. The reader of Christ Church 92 would have been able to incarnate Richard, to put him in its unfinished pictures as a model for Edward III.

By the time of Christ Church 92's production, Richard the crusader was everywhere in some form or fashion, except for in those pictures in the manuscript itself. As modern readers, trying to make manifest the line drawings not in retrospect but in real time, we have to perform significant reconstructive work to see him there, have to become fourteenth-century knowing readers. As knowing readers, now aware of what people were saying about Richard prior to and around the time of Christ Church 92's production, the drawings that fill its final quire appear to tell a relatively or entirely new narrative, for we have not yet heard or seen it elsewhere. But the drawings' placement and nature could equally demonstrate a hesitance to foreground Richard in the manuscript, to render him wholly present as a model for kingship. It is possible that the sketches in Christ Church 92 were in the process of becoming; it is also possible that they were not.

In England, Richard's identity had always been inextricable from his absence. While, as chapter 2 shows, the *quo warranto* period required the public to situate Richard within their individual narrations of descent, how

---

67. On the siege of Antioch, which occurred from October 1097 to June 2, 1098, see Tyerman, *God's War*, 132–43.

68. Tristram, *Wall Painting*, 1:215; and Tyerman, *England and the Crusades*, 117.

Richard's reign might fit into a collective—that is, into England's—narration of descent remained a work in progress. For litigants in the thirteenth-century eyre courts, Richard was a subject of talk precisely because situating him as a once significant insular presence required both effort and finesse. Richard would ideally, through firsthand or secondhand accounts, be in the foreground or background of litigants' personal narratives. This need presented practical problems, but also theoretical ones. The version of Richard in wide circulation, long before his reign was made legally significant to individual memory and family history, was of the model crusader abroad, not a model king in England, and the two vocations may well have been mutually exclusive not only in the minds of England's public, but in the minds of Edward's guardians. What Richard looked like as a crusader in retrospect may have been universally difficult to reconcile with what he looked like as a king.

In the earlier sections of Christ Church 92 that expressly instruct on good kingship, Richard is at best an absent presence. Three gold leopards on a red field, the arms of England whose earliest known representation dates from Richard's reign,[69] appear throughout the manuscript, including on Edward's tunic as he stands with Saint George—himself a visual reference to crusade and thus to Richard.[70] England's arms appear again in the manuscript's penultimate illuminated *bas-de-page* miniature depicting the gruesome battle whose weapons, armor, and participants are contemporary with Christ Church 92. Although his face is covered by a visor, the man leading the charge is presumably England's king: He wears England's arms on his tunic and his horse is similarly draped in them. Even with its "modern" identifications, the miniature evokes Richard. With his face covered and his body dressed in England's arms, Edward III could be mistaken for the version of his ancestor in combat on the Chertsey Tiles. At once everywhere and nowhere in Christ Church 92, Richard most closely resembles in its pages another absent presence in the manuscript, Edward II. Rather than disappearing the deposed king, the manuscript's up-to-the-minute cancellation of his kingship—a reminder of the rapidity and messiness of the shifting political landscape—only makes him a spectral anti-model. The line drawings, which conjure Richard but do not flesh him out, and the ghosts of Edward II, which like the rumors that he

---

69. See Alexander and Binski, *Age of Chivalry*, 57. The earliest known representation of the three leopards, or the lions passant guardant, is on the second Great Seal of Richard I, cut in 1195 and made public in 1198. In an exemplary case of retrospectively produced inheritance, the early thirteenth-century chronicler Matthew Paris went behind Richard's reign to attach the arms to England's previous kings, beginning with William the Conqueror.

70. Hanna, *London Literature*, 122.

still lived are never fully exorcised from Christ Church 92, exemplify a tension between the present and the past that pervades the manuscript.

Christ Church 92 trains its reader to read retrospectively, but in the manuscript's present time and place, the past signifies differently than it would, for instance, during the era of *quo warranto*. Double-edged signifiers of inheritance run throughout the visual program. The prominence of the Lancastrian arms in the battle miniature described above at once celebrate Edward III's repaired baronial allegiances and evoke the baronial uprising against a king that necessitated reparation.[71] In a response that possibly reproduces that of fourteenth-century readers, modern scholars have not been able to agree on what they see in the full-page miniature on fol. 4v. It could be Edward III and his mother, Isabella of France, or Edward III and Philippa of Hainault, enthroned side by side with the shield of England below the king and the split shield of England and France below the queen.[72] Even if one decides this image evokes the present moment of the young Edward's ascension to the throne, he here embodies a complex chronological position in which his form fits exactly in the outline of his father: a replication the manuscript elsewhere so vociferously works against. Moreover, by exactly replacing his father in the miniature, he sits as his mother's equal, at best. At worst, despite his title, the image reinforces the fact that she remains regent and he her child. M. A. Michael contends that to its contemporary royal viewers, this miniature would situate Edward III and Isabella within a pictorial tradition of legitimately ruling mothers and sons. The young king alongside his mother "recalls the image prefacing the *Bible moralisée* fragment in the Morgan Library, which is usually thought to depict Blanche of Castile seated with her son Louis of France. This analogy would not have been lost on Queen Isabella."[73]

The miniature calls to mind another possible analogy: the paradigmatic mother and son duo of Eleanor of Aquitaine and Richard, similarly active

---

71. The final illumination before the pen sketches is a half-page miniature on fol. 60v that would prove problematic in retrospect. It shows the young Edward with his contemporaries, identifiable by their heraldry. They include John de Boun, Earl of Hereford; Thomas Lord Wake of Lydell; and Edmund of Woodstock, Earl of Kent. In 1330, Parliament indicted Edmund of Woodstock, Earl of Kent and half-brother to Edward II, and then publicly executed him at Winchester Castle as a traitor. In the words of Michael Camille, "One of the problems of seeing images as mirrors of history is that history does not stand still long enough to get its portrait painted." See Michael Camille, *Mirror in Parchment: The Luttrell Psalter and the Making of Medieval England* (Chicago: University of Chicago Press, 1998), 67. On Edmund of Woodstock, see, for example, Prestwich, *Three Edwards*, 99 and 131.

72. Michael, "Iconography," 37–38, argues convincingly that this miniature depicts Isabella rather than Philippa of Hainault.

73. Michael, "Iconography," 38.

some 150 years earlier. While still a prince, Richard twice engaged in questionable uprisings against his father, Henry II. In 1173, Richard joined forces with his brothers and mother, and in 1189, with Philip Augustus of France and with Eleanor's support, he again challenged his father. Eleanor was under surveillance in England on her husband's order when, shortly before his death in July 1189, Henry II acquiesced to his son's terms. Richard immediately invested Eleanor with the full authority of the Crown until he could return to England from Anjou.[74] The readers of Christ Church 92 would have been prompted to remember Richard in this context of kingship—retrospection that would have thrown into relief either England's instability during his absence or the absence itself. The uncaptioned and unfinished nature of the line drawings could signify a story of Richard already so well known that it was recognizable on sight, but the circumstances of the drawings might equally demonstrate some ambivalence about whether Richard should be brought back fully from his perpetual state of absence.

The late thirteenth century's consternated public talk about Richard did not settle questions about Richard's time in England, nor did it yield a standard or authoritative narrative of that time on which everyone could agree. This unsettledness around Richard's time in England and his place in its collective memory was partly a function of attempting to address such issues in legal court. One narrative was countered by another. Richard acquired qualities that persisted across individual narrations of descent, but no portable narrative skeleton of his presence in England emerged. Questions remained open, narratives multiple. Legal memory attached new stakes to this narrative puzzle in the late thirteenth century, but how Richard should be brought into the picture as a present king, not an absent crusader, was a problem as old as Richard's reign itself. In retrospective texts that predate both Christ Church 92 and the height of relevant narrations of descent, text-makers found ways around synthesizing king and crusader into a single body, and established a narrative form for Richard's reign that failed, or did not try, to integrate events at home during his reign with the crusade abroad.

In these texts, the narrative of Richard's reign has a binary form. Cambridge, Corpus Christi College, MS 339, a book dated to the late twelfth century, contains the autograph manuscript of a Latin chronicle by a monk of St. Swithun's, Winchester, who remained in England during the Third Crusade. He identifies himself in his chronicle as Richard of Devizes.[75] We cannot

---

74. Appleby, *England without Richard*, 1–2.

75. On Richard of Devizes's chronicle in CCCC MS 339, its visual representation of Richard's reign, and the difficulties of writing about a geographically distant crusade in real time, see my article, "The Function of Form in the Chronicle of Richard of Devizes" (forth-

know if the Corpus autograph is a foul or a fair copy, but in it, Devizes conceives of Richard's reign as bifurcated. The chronicle begins with Richard's coronation in 1189 and ends with his plans to leave the Holy Land in October 1192. However, after Richard sails from the Continent in 1191, Devizes separates Richard's narrative from England's by moving the king's adventures on crusade into the manuscript's wide margins. The chaotic events occurring at home in England, without Richard, appear in the text block. This polyvocal *mise-en-page,* in which Richard's reign is split into two narratives that operate simultaneously but separately, continues for nearly the balance of the chronicle.[76] That Devizes, unlike his better known and studied contemporaries, such as Roger of Howden or Ambroise, remained in England surely informed his view of, access to, and inscription of Richard.

During Richard's reign in absentia, rumor was a productive, indeed an essential, mode of history-making. To write while in England about Richard's contemporaneous exploits outside of it was essentially to wait for and then to write down rumor: circulating pieces of talk about an absent person or thing that together constitute a perpetually alterable whole. For those who, like Devizes, remained in England, what was known of Richard—his person and his actions—during his prolonged absence came mostly by way of especially far-flung rumor.[77] The writing of contemporary history and the writing of rumor were thus not mutually exclusive endeavors in the late twelfth century. This reality, in which Richard's absence was filled by rumors about him, was so pervasive that for us, looking back at his reign, it is effectively invisible. For Devizes and his contemporaries in England, it was a fact of life. Through his chronicle's bifurcated form, Devizes conveys that for those like him who remained at home, England was unruly during the Third Crusade in large part because it was without a ruler: Its king was, at best, an absent presence. This organization of narrative content and visual layout forces his chronicle's

---

coming). Devizes's chronicle also survives in one slightly later manuscript, London, British Library, MS Cotton Domitian A.xiii.

76. Richard of Devizes, *Chronicle,* 35–36. Devizes first moves Richard's narrative to the outer margin on fol. 33r, when Richard and his fleet depart Messina: "The fleet of Richard, king of the English, sailed on the open sea and proceeded in this order" (*Classis Ricardi regis Anglorum altum legebat, et hoc ordine procedebat*).

77. A growing field of scholarship is addressing the transmission of information during the crusades. See, for example, Carol Symes, "Popular Literacies and the First Historians of the First Crusade," *Past and Present* 235 (2017): 37–67; and Sophia Menache, "The Crusades and Their Impact on the Development of Medieval Communication," in *Kommunikation zwischen Orient und Okzident Alltag und Sachkultur: internationaler Kongress, Krems an der Donau 6. bis 9. Oktober 1992,* ed. Helmut Hundbichler (Vienna: Österreichischen Akademie der Wissenschaften, 1994), 69–90.

reader to contemplate, as Devizes must have done, the long-term and day-to-day, the ideological and very real, effects of Richard's absence on England.

Devizes's use of *mise-en-page* to accommodate two simultaneous narratives—narratives whose events bear on each other but do not precisely coincide—embodied the ruptures in Richard's reign in real time. In retrospective texts, the legacy of this bifurcated form can be seen in fragmentation and modularity, which are instrumentalized as tools with which to reconstruct Richard's reign. The single manuscript in which a complete copy of Ambroise's *Estoire de la Guerre Sainte* survives, Vatican City, Bibliotheca Apostolica Vaticana, MS Reg. lat. 1659,[78] was copied in the second half of the thirteenth century, making it roughly contemporary with the setting of Richard's reign as the new *terminus post quem* of England's legal memory during the *quo warranto* era. The Vatican manuscript's text is written on parchment, in two columns. Corrections have been made in the scribe's own hand. That hand is also responsible for another text that begins in the same column immediately after the *Estoire* ends: the music and words for the first two strophes of the *planh* or lament on the death of Richard, composed by the late twelfth-century troubadour Gaucelm Faidit.[79] The narrative of the *Estoire* ends in 1192, well before the end of Richard's life in 1199. The scribal-reader's impulse here, it seems, was to present a more complete written picture of Richard by reconstructing Richard's life and death from recoverable remnants. The scribe pieced together fragments of Richard's story that were in circulation to produce a new whole.

Robert of Gloucester, writing around 1300, grapples in his Middle English metrical chronicle—much like Richard of Devizes did a century earlier—with how to manage two simultaneous storylines, one about England and the other about its king abroad. A distinct problem of retrospectivity is visible in Robert's work.[80] Where Richard of Devizes at most solves, and, at least, accommodates this problem visually, and the Vatican manuscript's

---

78. Dean, *Anglo-Norman Literature*, 38, no. 56.1.

79. Ambroise, *The History*, 1:xi. On Faidit, see R. T. Hill and T. G. Bergin, *Anthology of the Provençal Troubadours*, 2nd ed., 2 vols. (New Haven: Yale University Press, 1973), 1:130–31 and 2:44–45. See also Jean Mouzat, ed., *Les Poèmes de Gaucelm Faidit, troubadour du XIIe siècle* (Paris: A. G. Nizet, 1965), 415–24.

80. As editor of Robert of Gloucester's chronicle for the Rolls Series, Wright tracked down many of the textual sources behind the "original" chronicle, for instance, Brutus to the death of Henry I, as well as parts of Robert's continuation up to 1270. For the account of Richard's reign in the longer recension, Wright specifies probable sources, such as Roger of Howden and the Annals of Waverly and Tewkesbury for the period from Richard's coronation to his victory at Acre, but admits that "for the rest of Richard's reign it is almost impossible to say what authority the writer followed in his brief summary"; see Robert of Gloucester, *Metrical Chronicle*, 1:xxx.

scribe implements fragmentation as a productive mode of text-making, Robert of Gloucester conceives of Richard's reign—England, crusade, absence, presence—in modular and thus neatly separable and movable parts. As readers of Robert's chronicle, for instance, we are in London in 1189 for Richard's coronation and the massacre of the Jews across England so closely associated with it. We are present as England hears of the circumstances in the Holy Land that precipitate the Third Crusade. And we are with England's men, including Richard, as they take the cross. Robert's narrative then shifts focus, leaving England behind to follow Richard as he travels quickly through Cyprus to Acre and, once there, as he and Philip conquer that city. When Philip, angry that he has not gotten enough credit for the victory, departs impulsively for France, we remain with Richard through a few more couplets. In these lines, Robert showers England's king with rote praise for his prowess as a knight.

Robert of Gloucester then abruptly advises his readers that if they desire a more detailed account of these events and the rest of Richard's time on crusade, they should turn to a different source: "in romance of him imad . me it may finde iwrite."[81] No "romance" about Richard contemporary with Robert's chronicle survives, so it is impossible to know precisely what that romance contained or if it resembles our extant romance about Richard. But, after directing his readers elsewhere if curious, Robert's narrative does not remain with the king abroad. Leaving Richard in the Holy Land, the narrative immediately returns to England, the site of John's "tricherie" in his brother's absence. The reader accompanies John "ouer se" to France, where he harnesses Philip's jealousy in a campaign against Richard, "So þat þe king & he . king richardes lond . / Destruede vaste in normandie . & here in engelond."[82] Within six more lines, Richard and his men in Syria have received "word" of John's betrayal and have undertaken their journey home. During that trip, Richard is captured outside of Vienna.[83] What reads as a disjointed picture of Richard's reign in this, the longer version of Robert of Gloucester's chronicle, signifies in its shorter version, probably written by someone other than Robert, as an efficient and even *de rigueur* treatment of the period:

Richard his sone þat vlke ʒer . was ycrouned king
Þat noble man was after . & hende in alle þing
Ac of his chiualeriʒe . who so wole y wyte
Rede on þe cronikes . þat buþ of him ywrite
Þat haþ maistre huwe . of howedene ywrout

---

81. Robert of Gloucester, *Metrical Chronicle*, vol. 2, line 9987.
82. Robert of Gloucester, *Metrical Chronicle*, vol. 2, lines 9989, 10000–10001.
83. On his capture, see chapter 1.

> Vor al his chiualeriȝe . þer inne is wel ibrout
> Þar fore on þis boke . nis hit nout ywrite
> Ac of his endinge . me schal her inne ywite.[84]

After readers are directed beyond the bounds of the present text to the Latin chronicle of "maistre huwe of howedene" (Roger of Howden), the narrator provides a detailed description of the circumstances of Richard's death and John's ascent.[85] Richard's absence as a crusader was an undeniable characteristic of his reign, but how that absence could be reconciled with the practice of kingship, and, further, could be told in the form of a fully synthesized and forward-moving narrative proved a practical and theoretical problem—a problem that persists on the pages of Christ Church 92.

Following the late thirteenth-century legal narratives in which Richard coincided with individuals' histories and memories, and sometimes with the histories of local communities, Christ Church 92 poses the question of how England should understand Richard's inheritance on a larger scale. It queries how his reign should fit within England's own narration of descent. The line drawings of Christ Church 92 were first identified by Ralph Hanna as glosses of the extant textual answer to that question, the Middle English romance *Richard Coeur de Lion*.[86] There are three moments in Auchinleck's *King Richard*, the copy of the romance most chronologically and geographically proximate to Christ Church 92, that would seem especially familiar to anyone who knows the drawings in Christ Church 92. First, after Richard arrives outside the walls of Acre, he is greeted by the recently arrived French king, Philip, and many other men, including the archbishop of Pisa, who, as a long-suffering member of the crusading party lodged beyond the city walls, informs Richard of the misery they have already experienced. Richard is driven first to sorrow ("King Richard wepe wiþ eȝen boþe")[87] by the archbishop's tale, and then to action. He goes to his forces, commands that a "mangonel," or siege weapon,

---

84. Robert of Gloucester, *Metrical Chronicle*, vol. 2, appendix xx, lines 515–22.
85. Robert of Gloucester, *Metrical Chronicle*, vol. 2, appendix xx, lines 523–58.
86. See Hanna-Rundle, 194; as well as Hanna, *London Literature*, 116–23: "The most proximate source for the depiction would be an English romance on this subject, one which lacks either Anglo-Norman or continental French analogue. This source, *Richard Coer de Lion*, although now mainly excised, was once present in the Auchinleck MS and there, as [G. V.] Smithers points out, in a language consonant with poems associable with London authorship. One may feel reasonably confident about this association of London vernacular romance with Latin royal book because the image fuses at least two separate depictions from the poem" (120). On Auchinleck, see chapter 4.
87. *King Richard*, line 975.

be set up, and then calls for the bees he has apparently (and farsightedly) brought with him on crusade:

> & King Richard i[n] Acres cite
> Lete cast be-hyues gret plente.
> Þe weder was hot i[n] someres tide,
> Þe ben brust out bi ich a side,
> & were atened & ful of grame,
> & dede þe Sarraȝins michel schame.[88]

The use of bees as siege weapons resonates for a reader of Christ Church 92. The image on fol. 74r, which depicts two soldiers manning a four-armed device with each arm holding a ball of fire to be launched across the page, and the image on fol. 76r, which pictures a bowman pulling back on a fiery arrow, could well correspond to the "Greek fire" Richard launches into the sky from his ships as he approaches Acre (Þo king Richard out of his galye / Kast wilde fire into þe sky / & fer Gregeys into þe see").[89] The folio opening that contains the bees is followed on fol. 75v by an image of soldiers attacking a city's wall with mining operations, a common siege tactic that the bees clear the way for in Auchinleck:

> Anoþer gin Richard vp sett,
> Þat was ycleped Robinett;
> A strong gine for þe nones,
> Þat cast into Acres hard stones.
> King Richard þe conquerour
> Cleped on hast his minour
> & bad him mini vp þe tour
> Þat was ycleped Maudit Colour,
> & swore his oþ bi seyn Simoun,
> Bot it were brouȝt adoun
> Ar none, & þe vtmast wal,
> He schuld hewe his bodi smal.
> Þe minours gun to mini fast
> & þe ginours ben & stones cast.
> Þe Sarraȝins þan hem armed al,
> vrn on hast to þe wal.[90]

---

88. *King Richard*, lines 999–1004.
89. *King Richard*, lines 751–53.
90. *King Richard*, lines 1011–26.

Hanna is surely correct that Christ Church 92 and Auchinleck both depict versions of a story about Richard that was in circulation in London in the first half of the fourteenth century. But the paradigm of textual priority, that is, the prioritization of Auchinleck's later text or of any written version of the romance at all, over Christ Church 92's earlier images, prompts us to engage those earlier images as secondary, when the most plausible direct relationship would be the reverse. Christ Church 92's images are our earliest extant evidence of the story's circulation, and Auchinleck's text glosses those images.

If not read through the lens of Auchinleck, both the line drawings and the talk of Richard circulating around them become substantial precisely because of their ephemerality. His absent presence was a rich uncertainty and indeterminacy, generative rather than reductive. In a state between air and that which is solid, multiple Richards could be conjured to reveal and to obscure multiple pasts and therefore to gesture at any future. Standing in Henry III's painted chambers, Richard's image would have signified differently for Edward I in the thirteenth century than for his grandson, Edward III, in the fourteenth. For Edward I, Richard confirmed individual identity, including Edward's own, through inheritance and as a model of the crusader Edward had hoped to be and the conqueror he was, complexly and closer to home in Scotland and Wales. At a further remove genealogically and chronologically from Richard, for a young Edward III, Richard's absence was not to be emulated, but it could be nostalgized. Just visible in the images and barely audible around them is the idea that, where a collective memory of England is concerned, it is precisely the sites of Richard's absence—the start of the Third Crusade nearly consonant with the start of Richard's reign, and the siege of Acre—that could constitute a new narrative beginning for Richard and for the idea of England.

FOUR

The Conversant Codex

IN A LETTER dated October 17, 1802, addressed to the antiquarian George Ellis in London, and dispatched from Abbotsford House, Scotland, Sir Walter Scott recorded his recent discovery:

> There is in the Auchinleck Ms. a fragment of King Richard. It consists only of two leaves & these not continuous: moreover the first page of the three is nearly obliterated. Nevertheless I do not think it the same with the poem you are abridging [from Cambridge, Gonville and Caius College, MS 175/96] & therefore I will endeavor to give you some account of the fragment imperfect as such account must be. There is an illumination prefixed of K. Richard in his Galley with his battle axe in hand rowing on to attack a castle mand by Saracens. The introduction seems so much to your purpose that I have bestowed much India rubber & stale bread to render it legible. It runs thus. . . .[1]

---

1. See Grierson, *Letters*, 12:219–24; Grierson omits Scott's partial transcription of *King Richard*. Scott's letter of October 17, 1802, is now New York, Morgan Library, MA 426.16 (1–3). Scott changes pen after "by Saracens," perhaps indicating that he suspended work on the letter at that juncture and took it up again when he had Auchinleck at hand to transcribe from directly. In addition to Scott's transcription, Grierson also omits Scott's assertion that *King Richard* shares text in common with another of Auchinleck's items, its copy of what we now call the *Anonymous Short English Metrical Chronicle*. As far as I know, Scott was the first to note this connection in writing. On its extant copies and relationship to *King Richard*, see

Walter Scott knew the "Auchinleck Ms.," now Edinburgh, National Library of Scotland, MS Advocates 19.2.1, because it was for him a local book.[2] In 1744, Alexander Boswell, a legal advocate by training and the Lord Auchinleck by birth, donated a cache of nonlegal materials to the Advocates Library, including the fourteenth-century manuscript now called after him.[3] Precisely how the Auchinleck manuscript came to be a local book for collectors and readers such as Boswell and Scott remains an open question. It appears to have been made with an entirely different set of readers in mind.

The Auchinleck manuscript is a demonstrably English book: nearly monolingual in an age of multilingual books, texts, and readers, and, according to internal and external evidence, probably produced in London between 1331 and 1340.[4] Auchinleck contains 334 folios and forty-four items, the majority of which are the earliest or only copies of texts that constitute a significant portion of our Middle English literary corpus.[5] It once contained even more material. Stubs of some leaves remain while other leaves are missing entirely. Quires (many, probably) have been lost,[6] and large squares, now patched, once

---

Ewald Zettl, ed., *An Anonymous Short English Metrical Chronicle*, EETS OS 196 (London: Oxford University Press, 1935), xcv–xcviii; and below, in this chapter.

2. When he wrote to Ellis, Scott was editing Auchinleck's unique copy of *Sir Tristrem* for publication. See Thomas of Ercildoune, *Sir Tristrem, a Metrical Romance*, ed. Sir Walter Scott (Edinburgh: Archibald Constable and Co., 1804), cvii–cxxvii. In his letter to Scott dated October 12, 1802, Ellis refers to Auchinleck's copy of the romance as "Your Sir Tristrem"; see Grierson, *Letters*, 12:221 n. 1.

3. See Pearsall-Cunningham, vii; and Burnley-Wiggins, "History and Owners." On a possible northern provenance, see Ann Higgins, "Sir Tristrem, a Few Fragments, and the Northern Identity of the Auchinleck Manuscript," in Fein, *The Auchinleck Manuscript*, 108–26.

4. On Auchinleck's date, see Turville-Petre, *England the Nation*, 111; and Cooper, "Lancelot," 95. On its provenance and production, see Laura Hibbard Loomis, "The Auchinleck Manuscript and a Possible London Bookshop of 1330–1340," *PMLA* 57 (1942): 595–627; Timothy A. Shonk, "A Study of the Auchinleck Manuscript: Bookmen and Bookmaking in the Early Fourteenth Century," *Speculum* 60 (1985): 71–91; Ralph Hanna, "Reconsidering the Auchinleck Manuscript," in *New Directions in Later Medieval Manuscript Studies: Essays from the 1998 Harvard Conference*, ed. Derek Pearsall (York: York Medieval Press, 2000), 91–102; and Helen Marshall, "What's in a Paraph? A New Methodology and Its Implications for the Auchinleck Manuscript," *Journal of the Early Book Society* 13 (2010): 39–62.

5. On Auchinleck's significance to scholars, see Margaret Connolly and A. S. G. Edwards, "Evidence for the History of the Auchinleck Manuscript," *The Library* 18 (2017): 292. On its earliest and unique copies of texts, see Pearsall-Cunningham, viii.

6. For example, Hanna, "Reconsidering," 92, estimates that more than eighty leaves and fifteen to twenty additional texts have been lost. On Auchinleck's possible losses, see Shonk, "A Study," 71–72; and Pearsall-Cunningham, xii–xiii.

contained illuminated miniatures.[7] Of at least nineteen miniatures once present in the manuscript, four survive. Very little is known of Auchinleck's movements after its production and before 1740,[8] by which time Boswell owned the manuscript, as a dated and signed inscription on one of its flyleaves attests. We can be almost certain that before coming into his possession the manuscript had circulated in Scotland for some time. Pieces of it continued to turn up there well after the book had entered the Advocates' collection. By 1837, David Laing had acquired four leaves—two from Auchinleck's *King Richard* and two from another of the manuscript's romances, *Kyng Alisaunder*—all of which had been covers for the notebooks of a professor at St. Andrews roughly one hundred years earlier. Around the middle of the twentieth century, Neil Ker discovered two more fragments of *Kyng Alisaunder*. Ker, along with G. V. Smithers, subsequently confirmed the identity of another bifolium of Auchinleck's *King Richard,* which had been found by the university librarian of St. Andrews in the binding of an eighteenth-century notebook.[9] The fragments of *King Richard* add seven hundred lines—remarkably, nearly consecutive lines—to what survives in the manuscript proper.

When Scott examined Auchinleck in the first years of the nineteenth century, its forty-third and penultimate item, *King Richard,* or "K. Richard" as he calls it in his letter to Ellis, consisted of fewer than four hundred lines: a single bifolium, fol. 326r–v and 327r–v, constituting the outer leaves of the manuscript's forty-eighth quire. *King Richard* begins perfectly at the top of that bifolium's first recto. All of the nearly consecutive fragments of *King Richard* that were later recovered are from this first quire. The quire itself is now missing probably only one bifolium.[10] Each leaf is bicolumnar and ruled for about forty-four lines, and, as in the rest of the manuscript, *litterae notabiliores* pointed in red begin each line, and red and blue paraphs alternate down the page. The boxy "illumination prefixed" above the first column on

---

7. On Auchinleck's excised miniatures, see Pearsall-Cunningham, xv; and Maidie Hilmo, "The Power of Images in Auchinleck, Vernon, Pearl, and Two *Piers Plowman* Manuscripts," in *Opening Up Middle English Manuscripts: Literary and Visual Approaches,* by Kathryn Kerby-Fulton, Maidie Hilmo, and Linda Olson (Ithaca, NY: Cornell University Press, 2012), 158–65.

8. See Connolly and Edwards, "Evidence," 297–304; and chapter 5.

9. On these fragments' discovery and identification, see Smithers, "Two Newly Discovered Fragments," 1–3. The earliest fragments to have been discovered are Edinburgh, University Library, MS 218 (the "Edinburgh fragments"). The rest are St. Andrews, University Library, MS PR.2065 A.15 and R.4 (the "St. Andrews fragments"). See also Pearsall-Cunningham, vii. Two further folios once belonging to Auchinleck's copy of the romance *Kyng Alisaunder* are now London, University of London Library, MS 593; on these, see Bridges, "Absent Presence," 88–107.

10. This would make it an eight-leaf quire, bringing it into line with all other extant quires in Auchinleck; see the collation diagram in Pearsall-Cunningham, xii–xiii.

fol. 326r and just below the rubricated title "King Richard," written in the text's scribal hand, measures 42 x 68 mm, is outlined in green and red, and is about nine text lines high. Although a full couplet, which declares Richard conqueror of Acre and offers a satisfying conclusion to the narrative, occupies the final two ruled lines of fol. 327vb, the bottom margin contains a hanging catchword, "þe sarraȝins seyȝe þai." These "sarraȝins" are seemingly related to Richard's preceding siege of Acre, provoking speculation among scholars that the catchword evinces significant loss at *King Richard*'s end.[11] In his letter to Ellis, Scott characterizes *King Richard* as a text mostly lost rather than newly found. He begins his description in negative terms, leaving his reader to form a positive picture of what survives by way of what does not. It is a "fragment," "only two leaves . . . not continuous"; "the first page . . . is nearly obliterated." He describes his own transcription of the text's "introduction" (following "It runs thus") as the product of erasure: He "render[ed] it legible" by "India rubber & stale bread." Scott's is perhaps the earliest extant description of Auchinleck's *King Richard*,[12] and although the additional fragments that have since been recovered now constitute a text of 1,046 nearly consecutive lines, our impression and treatment of *King Richard* has not advanced much beyond Scott's construal of it.

Auchinleck's *King Richard* has received little individuated attention from scholars. Following Scott, albeit with multiple intermediaries, Geraldine Heng characterizes Auchinleck's *King Richard* (including its recovered folios) as a "mere fragment,"[13] and argues that the transmission of *Richard Coeur de Lion* constitutes a "collective authoring" over the centuries, a process by which the "fragmentary" story contained in Auchinleck was added to over time:

> Prominently, the consolidation of *RCL* as a literary text spans three centuries of collective authorship, as copyists, redactors, editors, and others cumulatively make its text: This most medieval of romances, whose creation richly exemplifies medieval textual culture and literary production at work, can be read only as a sedimented repository of cultural patterns, investments, and obsessions that were deemed important enough to be inscribed, and reinscribed, over a span of centuries—witnessed through the hands

---

11. Scholars often "complete," either theoretically or actually, *King Richard* with "the rest" of *Richard Coeur de Lion* extant in other manuscript copies or in *Richard Löwenherz*. See, for example, Bliss, "Notes on the Auchinleck Manuscript," 656.

12. An early assessment of Auchinleck and transcription of its copy of *King Richard* appear in Eugen Kölbing, "Vier romanzen-handschriften," *Englische Studien* 7 (1884): 178–91; and Kölbing, "Kleine publicationen," 115–19.

13. Heng, *Empire of Magic*, 333 n. 1.

and intelligences that compiled its dual textual traditions—and not as the inspired autographic production of a single authorial genius, anonymous or attested by signature. Because the text of *RCL is* collectively produced, a reading of *RCL* is thus truly a reading of the sedimented locations of culture—of aggregated cultural markings felt by many to be necessary to lodge—over the long period that produced the distinctive spoor and text of this romance.[14]

Heng's wide-ranging work on *Richard Coeur de Lion* has revitalized scholarship on the romance in the twenty-first century. I quote this part of her argument at length because the scenario of production and survival she posits has greatly influenced recent scholarship on the textual tradition of *Richard Coeur de Lion,* and the transmission of romances more generally. To assess this scenario, it is crucial to note that Heng conflates "*RCL*" and Brunner's edition, *Richard Löwenherz* ("Brunner's edition, henceforth *RCL*"),[15] making it impossible to distinguish between the extant manuscript copies of *Richard Coeur de Lion* and *Richard Löwenherz* in her argument. As chapter 1 of the present book shows, Brunner's edition is neither an exemplary nor a comprehensive embodiment of the textual tradition of *Richard Coeur de Lion*. It is a retrospective text responsive to and shaped by the local talk and cultural memory that circulated in the time and place of its production, fin-de-siècle Vienna. As this chapter and the next demonstrate, my own evidence and arguments for how the extant copies of *Richard Coeur de Lion* were made, read, and should now be studied fundamentally disagree with Heng's model of medieval manuscript culture. My evidence and arguments, grounded in book history, disagree, too, with the assertion that we should, indeed that we can "only," regard *Richard Coeur de Lion* as the product of aggregation, agglomeration, consolidation. As concerns the present discussion, that is, the nature of *King Richard*'s status as fragment, while Heng's model is explicitly progressive, it is implicitly binary. To privilege the aggregated product is to put "fragmentary" and "complete" into opposition, and consequently to dismiss earlier or seemingly partial copies of a textual tradition in favor of later and ostensibly more substantive copies.

This chapter and the next argue that material and narrative fragmentation, modularity, and excision were purposeful and productive tools with which medieval text-makers and readers produced their retrospective texts. In this chapter, I read the surviving 1,046 lines of *King Richard* as a copy relative to

---

14. Heng, *Empire of Magic,* 67.
15. Heng, *Empire of Magic,* 333 n. 1.

its time, place, and manuscript—that is, as a text that can tell us something. This approach runs counter to the usual treatment of *King Richard*. In its specific case, and in manuscript studies more generally, we look to later and longer copies of a textual tradition to show us what earlier and less "complete" copies once contained or were meant to contain. I call this praxis "proleptic reading": We identify a copy's narrative or material loss or damage, and then use later or longer copies to repair, either in theory or on paper, the "imperfect," incomplete," or "fragmentary." Reading proleptically can certainly help us to envision how a text might have been materially and narratively constituted in its extant and lost copies. (Indeed, I sometimes pointedly employ this method in the next chapter to estimate the number of leaves that a given copy may have lost.) But it is also possible that no repairs are needed, or that by moving so quickly to "complete" a text, we fail to comprehend the richness of the copy presently before us. Although much can be gained from proleptic reading, it can produce a loss of meaning relative to a copy's contemporary milieu. By removing that incomplete, imperfect, or fragmented manuscript copy from its local contexts, we neglect the situated exigencies from which, and perhaps because of which, it emerged. Even a fragment has the potential to disclose the intangible daily life that existed around it.

King Richard preserves the ways in which Auchinleck's makers grappled with and responded to talk as a context essential to medieval textual production. Situated in the political and cultural networks of fourteenth-century London, Auchinleck's makers constructed *King Richard* and associated texts in the manuscript from and in response to the local talk and historical rumor in circulation around them. The result is a Richard whose historical and literary parts are indiscernible, whose relevance to Auchinleck's fourteenth-century moment is clear, and who is positioned to do incursive political and cultural work among its readers in that moment. To demonstrate these processes of production and reception, this chapter first lays out the social contexts in which Auchinleck was made and into which it was dispatched in order to consider the ways *King Richard* responds to those contexts. These responses include attempts to overwrite old talk about Richard, to prompt new talk about him and his relationship to England, and to reconstruct the past on the page using talk already in circulation. In Auchinleck, we see how England's text-makers could harness local talk and cultural memory to make meaning. But such meaning-making was, and is, collaborative. Auchinleck's makers, *King Richard* evinces, anticipated knowing readers, conversant in local talk and historical rumor, who would bring their knowledge with them to the manuscript. Given the reader's role in this project, the chapter turns from how *King Richard* and associated texts were made to how they were read. While

Auchinleck's makers used talk in the air as exemplar, its readers used that talk as extratextual gloss. The year 1189 was the *terminus post quem* for individuals' retrospective reconstruction of Richard's reign—a project that threw new fictions about him and the old, intractable facts of his absence into circulation. In *King Richard,* the Third Crusade's siege of Acre is communally reconstructed as the origin of England's narration of descent, and the fragments of talk about Richard together form a new collective inheritance.

Outside of the royal palaces and books of Edward III, talk among the public in fourteenth-century London concerned the sites of Richard's absence: the siege of Acre, and the conquests of Messina and Cyprus that preceded it. Written and unwritten material in circulation evinces an ongoing reckoning with this part of the past. This material includes the "romance of him imad,"[16] which Robert of Gloucester urges his readers to locate if they wish to know more about the siege of Acre, and Robert Mannyng's mention in his Middle English chronicle of what a "romance" in circulation says about Richard's siege machines at Acre.[17] It includes, too, the stories about Messina, Cyprus, and Acre that Edward II's biographer describes circulating in the air, and the story that the line drawings in Christ Church 92 tell, if obliquely.[18] However ubiquitous, these pieces of evidence form an unsettled picture. Unlike the established visual programs of Richard on crusade that could apparently be ordered by name in the thirteenth-century reign of Henry III, no standard visual depiction of Messina, Cyprus, and Acre survives from early fourteenth-century London, and there is no evidence that one was in circulation. Auchinleck's *King Richard* miniature, which depicts Richard aboard ship outside of Acre, for instance, bears no resemblance to the drawings in Christ Church 92 and, like those drawings, has no known visual analogue or precedent. What survives from or is rumored to have once existed in fourteenth-century London indicates that talk about Acre, especially, was occurring, and that the memory of England's late twelfth-century past—the utility and constituent parts of Richard's reign—was in flux.

Cross-reading Christ Church 92's line drawings with Auchinleck's Richard material, including its miniature, makes audible versions of at least one story about Richard circulating in unwritten or written form, or both, in fourteenth-century London. The moment a picture or text is inscribed rarely, if ever, coincides with the moment of inception. I say "Richard material" because in addition to *King Richard,* Auchinleck's fortieth item, a copy of the

---

16. Robert of Gloucester, *Metrical Chronicle*, vol. 2, line 9987; and see chapter 3.
17. Robert Mannyng, *The Chronicle*, pt. 2, line 3870.
18. See chapter 3.

so-called *Anonymous Short English Metrical Chronicle* (*Short Chronicle*), contains over one hundred unique lines on Richard's reign.[19] The two texts in Auchinleck are related but distinct. They share phrases, lines, and scenes at certain points,[20] but the *Short Chronicle*'s material is necessarily briefer, and offers a fundamentally different description of events. After *King Richard*'s introductory lines, both texts begin by ascribing Jerusalem's fall to French treachery. Richard then makes preparations for crusade and sets sail for the East; both texts exploit the contemporaneously documented discord between Richard and the French king, Philip Augustus, as the English and the French travel together.[21] *King Richard* defers Richard's arrival at Acre. It details his conquering of Messina, Cyprus, and an encounter with a dromond; includes the archbishop of Pisa's long account to Richard of the hardships crusaders have suffered outside Acre's walls; and concludes with Richard's strangely spectacular arrival at Acre and its siege. During that siege, Richard slings loaded beehives over the city's wall. The *Short Chronicle* proceeds straight from England to the waters beyond Acre. There, from his ship, Richard constructs a tower on which he situates a "mangonel" to launch beehives.[22] Victorious, the French and English armies proceed to Jerusalem's outskirts, where a quarrel over credit for the crusade's (limited) success occurs between Richard and Philip. Richard returns to England.

From the images in Christ Church 92, as well as the text of Auchinleck's Richard material and the single miniature associable with it, we can discern that at least three different versions of the bee-casting episode were in circulation.[23] The drawing in Christ Church 92 of a windmill flinging beehives resembles scenes in both *King Richard* and the *Short Chronicle*, but does not replicate them exactly.[24] Auchinleck's *King Richard* and *Short Chronicle* tell of the English launching beehives into Acre with "mangonels." *King Richard* never mentions a windmill. The *Short Chronicle* does include mills among

---

19. Unless otherwise specified, all subsequent citations of Auchinleck's *Short Chronicle* refer to Burnley-Wiggins: *Short Chronicle*, lines 2038–2188, for Richard's reign. Unique material from each of the text's seven manuscripts is appended in Zettl, *Short Chronicle*, 46–91.

20. Zettl, *Short Chronicle*, xcvi, offers a side-by-side comparison of the bee episodes.

21. On Philip's propaganda campaign, see *Richard I*, 222–53.

22. On the bees as English signifiers, see Heng, *Empire of Magic*, 102.

23. Several other sources evince the windmill story's circulation in written or unwritten form, possibly but not necessarily, contextualized within a longer story. Mannyng's chronicle, written before 1338, includes in its description of Richard's entrance into Acre "blak & blo" and "rede & grene" "sailes" (pt. 2, lines 4303–05). As Hanna notes in *London Literature* (144 n. 22), windmills are present in Dante's *Inferno*. In his late thirteenth-century chronicle, Langtoft, *Chronicle*, 79–81, describes stone-casting "mills to be raised in barges and galleys" (*En barges et galayes fet lever molyns*) at Richard's direction outside of Acre.

24. Hanna, *London Literature*, posits that in this image, Christ Church 92's Artist 1 "fuses at least two separate depictions from the poem" (120).

Richard's odd weaponry, though how precisely they qualify there as weaponry remains unclear. They are, the *Short Chronicle* tells us, "a queynter þing" of Richard's own making: "Windemilles in schippes houend on water / Sailed about wiþ brenand tapre, / Honged wiþ vice made wel queynt." Their sails are tinted red, yellow, and green—"Wel griseliche þing ariȝt to sen."[25] Either another unattested version of the episode was in circulation—a version that construed the windmill as a weapon or catapult—or in his line drawings at the back of Christ Church 92, Artist 1 sketched a new version of what he had heard or read.[26] This episode, in its various forms, did not necessarily circulate within a longer account. Its presence in Christ Church 92 shows that it can be extricated from a text. It is impossible to know whether the "romance" of Richard to which Robert of Gloucester refers at the turn of the fourteenth century contained versions of the talk in the air now preserved in Christ Church 92's line drawings and in Auchinleck's Richard material. The "romance" Robert knew almost certainly included, or perhaps even began with, the siege of Acre. His external reference intervenes in his narrative at the precise moment the siege would have begun, but that romance's account of the siege may have been significantly different from what survives.

The proliferation of varying written and unwritten accounts of Richard at Messina, Cyprus, and especially Acre—a proliferation that predates Auchinleck—is expressly addressed in its *King Richard*. The first lines of Auchinleck's *King Richard* speak of a lack of memorial fixedness and its ramifications, and of the spreading of false rumor:

Lord Ihesu, kyng of glorie,
Swiche auentour & swiche victorie
Þou sentest king Richard,
Miri it is to heren his stori
& of him to han in memorie
Þat neuer no was couward.[27]

---

25. *Short Chronicle*, lines 2109–14.

26. If the images commissioned for walls, tiles, and books tell us that Richard was a subject of reflection and talk in royal households, then they tell us, too, that the same subject was discussed and considered among a very different group of people. Those employed to make such images no doubt talked about the late twelfth-century past in the course of their work depicting it. If they also made decisions about how that past was portrayed, then they played an important role in the development of the common knowledge about that past. How much agency over image and design any single artist in London had is an unsettled question. For a recent discussion of the possible contact among artists and instructions to illuminators working on English manuscripts in later medieval London, see Sonja Drimmer, *The Art of Allusion: Illuminators and the Making of English Literature, 1403–1476* (Philadelphia: University of Pennsylvania Press, 2019), 21–37.

27. *King Richard*, lines 1–6.

These lines—the first six of a twenty-four-line tail-rhyme prologue unique to *King Richard*—seemingly respond to a textual context that includes written and unwritten discourse, and exhibit more concern with what people are saying about Richard than with Richard himself. The lines describe a transmission process in which texts play no explicit part. They focus instead on "hearing" and "remembering" the "stori" of Richard. Spoken word and memory, unstable archives both, are thus prominent. If the source of the hearing is a text read aloud, we are not shown its part in the process. The absence of the language in which the "stori" is told and heard—especially in a prologue that, like several other romance prologues in Auchinleck, will momentarily be preoccupied with multilingualism and its opposite—leaves the reader to imagine a multiplicity of dialects and languages. This initial presentation of a malleable, fleet-footed, and variously unfixed "stori" about Richard is the enabling premise for the existence of *King Richard* itself: the codification of Richard's "story" and "memory" in Auchinleck. In *King Richard,* then, some rumors can be silenced: Richard "neuer was no couward." This contention registers as an oddly defensive non sequitur for which there are at least two possible explanations. Either this line anticipates some defect the reader will find in Richard's story, or it rebuffs charges of cowardliness or foolishness lodged against Richard elsewhere, perhaps in circulation outside of the manuscript.

King Richard models what a retrospective romance does, indeed what any retrospective text, can do: reconstruct the past on the page. Like litigants in the thirteenth-century eyre courts, the makers of *King Richard* are engaged here in a project of retrospective inheritance, making specific decisions about how Richard should be reconstructed, and to what end. The romance's opening lines frame all that follows as at once old and new, as the late twelfth-century truth being heard for the first time. While in codicological terms *King Richard* begins "perfectly," that perfect beginning preserves an instance of historical fragmentation. The romance's reconstruction of the late twelfth-century king commences not with his birth, but with his birth as a crusader. This choice of narrative beginning requires all readers of *King Richard* to remember certain parts of the past and to forget others. In turn, this selective retrospection requires us to ask what new cultural memory was being made by the manuscript among its fourteenth-century readers.[28] Auchin-

---

28. There were earlier and probably less desirable signal moments in Richard's reign. During Richard's coronation festivities in London, Jews attempting to bring the king gifts were murdered by crusaders, an event that sparked massacres of Jewish communities across England, and culminated with the horrific massacre at York in 1190. By then—conveniently or dispassionately—Richard had already sailed. See, for example, *Richard* I, 104–5; and Richard of Devizes, *Chronicle,* 3–4, for a notable contemporary account.

leck's Richard material is in the hand of the manuscript's "Scribe 1," who was responsible for over seventy percent of Auchinleck's contents and who was, at least, the manuscript's editor and, at most, something closer to an author—a hypothesis supported by the unique, earliest, and expanded Richard material he inscribes.[29] In Scribe 1's hand, Richard is reconstructed as a romance hero if not for all time, then certainly for the present moment.

Auchinleck was made in, and *King Richard* dispatched into, political and social tumult, partially preserved for us in the local talk and retrospective texts of early fourteenth-century London. Auchinleck was made and initially read in an England recovering from internal conflicts and anticipating, and then fighting, a war with France. Civil strife needed to be either genuinely repaired or temporarily forgotten. The coup by which Edward III came to power and the regicide of his father that followed closely behind it would have still been fresh in the public's mind. Only sixty years earlier, England had been in the midst of its most recent civil war, after "the Anarchy" in the first half of the twelfth century and the First Barons' War, which occurred between 1215 and 1217 as a result of John's resistance to Magna Carta.[30] The Second Barons' War, likewise fought over the resistance of England's king, Henry III, to the provisions of Magna Carta, lasted from 1264 to 1267.[31] How that most recent war should be remembered was the subject of popular debate long after the rebel leader Simon de Montfort's death at the Battle of Evesham in 1265 and the declaration of terms for the rebel barons' reabsorption into society at Kenilworth Castle in 1266.[32] A cold war of popular songs, texts, and debates outstripped the physical battle and its immediate aftermath.

On one side, surviving pro-baronial songs, poems, and liturgies continued to be transmitted into Auchinleck's fourteenth-century milieu,[33] some-

---

29. On Scribe 1's role in general, see Hanna, "Reconsidering," 93–94; Shonk, "A Study," 72–74; and Hanna, *London Literature,* 104–5. Zettl, *Short Chronicle,* xcv–xcvii, hypothesizes that material in the *Short Chronicle* was "borrowed" from *King Richard.* Other theories have been advanced recently, including by Fisher, *Scribal Authorship,* 158–67, who posits that Scribe 1 had multiple exemplars of *King Richard* to hand. Smithers, *Kyng Alisaunder,* 2:41, suggests, though without specific evidence, common (not scribal) authorship for several of Auchinleck's texts.

30. Holt, *Magna Carta,* 188–266.

31. On the prince Edward's wartime conduct, see, for example, Powicke, *Thirteenth Century,* 186–90; and chapter 2.

32. Knowles, "Resettlement," 26–27. Over three hundred rebels were affected by formal disherison between the time of Simon de Montfort's death at Evesham in 1265 and the promulgation of the Dictum of Kenilworth on October 31 of the following year; these are the recorded numbers only.

33. "The Song Against the King of Almaigne," a Middle English "political song" dated to the Second Barons' War, continued to circulate well into the fourteenth century, when it

times despite the Crown's express injunctions.[34] On the other, extant chronicle accounts preserve local memories of "the many evils done in the burning of [the property of] the rich and the spoliation of the poor."[35] Scholarly opinion is split on the rapidity with which equilibrium returned.[36] The rebels, most of whom had been stripped of their lands and needed money to regain them, accounted for a large percentage of all barons, making their rehabilitation essential, ongoing, and public.[37] After a former rebel had gained a right of seisin, the most common mode of payment was by installment in person at, for instance, New Temple, London; once seised, a baron could raise funds however he wished, from selling wood on his estate to borrowing money from Jewish lenders. Many of those accused of rebellion who contested the charge did so immediately in the eyre courts. But in the late thirteenth-century eyre courts of Edward I, justices were still being reminded that offences in wartime and peacetime should be distinguished, and the restitutive provisions of Kenilworth applied where appropriate.[38] While the Second Barons' War and its aftermath were within living memory or just beyond it for most, if not all, of Auchinleck's readers and makers, the present and near future held the

---

was copied into the multilingual miscellany London, British Library, MS Harley 2253. Harley 2253 was produced probably only shortly before or roughly contemporaneously with Auchinleck, and its "Song Against the King of Almaigne," as well as the Latin "Battle of Lewes," which survives in London, British Library, MS Harley 978, are two of the most famous examples of pro-baronial political songs contemporary with the Second Barons' War. They, along with the Anglo-Norman lament for Simon de Montfort also in Harley 2253, are included in Coss, *Political Songs*, 69, 72, and 125, respectively. On Harley 2253, see, for example, Susanna Fein, ed., *The Complete Harley 2253 Manuscript in Three Volumes*, with trans. and collaboration of David Raybin and Jan Ziolkowski (Kalamazoo, MI: Medieval Institute Publications, 2014–2015). On "The Song against the King of Almaigne," see also chapter 5.

34. See Powicke, *Thirteenth Century*, 174–77; and Maddicott, *Simon de Montfort*, 347, 367–68. After the death and subsequent dismemberment of Simon de Montfort, he became the focus of local cults throughout England and the hero of pro-baronial political songs.

35. Maddicott, *Simon de Montfort*, 347–48, where he quotes from the *Annales de rebus praecipue Anglicis*, preserved in London, British Library, MS Cotton Faustina B.vi, fol. 75.

36. For example, Knowles, "Resettlement," 25, but see Sutherland, *Quo Warranto*, 145. During the war, the barons figuratively divided England, and after they capitulated, Henry III divided it literally through the official and unofficial usurpation of baronial lands, the division of their estates, and the redistribution of all of it among his loyalists. The dislocation and despair such widespread disherison wrought was assuaged, partially and slowly, by the terms of Kenilworth: namely, that rebel barons could buy back their lands.

37. See Knowles, "Resettlement," 31–33.

38. I. J. Sanders and R. F. Treharne, ed. *Documents of the Baronial Movement of Reform and Rebellion, 1258–1267* (Oxford: Clarendon Press, 1973), 319–33, esp. 325; Maddicott, *Simon de Montfort*, 365. On Kenilworth's immediate and lasting effects, see chapter 2, and, for example, Powicke, *Thirteenth Century*, 210: "It arrested, and so far as was possible dissolved the effects of, a social revolution."

Hundred Years' War between England and France. Long in coming, its official beginning arrived in 1337, during the period of Auchinleck's production.[39]

A statute issued by Edward III in 1340, and thus roughly concurrent with perhaps the last year(s) of Auchinleck's production, sheds further light on the milieu of talk and text into which the manuscript emerged. In the third statute of the fourteenth year of his reign, Edward III promises his people that they will never be made subject to the king of England in his (anticipated) capacity as king of France.[40] The statute clarifies that this declaration does not preempt, but rather responds to the public murmuring: "Know Ye, That whereas some People do think . . ." it begins. It then repeats and attempts to quiet the rumor that if Edward were to be recognized as the heir to France, England would be put "in subjection of the King and of the Realm of France in time to come."[41] Edward may have felt in April 1340, when the statute was issued, that he needed to manage this talk. It is a decision that conveys, if not how concerned England's public was about England and France, then at least how talkative people were on the subject.

Auchinleck's *King Richard* responds directly to this multifaceted context: the recent past, the no less tumultuous present, and that which was being remembered, written down, and said about both. The war with France becomes, in the fifteen lines at the prologue's heart, a war of culture and identity in which the old "Freyns" knights of "romaunce" are simultaneously dead and canonized:

Romaunce make folk of Fraunce
Of kniȝtes þat were in destaunce
Þat dyed þurth dint of sward:
Of Roland & of Oliuer
& of þe oþer dusseper
Of Alisander & Charlmeyn
& Ector þe gret werrer
& of Danys le fiz Oger,
Of Arthour & of Gaweyn.
As þis romaunce of Frenys wrouȝt,
Þat mani lewed no knowe noȝt,

---

39. On the possibility that the manuscript remained disbound for some time, see Hanna, "Reconsidering," 91–92; Connolly and Edwards, "Evidence," 299–304; and chapter 5.

40. *Statutes of the Realm*, 1:292. A variant copy noted by the *Statutes* editors dates the statute to April 16.

41. *Statutes of the Realm*, 1:292: "Sachietz q̄ come ascuns gentz entendont . . . en subjeccion du Roi & du Roialme de France, en temps avenir."

In gest as-so we seyn;
Þis lewed no can Freyns non;
Among an hundred vnneþe on,
In lede is nouȝt to leyn.⁴²

The intensifying opposition between England and France comes to complete, if seemingly simple fruition in these lines.⁴³ Englishness is evoked as capacious in its absence, while Frenchness is carefully circumscribed. "French" means here both a language and a "folk," distinct from, or perhaps encompassing, Anglo-Norman.⁴⁴ This Frenchness is rejected by (English)men, whose own "lewedness" renders them simultaneously insurgent and bookishly demanding. Their linguistic inability to access "French" texts most immediately precipitates the call for new and better English ones, as the prologue continues:

Noþeles, wiþ gode chere
Fele of hem wald yhere
Noble gestes, ich vnderstond,
Of douȝti kniȝtes of Inglond.
Þerfore now ichil ȝou rede
Of a king douhti of dede,
King Richard, þe werrour best
Þat men findeþ in ani gest.⁴⁵

The impulse to inscribe English romances and English heroes in response to the inexact declaration that "Romaunce make folk of Fraunce" troubles the carefully policed boundary between Englishness and Frenchness the prologue has constructed. French folk make romances, but their collective identity has been, the line implies, reciprocally made or informed by these same romances. The recognition of this fact by the prologue's "I" compels him to tell his

---

42. *King Richard,* lines 10–24.
43. The prologue has been variously interpreted as speaking to a monolingual audience, registering a shift in the hierarchy of languages, and presaging the literal and ideological beating the French take from the English within *King Richard.* See Carole M. Meale, *Readings in Middle English Romance* (Cambridge: Cambridge University Press, 1994), 114–15; Rhiannon Purdie, *Anglicising Romance: Tail-Rhyme and Genre in Medieval English Literature* (Cambridge: D. S. Brewer, 2008), 100–101; and Salter, *Fourteenth-Century English Poetry,* 27–28.
44. The project of differentiating "English" from Anglo-Norman identity was underway in England from the mid-twelfth century; see John Gillingham, "Foundations of a Disunited Kingdom," in *Uniting the Kingdom? The Making of British History,* ed. Alexander Grant and Keith J. Stringer (London: Routledge, 1995), 54.
45. *King Richard,* lines 25–32.

audience, either by reading aloud or by recounting,[46] a similarly generative English romance about an English knight and king—a romance that aims to replace rather than reside among those old "French" romances it emulates.

It is precisely this productive and locally driven tension between displacing Frenchness and harnessing its cultural production that characterizes *King Richard* in the Auchinleck manuscript. Even as we are told about the "kniȝtes þat were in destaunce / Þat dyed þurth dint of sward," they are resurrected by name: Roland and Oliver, the Twelve Peers; Charlemagne, Ogier le Danois, Arthur and Gawain. The seemingly counterintuitive proliferation of French heroes and French genres triggers the memory of its readers. That the prologue anticipates its readers already know Charlemagne, Roland, and the other heroes of *chanson de geste* is clear. Despite the rhetorical construction of long-suffered inaccessibility to un-English things, one does not get the sense that these French stories and characters are anything but well worn. The reader is already thinking, then, about the matter of France broadly construed, and about *chanson de geste* specifically, when told that the material about King Richard can be found "in ani gest." This claim is more rooted in the truth than has previously been realized. On the brink of war with France and with a civil war within living memory, the makers of *King Richard* harnessed the old, familiar French network of talk and text. And with it, they reconstructed "the time of King Richard," making the late twelfth-century past not only relevant to the present moment, but able to intervene in it.

Auchinleck's *King Richard* does not derive from a single lost Anglo-Norman source about Richard, as has long been rumored.[47] Rather, behind Auchinleck's Richard material is a network of stories about Charlemagne and Roland that had been circulating in England since at least the second quarter of the twelfth century, when the earliest extant copy of the Anglo-Norman *Chanson de Roland* was written down in Oxford, Bodleian Library, MS Digby 23.[48] Dispersed throughout Scribe 1's work in Auchinleck's *King Richard* and *Short Chronicle* are narrative and verbatim echoes of Charlemagne material popular in medieval England. That material survives now in a surprising place: the Old Norse *Karlamagnús saga* (*Klm*),[49] a ten-branch prose cycle

---

46. *MED*, "rede" (v. (1)), 2a and 5a.

47. In twentieth- and twenty-first-century scholarship, the most oft-cited source of this claim is L. H. Loomis, *Medieval Romance*, 147.

48. Unless otherwise noted, subsequent citations to *La Chanson de Roland* refer to Ian Short's edition of Oxford, Bodleian Library, MS Digby 23 ("Oxford Version"), contained in volume 1 of Joseph J. Duggan et al., eds., *La Chanson de Roland; The Song of Roland: The French Corpus*, 3 vols. (Turnhout: Brepols, 2005). For Short's date of the copying of *Roland* into Digby 23, see 1:19–20.

49. This abbreviation is given in *ONP*.

compiled and translated largely from Anglo-Norman *chansons de geste* about Charlemagne, Roland, and other "kni3tes" named in Auchinleck's unique prologue to *King Richard*.[50]

The exemplars that facilitated the extensive *Klm* project were almost certainly among the texts that Hákon Hákonarson IV, Norway's king from 1217 to 1263 and an Anglophile, solicited from Britain. He admired the court of Henry III as a model of courtesy, cultivated an expertise in the material culture of England and France, and engaged in a selective book trade, demanding copies of verse texts that were in fashion at the beginning of the thirteenth century in England or France.[51] Those texts, whose surviving Norse copies confirm their popularity in thirteenth-century England, include the *Roman de Tristan* of Thomas d'Angleterre; works of Chrétien de Troyes such as *Érec et Enide*, *Yvain*, and *Perceval*; a collection of Breton lais attributed to Marie de France; *Floire et Blancheflour*; and *Beuve de Hantone*.[52] The Charlemagne material, in Anglo-Norman and Latin exemplars, most likely came to Norse and Icelandic scribes from Britain independently. Those exemplars, including a *Vie de Charlemagne*; a *chanson de geste* resembling the *Chevalerie Ogier de*

---

50. Although exemplars are sometimes referred to as occurring in "Old French," internal manuscript evidence supports specifically Anglo-Norman sources behind most branches. On this issue, see, for instance, Povl Skårup, "Contenu, sources, rédactions," in *Karlamagnús saga: Branches I, III, VII, et IX*, ed. Knud Togeby et al. (Copenhagen: La Société pour l'étude de la langue et de la littérature danoises, 1980), 334; Henry Goddard Leach, *Angevin Britain and Scandinavia* (Cambridge, MA: Harvard University Press, 1921), 248; and Constance B. Hieatt, trans., *Karlamagnús saga: The Saga of Charlemagne and His Heroes*, 3 vols. (Toronto: The Pontifical Institute of Medieval Studies, 1975), 1:23. My work on the Oxford *Roland* and *Klm* is deeply indebted to the scholarship and intellectual generosity of Joseph J. Duggan.

51. Daniel W. Lacroix, trans. *La Saga de Charlemagne: Traduction française des dix branches de la Karlamagnús saga norroise* (Paris: Librairie générale française, 2000), 9. There is a critical consensus around Hákon's involvement in the Norse acquisition of the Charlemagne material, and thus a consensus around the dating of its earliest circulation in Norway and Iceland; see *Saga*, 9–10. Internal evidence for this dating relies heavily on the Norse translation's formal style ("translator's prose") common prior to c. 1300. After the turn of the fourteenth century, a more otiose style ("court prose") became popular; see E. F. Halvorsen, *The Norse Version of the Chanson de Roland* (Copenhagen: Ejnar Munksgaard, 1959), 75. Peter Foote has argued that translations from Latin sources conveyed to Scandinavia from England may have been made in Iceland as early as 1190 to 1220; see Foote, *The Pseudo-Turpin Chronicle in Iceland: A Contribution to the Study of the Karlamagnús saga* (London: London Medieval Studies, 1959), 47.

52. See Lacroix, *Saga*, 9–10, for additional examples; see also Leach, *Angevin Britain*, 152. These and other works are well known to us in Old French and Middle English, in their continental and insular manuscript contexts, including Auchinleck, which contains English translations of the *Lay le Freine*, *Sir Tristrem*, *Floris and Blancheflour*, and *Bevis of Hampton*, as well as Arthurian material.

Danemarche; the *Chanson d'Aspremont*; a version of the *Pseudo-Turpin*; a *chanson de geste* about Charlemagne's war with the Saxons; a *Chanson d'Otinel*; the *Pèlerinage de Charlemagne*; *La Chanson de Roland*; and a *Moinage Guillaume*, were then translated and compiled before 1300 into something resembling a unified prose cycle.[53] After the turn of the fourteenth century, *Klm* was continuously revised to include newly acquired stories about Charlemagne.[54]

No definitively "complete" copy of *Klm* survives,[55] though extant manuscripts and records of now lost copies attest to its long textual tradition. Besides early fragments, including the Norse *Roland* dated to the second half

---

53. Halvorsen, *Norse Version*, 64–66, constructs a list that largely reflects the critical consensus on sources. On the Latin *Pseudo-Turpin* and the *Pèlerinage de Charlemagne*, see Annalee C. Rejhon, *Cân Rolant: The Medieval Welsh Version of the Song of Roland* (Berkeley: University of California Press, 1984), esp. 71–72. The *Pseudo-Turpin* and *Pèlerinage* were probably circulating in Scandinavia during the reign of Hákon's predecessor, Inge II. The number of scribes and translators at work on the project remains an open question, but for a summary of arguments and possibilities, see Skårup, "Contenu," 334–35.

54. On the transmission of Charlemagne texts, see Rejhon, *Cân Rolant*, 68–74. Rejhon's insightful work on the Welsh Charlemagne materials offers a useful parallel for the Norse *Klm*. See also Sif Rikhardsdottir, *Medieval Translations and Cultural Discourse: The Movement of Texts in England, France, and Scandinavia* (Cambridge: D. S. Brewer, 2012), 53–75.

55. Since C. R. Unger's first edition of *Klm* in the late nineteenth century, several additional early fragments have been recovered. Nevertheless, Unger's manuscript sigla, provided below, remain standard; see Unger, ed., *Karlamagnús saga ok Kappa Hans* (Christiana: H. J. Jensen, 1860), xl. Some scholars put the manuscript total at four, but following the recent work of Lacroix, I include Copenhagen, University of Copenhagen, AM, MS 180e fol. The manuscripts have been divided into two recensions: The "alpha" group is considered most representative of an original Norse Charlemagne cycle, while the "beta" group is thought to be a later revision because it features a significant amount of material not in the alpha manuscripts, and shows evidence of attempts to correct contradictions and repetitions that occur among branches in the alpha manuscripts; see Agnete Loth, "Les manuscrits norrois," in Togeby et al., *Karlamagnús saga*, 358–59. The five extant manuscripts are now (a) Copenhagen, University of Copenhagen, MS AM 180a fol., dated to *c.* 1450–1500; (A) MS AM 180c fol., *c.* 1400; (B) MS AM 180d fol^x, *c.* 1700 (a scholarly reproduction of an Icelandic manuscript dated to the fourteenth century on the basis of spelling and word forms); (b^1) MS AM 531, *c.* 1700 (a copy of a now lost medieval manuscript thought to have been copied from the same exemplar as MS AM 180d fol); (b^2) MS AM 180e fol., *c.* 1700 (a copy of a medieval manuscript, now lost, that contained a translation into Icelandic of portions of the Danish *Karl Magnus Krønike*). There are also five fragments, each significantly earlier than the extant manuscripts: Oslo, Norsk Riksarkivet, MS 61, in verse and dated to *c.* 1250, contains material from branch viii and was probably copied in Iceland; Oslo, Norsk Riksarkivet, MS 62, dated to the first half of the fourteenth century, localized to Iceland, and containing passages from branches iv, vi, and vii; Oslo, Norsk Riksarkivet, MS 63, from an Icelandic manuscript dated to the second half of the fourteenth century, and containing portions of branch vii. The final two fragments include one dated to the fourteenth century, and another not published as yet. See Halvorsen, *Norse Version*, 32–36, as well as Lacroix, *Saga*, 19–21. For a convenient publication history of *Klm* up to 1980, see Skårup, "Contentu," 334.

of the thirteenth century,[56] *Klm* comes down to us in a stream of manuscript copies behind which are the rumors of more copies: fourteenth-century manuscripts thought to exemplify their thirteenth-century predecessors, and seventeenth-century diplomatic reproductions of fourteenth- and fifteenth-century manuscripts destroyed in the Copenhagen Castle fire of 1728. Inventories and library records dating from the medieval period through the eighteenth century suggest that there was once much more. Prior to 1728, the book collector Árni Magnússon possessed at least five copies. In his records, Magnússon refers to one of the completely destroyed manuscripts as "the old codex," suggesting that if it had survived, it would have been older than any *Klm* fragment or manuscript we now have.[57] Norse and Icelandic manuscript exemplars that appear to lay behind surviving Swedish and Danish copies of *Klm* have also been lost.[58]

The Charlemagne material in *Klm* that is associable with Auchinleck's Richard material occurs in two places in the Norse saga. The first is branch i, the "Life of Charlemagne," which consists of an abridged life thought to be the oldest material extant in *Klm*. It includes a brief account of Charlemagne's war against the Saxons.[59] The second is branch v, or "Guitaclin the Saxon," a fifty-five-chapter account of Charlemagne's Saxon war, derived from a different source than branch i.[60] That two distinct versions of Charlemagne's

---

56. See Halvorsen, *Norse Version*, 34. The fragment consists of two leaves—the upper half of one and the lower half of another—probably from the middle of a gathering. Although written in inner-southwest Norwegian, the fragment contains two Icelandic forms, indicating an Icelandic translator.

57. For Magnússon's inventory and the monastic library records, see Halvorsen, *Norse Version*, 32–41 *passim*; and Hieatt, *Karlamagnús saga*, 1:20–23. On Magnússon's book collecting, see Sigurgeir Steingrímsson, "Árni Magnússon," in *The Manuscripts of Iceland*, ed. Gísli Sigurðsson and Vésteinn Ólason (Reykjavík: Árni Magnússon Institute in Iceland, 2004), 85–99.

58. See Skårup, "Contenu," 335. A Swedish translation of *Klm* also survives in four fifteenth-century manuscripts, and the Danish *Karl Magnus Krønike* survives in one manuscript dated to 1480, as well as in multiple sixteenth-century printed editions that are not based on the extant Danish manuscript; see also Halvorsen, *Norse Version*, 37.

59. Lacroix, *Saga*, 13–14. Paul Aebischer first argued that before it was added to *Klm* in the thirteenth century, the material that survives as branch i was in circulation around 1200 as a complete (and now lost) Anglo-Norman life of Charlemagne. Further, branch i then made its way to Norway, where it was translated, circulated, and, around 1250, abridged and folded into *Klm*. See Paul Aebischer, *Préhistoire et protohistoire du Roland d'Oxford* (Bern: Francke, 1972), 162–80. On Aebischer's influential work, see Ian Short and Maureen Thomas, "Karlamagnús and the Pre-History of the *Roland*," *Romance Philology* 30 (1976): 210–16. On the transmission and critical history of branch i, see also Lacroix, *Saga*, 36–38.

60. See Lacroix, *Saga*, 520–21. The Saxon war appears in both branch i and branch v of the "A" manuscript, thought to be the closest to the "original" thirteenth-century compila-

Saxon war survive in *Klm* attests to the suspected piecemeal compilation of the Norse saga, and to the war story's wider circulation in England before it reached—in multiple copies, iterations, and instances—the North. As further confirmation of the Saxon war story's ubiquity, it also has a continental relative in the late twelfth-century *Chanson des Saisnes* ascribed to Jean Bodel.[61] However, the contents of branch v, where Roland plays a crucial role, much more closely reflect Auchinleck's Richard material than does Bodel's work. In Bodel's version, the war occurs after Roncevaux, excluding Roland from the narrative. Moreover, branch v preserves traces of a specifically English provenance, including an early reference to Roland's horn Oliphant and the Norse translator's fragmentary comments about his Anglo-Norman source.[62]

The episodes in which Charlemagne's words, actions, and ingenuity are most obviously translated to Auchinleck's Richard constitute a set piece in both *King Richard* and the *Short Chronicle*, as well as in all later extant copies of *Richard Coeur de Lion*: Richard's strange and spectacular siege of Acre. In the *Short Chronicle*, Richard ascends the throne and immediately begins preparations for his journey to Acre, charging ships and then building on his own ship a castle with high towers from which the English can spy on their enemies.[63] This scene closely recalls Charlemagne's preparations for war in branch v of *Klm*. There, Charlemagne and his men build a great ship, on which they mount castles with towers, to cross the Rhine. They also fit the ship with a statue of Charlemagne, made and dressed in his likeness, but hollow, so that a man can stand inside and grasp and shake the statue's beard: an ingenious

---

tion. When branch v appears in other manuscripts, it does so alone, suggesting that *Klm* redactors omitted the repetitive Saxon war material of branch i.

61. Jean Bodel, *La Chanson des Saisnes*, ed. Annette Brasseur, 2 vols. (Geneva: Droz, 1989), 1:ix–x. Bodel's work has also been translated into modern French: Annette Brasseur, ed. and trans., *La Chanson des Saxons* (Paris: Librairie Honoré Champion, 1992). Paris, Bibliothèque de l'Arsenal, MS 3142, a deluxe codex from around 1285, is the earliest of the four manuscripts in which the text survives; see Bodel, *La Chanson*, 1:x–xi. That Bodel's *Chanson des Saisnes* and the Anglo-Norman text behind branch v share a common source has been widely accepted: See Halvorsen, *Norse Version*, 55; Hieatt, *Karlamagnús saga*, 3:6, Skårup, "Contenu," 336. Leach, *Angevin Britain*, 248, disagrees, claiming that branch v derives from an account of Charlemagne's war with the Saxons predating Bodel. As Lacroix, *Saga*, 521, rightly points out, while the material in *Klm* and Bodel's work are "proximate" or "close," no absolute proof of a common source exists.

62. On the Anglo-Norman French unique to manuscript A's text of branch v (in chapters fourteen and twenty-seven), and used to date the material's arrival in Norway to the thirteenth century, see Paul Aebischer, *Des annals carolingiennes à Doon de Mayence: nouveau recueil d'études sur l'épique française médiévale* (Geneva: Droz, 1975), 227; Hieatt, *Karlamagnús saga*, 3:8–12; and Lacroix, *Saga*, 522. The second textual remnant that points to an Anglo-Norman source also carries traces of its exemplar's assonance.

63. *Short Chronicle*, lines 2051–54.

"trick" (*Autre astuce de fabrication*).⁶⁴ The French place the statue on one of the ship's towers and turn it toward the Saxons. The man inside yells insults and the Saxons assail the statue with stones and other objects, but nothing harms what appears to them to be Charlemagne. Distressed and afraid, the Saxons discuss the situation and then cry out to one another that this "is not a man, but a devil whom weapons will not bite" (*Les païens dirent alors: "Ce n'est pas un homme, mais un diable sur lequel les armes ne mordent pas"*).⁶⁵

After Richard similarly constructs his castle aboard ship, fitting it with a stone-throwing windmill, the *Short Chronicle* specifies that the view from this castle affords Richard the opportunity to "seye in priuete / What Sarraȝines dede in þe cite."⁶⁶ Richard and his men then "make a queynter þing / Windemilles in schippes houend on water" that were "Wel griseliche þing ariȝt to sen." Then:

> Þe Sarraȝines seye þat mervaile,
> Þai no durst abide to ȝif batayle.
> Þai seyden hem ichon among,
> "Lordinges, to dyen it wer strong,
> For þis is þe deuel of helle
> Þat wil ous euerichon aquelle."⁶⁷

Like Charlemagne, Richard's enemies perceive him to be "no man, but a devil," and like the shifts in perspective in *Klm,* readers in Auchinleck are first with Richard aboard ship, and then, suddenly, with the Muslims behind Acre's wall. At the corresponding moment in *King Richard*, Richard sets up a "gin," an ingenious contraption called "Robinett," which "cast into Acres hard stones."⁶⁸ When Richard slings loaded beehives over the city's wall in the summer heat, the Muslims declare, in an echo of the Saxons' lament, that "King Richard is ful fel, / When his fleyȝen bite so wel."⁶⁹

In the least fantastic but most compelling moment of correspondence among the texts, Richard rallies his men against the emperor of Cyprus in *King Richard* by vowing on Saint Denis ("bi seyn Denis") that the English will be victorious. Charlemagne swears an almost identical oath in branch v

---

64. Lacroix, *Saga*, 578.
65. Lacroix, *Saga*, 578.
66. *Short Chronicle,* lines 2055–56.
67. *Short Chronicle,* lines 2115–20.
68. *King Richard,* lines 1011–14.
69. *King Richard,* lines 1009–10.

of *Klm* ("par Saint-Denis en France") that the French will conquer Saxony.[70] In *chansons de geste* and romances, Charlemagne swears by Saint Denis almost as frequently as he tugs at his beard in worry, and in Auchinleck's thirty-second item, a unique copy of *Otuel a Kniȝt*, the text introduces Charlemagne as "born in seint Denis / Nouȝt bote a litel fram Parys."[71] Richard's prayer to Saint Denis, in Charlemagne's image, to ensure England's victory subtly embodies the processes behind Richard's own textual reconstruction. The English king invokes the French saint to spur the English army, and in doing so evokes for the reader both the specter of Charlemagne and his "French" romances in Auchinleck.

At the height of the mid-twentieth-century's resurgent interest in Auchinleck, born largely of Laura Hibbard Loomis's work on the manuscript's production and contents, Ronald Walpole suggested an Anglo-Norman exemplar lay behind Auchinleck's own Charlemagne material, including *Roland and Vernagu*, for which Scribe 1 was responsible.[72] So too, the most immediate source for Scribe 1's material on the Saxon war might be an Anglo-Norman one, especially since original translations and complicated interpolations from Anglo-Norman exemplars occur elsewhere in his hand in the manuscript.[73] Yet, the possibility that Scribe 1 had one or more Old Norse sources to hand has become increasingly convincing. Ralph Hanna suggests that a scene unique to Scribe 1's *Bevis of Hampton* may have been adapted from a Scandinavian source, and Ann Higgins argues for Scribe 1's access to an Old Norse exemplar for Auchinleck's *Sir Tristrem*.[74] Regardless of the source material's language,

---

70. *King Richard*, line 370; Lacroix, *Saga*, 584. These textual associations between Richard and Charlemagne arguably enact an affiliation the historical Richard himself had in mind: See Joseph J. Duggan, "La France des Plantagenêts dans les versions rimées de la *Chanson de Roland*," in *Les chansons de geste: Actes du XVI congrès international de la Société Rencesvals, pour l'étude des épopées romanes, Granada, 21–25 juillet 2003*, ed. C. Alvar and J. Paredes (Granada: Universidad de Granada, 2005), 205–14. Beyond Duggan's evidence, the abbey at Charroux, where at his own orders Richard's brain and entrails were buried, claimed Charlemagne as its founder; see *Richard I*, 324–25.

71. Burnley-Wiggins, *Otuel a Kniȝt*, lines 10–11. See also S. J. H. Herrtage, ed., *The Taill of Rauf Coilyear . . . with the fragments of Roland and Vernagu, and Otuel*. EETS ES 39 (London: Trübner, 1882).

72. R. N. Walpole, "The Source MS of *Charlemagne and Roland* and the Auchinleck Bookshop," *Modern Language Notes* 60 (1945): 23. See L. H. Loomis, "The Auchinleck Manuscript," cited above.

73. Fisher, *Scribal Authorship*, 153–54.

74. Hanna, *London Literature*, 135, 147 n. 45. Higgins is cited above. On northern affiliations, see also Angus McIntosh, "Is *Sir Tristrem* an English or a Scottish Poem?," in *In Other Words: Transcultural Studies in Philology, Translation, and Lexicology Presented to Hans Heinrich Meier on the Occasion of His Sixty-Fifth Birthday*, ed. J. Lachlan Mackenzie and Richard Todd (Dordecht, Holland: Foris Publications, 1989), 85–95.

the matter of Charlemagne is too carefully woven throughout Auchinleck's unique material in the hand of Scribe 1 for that material to have been copied *ad litteram* from an exemplar.

Richard is not the only pointedly English figure in the manuscript to inherit the Matter of Charlemagne. As a library unto itself, Auchinleck was not necessarily read from beginning to end, but its chronologically earliest narrative echoes of Charlemagne survive in the character of King Hengist, a fictional king. The reign of "king Hengist of Jnglond" occupies over two hundred lines unique to Auchinleck's copy of the *Short Chronicle*, which is in Scribe 1's hand.[75] "King Hengist" is "our king," "a conquerour," "þe strong king, / Wele doinde in al þing."[76] He appears between King Belin, out of whose inept hands Hengist rescues England, and King Lear, who, as Auchinleck's *Short Chronicle* tells it, is one of Hengist's many sons. In written histories dating back to at least the eighth century, a Saxon called Hengist and his brother, Horsa, lead Saxon mercenaries hired by the British king, Vortigern.[77] Geoffrey of Monmouth's early twelfth-century *Historia regum Britanniae* contains the most well-known version of the story.[78] Given the survival of Geoffrey's *Historia* in more than two hundred manuscripts, the name "Hengist" would have carried the same associations for medieval readers of Auchinleck that it does for modern knowing readers.[79] Scribe 1, who appears to have intricately planned his reconstruction of Hengist, puts those associations to narrative use. Nowhere in Auchinleck's *Short Chronicle* does the "old" iteration of Hengist appear. It is he and not Merlin, as in other *Short Chronicle*

---

75. *Short Chronicle*, line 762, lines 655–876. On the uniqueness of Auchinleck's Hengist, see Zettl, *Short Chronicle*, lviii. The only other copy of the *Short Chronicle* to include Hengist is London, British Library, MS Royal 12 C.xii, where he resembles the treasonous Saxon in Geoffrey of Monmouth's *Historia regum Britanniae*, on which see below.

76. *Short Chronicle*, lines 782, 655–60.

77. On their history in England's literature and its retrospective configuration of language and conquest, see Ardis Butterfield, *The Familiar Enemy: Chaucer, Language and Nation in the Hundred Years War* (Oxford: Oxford University Press, 2009), 37–43.

78. See Geoffrey of Monmouth, *The History of the Kings of Britain: An Edition and Translation of De gestis Britonum [Historia Regum Britanniae]*, ed. Michael D. Reeve, trans. Neil Wright (Woodbridge: The Boydell Press, 2007). Hengist and Horsa first appear in Kent and in the text at bk. 6, pp. 124–25.

79. On the manuscripts and milieu in which Geoffrey worked, see the introduction to Reeve and Wright, *History*, vii–lxxvi, as well as, for example, John Gillingham, "The Context and Purposes of Geoffrey of Monmouth's *History of the Kings of Britain*," in *Anglo-Norman Studies 13: Proceedings of the Battle Conference*, ed. Marjorie Chibnall (Woodbridge: The Boydell Press, 1990), 99–118; and Jennifer Miller, "Laȝamon's Welsh," in *Reading Laȝamon's Brut: Approaches and Explorations*, ed. Rosamund Allen, Jane Roberts, and Carole Weinberg (New York: Rodopi, 2013), esp. 589–607.

redactions, who builds Stonehenge.[80] In Auchinleck's *Of Arthour and of Merlin* (item 26), the earliest extant copy of that text and also in Scribe 1's hand, the nobleman assisting Vortigern is a Frenchman called "Angis."[81] For a knowing reader of the fourteenth century, Hengist was a foundational English figure, and also a swindler. In Auchinleck, the questionable aspects of his identity are excised and his fundamental importance to English history is not only maintained but enhanced.

In Scribe 1's hand, Hengist, like Richard, is reconstructed from old French parts. Before Charlemagne builds a ship to cross the Rhine in branch v of *Klm,* he attempts to build a bridge with Roland's assistance, but the scheme goes awry. As he declares he will abandon the plan, two brothers from Spain, Elspalrath and Ealraath, appear and take on the project. In Auchinleck's *Short Chronicle,* Hengist, too, after naming London ("Hingisthom"), decides to build a bridge, not across the Rhine, but across the Channel in order to win Normandy from the French king, Selmin, who "schuld ȝeld him Normundye / As his ancesters hadde bifore."[82] Hengist "coniourd" three hundred "fendes of helle" as workmen, who, as in branch v of *Klm,* build the bridge from stone and, "Þer lete make a strong tour, / Wele yhoused & wele ybeld, / (T) chambers & halles wiþ mani teld."[83] Also reminiscent of branch v, where the sons of the Saxon king Guitaclin act as messengers, the messengers who move between the kings in the *Short Chronicle* are Selmin's sons. Hengist spends a great deal of time planning an attack on the French who threaten to invade England, and face-to-face negotiations between Hengist and Selmin occur, but the prospect of the bridge, coupled with Hengist's general impressiveness, terrifies the French king. Selmin peremptorily concedes defeat, draws up a charter, gives Hengist Normandy and Gascony, and personally leads Hengist into Paris as a conqueror.[84] "Our king" Hengist's reign over England and right to Normandy predates that of William the Conqueror and precedes even Julius Caesar's interest in Britain—a point emphasized by the detail that

---

80. *Short Chronicle,* lines 715–26. On Merlin building Stonehenge in other *Short Chronicle* redactions, see Zettl, *Short Chronicle,* 58.

81. Burnley-Wiggins, *Of Arthour and Of Merlin,* for example, line 147.

82. *Short Chronicle,* lines 738, 772–73. Turville-Petre, *England the Nation,* 109, calls this unique Hengist material "extraordinary nonsense, but its significance bears directly on the contemporary situation. Hengist is what Edward III ought to be." On the infrequency of bridge building in medieval epics and *chansons de geste,* see Bodel, *La Chanson des Saisnes,* 2:817, where Brasseur notes: "La construction des ponts n'est pas un thème épique, et rares sont les chansons de geste où l'on peut relever une mention, ne serait-ce que la plus fugitive, de telles édifications."

83. *Short Chronicle,* lines 739–59.

84. *Short Chronicle,* lines 760–836.

when Caesar enters London, the locals still call it "Hingisthom." Auchinleck's Hengist is Charlemagne's historical predecessor, and in a shrewd reversal, his textual predecessor, too: a builder of bridges and a hero worthy of, or at least demanding of, French tribute. Nearly 1,200 lines after the *Short Chronicle* notes Hengist's burial at Glastonbury, Richard ascends the throne. To return to the terms of this book's second chapter, the retrospective inheritance that Auchinleck claims is material, cultural, and vast. And the narration of descent that the codex posits is one in which England is both the ancestor of and the heir to the old French literary and historical landscape.

The fundamental success of this transaction depends upon a readership for Auchinleck different from the type we have imagined,[85] distinct from the "lewed" Englishman sketched in the prologue to *King Richard*. Auchinleck's makers here anticipate another kind of audience: readers who resemble Scribe 1 in their physical proximity to books and familiarity with a wide range of stories, written and unwritten.[86] Auchinleck's *Short Chronicle* contains a unique set of lines in which Lancelot and Guinevere steal away from Arthur in Nottingham Castle's underground caves and chambers. As Helen Cooper explains, this strange detail expressly recalls the recent events of 1330, when Edward III's mother, Isabella of France, and her lover, Roger Mortimer, barricaded themselves in Nottingham castle against her son and his men. These implicit associations between Isabella and Guinevere, Mortimer and Lancelot, and Edward and Arthur presume a particular kind of reader since, according to Cooper, Auchinleck's reference to the affair between Lancelot and Guinevere is the first trace of this story in English and yet the reader's knowledge of it is assumed.[87]

This parallel construction gives us insight into Scribe 1's ability to make a conversant codex. In his work, we can begin to conceive of local talk in the ways Scribe 1 and other text-makers might have: as its own type of exem-

---

85. For example, Turville-Petre, *England the Nation*, 109: "The wild invention of the Auchinleck's adapter relies on a pretty comprehensive ignorance in its readers, for Hengist is portrayed as the ideal *British* king."

86. A picture of such an audience has begun to emerge in scholarship. See, for example, Linda Olson, "Romancing the Book: Manuscripts for 'Euerich Inglische,'" in *Opening Up Middle English Manuscripts*, by Kathryn Kerby-Fulton, Maidie Hilmo, and Linda Olson (Ithaca, NY: Cornell University Press, 2012), 97–106; and Arthur Bahr, *Fragments and Assemblages: Forming Compilations of Medieval London* (Chicago: University of Chicago Press, 2013), 135.

87. Cooper, "Lancelot," 95–98. The connection between Auchinleck's unique *Short Chronicle* material and fourteenth-century current events is treated briefly in Turville-Petre, *England the Nation*, 111; Cooper contextualizes the anecdote within contemporary historical rumor and the Arthurian textual tradition in England, and she ascribes a new *terminus a quo* of 1331 to Auchinleck's production.

plar to be copied. And as an extratextual gloss with which knowing readers could interpret a text's meaning. Scribe 1's implicit reference to Isabella and Mortimer also reveals how attuned he was to the local talk of the day. There would scarcely have been enough time for the Nottingham antics to be transmitted widely via text between 1330 and Auchinleck's production. The fullest version of the Nottingham story survives in the second and longer chronicle of Geoffrey Baker, who according to his own text wrote in Oxfordshire around 1350. In Baker's telling, the original event and its narrative afterlife can be traced back to a rumor that "sprang up among the barons, which also came to the ears of the commons" (*Fit murmur inter magnates, quod ad aures populares avolavit*): Mortimer had plotted Edward III's imminent murder.[88] This rumor reached the king, who gathered his men to find and take into custody his mother and Mortimer. On October 18, 1330 (or the following Friday—both dates circulated simultaneously after the fact), Mortimer and Isabella, who in one version of the story had confiscated the castle's keys from its constable, were locked in their bedchamber when Edward and his men, having learned (also from the constable) of the castle's secret passages, entered through its underground caves and made their arrests.[89] Scribe 1 reports in Auchinleck's *Short Chronicle* that Lancelot held Guinevere at Nottingham for "þre ȝere and moneþes ten," a period of time "not found in any source, but which corresponds precisely to the period from the deposition of Edward II, in January 1327, to the date of the arrest of Mortimer [in late 1330]."[90] Scribe 1's source appears to have been talk—talk that he used to connect the present and the past, the historical and the literary.

Auchinleck's texts, especially those in the hand of Scribe 1, imagine readers conversant in the similarly complex old French stories about Charlemagne. The interplay between talk and textual production surrounding the Matter of Charlemagne in England not only provides more evidence that the related talk Auchinleck's makers used was ubiquitous, but also offers a model they might have known: a model of how a text generates talk. The Charlemagne material demonstrates the ways in which makers of texts could build expectations for

---

88. The *Chronicon Galfridi le Baker de Swynebroke* is quoted in Cooper, "Lancelot," 91: Geoffrey Baker provides "the most detailed and circumstantial account," which was written down "within a couple of decades of the events he describes." Geoffrey Baker's larger chronicle runs from 1303 to 1356, though Baker did not die until 1358. A similar story circulated in the prose *Brut*, and in Thomas Gray's *Scalacronica*, which ends in 1363: Sir Thomas Gray, *Scalacronica, 1272–1363*, ed. and trans. Andy King, Surtees Society 209 (Woodbridge: The Boydell Press, 2005), 103–7.

89. On the rumors that circulated around Isabella, see, for example, Camille, *Mirror in Parchment*, 74–75.

90. *Short Chronicle*, line 1087; Cooper, "Lancelot," 95.

readerly knowledge into their texts, and, moreover, could anticipate how those texts might shape future talk. Rumors about Charlemagne in England can be traced back, like *Klm,* to Oxford, Bodleian Library, MS Digby 23, which contains the earliest extant copy of the *Chanson de Roland,* written down in assonating Anglo-Norman in the second quarter of the twelfth century, and rediscovered in England in the nineteenth.[91]

Traces of what I call the "Charlemagne rumor" are embedded in the Oxford *Roland* at laisse 155, which begins by describing the mortally wounded archbishop Turpin before stating that Charles himself would one day tell honorific tales about these moments during which his archbishop, showing the enemy no mercy, fought to his death (*Puis le dist Carles qu'il n'en espargnat nul*).[92] The assertion that Charlemagne would be complicit in shaping his own memory is undercut by the bodiless voice of the text, which immediately reasserts its own authority as a document independent of Charlemagne's storytelling project. After the description of Turpin's death, the laisse concludes in an apparent non sequitur, with four lines of complex and coded rumor about Charlemagne that situate the Oxford *Roland* within a network of talk extending far beyond Digby 23:

> So says the story and he who was on the battlefield,
> the baron saint Giles, for whom God performs miracles
> and made the document in the church of Laon;
> anyone who does not know that much has not understood it at all.[93]

The extratextual gestures (*la Geste; la chartre*) would be as familiar to medieval readers as they are to modern ones who have read the types of texts that refer their audiences to a real or contrived originary textual source. It is not odd that the Oxford *Roland* contains these conventions, but the frequency and self-consciousness with which the reader is directed beyond the text's own pages here, twice within two lines and to two different documents, is remarkable.

These four lines of laisse 155 assume an audience of knowing readers who have already heard or read certain things about Charlemagne. The lines also

---

91. On this discovery and its ramifications for the idea of France, see chapter 1.
92. Short, "Oxford Version," line 2091.
93. Short, "Oxford Version," lines 2095–98: "Ço dit la Geste e cil ki el camp fut, / li ber seinz Gilie, por qui Deus fait vertuz / e fist la chartre el muster de Loüm; / ki tant ne set ne l'ad prod entendut." Each of the seven extant manuscripts of *La Chanson de Roland* includes some version, however garbled, of these lines. See the concordance of laisses prepared by Karen Akiyama in the 2005 edition by Duggan et al., 1:74.

address unknowing readers, who have "not understood it at all."[94] Early modern editors added another layer of rumor to laisse 155. By inserting punctuation and correcting "scribal errors," these editors have treated lines 2095 to 2098 precisely as one would treat rumor—open to intervention, disruption, alteration—in their attempts to make meaning out of what was thought to be nonsense.[95] The significance of these four lines from laisse 155 emerges not from what they say, but from what they presume: that their readers will contribute to the text's meaning by bringing to bear information already known, or will seek out someone who knows it and is willing to talk.

The Oxford *Roland* was constructed, like other retrospective texts, under the assumption that it would circulate among texts, talk, and images with which it could converse and to which its readers had access. The four lines of laisse 155 point to an episode in the legend of Charlemagne absent from all seven extant medieval copies and three fragments of the *Chanson de Roland*, but extant in the epic's Old Norse prequel.[96] The first branch of *Klm* contains the earliest extant textual disclosure of "Charlemagne's sin," to which laisse 155 alludes. Upon returning to Aix from his coronation in Rome, the newly crowned emperor sleeps with his sister, a sin that precipitates Roland's birth.[97] Charlemagne leaves his sister's bedroom in a state of panic and goes immediately to church to confess his sins, save that most recent mortal one. His confessor, Giles, unaware of the omission, blesses the king and goes to mass, where:

---

94. For example, the Oxford *Roland*, in keeping with the oral transmission of vernacular epics, belies a long tradition of oral/aural transmission: The matter of its text was intoned rumor, spoken and heard long before—and possibly contemporaneously with—its written transmission; see Short, "Oxford Version," 39–50.

95. Short, "Oxford Version," 308 n. 2097, summarizes the various ways in which the lines have been punctuated in previous editions, and the problems therein. For instance, placing a comma after "vertuz" forecloses a reading in which the document was sent by God; Short explains his own practice: "However, placing a comma after *fut*, having no punctuation after *vertuz*, and resisting the temptation to emend *e* 2097, allow the ambiguity of the passage to be safeguarded." In his 1990 edition of *La Chanson de Roland*, Short responds to the last four lines of laisse 155 by asking, "Faut-il comprendre que saint Gilles avait assisté à la bataille de Roncevaux et qu'il et fit le récit dans un document conservé au monastère de Laon?" Short is a knowing reader posing as unknowing here, and his gloss shrewdly performs the confusion the lines have engendered in modern editors. See *La Chanson de Roland*, ed. and trans. Ian Short (Paris: Librairie générale française, 1990), 152.

96. See, for instance, Gerard J. Brault, ed. and trans., *The Song of Roland: An Analytical Edition*, vol. 1 (University Park: The Pennsylvania State University Press, 1978), 233–35. On the extant corpus of *Roland*, see Duggan's general introduction to *La Chanson de Roland*, 1:5–40.

97. Lacroix, *Saga*, 109.

Gabriel, God's angel, appeared and placed a document on the paten. The document stated that Charlemagne had not confessed all of his sins: "He has slept with his sister and she will give birth to a son who will be named Roland; and he will give her in marriage to Milon d'Aiglent, but seven months after they share a bed, she will give birth. And he must know that he is both his son and his nephew; and he should see to it that the boy is well cared for because he needs him." Giles took the document from the paten, and went at once, still clad in his vestments, to king Charlemagne, and read it before him. He confessed, fell down on his knees, and asked for forgiveness; he promised that he would not commit that sin again and did all that the writ ordered: he married his sister to Milon and made him duke of Brittany. The child was born seven months later.[98]

While no Anglo-Norman or English copy of the prequel survives, we know that versions of this episode—versions that did not usually disclose the precise sin committed—circulated elsewhere in England not only in the source material for *Klm*, but by way of another ubiquitous text: the *vita* of Charlemagne's confessor, Giles.

The extant manuscripts containing the life of St. Giles bear extensive though only partial witness to the transmission of the rumor of Charlemagne's sin, both in England and France. In laisse 155 of the Oxford *Roland*, "the baron saint Giles, for whom God performs miracles / and made the document in the church of Laon," refers to the hermit saint born in the seventh century (roughly one hundred years before Charlemagne). The versions of Giles's *vita*, as well as the extant material witnesses to his cult in France, recognize him as a caregiver, patron of the sick, and, in his life's Charlemagne section called "the mass of St. Giles," as a possessor of intercessory power so profound that merely invoking him obviates the need for full auricular confession.[99]

---

98. Lacroix, *Saga*, 108–9: "Il se rendit ensuite à l'église et alla se confesser auprès d'Egidius de tous ses péchés, sauf celui-là. Egidius le bénit et il alla à la messe. Or tandis qu'il assistait à la messe basse, survint Gabriel, l'ange de Dieu, qui posa un écrit sur la patène. Il était dit dans l'écrit que le roi Charlemagne n'avait pas confessé tous ses péchés: 'Il a couché avec sa soeur et elle donnera le jour à un fils qui s'appellera Roland; il la mariera à Milon d'Aiglent, mais sept mois après qu'ils auront partagé le même lit, elle enfantera. Et il doit savoir qu'il est son fils, et pourtant celui de sa soeur; et qu'il veille à faire bien garder le garçon car il en aura besoin.' Egidius prit l'écrit de la patène, all immédiatement, revêtu des ornements auprès du roi Charlemagne, et le lut devant lui. Il avoua, tomba à ses pieds et demanda le pardon; il promit qu'il ne commettrait jamais plus ce péché et fit tout ce que l'écrit lui ordonnait: il maria sa soeur à Milon et fit celui-ci duc de Bretagne. L'enfant vit le jour sept mois plus tard."

99. See Eamon Duffy, *The Stripping of the Altars: Traditional Religion in England 1400–1580* (New Haven and London: Yale University Press, 1992), 155, 178. Crusaders are thought

An account of the saint's supposed encounter with Charlemagne was first written down in the tenth century. Many copies of the Latin *Vita Aegidii* dated to the tenth century survive, as does the twelfth-century *Vie de saint Gilles,* written in Anglo-Norman and circulated in England.[100] The presence of the life of St. Giles in the *Legenda aurea,* the collection of saints' lives attributed to the thirteenth-century Dominican prior Jacobus de Voragine and surviving in more than one thousand manuscripts, attests to the scope and type of audience able to access Giles's *vita* and the Charlemagne rumor.[101] In the *Legenda,* Giles learns Charlemagne's sin, but it is not disclosed to the reader. When William Caxton printed the first English translation of the *Legenda aurea* as the *Golden Legend* in 1483, Giles's *vita* had already been circulating in Middle English for more than one hundred years in the *South English Legendary* (*SEL*), which survives in at least fifty-two copies.[102] The life of St. Giles is extant in some of the earliest *SEL* manuscripts, including

---

to have been in part responsible for the transmission of the cult of Giles across Europe, and his popularity in England continued well into the fifteenth century. Most of the 162 British churches dedicated to Giles date from the eleventh and twelfth centuries. See Frances Arnold-Forster, *Studies in Church Dedications; or England's Patron Saints,* 3 vols. (London: Skeffington and Son, 1899), 2:46–51 and 3:15.

100. See Guillaume de Berneville, *La vie de saint Gilles: poème du XIIe siècle,* ed. Gaston Paris and Alphonse Bos (Paris: Didot, 1881), lxxii–lxxxix, xxxvi, and xlvii for the composition date; and see Françoise Laurent, ed. *Guillaume de Berneville, La vie de saint Gilles* (Paris: Champion, 2003), xi–xvii, for the internal evidence on which the composition date and provenance are determined. The *vie* survives in one complete manuscript of the thirteenth century, and one fragment dated to no later than the early fifteenth century; see Guillaume de Berneville, *La vie,* lii–liii. Many manuscripts of the *Vita Aegidii* are extant, dating from the eleventh to the fourteenth centuries: See Laurent, *Guillaume de Berneville,* xvii. See also Rita Lejeune and Jacques Stiennon, *La légende de Roland dans l'art du moyen âge,* vol. 1 (Brussels: Arcade, 1966), 145.

101. J. A. W. Bennett calls the Latin text's presence in medieval England "ubiquitous." See Bennett, *Middle English Literature,* ed. and completed by Douglas Gray (Oxford: Clarendon Press, 1986), 62. The earliest compilation of the *Legenda aurea* has been dated to around 1260; see Jacobus de Voragine, *The Golden Legend: Readings on the Saints,* trans. William Granger Ryan, 2 vols. (Princeton: Princeton University Press, 1993), 1:xiii–xviii. All translations of the *Legenda aurea* are from Ryan, 2:147–49.

102. See Charlotte D'Evelyn and Anna J. Mill, ed., *The South English Legendary,* EETS OS 235, 236, 244 (London: Oxford University Press, 1956–1959), 3:1–3; and Ralph Hanna, "Middle English Verses from a Bodleian Binding," *Bodleian Library Record* 17 (2002): 488–92. The earliest extant manuscript containing the *SEL,* Oxford, Bodleian Library, MS Laud Misc. 108, has been dated to the end of the thirteenth century, but the *SEL*'s transmission and circulation in England continued well into the fifteenth. No two *SEL* manuscripts are alike in either their list of saints or the ordering of their contents: See D'Evelyn and Mill, *SEL,* 3:1–2; and see Manfred Görlach, *The Textual Tradition of the South English Legendary* (Leeds: The University of Leeds School of English, 1974), 73–130 for manuscript descriptions, including fragments.

London, British Library, MS Harley 2277, dated to around 1300, and Oxford, Bodleian Library, MS Ashmole 43, dated to around the first decade of the fourteenth century.[103]

The irony of the mass of St. Giles, an irony medieval text-makers clearly understood and exploited in their retelling of the episode, is that one prays to Giles in order to avoid articulation, to suppress talk. Yet his *vita* demonstrates that the suppression of talk is counterproductive. We talk to fill silence. In the *SEL*'s vernacular retelling of the mass of St. Giles, this dynamic between talk and its suppression is centered:

Þe king of France þat was þo . Charles was is name
In a sunne he was þat he nemiȝte . noman telle for ssame
Of sein Gilis he hurde telle . þat he godman was
He wende to him & bad him ȝeorne . to helpe him of þat cas
Ich habbe he sede a sunne ido . þat i nemai for ssame telle
Þe ne non oþer man . þei ich euere be[o] in helle
Bidde oure Louerd por charite . þat he is me forȝiue
Þoru þi bone for i nemay for ssame . þer of be[o] issriue
Þe Sonedai þere after . as sein Gile masse song
Þe kinges sunne he hadde in munde . & þereuore bad among
An angel þer com wiþ a writ . as oure Louerd þuder sende
Þat writ he leide upe þe weued . & aȝen to heuene wende
Sein Gile radde þat writ anon . þer on he fonde iwrite
Þe kinges sunne þat was so luþer . þat noman ne ssolde iwite
Þat writ sede ek þat þulke sunne . þoru is bone was forȝiue
Ȝif þe king it bileuede & repentant were . & þat is issriue
And alle men þat sein Gilis . for eni sunne bede
Oure Louerd wolde hore bone ihure . ȝif he bileuede hore misdede
Swete a sonde was þis on . þat oure Louerd sein Gile sende
Hopie mai ech man þerto . þat is lif wilneþ amende
Sein Gilis nom þis holi writ . and king Charles gan bitake
Þo þe king isei is sunne iwrite . he nemiȝte noȝt forsake

---

103. *NIMEV* 2906; *DIMEV* 4605. *DIMEV* records thirteen *SEL* manuscript witnesses of the life of Giles. His *vita* appears regularly in extant manuscripts of the *SEL* from the late thirteenth century and the beginning of the fourteenth century, and through the later medieval period: for example, in London, British Library, MS Cotton Julius D.ix, dated to the first half of the fifteenth century, as well as in Oxford, Bodleian Library, MS Laud Misc. 463, dated to the late fourteenth century.

Ac sore wepinge he þer of ssrof . and þonkede God also
And þe holi abbot sein Gilis . þat it broȝte þerto.[104]

The wealth of extant material dating from the early thirteenth century and after that shows and retells this episode confirms not only the continued circulation of the rumor about Charlemagne's sin but also the public's continued interest in it.

The modularity of the mass of St. Giles, exemplified by its easy presence as a fully formed narrative extracted from its hagiographic context in this chapter, partially demonstrates how the episode was able to appear so frequently not only as rumor, but as a more broadly inscribed intrigue in a multiplicity of literary and visual contexts throughout England and France. The manuscript witnesses of the life of St. Giles constitute only a portion of the episode's circulation. In addition to the mass of St. Giles reference in *Roland* and the extant manuscripts of the *SEL* and the *Legenda aurea,* the mass of St. Giles was recontextualized in visual representations: removed from Giles's *vita* and inserted into depictions of Charlemagne's life. It survives on a mural at Le Loroux-Bottereau dated to around 1200, and as a miniature dated to about 1260, now at Liège.[105] The episode also appears with scenes from the Battle of Roncevaux on the early thirteenth-century Aachen casket, and most notably, the mass of St. Giles occupies a panel on the mid-thirteenth-century "Charlemagne Window" of Chartres Cathedral,[106] where its presence confirms that the majority of the public had, in the words of the Oxford *Roland,* "understood it well," and that those who did not soon would.[107] The Charlemagne

---

104. D'Evelyn and Mill, *SEL,* 2:388–89, lines 125–48.

105. Lejeune and Stiennon, *La légende,* 1:145–50; and Brault, *The Song of Roland,* 1:234. For the Latin and French *vitae,* see above.

106. On the Aachen casket, see Lejeune and Stiennon, *La légende,* 1:172; and Brault, *The Song of Roland,* 1:234. On the window, see Clark Maines, "The Charlemagne Window at Chartres Cathedral: New Considerations on Text and Image," *Speculum* 52 (1977), 801. The window has been dated more precisely to *c.* 1225. Maines, "Charlemagne Window," 818–21, identifies panel 22 as depicting the mass of St. Giles. By considering the entire panel sequence in its original order, Maines discovers that the original ordering does not reveal the details of Charlemagne's sin, but does "make a direct statement about, rather than an allusion to, the nature of Charlemagne's sin" (821). In their pre-1921 order, the sequence of panels depicting Charlemagne's third expedition to Spain begins with the mass of St. Giles and ends with a depiction of the announcement of Roland's death. Maines thus reads the whole sequence as a commentary on sin and forgiveness; however, the sequence also provides further evidence that Charlemagne's specific sin was widely known and remained a subject of public judgment contemporaneous with the window's thirteenth-century production.

107. Joseph J. Duggan asserted in private conversation that the episode's presence in the Charlemagne Window confirms that the mass of St. Giles had acquired "soap-opera status" by the mid-thirteenth century.

Window depicts Giles standing before the altar, looking up to receive the scroll from the descending angel; to the far left of this scene Charlemagne sits on his throne, bearded chin in hand. Clark Maines characterizes Charlemagne here as "pensive" and conjectures that the medieval public viewing the new window in the mid-thirteenth century would have known the details of the mass of St. Giles and the exact nature of Charlemagne's sin.[108] The old Charlemagne material now extant in *Klm* kept people, regardless of their firsthand access to books, talking.

Scribe 1's complex textual inventions of Hengist, Richard, and even Edward III in Auchinleck prove that old French rumor and romance can "make," at least partially, the folk of England. By the early fourteenth century, French stories, broadly construed, and the books that contained them had long been implicitly constitutive of England's identity. But the real and present fourteenth-century difficulty of what to do when your own cultural identity cannot be cleanly distinguished from that of your enemy—when you read and write and tell the same stories about the past—resides everywhere in Auchinleck. In answer to this problem, Auchinleck proposes that the old French canon and England's identity are inextricable rather than distinct or oppositional. Made partly of Charlemagne's textual corpus, Richard cries out in *King Richard* that England's enemies have "despised our naciouns."[109] This declaration at once unites his men around him and invokes a unified English body. It is one of the earliest usages, perhaps even the earliest usage, of "naciouns" in its modern sense,[110] and crucially, in what may be the text's most potent instrumentalization of Frenchness, it is the traitorous alliance between the French and the "Griffons" or Greeks of Messina that provokes England's articulation as a nation.

King Richard's textual reconstruction of the Third Crusade would have evoked the memory of a whole and unified England, a memory that would have doubled as an especially potent *exemplum* as Auchinleck was being produced and read in the fourteenth century. The homilies preached in local parishes during the late twelfth century may have advocated recovery of Jerusalem from Muslims, but Auchinleck's *King Richard* preaches a different enemy. The central front of the Third Crusade in Auchinleck's *King Richard* is the alternately hotly and coldly contested border between Englishness and Frenchness. This reconstruction of the late twelfth century vis-à-vis the exigencies of the present moment renders past and present projects coterminous. In

---

108. Maines, "Charlemagne Window," 818–21.
109. *King Richard*, line 264.
110. *OED*, "nation, n." 1 (a).

Auchinleck, the siege of Acre is the direct martial predecessor of the Hundred Years' War.

The Hundred Years' War necessitated a unified England. Collective investment had long been a crucial feature in the memory of the Third Crusade. From the late thirteenth century, England's formal participation in the Third Crusade at the beginning of Richard's reign had coincided with the universal *terminus post quem* enacted by Edward I. The Third Crusade no doubt figured directly or indirectly in every lay and ecclesiastical narration of descent because every English family and church had participated in the Third Crusade or been affected by it.[111] Exact numbers are difficult to ascertain—the accounts of participation are diffuse among extant records, including Pipe Rolls, mortgage charters, anecdotal accounts of returning crusaders, and mort d'ancestor assizes for crusaders who never returned. According to Christopher Tyerman, "the scale of the operation was massive"; "it was not a question of who took the cross but who did not."[112] England's fighting contingent consisted of a broad socioeconomic and geographic cross-section: *Crucesignati* included religious men, magnates or knights and their military households, serfs on behalf of or in the service of their lords, artisans, and even women.[113] Recruitment, first undertaken by Henry II with his implementation of the Saladin Tithe—a tax of ten percent on moveable goods that could only be avoided by taking the cross—and then by Richard, whose own court became the crusader army's core, was both a model for and the envy of other Western monarchs.[114] The Third Crusade also implicated those who remained at home. Rallying support and recruiting participants were twin aims of papal bulls, royal resolutions, and preaching. A part of that personal and locally conveyed urging was aimed specifically at the wives of potential crusaders, in the hope that they

---

111. For instance, Tyerman, *God's War*, 437–38: "Richard's crusade preparations exposed the existence of a wider political community beyond the nobility, knights, and urban elites. The combination of fundraising, recruitment and revivalist crusade preaching created wide public involvement with occasionally violent consequences."

112. Tyerman, *England and the Crusades*, 65–66.

113. Tyerman, *England and the Crusades*, 64–75, provides the most thorough account of England's crusaders and the processes by which they were recruited; he is careful to clarify that "the image of a peasant leaving his field to fight for the cross is a myth. . . . Serfs, for reasons economic, financial, and legal, did not go on crusade except in the service of their lords or as proxies" (72–73). On the recruitment of artisans and women, see Tyerman, *God's War*, 396–97: "Women fought at Acre, to the admiration of western sources and the fascinated horror of Arabic ones. In a list of forty-seven Cornish recruits there were at least four *crucesignatae*."

114. Tyerman, *God's War*, 382, 390–95.

would agree to an endeavor that would leave them certainly vulnerable and potentially widowed.[115]

Even the end of the Third Crusade was marked by and remembered for institutionally mandated collective participation.[116] When, while returning from crusade in 1192, Richard and his companions were captured in the lands of the English king's German and Austrian enemies, "the whole" of England, as chronicler Roger of Howden reports, was held responsible for procuring the necessary ransom.[117] Like the siege of Acre, stories about this collective undertaking on behalf of England and its king continued to be sites of interest and reconstruction well after the fact. Writing around 1300, Robert of Gloucester casts the story of England's collective sacrifice for its king in the more topical terms of inheritance. As Robert tells it, for Richard's sake the English people were not taxed impersonally on their "rents" and "properties," but instead forfeited very particular items, personal objects that often signify as ancestral heirlooms and talismans in medieval England's cultural parlance:

Oþer vorewarde he bed him ek . ac he it euere vorsok .
So þat atte laste . þe vorewarde me tok .
Þat an hundred þousend marc . & vifti þousend þerto .
King Richard ssolde ȝiue . of prison to ben ydo .
Þe hundred þousend marc were . ipaid biuore hond .
& wel narwe igadered . here in engelond .
Vor broches & ringes & ȝimmes al so .
& þe calis of þe weued . me ssolde þerto .
& greye monekes . þat newe come . & pouere þo were .
ȝeue al hor wolle . þerto of one ȝere .
Þo þe hundred þousend were . ipayd biuore hond .
King richard of þe oþer del . god ostage fond .

---

115. Tyerman, *God's War,* 383, explains: "Conjugal rights also could not, in theory, be ignored nor the very real dangers to life, limb and possessions to which abandoned crusaders' wives, widows and heiresses were liable." A selection of sermons from the twelfth through early fourteenth centuries is collected in Christoph T. Maier, *Crusading Propaganda and Ideology: Model Sermons for the Preaching of the Cross* (Cambridge: Cambridge University Press, 2000).

116. Appleby, *England without Richard,* 118–19. Very little evidence survives to tell us what this collection process looked like, but according to the chronicler William of Newburgh, three levies were imposed before enough money had been collected. William attributes the difficulty in raising ransom to the dishonesty of the collectors, not to any intense withholding from Richard's subjects, though Appleby notes the vocal unhappiness of the clergy.

117. Roger of Howden, *Chronica,* 3:210–11, 290.

& deliuered was of prison . & hiderward wende bliue .
Endleue hundred 3er of grace & ninty & fiue."⁸

Robert's retrospective account resonates with the connection forged in the last decade of the thirteenth century between Richard's reign and ancestral property. Robert's readers would have been able to imagine their ancestors' direct and collective participation in the effort not only to "deliver" Richard soundly to England, but also to render England, deeply politically troubled in Richard's absence, once again whole through the safe return of its king.

Auchinleck's *King Richard* does more than pointedly remember England's wholeness in a way that models for its readers how to forget England's divisions. It begins to perform the harder and more subtle work of defining the terms of English collectivity. The collective endeavor of the Third Crusade joined with England's narrative absence facilitates talk about and remembrance of England within *King Richard*. When on crusade, England must be evoked through memory, conjured through articulation, and defined against un-Englishness all around. Both purposefully and by necessity, England begins to emerge in Auchinleck's *King Richard* not as a concrete place, but as an idea, a "nacioun."

Auchinleck's Richard material calls its readers to reimagine the present moment by presenting them with a reconstructed and expediently positive precedent. As a retrospective text, *King Richard* intervenes in the accounts of England's past contained in both the textual record and cultural memory. The end of *King Richard* as it survives in Auchinleck coincides with England's victory at Acre and concludes with the lines:

Þat day so Richard sped þer
Þat he was holden conquerer,
For better he sped þat day ar none
Þan þe oþer in seuen 3er hadde done."⁹

In the space of a fragment, Auchinleck's contemporary readers and text-makers gained a nation and attributed its origins.

---

118. Robert of Gloucester, *Metrical Chronicle*, vol. 2, lines 10024–37. This description appears to be unique to Robert of Gloucester's chronicle; see Robert of Gloucester, *Metrical Chronicle*, 1:xxx–xxxi. The detail of "broaches, rings, and gems" does not appear in Howden's much drier account, which is also silent on the matter of any specifically Cistercian hardship.

119. *King Richard*, lines 1043–46.

FIVE

English Rumor and the Modular Manuscript

"ÞE SARRAЗINS SEYЗE ÞAI," a catchword, is apparently the final trace of *King Richard* in the Auchinleck manuscript. It sits in the bottom margin of fol. 327v, halfway between the leaf's edge and its last four lines. In their praise of Richard for his victory at Acre, these lines remind the reader that martial success had eluded the crusading armies encamped outside the city's wall for years prior to his arrival.[1] Catchwords were used in manuscripts to eliminate uncertainty about what came next; to ensure the order of a book's constituent parts when the time came for them to be stitched together; to render speculation unnecessary for the book's maker(s) and, sometimes, if catchwords were not cut off when a folio was cut down, for its reader. For as long as we have known of it, and possibly long before that, the *King Richard* catchword has had the opposite effect. The manuscript's subsequent folio begins a new quire, a new poem, and a new scribal stint with the earliest extant copy of *The Simonie* in the hand of Scribe 2.[2] A metrical complaint thought to have been

---

1. In Pearsall-Cunningham, xiii, the single quire containing *King Richard* is numbered forty-eight. The quire probably comprised eight leaves, including its outer bifolium, extant in Auchinleck, and its inner bifolia—four leaves that survive as the St. Andrews fragments and the Edinburgh fragments, and two lost leaves.

2. *The Simonie*, in Scribe 2's hand, ends imperfectly on fol. 334v. Auchinleck's texts are numbered in Roman numerals in Scribe 1's hand at the top of each recto, though much of that numbering was lost when the manuscript's leaves were cut down. *King Richard* is numbered "lvi," and while the slightest traces of numerals are visible on a few leaves of *The Simonie*,

composed during the reign of Edward II, *The Simonie* is now Auchinleck's final text.³ Instead of a siege, it begins with another kind of struggle: "Whij werre and wrake in londe and manslaught is icome, / Whij hungger and derþe on eorþe þe pore haþ vndernome."⁴ In *The Simonie* the English are engaged in a moral and ethical battle at home, against themselves, and they are losing. Faced with this seeming disjunction between the end of *King Richard* and the start of *The Simonie*, we have tried to make the *King Richard* catchword mean the way other catchwords do, both in and outside of Auchinleck, by asserting that it evinces the one-time presence of additional quires comprising "the remainder" of *King Richard*.

This assertion may well be accurate. Besides our knowledge of how catchwords were meant to work, other evidence supports the possibility of loss at the end of *King Richard*. Its catchword does not appear at the start of any completely separate text outside of the manuscript—at least, not one I could discover—and it is anomalous within Auchinleck as now constituted. Of the nine catchwords that precede the beginning of a new text in the manuscript, including four instances where a new scribal stint begins, it is the only catchword not "caught" in the subsequent quire.⁵ In many ways, it is an oddity, too,

---

they have been cut off so as to be completely illegible, to my eye. In Pearsall-Cunningham, the number of *The Simonie* is also designated with "(?)." Burnley-Wiggins notes in passing that *The Simonie* was numbered contemporaneously "lx," the sixtieth text. What might be the foot of "x" is just extant on fol. 330r. Still, how this conclusion was reached with certainty is unclear: See Burnley-Wiggins, "Damage, Condition, and Losses." *The Simonie* survives in three fourteenth- and fifteenth-century manuscripts, of which Auchinleck is the earliest: See *The Simonie: A Parallel-Text Edition, edited from MSS Advocates 19.2.1, Bodley 48, and Peterhouse College 104*, ed. Dan Embree and Elizabeth Urquhart (Heidelberg: Carl Winter, 1991).

3. One or more text(s) may have once followed *The Simonie*; the final folio of its quire has been lost. See Pearsall-Cunningham, xiii.

4. *The Simonie*, lines 1–2. All subsequent citations of *The Simonie* refer to Burnley-Wiggins.

5. Auchinleck has forty-nine extant quires and thirty-six catchwords. At least six of the missing catchwords can be attributed to the loss of a leaf. The nine catchwords that precede new texts occur between: fols. 38v and 39r; 69v and 70r; 107v and 107a (stub); 260v and 261r; 267v and 268r; 280v and 281r; 303v and 304r; 325v and 326r; 327v and 328r. These nine instances include four where the change in quire coincides with a new scribal stint, as is the case between *King Richard*, in Scribe 1's hand, and *The Simonie*, in the hand of Scribe 2: fol. 38v (Scribe 1)–fol. 39r (Scribe 2); 69v (Scribe 1)–70r (Scribe 3); 107v (Scribe 4, though the catchword is in Scribe 1's hand)–107a (a stub, but the remainder of the text is in Scribe 1's hand); 327v (Scribe 1)–328r (Scribe 2). I do not include a change of quire between fol. 267v, where Scribe 1's *Roland and Vernagu* ends, and fol. 268r, where *Otuel, A Knight*, begins. Whether *Otuel* is written in the hand of Scribe 1 or that of a sixth scribe whose only contribution to the manuscript was *Otuel* remains an open question in Auchinleck scholarship. I follow Parkes, Hanna, and my own assessment of Scribe 1's personal idiom in recognizing *Otuel* as Scribe 1's work. For the most recent published assessments, as well as an account of the ongoing debate, see Alison Wiggins, "Are Auchinleck Manuscript Scribe 1 and 6 the

among the work of Scribe 1, whose hand we know inscribed *King Richard*, and who would have been responsible for copying whatever comprised "the remainder" of the romance because scribal stints in Auchinleck coincide with the start of a new text rather than that of a new quire.[6] His hand, and possibly his temperament, are visible, expressly and intrinsically, at all stages of the manuscript's production,[7] revealing the orderly and possibly overbearing codicological identity of Scribe 1.[8] That he would write a catchword for material he did not intend to copy or had not already copied seems out of character.

Yet, additional pieces of evidence raise pressing questions. Would the post-catchword and ostensibly lost additional lines or quires of *King Richard* resemble our proleptic reading of "the rest" of the romance? Or might a fourteenth-century reader have encountered the single *King Richard* quire that we have before us as a separable text because no more of *King Richard* ever existed in the manuscript?[9] In the early twentieth century, A. J. Bliss speculated that the *King Richard* material purportedly lost after the catchword would have been "exactly enough to fill three complete gatherings."[10] That is, exactly enough to make Auchinleck's copy of the romance as "complete" as Brunner's *Richard Löwenherz*. That no surviving copy of *Richard Coeur de Lion* contains "þe sarraȝins seyȝe þai," however, troubles both easy supplementation of *King*

Same Scribe? The Advantages of Whole-Data Analysis and Electronic Texts," *Medium Ævum* 73 (2004): 10–26; and Ralph Hanna, "Auchinleck 'Scribe 6' and Some Corollary Issues," in Fein, *New Perspectives*, 209–21. Here and elsewhere in discussions of handwriting, I primarily use Parkes's terminology, collected as a glossary in Malcolm B. Parkes, *Their Hands before Our Eyes: A Closer Look at Scribes*, The Lyell Lectures Delivered in the University of Oxford 1999 (Aldershot: Ashgate, 2008), 149–55.

6. Shonk, "A Study," 73–77; and Hanna, "Reconsidering," 94.

7. Catchwords occur and are followed consistently throughout Scribe 1's stints. On scribal interaction, Shonk, "A Study," 74, asserts that "even the shared gatherings do not offer evidence of direct contact among the scribes." Yet it is evident that when Scribe 1 appears to have been near at hand, in body or in spirit, his colleagues were conscientious about technical considerations, for example, letter height.

8. On Scribe 1's "Type-A" management style, see Hanna, "Reconsidering," 93–94; and chapter 4. It would be easy to characterize Scribe 1 as "playing fast and loose" with several of the texts he copied and altered, but the changes and additions in his hand convey a precision similar to that seen in the manuscript's physical construction.

9. One bifolium of *King Richard*'s extant quire remains lost. In this case, enough of the episodes begun/continued on the leaves of that lost bifolium remain on extant leaves that it is possible to make a highly informed guess at what they contained. See below in this chapter.

10. Bliss, "Notes on the Auchinleck Manuscript," 656: "Gatherings 49–51 are justified by a consideration of the other versions of *Richard Coeur de Lion*. The complete romance contains about 4,200 lines beyond the end of the Auchinleck text, exactly enough to fill three complete gatherings." On the basis of Bliss (and Brunner), Pearsall-Cunningham, xii, likewise posit that three additional *King Richard* quires have been lost, a supposition often mistaken for fact.

Richard with *Richard Löwenherz* and any assumptions about what would have come next in Auchinleck's copy.[11] This discrepancy does not prove that no additional folios of *King Richard* have been lost, but it does undermine scholarly certainty about what they may have contained.

Other things, too, rankle the settled wisdom on the copy's material and narrative loss. The present ending of *King Richard* is materially and narratively neat: No stubs remain between it and *The Simonie*. And if an explicit were present, or if the catchword were about something other than "Saracens," a group whose city Richard has just laid siege to in the text, the final four lines of *King Richard* in Auchinleck would register as a logical, and a narratively and formally satisfying, ending to the story that precedes them:

Þat day so Richard sped þer
Þat he was holden conquerer,
For better he sped þat day ar none
Þan þe oþer in seuen ȝer hadde done.[12]

These final lines form two full couplets, fill the final four ruled lines of the quire, and make narrative sense as a conclusion. As concerns Scribe 1, while it is true that he has a fastidious codicological identity, the unique texts and changes that appear in his hand, both in *King Richard* and throughout Auchinleck,[13] emphasize his *writerly* identity: equal parts canniness, bookishness, and inventiveness. However unlikely it seems that he would not follow his inscription of a catchword with expressly related text, Scribe 1 made

---

11. *King Richard*'s closest companion is the unique Richard material in the manuscript's *Short Chronicle*, which contains a line that resembles the *King Richard* catchword: "Þe Sarraȝins seye þat mervaile" (2115). That "marvel" in the *Short Chronicle* are the English ships that compass the city with lighted candles and colored sails prior to the siege of Acre. On the *Short Chronicle*, see chapter 4.

12. *King Richard*, lines 1043–46.

13. Here I refer not only to the complex processes of *inventio* and *translatio* behind the manuscript's Richard material, but also to, for example, the vast amounts of unique material in Auchinleck's *Short Chronicle* (see Zettl, *Short Chronicle*, 46–91), and the "unlacing" and "re-lacing" of the Guy of Warwick material—as first discussed in L. H. Loomis, "The Auchinleck Manuscript," 609–27, and more recently examined in Jamie DeAngelis, "Reading across Languages in Medieval Britain" (unpublished PhD diss., University of California, Berkeley, 2012), 30–74. So too, the decision to make such a hyper-English book signify visually as an Anglo-Norman production: a translation of form that parallels Auchinleck's linguistic and rhetorical translations from Anglo-Norman French to English. On the organization of material and its layout in medieval manuscripts more generally, see Malcolm B. Parkes, "The Influence of the Concepts of *Ordinatio* and *Compilatio* on the Development of the Book," in *Medieval Learning and Literature: Essays Presented to William Hunt*, ed. J. J. G. Alexander and M. T. Gibson (Oxford: Clarendon Press, 1976): 115–41; on Auchinleck's aspect and Anglo-Norman inheritance, see, for example, Hanna, "Reconsidering," 98.

equally unusual and unexpected choices about content elsewhere in the manuscript. Also of note is the strangely fortuitous recovery of nearly consecutive *King Richard* leaves in Scotland.[14] Despite the possibility that more is lost from Auchinleck's *King Richard* than survives, the leaves that were discovered in the nineteenth and twentieth centuries do not come from any of the post-catchword quires assumed lost, but rather from *King Richard*'s first quire, whose outer bifolium survives in the manuscript.

It is possible that what survives of *King Richard* in Auchinleck was recognized as a self-contained story, separable in theory or in practice from other material about Richard in the minds and hands of Auchinleck's readers and makers. The content of the *King Richard* quire, including its outer bifolium extant in the manuscript and the inner bifolia discovered in Scottish notebooks, precisely codifies the stories about Richard conquering Messina, Cyprus, and Acre that were circulating in early fourteenth-century London and its environs. These stories evince a public whose members were uninterested, or at least disinterested, in remembering collectively Richard's life before he became a crusader: In talk, text, and image the beginning of his kingship was made to coincide not with his coronation, but with his absence—his departure from England.

A new scenario of how contemporary readers might have accessed Auchinleck has recently been posited by Margaret Connolly and A. S. G. Edwards. Based on the texts surviving in Auchinleck and its fragments recovered elsewhere, they hypothesize that the manuscript, costly to make and to bind, "remained initially unbound once it was completed,"[15] its contents circulating for some amount of time in "definable codicological units," or booklets.[16] As Connolly and Edwards point out, the recto of *King Richard*'s first folio, 326, carries the marks of particularly heavy wear—the sort of wear the first leaf of a booklet circulating outside of its manuscript would likely incur.[17] Although

---

14. On Auchinleck's leaves and fragments recovered in the nineteenth and twentieth centuries, see chapter 4.

15. Connolly and Edwards, "Evidence," 303; see also 298–304. Their evidence includes careful study and dating of the various sets of binding holes visible on, and in at least one instance absent from, the bifolia and other recovered fragments.

16. Connolly and Edwards, "Evidence," 304, where they also note that the cleanness of most of Auchinleck's folios (unusual, especially on the outer leaves of booklets, if circulated outside of their binding) might be explained by temporary protective wrappers made of parchment whose use has been documented for other manuscripts in similar circumstances. The possibilities raised in the article are new and compelling, even though, as the authors themselves say, "these factors are not, of course, conclusive, but they may have a degree of circumstantial weight" (304).

17. Connolly and Edwards, "Evidence," 304.

booklets are usually made up of multiple quires,[18] the extant bifolium's final leaf, 327v, which would have been the last leaf of *King Richard*'s first quire, also shows wear—less than fol. 326r, but more than most other folios in the manuscript. Whether or not more of the romance once existed in Auchinleck, we must at least entertain the possibility that the extant *King Richard* quire was read in the fourteenth century, by choice or by chance, more or less as it must be read now: as a self-contained unit, from its rubricated title and decorated miniature to its hanging catchword.

I begin this chapter with Auchinleck's catchword, a diminutive object on which to build an argument, for two reasons: First, to start unsettling our settled wisdom about narrative and material imperfection, loss, and fragmentation. This chapter uses the textual tradition of *Richard Coeur de Lion* to propose and to practice a new kind of book history for medieval England's retrospective texts whose narratives, like *Richard Coeur de Lion,* were rooted in rumor or speculative talk about the past. Although the scholarly rumor of *Richard Coeur de Lion* characterizes Auchinleck's *King Richard* as a "mere fragment," the matter of Auchinleck's "fragment"—the stories about Messina, Cyprus, and the siege of Acre, stories from which the idea of England as a "nacioun" emerges—was in fact the narrative heart of the textual corpus of *Richard Coeur de Lion* in the fourteenth and fifteenth centuries. Together these stories constitute something like a "core rumor" around which other rumors were added, altered, and excised in copies of *Richard Coeur de Lion,*[19] relative to each manuscript copy's time and place. My second reason for beginning with the catchword, then, is that it throws into relief the slippage between medieval England's continued centering of the matter of Auchinleck's *King Richard* and our own marginalization of that matter, between their rumor about Richard and our rumor about *Richard Coeur de Lion.*

In this chapter's first half, I discuss the core rumor that circulated in medieval England, and the insular ramifications of its meaning and function. Building on those ramifications, the second half of the chapter intervenes in

---

18. P. R. Robinson, "The 'Booklet': A Self-Contained Unit in Composite Manuscripts," *Codicologica* 3 (1980): 46–69; see Ralph Hanna, *Pursuing History: Middle English Manuscripts and Their Texts* (Stanford: Stanford University Press, 1996), 21–34, esp. 21–24, where Hanna urges an awareness of approach in the study of booklets: "One can consider booklets from two perspectives—that of the vendor or owner of books and that of the producer of books" (22). I am primarily interested in the latter perspective here and in the balance of this chapter, where I identify other codicological and textual units whose separability, like that of booklets, was essential to the production of medieval manuscripts and their texts.

19. Schellekens, "An Edition," 2:32, independently arrives at a similar conclusion about the stability of these episodes across manuscripts, isolating them primarily on the basis of dialect.

our codicological approach to the textual tradition of *Richard Coeur de Lion* and retrospective textual traditions more generally. We often elide the effects of medieval manuscript culture's instability—narrative and material fragmentation and excision—to produce a representative text for study and teaching, or to make a "complete" text in line with modern expectations. But, as this chapter demonstrates, the literary "Matter of Richard I" was not a product of agglomeration, nor did its makers aspire to its "completion." Its power was located in its instability. The practices dismissed by traditional book history as errors or evidence of failure not only characterize the extant copies of *Richard Coeur de Lion,* but constitute a set of tools deployed by text-makers to make each copy of the romance flexible: relevant to its time and place and amenable to the addition and excision, the repeating and suppressing, of local talk and rumor.

In the manuscript copies of *Richard Coeur de Lion,* the core rumor of Richard begins with the treason of French crusaders that precipitates the fall of Jerusalem; the English and French armies convening at Marseille; Philip's circulation of rumors about Richard in Messina; and Richard's meeting there with Tancred, king of Puglia, to undo Philip's treachery.[20] It culminates in the battle between Messina's Greeks (and the French) and the English, the shipwreck of English crusaders on the coast of Cyprus, Richard's subsequent extended siege of that island and the humiliating defeat of its emperor, and the at-sea capture of a supply vessel on its way to Acre. The core rumor ends with Richard cutting Acre's defensive chain,[21] the English fleet's spectacular entrance into that city, the archbishop of Pisa's tale of the crusaders' hardship at Acre prior to Richard's arrival, and the ensuing siege of Acre, with beehives flung from catapults in the summer heat.

Given its placement in the royal book Oxford, Christ Church, MS 92,[22] where the hives are pictured being launched by a windmill's arms, this is perhaps the oldest and most well-worn strand of the core rumor. The language and images in the core rumor's siege of Acre—the "mangonel" in Auchinleck's *King Richard,* the "sails" in its *Short Chronicle,* the depiction of the windmill in Christ Church 92, and even the name "Richard" itself—respond expressly to a "political song" that began to circulate during the Second Barons' War, after the Battle of Lewes in May 1264. *King Richard* appropriates the key terms and images of this "song" or poem, which circulated until at least the early fourteenth century, and it perverts them in Richard's siege of Acre to

---

20. See chapter 1.
21. This is the scene depicted in Auchinleck's *King Richard* miniature, on which see chapter 4.
22. See chapter 3.

produce an alternate rumor, as if the final voice in a high-stakes game of telephone. The song, which Thomas Wright printed in his collection of *Political Songs* as the "Song Against the King of Almaigne" survives as a unique copy in London, British Library, MS Harley 2253, a manuscript produced in Ludlow roughly contemporaneously with Auchinleck. Its first three (of eight) stanzas are as follows:

> Sitteth alle stille ant herkneth to me!
> The Kyng of Alemaigne, bi mi leaute,
> Thritti thousent pound askede he
> Forte make the pees in the countre,
> Ant so he dude more.
> *Richard,*
> *Thah thou be ever trichard,*
> *Tricchen shalt thou nevermore!*
>
> Richard of Alemaigne, whil that he wes kyng,
> He spende al is tresour opon swyvyng,
> Haveth he nout of Walingford o ferlyng;
> Let him habbe ase he brew, bale to dryng,
> Maugre Wyndesore.
> *Richard,*
> *Thah thou be ever trichard,*
> *Tricchen shalt thou nevermore!*
>
> The Kyng of Alemaigne wende do ful wel,
> He saisede the mulne for a castel,
> With hare sharpe swerdes he grounde the stel.
> He wende that the sayles were mangonel
> To helpe Wyndesore.
> *Richard,*
> *Thah thou be ever trichard,*
> *Tricchen shalt thou nevermore!*[23]

---

23. Fein, *Harley 2253*, 2: Art. 23, under the title "Sitteth alle stille ant herkneth to me." John Scattergood describes it as "the earliest surviving English *sirventes*"; quoted in David Matthews, *Writing to the King: Nation, Kingship and Literature in England, 1250–1350* (Cambridge: Cambridge University Press, 2010), 35, where Matthews also calls it "the sole complete" vernacular pro-baronial "song" from the period.

In the balance of its stanzas this pro-baronial song criticizes John de Warenne and Edward I, still a prince during the war, and praises Simon de Montfort, leader of the barons' rebellion. "Richard" here is Richard, Earl of Cornwall, brother to Henry III, and, from 1257, king of Germany. The Montfortians captured him, as the poem depicts, hiding in a windmill.[24] In the song's third verse, Richard of Cornwall holds the "mulne" or mill as his castle or fortress. An absurd miller, he and his men defend it with "sharpe swerdes," and they mistake its "sails" or arms for a "mangonel," or siege engine.

The poem's survival in a unique copy belies its fame—or its infamy, depending on one's side in the civil war that precipitated its composition—for its presence in Harley 2253 confirms that it was still circulating in talk and text during the early fourteenth century. Eighteenth-century rumor had it that the song's circulation was so ubiquitous and persistent in both the immediate aftermath and longer wake of the Second Barons' War that the rare libel law Edward I issued in 1275 was in direct rebuke:

> Forasmuch as there have been oftentimes found in the Country [Devisors] of Tales, whereby discord [or occasion] of discord, hath many times arisen between the King and his People, or Great Men of this Realm; for the Damage that hath and may thereof ensue; It is commanded, That from henceforth non be so hardy to tell or publish any false News or Tales, whereby discord, or [occasion] of discord or slander may grow between the King and his People, or the Great Men of the Realm; and he that doth so, shall be taken and kept in Prison, until he hath brought him in to the Court [which was the first Author of the Tale.]
> (Statute of Westminster, I, 3 Edw. I, c. 34.)[25]

The *Statutes of the Realm*, from which the copy of this statute is taken, translates "contier" as "to publish," but "to tell" or "to account," as in, "to give an account of," would be a more accurate meaning. Presumably, and ironically, the first tellers of false tales would be brought to the eyre courts, where their

---

24. Matthews, *Writing to the King*, 35–37.

25. *Statutes of the Realm*, 1:35: "Purceo q̄ plusors unt sovent trove [& Conte com troveurs] dont descord & manere de descord ad este sovent entre le Rey e son pople, ou [aukuns homes] de son reaume, est defendu pur le damage q̄ ad este e uncore purreit avenir, q̄ desorenavaunt nul ne seit si hardi de dire ne de contier nule fause novele ou controveure, dont, nul descord ou manere de descord ou desclaundre puisse sourdre entre le Rey e son pople, ou les hauz houmes de son reaume: Et ki le fra seit pris e detenuz en p'son, jseqes taunt q̄ il eit trove celuy en la Court dont la parole serra meu." On this statute in its longer legal context, see Van Vechten Veeder, "The History and Theory of the Law of Defamation," *Columbia Law Review* 3 (1903): 546–73, esp. 551–61.

tales would no doubt be told again, officially, when the charge was read out, and repeated by those who heard it. Such legislation is one approach to silencing certain kinds of talk. The circulation of King Richard's siege of Acre takes an alternate tack: the overwriting, or talking over, of one vernacular political rumor with another. By at least the early fourteenth century, when images of windmills and crusade appear together in Christ Church 92, the alternate rumor about "King Richard" using a "mangonel," "sails," and a windmill to set siege to Acre was in the air. With the circulation of this counter-rumor, Richard of Cornwall would have become only "a" Richard, not "the" Richard.

"The" Richard—King Richard, uncle to Richard of Cornwall—is bluntly presented in the opening lines of Auchinleck's *King Richard* as not a "coward," a claim that, as noted in the previous chapter, anticipates some accusation against Richard external to the romance itself. In light of Richard of Cornwall, however, the too-eager refutation of Richard's cowardice also reads as a response to the sonic and therefore notional sameness of "Richard" and "trichard," a word whose sole attestation is the refrain of the "Song Against the King of Almaigne."[26] It is impossible to say how much the pro-Richard, royalist rumor was elaborated upon in Auchinleck, though given the manuscript's repurposing of England's Charlemagne material, the account of Richard's mangonel underwent significant expansion and embellishment in the hands of Scribe 1. The pro-baronial talk to which Auchinleck's Richard material responds, and thus evokes, further enriches the manuscript's textual invention and political deployment of its crusader king. Rather than rending England from itself, Richard unites it by bridging the baronial and royalist factions as a king with palpable baronial qualities. He fights alongside of and leads his men, and together they constitute a single body, a single "nacioun."

As far as I am aware, no argument has been made for a purposeful juxtaposition of Auchinleck's *King Richard* and *The Simonie*; the assumption has always been that other texts intervened. For a knowing reader of Auchinleck, as well as a text-maker like Scribe 1, *The Simonie* acknowledges the specter of the Second Barons' War raised in *King Richard*. *The Simonie* oscillates between vagueness and precision with enough skill to render its description of England's infighting, self-destruction, and waywardness a timeless spectacle. Near its end, *The Simonie* gestures at what around 1330 would have sounded like an echo of the Second Barons' War: the death (many said martyrdom) of Thomas of Lancaster, who led a baronial revolt of mainly marcher lords against Edward II in 1322.[27] In the hands of Scribe 1, political talk and the

---

26. *MED*, "trechard" n. Also *trichard*.

27. See Coss, *Political Songs*, xliii–xlvi; Turville-Petre, *England the Nation*, 132; and *The Simonie*, lines 428–45. On Thomas of Lancaster, see, for example, Camille, *Mirror in Parch-*

baggage it carries is made to do nuanced retrospective work. The two texts together raise the question of English identity and insist that the fourteenth-century reader exists in a crucible of choice.

The idea of English collective identity is embodied in the core rumor and thus sits at the heart of all copies of *Richard Coeur de Lion*. The "nacioun" Richard and his men embodied abroad could be anything the present moment and its public called for in retrospect: ingenious, victorious, proselytizing, vengeful; nostalgic, yearning for home. That home—that England—could likewise be, according to Richard and according to the reader of his romance or the painter viewing his own work on the palace wall, anything they imagined. In the core of *Richard Coeur de Lion*, England's identity is largely contingent upon the talk among crusaders and on the talk of those who read about them retrospectively; upon saying and "mis-saying," articulating an imagined community, telling stories from a shared archive, and speaking a single language. For instance, at wintertime, the French and the Greeks are lodged within the city wall of Messina, while the English have stoically set up their pavilions outside of the city ("þe kynge of Fraunce wiþouten wene / Lay in þe cite of Messene / And þe kinge Richarde wiþouten þe wal").[28] When a disagreement between the English and the people of Messina shows signs of erupting into a full-fledged fight, the text draws a sharp and multifaceted distinction between the English and everyone else. Those lodged within the city wall:

---

ment, 72–75; and J. R. Maddicott, *Thomas of Lancaster, 1307–1322* (Oxford: Oxford University Press, 1970). It is also worth noting that taken together, *King Richard* and *The Simonie* fix the fourteenth-century's nostalgic gaze on the twelfth century, looking back to the early days of the Third Crusade in *King Richard*, and in *The Simonie*, if only fleetingly, to the martyrdom of Thomas Becket:

> But certes, holi churche is muchel ibrouht þer doune
> Siþþen seint Thomas was slain and smitten of his croune.
> He was a piler ariht to holden vp holi churche.
> Þise oþere ben to slouwe and feinteliche kunnen worche,
> Iwis. (lines 37–40)

In a poem that otherwise condemns almost every social group and institution that structured fourteenth-century life, especially the transhistorical Church stretching from Rome to England and the people who actively propped it up or passively went along to get along, the solace located in the past, and specifically in a twelfth-century past not of Henry II or John but of Richard and Becket, takes readers out of the poem and, indeed, out of the present in which they are reading it. Henry II and John both appear in Auchinleck's *Short Chronicle*, and neither fares well there. Henry's long and eventful reign is compressed into six lines, one giving Henry's burial place and four on Becket's death: "In his time seyn Thomas / For Godes loue martird was / At Caunterbiri toforn þe auter ston. / He doþ miracles mani on" (lines 2033–36).

28. *King Richard*, lines 181–83.

    shet hastiliche þe gate
Wiþ barres þat þai founde þerate,
& vrn on hast to þe wal
& schoten wiþ speres & springal
& crid to our folk saunfeyl
"Goþ hom dogges wiþ ȝour tayl.
For ȝour bost & ȝour orgoyl
Man schal þrest in ȝour coyl."
Þus þai misdeden & misseyd;
& king Richard sore atreyd.²⁹

The collectivity of the English is emphasized here not only by that group's locational differentiation from the Greeks and the French—the English encampment is an England in microcosm, an isolated island itself on the island of Sicily—but also by their externally perceived and articulated difference. They collectively endure the old insult that Englishmen are tailed,³⁰ an insult described in *Richard Coeur de Lion* as explicitly a problem of language, of "mis-saying." The text implicates its readers in this double-edged insult and badge of collective identity in a way that simultaneously imagines and produces an English community. That community encompasses not only the English encamped at Messina but also all English readers and writers of *Richard Coeur de Lion* present in England over the course of the fourteenth and fifteenth centuries. These are "our men" in Cambridge, Gonville and Caius College, MS 175/96; "our Englissh men" in London, College of Arms, MS Arundel 58; "owre Englysche-menne" in London, British Library, MS Harley 4690; and "our folk" in the Auchinleck manuscript.

    The transhistorical idea of England is brought into being through reading, and talking. Similar scenes occur frequently within the core rumor, and

---

    29. *King Richard,* lines 241–50.

    30. This scene has often been raised in discussions of the romance's monstrosity, including the cannibalism episodes, and the growth of the idea of England and English identity. Turville-Petre, *England the Nation,* 123, goes so far as to call "the Englishman's tail, referred to again and again, [the] real subject of the first half of the story." Historically the insult was primarily deployed by the French and the Scots, but it is first recorded in twelfth-century stories about the English, including one in which Kentishmen tie rays' tails to St. Augustine of Canterbury's cope; they along with their descendants are marked for the sin by developing biological tails. See, for example, George Neilson, *Caudatus Anglicus: A Medieval Slander* (Edinburgh: G. P. Johnston, 1896), 2 and 18–19. Neilson notes that the rumor circulated in the fifteenth century by way of *The Golden Legend.* See also P. Rickard, *Britain in Medieval French Literature 1100–1500* (Cambridge: Cambridge University Press, 1956), 165–66.

they remain stable throughout the romance's centuries-long transmission.³¹ These scenes become opportunities for the English to (re)define themselves and the terms by which they are identified, through a more skillful wielding of language within the narrative, and through its composition. Anticipating the imminent fight at Messina, Richard leads his army to the base of the city wall, and

> His ost he ded at ones crie,
> Men mi3t it here into þe skie
> "Now lasse cum Freyns musardes
> & 3if bateyl to þe teylardes."³²

The English use "teylardes" here to refer to themselves, and in doing so, they not only take possession of the term, they also redefine it through recontextualization. Here the "teylardes" are a pack of aggressive—and, as we know, soon to be victorious—warriors. Indeed, throughout its core rumor, *Richard Coeur de Lion* repeatedly yokes the image of the tailed Englishmen to English victory in battle. The insult becomes a provocation, and because the English usually win in the romance, the language also becomes inextricably tied to the image of collective achievement, through either strength or cunning. The justices of France "chide" Richard, calling him a "teylarde." He immediately bears arms and violently beats them for, again, "mis-saying." In the romance, talk has stakes situationally and ideologically for individual and collective identity.

Two further episodes are crucial to the core rumor's project of conjuring, articulating, and reconstructing England as a collective "nacioun" abroad. The first comprises the conclusion of the battle against the French and Greeks at Messina. Richard and his men ride toward one of the city's unguarded gates and there encounter the Greeks and, unexpectedly, the French. At this moment, Richard repeatedly calls attention to the French army's treachery: "And euer cryed Kynge Richarde / Slee downe righte the Frensshe cowarde, / And ken them in batayl / That ye have no tayl."³³ A battle ensues, which the English are winning. Philip then appears on horseback and begs for mercy.

---

31. For instance, *Richard Löwenherz*, lines 1869–78, also at Messina: "The knyghtes framed the tre-castell / Before the cyte vpon an hyll. / All this sawe the Kynge of Fraunce, / And sayd: 'Haue ye no doutaunce / Of all these Englyssh cowardes ["taylardes" in MSS. Harley 4690, Arundel 58, and Douce 228], / For they ne be but mossardes; / Drisses now your mangenell, / And caste to theyr tre-castell, / And shote to them with arblast, / The tayled dogges for to agast!"

32. *King Richard*, lines 299–302; *Richard Löwenherz*, lines 1883–86.

33. *Richard Löwenherz*, lines 1957–60. I cite *Richard Löwenherz* rather than *King Richard* here and in several subsequent notes because this scene is partially contained in Auchinleck's

Richard takes pity on the French king and halts the battle, whereupon Philip asks that Richard be his confessor and offers him treasure in repayment for his treatment of the English. Richard rejects this offer, saying that it cheapens their crusading oath, but he agrees to honor that oath by continuing his journey with Philip to the East. Immediately after this:

> Whan abbated was that dystaunce,
> There came two justyces of Fraunce
> Upon two stedes ryde,
> And Kynge Rycharde they gan chyde.
> That one as hyght Margaryte,
> That other Syr Hewe Impetyte.
> Swythe sore they hym trayde,
> Cleped hym taylarde and hym myssayde.
> Kyng Rycharde helde a tronchon tewe,
> And to them two he hym drewe;
> Sir Margaryte he gaue a dente than
> Aboue the eye vpon the pan;
> The skulle braste with that dente,
> The ryght eye flewe out quytemente,
> And he fell downe deede in haste.
> Hewe of Impetyte was agaste,
> And prycked away withouten fayle,
> And Rycharde was soone at his tayle
> And gaue hym a stroke on the molde,
> That deed he thought be he sholde.
> Ternes and quernes he gaue hym there,
> And sayd: "Syr, thus thou shalt lere
> To myssaye thy ouerhedlynge!
> Go playne now to your Frensshe kynge!"[34]

After Richard again grants the French mercy, the text explains, "To this daye men may here speke / How the Englysshe were there awreke."[35] To put it another way, talk preserves the past.

Edinburgh fragments and was thus presumably continued on the first leaf of the lost bifolium of Auchinleck's forty-eighth quire.

34. *Richard Löwenherz*, lines 1999–2022.
35. *Richard Löwenherz*, lines 2031–32; the language and narrative of this episode are remarkably stable across all manuscript copies.

The second episode in which the idea of England is codified abroad occurs while the English are at sea, en route from Cyprus to Acre. One night, in the middle of a storm at sea, Richard spots a "dromond," or a large and fast ship, weighed down with provisions, and sailing—like the English ships—toward Acre. Richard calls on one of his men, "Aleyn Trenchemer," to go out, row alongside this strange ship, and inquire after its sailors' identity and purpose. Aleyn does this, and a man on the mysterious ship replies that they are transporting the French king's provisions from Puglia to Acre. After another brief exchange, Aleyn remains skeptical:

Þenne sayde Alayn sone anon:
"I here off ȝow speke but on;
Let stande vp alle in ffere,
Þat we now myȝte moo here,
And knowe ȝoure tungge afftyr þan;
Ffor we wole nouȝt leue oo man."[36]

When the man refuses this order, saying that the ship's other men are asleep, Aleyn's suspicions are confirmed and he declares: "To Kyng Rychard j wole seyn / That ȝe aren alle Sarezynes euerylkon."[37] He does this, and a battle aboard ship follows; the English are victorious and lay claim to the ship's provisions, which were presumably intended for the Muslims of Acre.

Aleyn's distrust of a single man, in this case an English-speaking (or French-speaking?) one representing a group, encapsulates the romance's views on collective identity and talk. It is difficult to know why Aleyn does not "believe" the lone speaker on the strange ship: because his original "tongue" must be determined to define his true identity? Or because he is unable or unwilling to produce a like-minded and like-speaking community when pressed? In retrospective texts, talk about the past can be talk about the present and the future. If Richard became a mechanism for reconstructing England's past in the thirteenth-century eyre courts, he becomes a signifier of its present and a prophet of its future in the core rumor of *Richard Coeur de Lion*. From the vantage point of Richard abroad, England becomes a distant island, an idea, a memory to be made. Richard was kept in mind and memory precisely because of the deep utility of his narrative in its flexible iterations of the idea of England.

---

36. *Richard Löwenherz*, lines 2499–504.
37. *Richard Löwenherz*, lines 2510–11.

The theorization of a shared lexicon about the present and the past, a vocabulary fundamental to the formation of England's identity, is the conversation in which *Richard Coeur de Lion* most consistently participates by way of its core rumor. This core rumor upsets the logic of Karl Brunner's *a* and *b* manuscript groups because the material deemed marginal according to Brunner's rationale is in fact essential. The discrepancy between our rumor and the core rumor makes it incumbent upon us to evaluate Brunner's configuration of manuscript copies and to reexamine the ways in which the romance was transmitted and the memory of Richard kept in mind throughout England. *Richard Coeur de Lion*'s extant manuscript copies exemplify a model of textual production in which narrative and material instability was confronted and then converted into a productive nimbleness. This model stands in direct opposition to Brunner's valuing of volume, and it challenges both the recent championing of what we might call the "agglomerative" model and the perennial scholarly impulse to make the past whole and coherent in the medieval memory, and in our own. Brunner's composite edition misconstrues the importance and productivity of narrative discrepancy and material fragmentation. In the manuscript copies of *Richard Coeur de Lion,* these and other strategies of textual production, dismissed in traditional book history as the failure of scribe, transmission, or preservation, constitute a collection of literary and text-making tools deployed by medieval scribes, bookmakers, and readers of retrospective texts. The form and function of retrospective texts therefore necessitate a reimagining and rearticulation of their textual traditions. Instead of finite "completeness," these textual traditions are grounded in productive instability. The aim of medieval writers and redactors would not have been to move back to an "original" iteration of a text or to stabilize its content, but to produce locally and historically contingent, and thus expressly relative and relevant, texts.

We must, then, bracket Brunner's stemmatic groups in order to reconceive of *Richard Coeur de Lion*'s textual transmission in terms of its chronological development: its transmission and reconstruction over time, as it was exposed to new talk about the present time and place, and new rumors circulating about the late twelfth-century past. This chronological model does not reveal an unceasing agglomeration of text over time, or a medieval notion of completeness that aligns with Brunner's ideal of the longest and therefore the best copy. Rather, it shows that the extant manuscript copies of *Richard Coeur de Lion* are not the products of ongoing accretion, but of pointed addition, excision, and revision over time.

While no extant manuscript containing *Richard Coeur de Lion* demonstrates a direct connection to any other, if we remove the manuscripts from

Brunner's stemma and organize them chronologically, the conversation about *Richard Coeur de Lion,* and thus about Richard, that was continuously occurring among its manuscripts and in the air becomes more audible. If Auchinleck's "fragment" marks the *terminus post quem* for the textual codification of public talk about Richard, then the fourteenth- and fifteenth-century manuscripts in which *Richard Coeur de Lion* survives resemble the eyre court records of the thirteenth century: They are repositories of local insular talk. Auchinleck itself at some point made its way from London to Scotland.[38] London, British Library, MS Egerton 2862 was written and probably remained in southeastern Suffolk.[39] The independent fragment, Gloucester, Gloucestershire Archives, MS D2700/V/1 No. 8 (*olim* Badminton, Duke of Beaufort, MS 704.1.16.), or the "Beaufort fragment," belonged to a manuscript probably copied in the area of the southwest Midlands and Gloucestershire, before it was perhaps excised from its manuscript and sent further west, to Wales.[40] The London Thornton manuscript and Cambridge, Gonville and Caius College, MS 175/96, were both copied and presumably both read in northern England: Yorkshire and Lincolnshire, respectively.[41] London, College of Arms, MS Arundel 58 has been located to Wiltshire in the southwest,[42] and London, British Library, MS Harley 4690 has also been located to the southwest of England, perhaps Somerset or southern Gloucester.[43] On the basis of dialectal and other internal evidence, Oxford, Bodleian Library, MS Douce 228 has been located to Norfolk.[44]

The earliest extant manuscript witnesses of *Richard Coeur de Lion*—Auchinleck, Egerton 2862, and the Beaufort fragment—contain (and in the

---

38. *LALME,* 1:88 (for "Hand A"), LP 6510 (London-Middlesex border).

39. On Egerton 2862, see *LALME,* 3:485, LP 8360, Grid 623 248; Guddat-Figge, *Catalogue,* 182–84; and M. Johnston, *Romance and the Gentry,* 94 n. 12, 110–14, esp. 111 n. 43.

40. Davis, "Another Fragment," 451.

41. For Additional 31042, see *LALME,* 1:101, and for Gonville and Caius, MS 175/96, see *LALME,* 1:63, LP 512. On Robert Thornton and the making and reading of his manuscripts, see, most recently, M. Johnston, *Romance and the Gentry,* 159–205. On the provenance of Gonville and Caius 175/96, see my article "Douce 228, *Richard Coeur de Lion,* and *The King of Tars," Notes and Queries* 65 (2018): 11.

42. *LALME,* 1:117, LP 5411.

43. Harley 4690 and Arundel 58 both appear in manuscripts that also contain the only extant copies of the "Mandeville translation" of the Anglo-Norman prose *Brut;* see Lister M. Matheson, *The Prose Brut: The Development of a Middle English Chronicle* (Binghamton, NY: Medieval and Renaissance Texts and Studies, 1998), 332–34. On Harley 4690, see also Guddat-Figge, *Catalogue,* 205–6.

44. *LALME,* 1:147, LP 4564. On the local context of Douce 228, see Beadle, "Prolegomena," 106; and on the milieu of talk and text that the manuscript preserves and responds to, see my article, "Douce 228," 8–11.

cases of Auchinleck and Beaufort consist of) the core rumor. The next manuscripts produced—the Caius manuscript that Brunner copied and the miscellany in Robert Thornton's hand (London Thornton)—contain the most expansive copies of *Richard Coeur de Lion*. Their text-makers added episodes, such as those involving Richard's mother and Richard's cannibalism, around the stable core of episodes found in the earlier manuscripts. The three latest extant manuscripts, Arundel 58, Harley 4690, and Douce 228, also contain the earliest manuscripts' core rumor, but the material in these later manuscripts is significantly pared down. They contain no substantial new material and no elaboration of old material. Narrative repetition is mostly absent from these copies, and some episodes have been simplified while others are absent altogether.

The Caius and London Thornton manuscripts, which survive from the chronological middle of the tradition, are longer than other copies of the romance because they contain new material around the core rumor, and also because they contain a great deal of unique narrative repetition. An episode the reader has already encountered will often be retold in detail by at least one of the text's characters, and therefore from his or her slightly altered perspective.[45] A lengthy description of a tournament sponsored by Richard and set in England during the early part of his reign, for instance, is added in Caius and London Thornton before the core rumor begins. In addition to a first description of the tournament, the entire story of the tournament is immediately retold within the narrative by one of Richard's knights.[46] The effect of such repetition is paradoxical, at once stalling the forward movement of the narrative and self-consciously portraying the process of oral transmission. Narrative repetition becomes an aesthetic principle in these manuscripts.

Other episodes in either Caius or London Thornton, and sometimes in both, have been added around the core rumor. On one side of the core, these include Richard's fantastical origin story: his parents' meeting and details about Richard's mother, an Antiochian princess who cannot bear the sight of the Eucharist; a jousting tournament at Salisbury, where Richard disguises himself in strange armor; the tournament scene's retelling and Richard's suggestion that he and his two best knights go to the East; the pre-crusade reconnaissance mission subsequently undertaken by Richard with "Fulk Doly"

---

45. On shifting perspectives in Caius and London Thornton, see Torpey, "Of Cannibalism and Kings," 111–12.

46. *Richard Löwenherz*, lines 251–450 for the first version; lines 451–590 for the second version, from the knight's perspective.

and "Thomas Multon,"[47] and Richard's capture. On the other side of the core are Richard's cannibalism and multiple long descriptions of several almost identical battles after Acre, battles that often end with the, alternatively forced and willing, conversion of Muslims in exchange for their lives. These copies thus develop an assimilative imaginary through the inclusion of these scenes of conversion and Richard's cannibalism. The conversion episodes are unique to Caius and London Thornton, suggesting an explicit religious interest or agenda not as overtly present among earlier manuscript copies, nor transmitted or sustained in later copies of the text.

Having emerged from the same fifteenth-century geographical milieu, Caius and London Thornton shared a store of local rumor. Extant images evince that several of the episodes the two manuscripts have in common were circulating contemporaneously in the area. Visual representations associable with Richard's imprisonment in "Almayne," as depicted in the northern copies of the romance, survive from southern Lincolnshire and Peterborough, and from Norwich, further east. They include an image in the early fourteenth-century book, Brussels, Bibliothèque royale de Belgique, MS 9961-62, or the Peterborough Psalter, of a bearded king standing before a crowd of people while pulling the heart out of a lion (fol. 33r), and an early fifteenth-century boss in the cloister of Norwich Cathedral. M. R. James posits that the man who raises a dagger in boss VI is Richard, and that the image relates to Richard's acquisition of an "Irish knife" in the romance while imprisoned in Almayne.[48] In 1915, R. S. Loomis inventoried these visual depictions, but without realizing the full significance of their geographical proximity to the fifteenth-century copies of *Richard Coeur de Lion* that appear to gloss them.[49] The addition of these episodes in Caius and London Thornton puts their copies of the romance in conversation with these local images: the local version of Richard in the air.

The copies of *Richard Coeur de Lion* in its three chronologically latest manuscripts, Arundel 58, Harley 4690, and Douce 228, are shorter than their predecessors, in part because they do not include the repetition common in both Caius and London Thornton. These three manuscripts exhibit the transmission of many of the stories added around the core rumor in the Caius

---

47. Finlayson, "*Richard Coer de Lyon*," 166, notes that both a Fulk d'Oilly and a Thomas Moulton "did exist"; L. H. Loomis, *Medieval Romance*, 148–49, suggests that the families of Multon and "Oilli" were "connected through the marriage of Lambert de Multon (d. 1247) with the widow of Geffrey de Oilli." See also Schellekens, "An Edition," 2:89, which places the former family in Yorkshire and the latter in Lincolnshire, and locates the dialect of the relevant passages to Lincolnshire.

48. Cited in R. S. Loomis, "*Richard Coeur de Lion*," 521 n. 18.

49. R. S. Loomis, "*Richard Coeur de Lion*," 520–22.

and London Thornton copies, but several other episodes added in those two copies are cleanly absent from the Arundel, Harley, and Douce manuscripts. All three manuscripts preserve the tournament scene, the pre-crusade pilgrimage, Richard's subsequent imprisonment, and the English victory at Jaffa around the core rumor of Messina, Cyprus, and Acre. But in these manuscripts the years of Richard's kingship are recentered. The story of Richard's birth is not present in these manuscripts, nor do they contain the most sensational or overtly didactic rumors of their manuscript predecessors. The cannibalism scenes and the violent conversion narratives are not now and never were present in these latest extant manuscript copies of *Richard Coeur de Lion*.

That such changes around the core rumor were purposeful and planned for is confirmed by *Richard Coeur de Lion*'s narrative form, which I call "modular." Discrete episodes can be dropped in or entirely eliminated around the core rumor without disrupting the narrative's sense. This episodic modularity allows for fluidity, and for the production of a bespoke narrative sensitive to time and place. The core rumor's essentialness to *Richard Coeur de Lion*, and the modularity of the romance's other parts around that core, interrupt our scholarly rumor. The parts of the romance that we talk about were not the same parts that its medieval makers and readers were consistently circulating, at least not according to the manuscript copies that survive. The fundamental parts of our rumor of *Richard Coeur de Lion*—Richard's Antiochian mother, his cannibalism—survive in a minority of manuscripts and, without exception, bear various signs of contestation. In Arundel, Harley, and Douce, the romance's modular form allowed for a reckoning with the cannibalism episodes.

The first cannibalism scene was never present in these manuscripts. Instead, their narratives simply move from one event to the next at Acre, eliminating Richard's illness altogether. In place of the second cannibalism episode, in which Richard invites Saladin's messengers to dinner and personally provides the recipe for preparing Muslims that his own English cook should follow, Arundel and Douce instead contain an episode involving a game of chess between Philip and Richard.[50] At line 3,346 in *Richard Löwenherz*, Richard has finally conquered Acre after a discussion with Philip of France over how the "tresore" ought to be divided between them, leaving Philip less than pleased with his own portion of the reward. At this point, the Caius and London Thornton manuscripts move into the second cannibalism episode. Arundel and Douce do not. Instead, they contain thirty-six lines of further dialogue between Richard and Philip over a game of chess. Philip revisits the

---

50. *Richard Löwenherz*, lines 3348ff. By this point, Harley 4690 has ended imperfectly at *Richard Löwenherz*, line 2775.

arrangements the men had previously made about the treasure of Acre, and tempers fly.[51] These unstable moments embody the rumors about Richard that themselves flew as soon as he departed England as a crusader—those separable pieces of speculative talk that together constitute a perpetually alterable whole.[52]

The romance's modularity suggests that the retrospective conversation about Richard throughout England was similarly unstable. Aspects of the medieval memory of Richard were flexible: Around the romance's core, new rumors were assembled, added to, and excised. Auchinleck's effort to reconstruct a memory of Richard relative to fourteenth-century London was mimicked to some degree by the maker of each subsequent copy of *Richard Coeur de Lion*. While the romance's core forged in Auchinleck remained stable, changes were made around it by way of the romance's modular pieces. The romance's narrative modularity thus continues the historiographical negotiations vis-à-vis Richard's reign that writers such as Richard of Devizes had entered into while Richard lived. Manuscripts offered possibilities for reconstructing Richard's reign that print culture does not, such as Devizes's bifurcated *mise-en-page*. Where Robert of Gloucester had produced a text that displayed the "seams" inherent in the reconstructive project,[53] those involved in the textual transmission of *Richard Coeur de Lion* reconstructed his reign rather more seamlessly. In making and remaking the text, they made a virtue of the instability of manuscript culture.

The copies bear the marks of text-makers keenly aware of the productive flexibility and instability of Richard's textual corpus. Here rumor functions both as a formal device, a means of rendering the past newly relevant, and a way of implicating the reader in a shared retrospective project. *Richard Coeur de Lion* exemplifies this modular form, but other retrospective texts similarly embody this productive instability. For instance, the *SEL,* both at the level of its overall composition and within its individual lives, is fundamentally modular. The contents of the *SEL* vary radically from manuscript to manuscript, but not arbitrarily. The time and place of a copy's production often dictated its contents so that local saints were included and other saints excluded. One of the *SEL*'s longer lives, that of Thomas Becket, is, like *Richard Coeur de Lion,* formally modular. Its various "historical" and miraculous episodes can be added and excised, including its romance-like introduction in which Thomas's

---

51. A compact version of the chess scene survives in the Richard material unique to Auchinleck's *Short Chronicle* at lines 2157–74.

52. On rumor contemporary with Richard, see esp. chapters 1 and 3; and *Richard I,* esp. 5–9 and 226–30.

53. On the chronicles of Richard of Devizes and Robert of Gloucester, see chapter 3.

Muslim mother wanders England repeating her only "Engliss" word: "Londone, Londone."[54] Through modularity, the details of retrospective texts could vary according to the local talk, common knowledge, and situated exigencies that contextualized a given manuscript copy.

The modular form of retrospective texts can be ascribed to the makers of those texts, but in more unofficial ways Richard's textual corpus in England resembles that of his remains abroad: fragmented and distributed as monuments to his memory. Different types of fragmentation, narrative and material, appear in the extant copies of *Richard Coeur de Lion*. The first of these is historical fragmentation, exemplified by the choice to begin Auchinleck's copy with Richard taking the cross rather than being born or being crowned king. The water damage at the start of Egerton 2862 exemplifies a second type, inadvertent fragmentation. The third is purposeful fragmentation: fragmentation whose pattern across the extant copies of *Richard Coeur de Lion* renders coincidence and chance insufficient explanations for the manuscripts' present material states.[55] We often ascribe material loss to accident, but the recovered fragments and extant fragmented manuscripts of *Richard Coeur de Lion* potentially preserve an active readerly contestation over how the past should be reconstructed and narrated.

The repeated fragmentation around *Richard Coeur de Lion*'s narrative of the English journey to Acre and the English experience once there appears to be a manifestation not of haphazard intervention, but rather of more than one reader taking matters into his or her own hands, and modifying the contours of this specific rumor about the past. The textual remains of *King Richard* in Auchinleck and in all recovered fragments of *Richard Coeur de Lion*— whether dated to the early fourteenth or early fifteenth century; whether textually localizable to London, Suffolk, or the Midlands; whether discovered on a university professor's notebook in Scotland or in Badminton among the possessions of the Duke of Beaufort—preserve the rumor about Richard and Acre. In Egerton 2862 and the Beaufort fragment, the two earliest witnesses after Auchinleck, the text around the siege of Acre has been physically reconstructed to form more desirable, or at least alternative, versions of what happened on the Third Crusade from one English perspective. That which scholars now deem a major "loss" of quires at the end of Auchinleck's *King Richard* may alternatively be read as purposeful fragmentation, as a decision

---

54. D'Evelyn and Mill, *SEL*, 2:613, lines 73–75.

55. My thinking about the material fragmentation of the manuscripts of *Richard Coeur de Lion* has been shaped by Jennifer Miller's general conceptualization of "purposive fragmentation," which can apply to many medieval texts and scribal contexts.

taken and acted upon to excise everything but that which centered on *King Richard*'s account of Acre.

Even at a chronological remove of roughly half a century from Auchinleck's production, and at some geographical distance from London, Egerton 2862 and the Beaufort fragment, which consists of a parchment bifolium with the outer half of the first leaf cut off,[56] begin not in some new and anticipated crusading locale, but in familiar terrain: Acre. *Richard Coeur de Lion* is the first of seven items in Egerton 2862 and occupies fols. 1–44v.[57] However, Egerton has suffered a loss of several leaves at its beginning, and its first thirteen extant leaves have sustained severe water damage and tears, making them mostly illegible.[58] As a result of Egerton's damage and initial fragmentation, no sustained attention has been paid to the beginning of the manuscript, and so to the beginning of its copy of *Richard Coeur de Lion*, where the first voice to emerge from these damaged folios is in fact that of Richard, ordering his men to arm their ships in preparation for a battle against the Greeks and the French. This is a trace of the now familiar episode in which the English fight against the Greeks, surreptitiously aided by the French, in Messina.[59] On fol. 4r it is apparent that Richard and his men are in the midst of battle against the Cypriot emperor; on fol. 5r the English are victorious, demanding "his clothes and his tresoure"[60]; and by fol. 9v, where the legibility of Egerton's text improves significantly, Richard and his men have landed at Acre's port and are being welcomed by the Christian kings and emperors awaiting the English army there.[61] Egerton has been rebound so tightly that determining

---

56. Egerton 2862 has suffered losses at both ends and can be dated to the last quarter of the fourteenth century. For a fuller description, see Guddat-Figge, *Catalogue*, 182. Egerton 2862 is also described in Kölbing, "Vier romanzen-handschriften," 191–93. The Beaufort fragment has been described, dated, and localized by Norman Davis in "Another Fragment," 447–48, 451.

57. Egerton 2862 contains metrical romances. In addition to *Richard Coeur de Lion*, these include *Bevis of Hampton, Sir Degaré, Florence and Blanchfleur, The Siege of Troy, Amis and Amiloun*, and *Sir Eglamour*.

58. The text of Egerton 2862's first two extant folios remains largely illegible under UV light.

59. What remains of this scene in Egerton 2862 corresponds roughly to lines 273ff. of Auchinleck's *King Richard*. Although Egerton 2862's *mise-en-page* is not consistent across texts, *Richard Coeur de Lion* is consistently written in one column per folio, forty lines per column. Rubricated initials were planned for (guide letters are visible), but were never executed.

60. Egerton 2862, fol. 5r, line 1.

61. These episodes correspond to lines 540ff. and 733ff., respectively, in Auchinleck's *King Richard*.

its collation is at best highly speculative business.[62] Yet that it is missing leaves at the beginning of *Richard Coeur de Lion*,[63] and that those missing leaves mean the narrative begins with the core rumor, are both certainties.

The Beaufort fragment consists of the inner bifolium of a gathering whose original manuscript remains lost. Held in a private collection since the late 1960s, the fragment was discovered in the Duke of Beaufort's house and sent among a sheaf of loose manuscript leaves to Oxford's Bodleian Library for identification. After it was identified as having come from a text of *Richard Coeur de Lion* that could not be ascribed to any known manuscript, the Bodleian returned the fragment to Badminton and the Duke of Beaufort's private collection, where it remained until very recently.[64] It contains roughly 240 lines of text, though not entirely consecutive as a result of excision and damage.[65] Despite its condition, Beaufort's first lines preserve a familiar story, or more accurately traces of a familiar voice: the archbishop of Pisa, in the midst of telling Richard about the demoralization and bodily harm the crusader armies encamped at Acre have suffered. As we have already heard from Auchinleck, the archbishop's tale launches a weeping Richard into action, rallying his men, preparing his siege tower Mate-Griffon, and catapulting beehives into Acre, episodes that form a large part of the Beaufort fragment's contents.

The fragment contains more clues about its chain of custody than do many other extant copies of *Richard Coeur de Lion*. It apparently passed through hands interested in recording the processes by which it was taken from its original manuscript context and transmitted. Like Auchinleck's fragments, the Beaufort fragment was used as a wrapper or a binding for estate records

---

62. Determining Egerton 2862's collation is difficult in its current state. In addition to water damage on its first extant folios, margins that might have contained additional catchwords have been cut down, and the manuscript's rebinding and supports make it difficult to discern quire divisions. The first quire is perhaps wanting two leaves, which would bring it in line with the eight-leaf quires in much of the rest of the manuscript.

63. Egerton 2862's copy of *Richard Coeur de Lion* is titled "Kyng Richard." That Egerton does not begin perfectly is demonstrated most simply by "Richard," part of the text's running title visible in the upper margin. This indicates that there is at least one now lost preceding leaf that had "Kyng," the first word in the running title, above top line. The recto of that leaf would either have "Richard" at its top, indicating another prior leaf lost (this could go on endlessly), or "Kyng Richard" to mark the beginning of the text. See, for example, Bevis of Hampton in the manuscript, where "Bevis of Hampton" appears on fol. 45r, and then for the text's remainder is split above top line on recto and verso, for example, "Bevis" on fol. 45v and "of Hampton" on fol. 46r.

64. Davis, "Another Fragment," 447.

65. Davis, "Another Fragment," 447–48, describes the fragment's aspect in detail. I have worked from a color facsimile kindly provided by Andrew Parry of the Gloucestershire Archives.

until the nineteenth century. At least three different hands have marked it: The most recent wrote "1437" vertically up the left margin in pencil. Norman Davis, who examined the Beaufort fragment in 1969, has dated this hand to the eighteenth or nineteenth century. Below it, a second, earlier hand wrote "Raglan rent roll 15 Henry 6" (that is, 1437) in ink, and between text columns, a "careless hand which seems likely to be of the sixteenth century" has written in ink, now faded, "Rent Rolles of Ragland."[66] These could be just textual manifestations of the fragment's own rumor, made increasingly precise over time until the vaguer "Rent Rolles of Ragland" was specified to "1437." But there is little reason to think that we know more about the fragment's history than those more proximate to its fragmentation and circulation. Davis tentatively suggests that 1437 might be a *terminus ad quem* for the separation of the bifolium from its manuscript,[67] a suggestion that, if at all accurate, would mean that the copy of *Richard Coeur de Lion* to which the Beaufort fragment once belonged was mutilated (and possibly traveled from Gloucester to Raglan Castle in Monmouthshire, Wales) very soon after it was copied in the first quarter of the fifteenth century.[68] Such a situation would be remarkable because we so often assume a longer time between a manuscript's making and unmaking. It would be remarkable, too, because of the potential implications of the relative rapidity with which the manuscript's fragmentation might have occurred. This scenario of fragmentation could signify the only short-lived success, or the fundamental lack of success, of the copy of *Richard Coeur de Lion* to which the Beaufort fragment bears witness.

The fragment's particular contents should also give us pause. Beaufort very closely recalls the portions of Auchinleck's *King Richard* recovered in the Edinburgh fragments. Both the Beaufort and the Edinburgh fragments contain the archbishop of Pisa's lament, which over the space of two hundred lines details the destruction and humiliation of the crusader armies by the Muslims of Acre. It is a section of the romance that has the dual inner-textual effects of setting Richard up for martial greatness at Acre and emphasizing the deep disgrace and loss of the crusaders, English among them, who had

---

66. Davis, "Another Fragment," 447.
67. Davis, "Another Fragment," 448.
68. As Davis, "Another Fragment," 448, points out, "The oldest of the inscriptions 'Rent Rolles of Ragland,' might be thought to imply that [the fragment] was probably not at Raglan itself, though this need not be so"; however, as Davis also reports, in the fifteenth century, Raglan Castle was expressly related to the future Dukes of Beaufort (447). It is also worth noting that the Dukes of Beaufort descended from the Plantagenet's male line through John of Gaunt and Edward III, thus connecting, however indirectly, Edward III to another book about his ancestor, Richard.

preceded him there.⁶⁹ Once home from the Third Crusade, Roger of Howden memorialized some of the Englishmen who had died at Acre between 1190 and 1192, recording their names in his chronicle.⁷⁰ When compared with Roger's firsthand description of these events, the dire situation the archbishop relates rings true, but it may also have continued to resonate uncomfortably into the fourteenth and fifteenth centuries. The continued unsettledness of this part of the text and its narrative suggest a more purposeful, and in Auchinleck's case, potentially earlier, fragmentation of *Richard Coeur de Lion* than has previously been considered.

Whether or not the archbishop's talk of those events at Acre became a point of contention for *Richard Coeur de Lion*'s readers, whose own ancestors may have suffered the sorts of crusading losses Roger of Howden documents, the extant Auchinleck, Egerton, and Beaufort fragments of *Richard Coeur de Lion* all preserve the text's account of Acre, both the unexpectedly fraught journey to Acre and what happened once Richard and his forces arrived at the city's port. Together, Auchinleck's recovered St. Andrews fragments and Edinburgh fragments contain the skirmishes with the Greeks and the French at Messina; the battle of armies and wits waged between Richard and the Cypriot emperor; the final few lines of the sea-staged episode involving the dromond laden with supplies; Richard's spectacular arrival at Acre and a portion of the archbishop of Pisa's tale. Without Auchinleck's recovered fragments repositioned in the middle of the manuscript's *King Richard* quire, Auchinleck's narrative would take us from England to Messina, where Richard clears up the rumor the French king has spread about him, and then straight on to Acre and the siege, important in its own right and also the moment at which he, according to the romance's telling, exacts revenge on those who were responsible for the suffering of the crusaders encamped outside of Acre's wall. By excising any preceding difficulties that the advance guard faced, Auchinleck's fragmentation narratively hastens England's victory at Acre. Similarly, the Beaufort fragment commences with the last 150 lines or so of the archbishop's tale and contains Richard's beehive assault of Acre, as well as the crusaders' subsequent mining. After the Beaufort fragment was removed from its copy of the romance, that copy might have resembled the *King Richard* bifolium that survives between Auchinleck's boards.

---

69. The Beaufort fragment joins the archbishop's account later than the Edinburgh fragment does—at about line 830 in Auchinleck's *King Richard*, roughly the beginning of Edinburgh fragment fol. 4v—but it also contains more of the archbishop's direct speech than Auchinleck does.

70. Roger of Howden, *Gesta*, 2:148–50.

The provocative rumors of Richard's mother and his cannibalism also exhibit signs of pointed intervention. The episode containing an extended description of Richard's childhood and parents, Henry II and Cassodorien, a princess of Antioch, occurs in full only in the London Thornton manuscript. There Henry marries Cassodorien and they have three children: Richard, John, and a girl, Topyas. One day in church:

> Whene þe belle beg*an* to ry*n*g,
> The prest scholde make þe sakery*n*g,
> Out off þe kyrke sche wolde away.
> Þe erl "For gode, sayde, nay,
> Lady, þou schalt her*e* abyde,
> Ffor ony þyng þat may betyde."
> Sche took here douȝter i*n* her*e* hond,
> And Johan her sone she wolde not wonde;
> Out of the rofe she gan her dyght,
> Openly before all theyr sight.
> Johan fell frome her in that stounde,
> And brak his thygh on the grounde.
> And with her doughter she fled her waye,
> That neuer she was isey.
> The kynge wondred of that thynge,
> That she made suche an endynge,
> For loue that he was serued so;
> Wolde he neuer after come there ne go.
> He let ordeyne, after his endynge,
> His sone Rycharde to be kynge.[71]

This is a "new" version of several old rumors: that Eleanor of Aquitaine was in actuality a devilish fairy, and that the Plantagenet line descended from demons.[72] Richard himself apparently repeated the latter rumor in moments

---

71. *Richard Löwenherz*, lines 221–40. I use *Richard Löwenherz* here and in subsequent citations because at the time of this book's publication, it remains the only published critical edition of the poem to which my readers will be able to refer.

72. Helen Cooper, *The English Romance in Time: Transforming Motifs from Geoffrey of Monmouth to the Death of Shakespeare* (Oxford: Oxford University Press, 2004), 382: "The legend offers a retrospective explanation for the towering and unconventional personality of Eleanor of Aquitaine (though she is given a different name and biography in the text); for Richard's exceptional savagery, of a kind to be wondered at rather than imitated (his byname supposedly derives from his tearing the heart out of a lion that attacked him; the romance describes his fondness for eating roast Saracen); and perhaps also for the inadequacies of her

of either lightheartedness or stratagem.[73] Brunner produces a full version of the Cassodorien episode in *Richard Löwenherz*, but only by supplementing the Caius manuscript with Wynkyn de Worde's 1509 edition. Cassodorien's story is only partially present in Caius, and the moment at which she shoots up through the church roof is absent altogether. Rather, Cassodorien's final extant action in the Caius copy is to take "her douȝtyr *in* her hond."[74] This is the final line, which completes a couplet, on the second leaf's verso. Narrative disjunction then occurs. The facing recto begins with another full couplet involving a hand, but here the hand belongs to an adult Richard, who leads two knights away to speak privately: "In eyþyr hond he took on / Into a chau*m*byr he bad hem gon."[75] Between the two disjunctive episodes, probably four leaves are missing.[76] These leaves may have contained Cassodorien's aversion to the Eucharist and a narrative jump in time to Richard as a new king, holding a tournament and meeting privately with two of his favorite knights.[77]

---

youngest son, the future King John, whom she dropped as she made her final disappearance through the church roof." In their correspondence, Walter Scott and George Ellis also discuss the roots of this legend. On October 17, 1802 (New York, Morgan Library, MS 486.16), Scott writes: "Your recollection has not deceived you about the descent of the Kings of England from the Devil. The pedigree is traced by Bowmaker the continuator of Fordun from a marriage of Geoffrey Anjou with a fiend." See also, Blurton, *Cannibalism*, 177 n. 55.

73. See Ambrisco, "Cannibalism and Cultural Encounters," 506–7, where he quotes twelfth-century writers, including Gerald of Wales: "Moreover, King Richard was often accustomed to refer to this event; saying that it was no matter of wonder, if coming from such a race, sons should not cease to harass their parents, and brothers to quarrel amongst each other; for he knew well that they all had come of the devil and to the devil they would go."

74. Gonville and Caius College, MS 175/96, p. 4b, line 30.

75. Gonville and Caius College, MS 175/96, p. 5a, lines 1–2.

76. Gonville and Caius's copy of *Richard Coeur de Lion* is ruled for bicolumnar text at roughly thirty lines per column, and thus roughly sixty lines per side. About four leaves, or around 240 lines, would be almost precisely enough space to contain the episodes that intervene in Wynkyn de Worde's 1509 edition. Four leaves between pages 4 and 5 (leaves two and three) in the manuscript would make a first quire of eight leaves, with the quire's catchword on the present page 8. Caius's second quire appears to be wanting one leaf, its first—the addition of which would make quire two also an eight-leaf quire. On Caius's second quire, see chapter 1. See also James, *A Descriptive Catalogue*, 199, where his collation speculates loss of an unknown number of leaves in the manuscript's first quire and the possible loss of one leaf in its second quire.

77. Another moment in the Caius copy exhibits ways in which the text's narrative lends itself to narrative and thus possibly material modularity. In his collation, James hypothesizes that the manuscript's third quire, with the catchword on page 26 caught on page 27, is missing any number of leaves, save its first and its last. When read against *Richard Löwenherz*, which supplements material—specifically the entire episode in which Richard conquers Cyprus en route to Acre (733 lines)—from Wynkyn de Worde's edition between Caius pages 24 and 25, narrative loss can be hypothesized. However, if one had no access to another copy of the romance, loss or judicious editing would not necessarily be evident to a reader of Caius,

The copies in Harley, Arundel, and Douce are all described as beginning "imperfectly," a codicological term of art that connotes inadvertent fragmentation. Each copy begins with the tournament scene, and in each the episode or module of Cassodorien was probably never present. Harley's copy of *Richard Coeur de Lion* begins on the sixth line of the second column of a bicolumnar folio, the first column of which is blank.[78] There are multiple possible explanations for this situation: Here Harley could reflect the layout of its exemplar, or its scribe could have left a full column and six lines blank in anticipation of more of *Richard Coeur de Lion* or another text altogether. Whatever the reason for the blank space, Harley's "imperfect" beginning cannot be ascribed to loss, but rather to a choice on the part of Harley's scribe. Arundel 58, whose copy of the romance replaces the section on Richard in a copy of Robert of Gloucester's chronicle, is missing only one leaf of *Richard Coeur de Lion*, totaling 152 lines, at most.[79] This is possibly enough space for something resembling Auchinleck's introduction to *King Richard* and the beginning of the tournament episode, but not the episode involving Richard's mother as it exists elsewhere. Douce 228, which contains only *Richard Coeur de Lion*, appears to have sustained a loss of two leaves, that is, a loss of between 168 and 188 lines, at its start.[80] Its present first three leaves are badly worn, and although most of their writing remains visible, they are torn along their outer edges. Whatever has been lost, Douce begins at a modular break in the narra-

---

which exhibits no obvious material, formal, or narrative problem here: Richard announces to the Puglian king, Tancred, on the last line of page 24 that he will imminently set sail from Messina, where he and his men have lodged for the winter, and on the first two lines of page 25a are "þe vnleuenþe day þay saylyd in tempest / þat ny3t ne day hadde þey no rest."

78. In Harley 4690, *Richard Coeur de Lion* begins on fol. 109rb. Fol. 108v has no text and is not lined; fol. 109r is lightly lined for two columns. Of these, the first is empty and writing begins on the sixth text line of the second column. The romance ends on fol. 118rb at line 19 and the remainder of the column's lines (more than half) remain blank. This is the last leaf in the manuscript; its verso is blank.

79. In Arundel 58, *Richard Coeur de Lion* occupies fol. 252ra–fol. 275re (half a leaf, containing the "a" column only), ruled for bicolumnar text. The missing folio that once contained the beginning of *Richard Coeur de Lion* is the third in the quire; it may have held an illumination, thus explaining its loss. If an illumination were present, the folio would have contained fewer than 152 lines. Arundel's copy contains marginal drawings that echo the visual memory of Richard that had been in insular circulation since at least the early fourteenth century: Fol. 259r contains a drawing of Richard's ax, and fol. 266v holds a drawing of St. George's coat of arms. On the visual lexicon of Richard, in which Arundel 58 here evinces fluency, see chapters 3 and 4.

80. Each folio of Douce 228 is ruled for a single column containing between thirty-eight and forty-seven lines. The manuscript has four quires, the second and third complete with twelve leaves each. The first quire at present has ten, thus probably wanting two leaves; the fourth is wanting six.

tive, with the emergence of Richard for his tournament: "Kyng R*ich*ard cam owt of a valey."⁸¹ The two leaves missing from Douce's first quire would not provide enough space for the multiple opening episodes extant in the Caius and London Thornton manuscripts. Like Harley 4690 and Arundel 58, Douce 228's lost leaves probably did not contain the Cassodorien episode.

Only a single extant manuscript—Caius—contains both scenes of Richard's cannibalism.⁸² That at least one of the cannibalism episodes was in circulation by the last quarter of the fourteenth century is confirmed by the copy of *Richard Coeur de Lion* extant in Egerton 2862. It contains the second instance of cannibalism, but not the first. The first takes place when Richard falls ill at Acre and, as was apparently his custom when ill, requests that he be given pork to eat. Of course, no pork is available on crusade, and in a panic, his cook takes the advice of an old, anonymous knight:

> Takes a Sarezyn ȝonge *and* ffat;
> Jn haste þat þe þeff be slayn,
> Openyd, *and* hys hyde off fflayn,
> And sode*n* fful hastyly,
> Wiþ powdyr, *and* wiþ spysory,
> And wiþ saffron off good colour.
> When þe kyng feles þer off sauour,
> Out off agu ȝyff he be went,
> He schal haue þertoo good talent.
> Whenne he has a good tast,
> And eat*en* weel a good repast,
> And soupyd off þe broweys a sope,
> Slept afftyr, *and* swet a drope,
> Þorwȝ Goddes myȝt, *and* my counsayl,
> Sone he schal be ffresch *and* hayl!⁸³

These lines appear in Caius's copy, and a version of the same instructions survives in the London Thornton. In these manuscripts, Richard's men tell

---

81. Douce 228, fol. 1r, line 1.

82. The cannibalism episodes have understandably been the central subject of scholarship on *Richard Coeur de Lion*: See, most notably, Blurton's chapter on the romance in *Cannibalism*; Heng's chapter on the romance in *Empire of Magic*; and Akbari, "Hunger"; Ambrisco, "Cannibalism"; McDonald, "Eating People"; and Torpey, "Of Cannibals." See also Lee Manion, *Narrating the Crusades*, 19. That these episodes, and others, possibly provoked criticism in medieval England and called into question the difference between "legitimate and illegitimate violence" (5) is explored in Marcel Elias, "Violence, Excess, and the Composite Emotional Rhetoric of *Richard Coeur de Lion*," *Studies in Philology* 114 (2017): 1–38.

83. *Richard Löwenherz*, lines 3088–102.

him that they have located pork and urge him to eat and regain his strength. In the London Thornton copy, these lines ("Etis nowe and suppis þeroffe a souppe / And thurghe Cristys myghte it schall be thi bote") complete fol. 143vb,[84] but at the top of fol. 144ra the scene does not continue. Instead, the Muslim messengers who were sent to Richard are shown having returned to Saladin. They weep as they explain to him the horrific spectacle they were made to observe. Codicological evidence suggests that three leaves, perhaps bearing the second cannibalism episode, were at some point removed from the manuscript.[85] Between these two moments in the Caius manuscript, Richard eats, learns he has just eaten his enemy, and sets about organizing the lavish dinner for Saladin's messengers.

When the Muslim messengers come to Richard at Acre to negotiate terms for the release of Richard's prisoners, Richard invites them to dinner, and then the English king takes his marshal aside and instructs him to go to the prison, ascertain which hostages "be comen off þe ryhcheste kynne,"[86] and kill them. Richard continues:

"And ar þe hedes be of smyten,
Looke euery name be wryten
Vpon a scrowe off parchemyn;
And bere þe hedes to þe kechyn,
And in a cawdroun þou hem caste,
And bydde þe cook sethe hem ffaste;
And loke that he þer her off stryppe,
Off hed, off berd, and eke off lyppe.
Whenne we schole sytte *and* eete,
Loke that ʒe nouʒt fforgete
To serue hem herewiþ in þis manere:
Lay euery hed on a platere,
Bryng it hoot forþ al in þyn hand,
Vpward hys vys, þe teeþ grennand;

---

84. The London Thornton copy of *Richard Coeur de Lion* is bicolumnar and ruled for about forty-three lines.

85. See Thompson, *Robert Thornton*, 31. Three leaves would have contained about five hundred lines, enough to hold the second cannibalism episode as it appears in Caius. As Thompson, 31, states: "The assumption of this loss is supported by the evidence of the watermark patterns and the chain indentations." See also, Ralph Hanna and David Lawton, eds. *The Siege of Jerusalem*, EETS OS 320 (Oxford: Oxford University Press, 2003), xvi. That the lost leaves may have contained a version of the second cannibalism episode is supported by the fact that the messengers' recounting of the episode remains present in London Thornton at fol. 144ra-b.

86. *Richard Löwenherz*, line 3415.

> And loke þey be nothynge rowe!
> Hys name faste aboue hys browe,
> What he hy3te, *and* off what kyn born(e).
> An hoot hed bryng me beforn;
> As j were weel apayde wiþal,
> Ete þeroff ry3t faste j schal,
> As it were a tendyr chyke,
> To se hou the oþere wyl lyke."[87]

Events then proceed as Richard directed. After the English king welcomes Saladin's messengers, the head of a Muslim, with a lineage written below it, is placed before Richard and, we are told:

> þe messang*erys* were seruyd soo,
> Eu*ere* an hed betwyxe twoo,
> In þe fforhede wrete*n* hys name:
> þeroff they had all grame!
> What þey were whe*nne* they seye*n*,
> þe teres ran out off her*e* eyen.[88]

Compared to the core rumor in all manuscripts, these other stories, which have long been central to our scholarly rumor, are rare in our extant manuscripts. Rather than instinctively copied and carefully preserved, they were managed and contested through modularity and purposeful fragmentation, at least in their written transmission.[89] As retrospective readers, our instinct when faced with these episodes, and others like them in other textual traditions, has been to make the fragmentary whole in our own texts and talk. This is one way of managing the past.

An alternate approach, practiced in the romance itself, involves seeing the historical record as the artifact of productive fragments. This is a generative vision, one that perceives and tolerates multiplicity. Richard, as kept in the

---

87. *Richard Löwenherz*, lines 3417–38.
88. *Richard Löwenherz*, lines 3461–66.
89. John Lydgate knew the rumor of Richard's cannibalism: Richard "was crownyd kyng, called cuer de leon, / With Sarsyn hedys seruyd at his table, / Slayn at Chalus, bi deth lamentable." See John Lydgate, *The Minor Poems II*, ed. H. N. MacCracken, EETS OS 192 (Oxford: Oxford University Press, 1934), 714. It is impossible to know from these lines if Lydgate knew of the "Sarsyn hedys seruyd" from reading the romance or from rumor circulating in the air, or both. Regardless, that it was not included in all copies of *Richard Coeur de Lion*, indeed that an entirely alternate sequence of scenes could be used, confirms that the cannibalism episodes, no matter Lydgate's eagerness to repeat one of them, were not essential to the memory of Richard as it appeared and circulated in *Richard Coeur de Lion*.

mind's eye and the memory of medieval England, was not a single, still thing. In the Caius manuscript—the copy we have thought closest to our stable, representative text of *Richard Coeur de Lion*—Richard is made a fundamentally unstable figure. He poses a rhetorical question to his two hand-picked companions, Thomas and Fulk: "What i haue ordeynyd & þou3t?" Richard answers his own question about the physical and narrative excursion they are about to take:

þe holy lond to wende too,
We þree, wiþouten kny3tes moo
Al in palmeres gyse
þe holy lond for to deuyse.⁹⁰

Richard's words neither confirm the English rumors that he was an upstanding crusader-pilgrim nor deny the Austrian and German rumors of his treachery.⁹¹ "Gyse" can mean how one looks because of a put-on bearing or choice of fashion, and it can also mean how one really is.⁹² Do Richard and his men only look like pilgrims? Or are they pilgrims? "Devyse" contains both the actions of looking and thinking, but to understand to what end demands context.⁹³ Do Richard and his men go on pilgrimage to witness the wonders of the "Holy Lond," or do they go as would-be conquerors preforming reconnaissance?

As now knowing readers ourselves, able to bring to bear both the insular and the Continental rumors about Richard, we can interpret his actions in either way. Moreover, because Richard himself ostensibly makes these rhetorical choices—innocuously vague at best, pointedly duplicitous at worst—Richard's very character is left open to our interpretation, too. The subsequent twenty-four-line-long list of places he and his men visit gives no indication of what they did, merely where they went:

A noble schyp þey founde þare
Into Cyprys redy to fare.
Þe seyl was reysyd, þe schip was strong,
And in þe see þey were long;
And at þe laste, j undyrstande,

---

90. Gonville and Caius College, MS 175/96, p. 7a, line 26–7b, line 3. Here I provide my own transcription of Caius because Brunner's transcription is faulty at several points in these lines. Nevertheless, the corresponding lines in *Richard Löwenherz* are 592–96.
91. On these rumors, see chapter 1.
92. *MED*: "gise (n.)." Also guise, gwise.
93. *MED*: "devisen (v.)." Also devicen, divisen.

> At Ffamagos þey come to lande.
> Þere þey dwellyd fourty dawes,
> Ffor to lerne þe landes lawes;
> And seþen deden hem on þe see
> Toward Acres, þat riche cete;
> And so forþ to Massedoyne,
> And to þe cyte off Babyloyne,
> And fro þennes to Cesare;
> Off Nynyve þey were ware,
> And þe cyte off Ierusalem;
> And to þe cyte off Bedlem,
> And to þe cyte of Sudan Turry,
> And eke alsoo to Ebedy,
> And to þe Castel Orglyous,
> And to þe cyte of Aperyous,
> To Jaffe, *and* to Safrane,
> To Taboret, *and* to Archane.[94]

Only after this itinerary are we made the wiser that "Thus þey vysytyd þe Holy Land, / How þe myȝt wynne it to here hand."[95] Yet this couplet, too, has it both ways: They visited the "Holy Land" in one breath, and actively learned (or innocently intuited?) how they might conquer it in the next. The narrator of our retrospective text claims to reside in the reader's present, and therefore, whether he knows with certainty what the men did in the East itself remains an open question. With "I undyrstande," our narrator leaves a wide berth for his own fallibility on the one hand, and plausible deniability on the other.

In the time between Richard's invitation to his companions within the romance and the line in which the narrator gestures at their purpose, the reader has by necessity had to make a series of choices, even if subconscious ones, informed by external talk and texts—choices about what Richard did after docking in Cyprus; between arriving at Acre and departing "þat riche cete" for "Massedoyne"; while in "the cyte off Ierusalem." This Richard in the romance's lines does something the historical Richard did not do as either a pilgrim or a conqueror in life: enter Jerusalem. *Richard Coeur de Lion* perhaps puts a new rumor into circulation about where Richard did and did not go. It is the Richard in this episode—containing multitudes, capable of being everything and anything a reader has previously heard about him, capable of doing

---

94. *Richard Löwenherz*, lines 625–46.
95. *Richard Löwenherz*, lines 647–48.

entirely new things—that returns from the East to England via "Almayne" in the romance, in rumor, in history. The medieval memory of Richard continued to be kept in mind, to circulate by way of *Richard Coeur de Lion* precisely because they—the memory and the text—were not "complete" but fragmentary; not agglomerative but modular; not the work of text-makers who strove for a stable account, but a collaboration between text-makers and the public, whose participation made such stability impossible. Yet, even as our own history is similarly constituted by an assemblage of talk, we have tried to make medieval England's come from whole cloth.

In the space between the productively unstable medieval rumor of Richard and our own scholarly rumor of *Richard Coeur de Lion* resides, among other things, our reconstruction of medieval texts, a process that includes deciding upon a manuscript copy to transcribe and to transmit, and choosing how to go about that business. The theoretical and analytical work of all scholars of medieval literature fundamentally depends upon our approaches to this process. That is to say, what medieval literature consists of turns on whether we make and/or use an edition that is the product of nineteenth-century Lachmannian stemmatics, in which, to restore an archetypal text, we compare different readings among manuscripts while paying particular attention to their interpolations and errors in common, or an edition that employs Joseph Bédier's early twentieth-century response to Lachmann. In Bédier's method, we privilege and correct, with reference to other less good copies, a "best-text," ostensibly representative of all extant copies.[96] Through their respective

---

96. These are the two main systems by which medieval manuscript copies are critically edited: Lachmann's, which seeks to reconstruct the author's text, and Bédier's, which deems a single manuscript copy, with some editorial intervention, illustrative. The scholarly archive of the practice, theory, and critique of this binary is extensive. For a bibliography (to 1960) that addresses English manuscripts particularly, see William Langland, *Piers Plowman: The A Version*, ed. George Kane (London: Athlone, 1960); and, more recently, Douglas Moffat, "A Bibliographical Essay on Editing Methods," in *A Guide to Editing Middle English*, ed. Vincent McCarren and Douglas Moffat (Ann Arbor: University of Michigan, 1998), 25–60. A paradigmatic explanation of process is George Kane, "*Piers Plowman*: Problems and Methods of Editing the B-Text," *Modern Language Review* 43 (1948): 1–25. For more recent discussion, see Jerome McGann, *A Critique of Modern Textual Criticism* (Chicago: University of Chicago Press, 1983); Tim William Machan, *Textual Criticism and Middle English Texts* (Charlottesville: University of Virginia Press, 1994); G. Thomas Tanselle, "Textual Instability and Editorial Idealism," *Studies in Bibliography* 49 (1996): 1–60; D. C. Greetham, *Theories of the Text* (Oxford: Oxford University Press, 1999). On Lachmann himself, see Sebastiano Timpanaro, *The Genesis of Lachmann's Method*, ed. and trans. Glenn W. Most (Chicago: University of Chicago Press, 2005); on the origins of the "best-text," see Joseph Bédier, "La tradition manuscrite du *Lai de l'Ombre*. Réflexions sur l'art d'éditer les anciens textes," *Romania* 54 (1928): 161–96, 321–56. In opposition to the critical edition is the diplomatic edition, which reproduces a manuscript copy with minimal intervention;

means—collating multiple copies, eliding differences (preserving those differences as variants in critical editions, completely eliminating them in others), deeming one copy extrapolatable for all others—both approaches come to an end having produced a stable text: "the text." Or, as R. S. Loomis's review of *Richard Löwenherz* explains,[97] the essential textual monument that can be transmitted, studied, and discussed collectively and collaboratively. The deep value of such a text is difficult to argue against on the grounds of utility. But the stability we impose as producers and readers of medieval texts is at cross-purposes with the unstable bookmaking culture within which medieval producers of texts and manuscripts not only worked, but with which they knowingly grappled.

One of the most famous, and famously self-conscious, examples of such grappling comes at the end of Chaucer's *Troilus and Criseyde*. Chaucer (at this point indistinguishable from the poem's "I") simultaneously speaks to his "litel bok" and prays to God "that non myswrite the, / Ne the mysmetre for defaute of tonge; / And red wherso thow be, or elles songe, / That thow be understonde, God I biseche!"[98] An apparent Lachmannian in this instance, Chaucer projects reception of his work not only in the hands of what we might consider straightforward readers, but in the possession, too, of those who would transmit his text either by reinscribing it or by talking about it—by formally or informally retelling it aloud. Chaucer is here a knowing text-maker, to be sure. He imagines the nuances of transmission, even as he tries to ward them off. The textual traditions of *Richard Coeur de Lion* and other retrospective texts enumerate the intricacies Chaucer glosses over and cast the instabilities of transmission in a positive light: as possibilities for making and remaking identity, history, cultural memory.

---

it is rare for an entire textual tradition to be published in a series of diplomatic editions so that, as Leah S. Marcus argues about early modern editions, we can study "the specific forms" in which a text reached its readers. See Leah S. Marcus, "Textual Scholarship," in *Introduction to Scholarship in Modern Languages and Literatures,* 3rd ed., ed. David G. Nicholls (New York: Modern Language Association, 2007), 143; and see also Marcus, *Unediting the Renaissance,* 1, 11, respectively. There Marcus asks and offers our historical answers to the question fundamental to editions vis-à-vis the project of literary cultural recovery: "What is it that we hope to experience when we read a literary text from an earlier era?" "Part of the purpose of a good edition has traditionally been to bridge historical distance—to make a text and its cultural milieu accessible to people with different practices and assumptions. But that process always involves the risk of over-normalization, of making the past over to accommodate one's own, and one's readers', sense of what constitutes acceptable meaning."

97. See chapter 1.
98. Chaucer, *Troilus and Criseyde,* bk. 5, lines 1795–98.

EPILOGUE

Turning Up the Archive

THE PRESENCE and pressures of talk fundamentally reconstitute the relationships among text-maker, text, reader, and history by making us all—medieval and modern people with voices—subjects in the literary history we tell and inscribe from our present vantage points. In writing this book, I am also a text-maker influenced by talk. My earliest foray into what would become this book's central matter—though I was not aware that I was doing this work in that moment at all—began when talk of Richard I reemerged in the air, locally and globally. In this book's first chapter, I refer to my earliest encounter with *Richard Coeur de Lion,* not as a text but as the subject of talk, talk among senior medievalists as I began my graduate work, a year after September 11, 2001. Outside of academe, Richard, along with the Crusades and Saladin, entered post-9/11 global discourse vis-à-vis the so-called War on Terror.

This talk, which emanated most loudly (though certainly not solely) from the highest-ranking members of the US administration, circulated a version of history and cultural memory that suited the political exigencies of its Western place and time.[1] Racist, repugnant, and intellectually vacant, that sound-bite-ready talk provoked, among other things, more talk and textual

---

1. Traces of that talk are preserved and critiqued in a contemporaneously made text: See Bruce Holsinger, *Neomedievalism, Neoconservatism, and the War on Terror* (Chicago: Prickly Paradigm Press, 2007).

production, some of which attempted to critique or to correct: to put more accurate and more nuanced histories and a wider range of cultural memory into the air. Doing so remains urgent and difficult work. It is work that necessitates the conviction to picture the past differently and a willingness to reconstrue the present's relationship to that past. And it is also work that requires the development of methodologies that can complicate and detail a more comprehensive picture, and that, crucially, can be taught and shared with our students and each other. Innovative methodologies can steadfastly enrich our intellectual and material approaches to the project of cultural recovery.

The present is always unstable. Medieval people could not ignore that fact. To make medieval England's past stay still and act whole by eliding or discarding discrepancies and fragments, and by assuming its occluded spaces were or are silent, is to puppet the past into moving teleologically in a way no present ever does. This book theorizes talk's circulation and in doing so resists reconstructions of the past that aim for completism. The diversity of *Richard Coeur de Lion*'s manuscript copies, for instance, embodies different demands of textual production than the notional singularity that has been offered. What makes the cultural memory of Richard timeless is precisely the productive instability of each of the manuscripts preserving and responding to the generative context of talk.

The power to make history, identity, and cultural memory resided in, among other places, the bodies who talked and listened, who repeated and intervened in rumor, and who tried to make sense of the unsettled present by unsettling the past. Talk was and is powerful because of its ubiquity, and also, counterintuitively, because of its durability. If we look or, better, listen for it, or if we simply acknowledge the fact of it and make space for that fact in our project of cultural recovery—in our retrospective inheritance, in our literary history—both past and present figure differently. So too does our archive.

Fundamental to such a reconceptualization of the archive is a dedication to the development of new methods with which to study the unrecovered and unheard, and to make space in our imaginations for a past in which all people, to borrow Michel-Rolph Trouillot's phrase, are "fully historical" beings, engaged "simultaneously in the sociohistorical process and in narrative constructions about that process."[2] This landscape populated with fully historical people should be our common point of critical and imaginative departure. Acknowledgment of this fact—and of the fact of their existence—precedes the making of new methodologies. In turn, these methodologies will necessarily

---

2. Michel-Rolph Trouillot, *Silencing the Past: Power and the Production of History* (Boston: Beacon Press, 1995), 24. I am grateful to Christian Crouch for introducing me to Trouillot's book at a crucial moment in the writing of my own.

unearth new voices and new sites of cultural recovery, and will reposition us to hear and see different things, or to begin to notice what we have not seen, not heard. For humanities fields to advance—not because it is timely to do so, but because a full range of fully historical people is a fact of the past—new methodologies can manifest that which has been declared unrecoverable or has never been sought in the first place.

The archive looks different when we reposition ourselves in relation to it. New, and disruptive, considerations emerge. I have approached the study of talk's circulation in ways that my expertise in literary criticism, book history, and medieval languages makes possible. Even my readings and critiques that run against the grain arise from both the richness and the limitations of that expertise. Limitations can be generative. This book aims to provoke new conversations and projects. Projects about talk's circulation within and around medieval Acre. Projects about hearing-impaired and nonverbal people in medieval England, because this book's focus on those who could speak and hear throws into sharp relief the presence of those who could not.

Literary history that includes talk contextualizes the fascination late medieval England's text-makers, such as Langland and Chaucer, had with sound. A relationship between manuscript culture and the public is visible when we use new approaches to book history to attend to the connective tissue of talk. That textual culture was contested and produced by a broad public is not only probable but provable when we recognize and interrogate the seemingly silent spaces of the past. This book has focused on the retrospectivity of medieval England's public and its text-makers, but relics like the charts by which people calculated feast days hundreds of years into the future tell us that they also looked forward. They have left behind a record that preserves humanity in all of its complexity, and that asks us to try to see all of their bodies and hear all of their voices. We owe that richer archival inheritance to the future.

BIBLIOGRAPHY

MANUSCRIPTS CITED

Brussels, Bibliothèque royale de Belgique, MS 9961–62 (Peterborough Psalter)
Cambridge (MA), Harvard Law School Library, MS 12
Cambridge (UK)
    Corpus Christi College
        MS 145
        MS 339
    Gonville and Caius College, MS 175/96
    Trinity College
        MS B.14.39
        MS O.4.32
        MS O.9.34
    University Library
        MS Dd.2.5
        MS Dd.14.2
        MS Ff.5.48
Copenhagen
    University of Copenhagen
        MS AM 180a fol
        MS AM 180c fol

    MS AM 180d fol
    MS AM 180e fol
    MS AM 531
Durham, Cathedral Library, MS C.IV.27B
Edinburgh
    Advocates Library, Abbotsford Collection [Collection of English and French metrical romances]
    National Library of Scotland
        MS Advocates 19.2.1 (Auchinleck)
        MS Advocates 33.5.3
        MS 873
    University Library, MS 218
Gloucester, Gloucestershire Archives, MS D2700/V/1 No. 8 (Beaufort fragment)
Graz, Steiermärkisches Landesarchiv, cod. 894
Kew
    The National Archives
        CP 40/14
        JUST 1/302
        JUST 1/303
        JUST 1/1050
        JUST 1/1076
        JUST 1/1093
        KB 138/107
        KB 138/110
        KB 138/120
Lincoln, Lincoln Cathedral, MS 91 (Thornton)
London
    British Library
        MS Additional 31042 (London Thornton)
        MS Additional 47680
        MS Cotton Claudius D.vii
        MS Cotton Domitian A.xiii
        MS Cotton Faustina B.vi
        MS Cotton Julius D.ix
        MS Egerton 2862
        MS Harley 978
        MS Harley 2253
        MS Harley 2277
        MS Harley 4690
        MS Lansdowne 239
        MS Royal 12.C.xii

College of Arms, MS Arundel 58
University of London, Senate House Library, MS 593
New York, The Morgan Library, MA 426.16
Oslo, Norsk Riksarkivet, MSS 61–63
Oxford
    Bodleian Library
        MS Ashmole 43
        MS Bodley 779
        MS Digby 23
        MS Digby 168
        MS Digby 170
        MS Douce 228
        MS Fairfax 10
        MS Laud Misc. 108
        MS Laud Misc. 463
        MS Rawlinson B.180
    Christ Church, MS 92
Paris
    Bibliothèque de l'Arsenal, MS 3142
    Bibliothèque nationale, MS fr. 571
Prague, Strahov Monastery Library, MS DF III 1/4
St. Andrews
    University Library
        MS PR.2065 A.15
        MS PR.2065 R.4
Tokyo, Keio University, MS 170.X.9.11
Vatican City, Biblioteca Apostolica Vaticana, MS Reg. lat. 1659

PRIMARY SOURCES

Ambroise. *The History of the Holy War: Ambroise's "Estoire de la Guerre Sainte."* Edited by Marianne Ailes and Malcolm Barber. Translated by Marianne Ailes. 2 vols. Woodbridge: The Boydell Press, 2003.

Ansbert. *Historia de Expeditione Friderici Imperatoris.* In *The Crusade of Frederick Barbarossa: The History of the Expedition of the Emperor Frederick and Related Texts.* Crusade Texts in Translation 19. Edited and translated by G. A. Loud. Farnham, Surrey: Ashgate, 2010.

The Auchinleck Manuscript: National Library of Scotland, Advocates' MS 19.2.1. Introduction by Derek Pearsall and I. C. Cunningham. London: Scolar Press, 1979.

Bodel, Jean. *La Chanson des Saisnes.* Edited by Annette Brasseur. 2 vols. Geneva: Droz, 1989.

Brand, Paul, ed. *The Earliest English Law Reports.* 4 vols. London: Selden Society, 1996–2007.

Brasseur, Annette, ed. and trans. *La Chanson des Saxons.* Paris: Librairie Honoré Champion, 1992.

Brault, Gerard J., ed. and trans. *The Song of Roland: An Analytical Edition.* 2 vols. University Park: The Pennsylvania State University Press, 1978.

Brunner, Karl, ed. *Der mittelenglische Versroman über Richard Löwenherz.* Wiener Beiträge zur englischen Philologie 42. Vienna: Whilhelm Braumüller, 1913.

Burnley, David, and Alison Wiggins, eds. National Library of Scotland, Edinburgh. "The Auchinleck Manuscript." Version 1.1. Last modified March 15, 2004. http://auchinleck.nls.uk/.

Calendar of the Liberate Rolls, Henry III. 6 vols. London: H. M. Stationary Office, 1916–1964.

Calendar of the Patent Rolls, Henry III. 6 vols. London: H. M. Stationary Office, 1901–1913.

Cantle, A., ed. *The Pleas of Quo Warranto for the County of Lancaster.* Manchester: The Chetham Society, 1937.

La Chanson de Roland. Edited and translated by Ian Short. Paris: Librairie générale française, 1990.

Chaucer, Geoffrey. *The Riverside Chaucer.* Edited by Larry D. Benson. New York: Houghton Mifflin Co., 1987.

Chronicles and Memorials of the Reign of Richard I. Edited by William Stubbs. 2 vols. RS 38. London: Longman, Green, Longman, Roberts, and Green, 1864–1865.

Chronicon de Lanercost. Edited by Joseph Stevenson. Edinburgh: Maitland Club, 1839.

Chroust, Anton, ed. *Quellen zur Geschichte des Kreuzzuges Kaiser Friedrichs I.* MGH SRG NS 5. Berlin: Weidmansche, 1928.

Clanchy, M. T., ed. *Civil Pleas of the Wiltshire Eyre, 1249.* Devizes: Wiltshire Record Society, 1971.

Cockayne, T. O., ed. *Leechdoms, Wortcunning, and Starcraft of Early England.* 3 vols. RS 35. London: Longman and Green, 1864–1866.

Coss, Peter, ed. *Thomas Wright's Political Songs of England: From the Reign of John to That of Edward II.* Cambridge: Cambridge University Press, 1996.

Davis, Norman, ed. *Paston Letters and Papers of the Fifteenth Century.* 2 vols. Oxford: Oxford University Press, 1971–1976.

D'Evelyn, Charlotte, and Anna J. Mill, eds. *The South English Legendary.* 3 vols. EETS OS 235–36, 244. London: Oxford University Press, 1956–1959.

Duggan, Joseph J. et al., eds. *La Chanson de Roland; The Song of Roland: The French Corpus.* 3 vols. Turnhout: Brepols, 2005.

Edbury, Peter W., ed. *The Conquest of Jerusalem and the Third Crusade: Sources in Translation.* London: Scolar Press, 1996.

Eliot, T. S. *Collected Poems, 1909–1962.* New York: Harcourt Brace, 1991.

Ellis, George, ed. *Specimens of Early English Metrical Romances, Chiefly Written during the Early Part of the Fourteenth Century.* 2nd ed. 3 vols. London: Longman, Hurst, Rees, and Orme, 1811.

English, Barbara, ed. *Yorkshire Hundred and Quo Warranto Rolls.* Leeds: The Yorkshire Archaeological Society, 1996.

Farrow, Frederic R., and Thomas Blashill. "The Recent Development of Vienna." In *Transactions of the Royal Institute of British Architects,* 27–42. Vol. 4. New Series. London: Royal Institute of British Architects, 1888.

Fein, Susanna, ed. *The Complete Harley 2253 Manuscript in Three Volumes.* With translation and collaboration of David Raybin and Jan Ziolkowski. Kalamazoo, MI: Medieval Institute Publications, 2014–2015.

Figueredo, M. C. "*Richard Coeur de Lion*: An Edition from the London Thornton Manuscript." 2 vols. Unpublished PhD diss., University of York, 2010.

Fraser, Constance M., ed. *The Northumberland Eyre Roll for 1293.* Woodbridge: The Boydell Press for the Surtees Society, 2007.

Gallagher, Eric James, trans. and ed. *The Civil Pleas of the Suffolk Eyre of 1240.* Suffolk Records Society 52. Woodbridge: The Boydell Press, 2009.

Geoffrey le Baker. *The Chronicle of Geoffrey le Baker.* Translated by David Preest. With introduction and notes by Richard Barber. Woodbridge: The Boydell Press, 2012.

———. *Chronicon Angliae temporibus Edwardi II et Edwardi III.* Edited by J. A. Giles. 1847. Reprint, New York: Burt Franklin, 1967.

Geoffrey of Monmouth. *The History of the Kings of Britain: An Edition and Translation of De gestis Britonum [Historia Regum Brianniae].* Edited by Michael D. Reeve. Translated by Neil Wright. Woodbridge: The Boydell Press, 2007.

Geoffrey of Vinsauf. *Poetria nova.* Translated by Margaret F. Nims. With an introduction by Martin Camargo. Rev. ed. Medieval Sources in Translation 49. Toronto: Pontifical Institute of Medieval Studies, 2010.

Gervase of Canterbury. *The Historical Works of Gervase of Canterbury.* Edited by William Stubbs. 2 vols. RS 73. London: Longman and Co., 1879–1880.

Gray, Thomas. *Scalacronica, 1272–1363.* Edited and translated by Andy King. Surtees Society 209. Woodbridge: The Boydell Press, 2005.

Grierson, Herbert, ed. *The Letters of Sir Walter Scott.* 12 vols. London: Constable, 1932–1937.

Guillaume de Berneville. *La vie de saint Gilles: poème du XIIe siècle.* Edited by Gaston Paris and Alphonse Bos. Paris: Didot, 1881.

Hanna, Ralph, and David Lawton, eds. *The Siege of Jerusalem.* EETS OS 320. Oxford: Oxford University Press, 2003.

Herrtage, S. J. H., ed. *The Taill of Rauf Coilyear . . . with the fragments of Roland and Vernagu, and Otuel.* EETS ES 39. London: Trübner, 1882.

Hieatt, Constance B., trans. *Karlamagnús saga: The Saga of Charlemagne and His Heroes.* 3 vols. Toronto: The Pontifical Institute of Medieval Studies, 1975.

Hill, R. T., and T. G. Bergin. *Anthology of Provençal Troubadours.* 2nd ed. 2 vols. New Haven: Yale University Press, 1973.

Horwood, Alfred J., ed. and trans. *Year Books of the Reign of King Edward I.* 5 vols. RS 31. London: Longmans, Green, Reader, et al., 1863–1879.

Jacobus de Voragine. *The Golden Legend: Readings on the Saints.* Translated by William Granger Ryan. 2 vols. Princeton: Princeton University Press, 1993.

James, M. R., ed. *The Treatise of Walter de Milemete, De nobilitatibus, sapientiis, et prudentiis regum.* Oxford: Oxford University Press for the Roxburghe Club, 1913.

Johnston, R. C., ed. *The Crusade and Death of Richard I.* ANTS 17. Oxford: Blackwell, 1961.

Karlamagús saga: Branches I, III, VII et IX. Edited by Knud Togeby et al. Copenhagen: La Société pour l'étude de la langue et de la littérature danoises, 1980.

"King Richard's Ransom (From Our Own Correspondent)." *The Times* (London), November 28, 1928.

Kölbing, Eugen, ed. *Arthour and Merlin, nach der Auchinleck-hs.* Leipzig: O. R. Reisland, 1890.

———. "Kleine publicationen aus der Auchinleck-hs. III." *Englische Studien* 8 (1885): 115–19.

Kyng Alisaunder. Edited by G. V. Smithers. 2 vols. EETS OS 227 and 237. Oxford: Oxford University Press, 1952–1957.

Lacroix, Daniel W., trans. *La Saga de Charlemagne: Traduction française des dix branches de la Karlamagnús saga norroise.* Paris: Librairie générale française, 2000.

Landon, Lionel, ed. *The Itinerary of Richard I.* London: Pipe Roll Society, 1934.

Langland, William. *Piers Plowman: The A Version.* Edited by George Kane. London: Athlone, 1960.

Langtoft, Peter. *The Chronicle of Pierre de Langtoft, in French Verse, from the Earliest Period to the Death of King Edward I.* Edited and translated by Thomas Wright. 2 vols. RS 47. London: Longmans, Green, Reader, and Dyer, 1866–1868.

Larkin, Peter, ed. *Richard Coer de Lyon.* Middle English Texts. Kalamazoo, MI: Medieval Institute Publications, 2015.

Laurent, Françoise, ed. *Guillaume de Berneville, La vie de saint Gilles.* Paris: Champion, 2003.

Loud, G. A., ed. and trans. *The Crusade of Frederick Barbarossa: The History of the Expedition of the Emperor Frederick and Related Texts.* Crusade Texts in Translation 19. Farnham, Surrey: Ashgate, 2010.

Lydgate, John. *The Minor Poems II.* Edited by H. N. MacCracken. EETS OS 192. Oxford: Oxford University Press, 1934.

Magnus of Reichersberg, *Chronicon Magni Presbiteri.* Edited by Wilhelm Wattenbach. MGH SS 17. Hanover: Hahn, 1861.

Maier, Christoph T. *Crusading Propaganda and Ideology: Model Sermons for the Preaching of the Cross.* Cambridge: Cambridge University Press, 2000.

Mannyng, Robert. *The Chronicle.* Edited by Idelle Sullens. Binghamton: Center for Medieval and Early Renaissance Studies, State University of New York at Binghamton, 1996.

Matthew Paris. *Chronica majora.* Edited by H. R. Luard. 7 vols. RS 57. London: Longman and Co., 1872–1883.

Maxwell, Herbert, ed. and trans. *The Chronicle of Lanercost.* Glasgow: James Maclehose & Sons, 1913.

Mayer, Hans Eberhard. *Das Itinerarium Peregrinorum: Eine zeitgenössische englische Chronik zum dritten Kreuzzug in ursprünglicher Gestalt.* Stuttgart: Hiersemann, 1962.

Meekings, C. A. F., ed. *Crown Pleas of the Wiltshire Eyre, 1249.* Devizes: Wiltshire Archaeological and Natural History Society Records Branch, 1961.

Mouzat, Jean, ed. *Les Poèmes de Gaucelm Faidit, troubadour du XIIe siècle.* Paris: A. G. Nizet, 1965.

Nicholson, Helen J., ed. and trans. *Itinerarium Peregrinorum et Gesta Regis Ricardi; The Chronicle of the Third Crusade.* Aldershot: Ashgate, 2001.

Otto of St. Blasien. *The Chronicle of Otto of St. Blasien.* In *The Crusade of Frederick Barbarossa: The History of the Expedition of the Emperor of Frederick and Related Texts.* Edited and translated by G. A. Loud. Crusade Texts in Translation 19. Farnham, Surrey: Ashgate, 2010.

Placita de quo warranto. Edited by William Illingworth. London: Record Commission, 1818.

Ralph of Coggeshall. *Chronicon Anglicanum.* Edited by J. Stevenson. RS 66. London: Longman, 1875.

Richard of Devizes. *The Chronicle of Richard of Devizes of the Time of King Richard the First.* Edited and translated by John T. Appleby. London: Thomas Nelson and Sons Ltd., 1963.

Rigord. *Histoire de Philippe Auguste.* Edited and translated by Élisabeth Carpentier, Georges Pon, and Yves Chauvin. Sources d'histoire médiévale 33. Paris: CNRS Éditions, 2006.

Robert of Gloucester. *The Metrical Chronicle of Robert of Gloucester.* Edited by William Aldis Wright. 2 vols. RS 86. London: Eyre and Spottiswoode, 1887.

Roger of Howden. *Chronica Magistri Rogeri de Houedene.* Edited by William Stubbs. 4 vols. RS 51. London: Eyre and Spottiswoode, 1868–1871.

———. *Gesta Regis Henrici Secundi Benedicti Abbatis, The Chronicle of the Reigns of Henry II and Richard I*. Edited by William Stubbs. 2 vols. RS 49. London: Longmans, 1867.

Rotuli Parliamentorum; ut et petitiones, et placita, in parliament. Edited by John Strachey et al. 6 vols. London: 1767–1777.

Sanders, I. J., and R. F. Treharne, ed. *Documents of the Baronial Movement of Reform and Rebellion, 1258–1267*. Oxford: Clarendon Press, 1973.

Sayles, G. O. *Select Cases in the Court of the King's Bench under Edward I*. 3 vols. Selden Society 55, 57, 58. London: B. Quaritch, 1936–1939.

Schellekens, Philida M. T. A. "An Edition of the Middle English Romance: *Richard Coeur de Lion*." 2 vols. Unpublished PhD diss., Durham University, 1989.

Schmale, Franz-Joseph, ed. *Die Chronik Ottos von Blaisen und die Marbacher Annalen*. Darmstadt: WBG, 1998.

Scott, Walter. *Qalb al-Asad*. Edited and translated by Ya'qub Sarruf and Faris Nimr. Cairo: Matba'at al-Muqtataf, 1886.

———. *The Talisman: A Tale of the Crusaders, and Chronicles of the Canongate*. 1825. Reprint, London: George Routledge and Sons, 1876.

Short, Ian, ed. "The Oxford Version." In *La Chanson de Roland; The Song of Roland: The French Corpus*, edited by Joseph J. Duggan et al. 3 vols. Turnhout: Brepols, 2005.

The Simonie: A Parallel-Text Edition, edited from MSS Advocates 19.2.1, Bodley 48, and Peterhouse College 104. Edited by Dan Embree and Elizabeth Urquhart. Heidelberg: Carl Winter, 1991.

Statutes and Ordinances, and Acts of Parliament of Ireland, King John to Henry V. Edited and translated by Henry F. Berry. Dublin: Alexander Thom and Co., 1907.

Statutes of the Realm. Edited and translated by A. Luders et al. 11 vols. London: Record Commission, 1810–1828.

Strauch, Philipp, ed. *Jansen Enikles Werke: Weltchronik, Fürstenbuch*. MGH DC 3. Hanover: Hahnsche, 1900.

Stubbs, William. *Select Charters and Other Illustrations of English Constitutional History*. 2nd ed. Oxford: Clarendon Press, 1874.

Terrell, Katherine H., ed. and trans. *Richard Coeur de Lion*. Peterborough, Ontario: Broadview Press, 2019.

Thomas de Kent. *Le Roman d'Alexandre ou Le Roman de toute chevalrie*. Edited by Brian Foster and Ian Short. Translated by Catherine Gaullier-Bougassas and Laurence Harf-Lancer. Paris: Honoré Champion, 2003.

Thomas of Ercildoune. *Sir Tristrem, a Metrical Romance*. Edited by Sir Walter Scott. Edinburgh: Archibald Constable and Co., 1804.

A Transcript of the Registers of the Company of Stationers of London, 1554–1640 A. D. Edited by Edward Arber and Charles Rivington. 5 vols. London: Company of Stationers, 1875–1894.

Unger, C. R., ed. *Karlamagnús saga ok Kappa Hans*. Christiana: H. J. Jensen, 1860.

Vita Edwardi Secundi. Edited and translated by Wendy R. Childs. OMT Oxford: Clarendon Press, 2005.

Walter of Guisborough. *The Chronicle of Walter of Guisborough*. Edited by Harry Rothwell. Camden Third Series 89. London: Royal Historical Society, 1957.

Weber, Henry, ed. *Metrical Romances of the Thirteenth, Fourteenth, and Fifteenth Centuries*. 2 vols. Edinburgh: George Ramsay and Co., 1810.

William of Malmesbury. *Gesta Regum Anglorum*. Edited and translated by R. A. B. Mynors. Completed by R. M. Thomson and Michael Winterbottom. OMT. Oxford: Clarendon Press, 1998.

William of Newburgh. *Historia Rerum Anglicarum*. In *Chronicles of the Reigns of Stephen, Henry II and Richard I*. Edited by Richard Howlett. 4 vols. RS 82. London: Longman, 1884–1889.

Zettl, Ewald, ed. *An Anonymous Short English Metrical Chronicle*. EETS OS 196. London: Oxford University Press, 1935.

SECONDARY STUDIES

Aebischer, Paul. *Des annales carolingiennes à Doon de Mayence: nouveau recueil d'études sur l'épique française médiévale*. Geneva: Droz, 1975.

———. *Préhistoire et protohistoire du Roland d'Oxford*. Bern: Francke, 1972.

Akbari, Susan Conklin, "The Hunger for National Identity in *Richard Coeur de Lion*." In *Reading Medieval Culture: Essays in Honor of Robert W. Hanning*, edited by R. M. Stein and S. Pierson Prior, 198–227. Notre Dame: University of Notre Dame Press, 2005.

Alexander, J. J. G., and Paul Binski, eds. *Age of Chivalry: Art in Plantagenet England, 1200–1400*. London: Royal Academy, 1987.

Allport, Gordon W., and Leo Postman. *The Psychology of Rumor*. New York: Henry Holt and Co., 1947.

Ambrisco, Alan S. "Cannibalism and Cultural Encounters in *Richard Coeur de Lion*." *Journal of Medieval and Modern Studies* 29 (1999): 499–528.

Appleby, John T. *England without Richard, 1189–1199*. Ithaca, NY: Cornell University Press, 1965.

Arnold-Forster, Frances. *Studies in Church Dedications; or England's Patron Saints*. 3 vols. London: Skeffington and Son, 1899.

Bahr, Arthur. *Fragments and Assemblages: Forming Compilations of Medieval London*. Chicago: University of Chicago Press, 2013.

Bailey, S. J. "Warranties of Land in the Reign of Richard I." *The Cambridge Law Journal* 9 (1946): 192–209.

Bardsley, Sandy. *Venomous Tongues: Speech and Gender in Late Medieval England*. Philadelphia: University of Pennsylvania Press, 2006.

Barron, W. R. J. *Medieval English Romance*. New York: Longman, 1987.

Barrow, G. S. W. "The Aftermath of War: Scotland and England in the Late Thirteenth and Early Fourteenth Centuries." *Transactions of the Royal Historical Society* 28 (1978): 103–25.

———. *Robert Bruce*. 1965. 4th ed. Reprint, Edinburgh: Edinburgh University Press, 2005.

Barrow, Julia. "The Chronology of Forgery Production at Worcester from c. 1000 to the Early Twelfth Century." In *St. Wulfstan and His World*, edited by Julia Barrow and Nicholas Brooks, 105–22. Aldershot: Ashgate, 2005.

Bartlett, Robert. *England under the Norman and Angevin Kings, 1075–1225*. Oxford: Clarendon Press, 2000.

Baswell, Christopher. "Multilingualism on the Page." In *Middle English: Oxford Twenty-First Century Approaches to Literature*, edited by Paul Strohm, 38–50. Oxford: Oxford University Press, 2007.

Baugh, Albert C. Foreword in *Studies in Medieval Literature: A Memorial Collection of Essays*, by Roger S. Loomis, v–vi. New York: B. Franklin, 1970.

Beadle, Richard. "Prolegomena to a Literary Geography of Later Medieval Norfolk." In *Regionalism in Late Medieval Manuscripts and Texts: Essays Celebrating the Publication of "A Linguistic Atlas of Late Medieval English,"* edited by Felicity Riddy, 89–108. Cambridge: D. S. Brewer, 1991.

Bédier, Joseph. "La tradition manuscrite du *Lai de l'Ombre*. Réflexions sur l'art d'editer les anciens texts." *Romania* 54 (1928): 161–96, 321–56.

Beller, Steven. *A Concise History of Austria*. Cambridge: Cambridge University Press, 2006.

Bennett, J. A. W. *Middle English Literature*. Edited and completed by Douglas Gray. Oxford: Clarendon Press, 1986.

Blau, Eve. "'A Capital without a Nation': Red Vienna, Architecture, and Spatial Politics between the World Wars." In *Power and Architecture: The Construction of Capitals and the Politics of Space*, edited by Michael Minkenberg, 178–207. New York: Berghahn Books, 2014.

Bliss, A. J. "Notes on the Auchinleck Manuscript." *Speculum* 26 (1951): 652–58.

Blurton, Heather. *Cannibalism in High Medieval English Literature*. New York: Palgrave Macmillan, 2007.

Bly Calkin, Siobhain. *Saracens and the Making of English Identity: The Auchinleck Manuscript*. New York: Routledge, 2005.

Boynton, Susan, Sarah Kay, Alison Cornish, and Andrew Albin. "Sound Matters." *Speculum* 91 (2016): 998–1039.

Brand, Paul. *Kings, Barons and Justices: The Making and Enforcing of Legislation in Thirteenth-Century England*. Cambridge: Cambridge University Press, 2003.

———. "The Languages of the Law in Medieval England." In *Multilingualism in Later Medieval Britain*, edited by D. A. Trotter, 69–76. Cambridge: D. S. Brewer, 2000.

———. "Origins of the English Legal Profession." *Law and History Review* 5 (1987): 31–50.

———. "'Quo Warranto' Law in the Reign of Edward I: A Hitherto Undiscovered Opinion of Chief Justice Hengham." *Irish Jurist* 14 (1979): 124–72.

———. "'Time Out of Mind': The Knowledge and Use of the Eleventh- and Twelfth- Century Past in Thirteenth-Century Litigation." In *Anglo-Norman Studies 16: Proceedings of the Battle Abbey Conference, 1993*, edited by Marjorie Chibnall, 37–54. Woodbridge: Boydell Press, 1994.

Bridges, Venetia. "Absent Presence: Auchinleck and *Kyng Alisaunder*." In *The Auchinleck Manuscript: New Perspectives*, edited by Susanna Fein, 88–107. York: York Medieval Press, 2016.

———. *Medieval Narratives of Alexander the Great: Transnational Texts in England and France*. Cambridge: D. S. Brewer, 2018.

Brooks, Lisa. *The Common Pot: The Recovery of Native Space in the Northeast*. Minneapolis: University of Minnesota Press, 2008.

Brunner, Karl. "Middle English Metrical Romances and Their Audience." In *Studies in Medieval Literature, in Honour of Professor Albert Croll Baugh*, edited by MacEdward Leach, 219–27. Philadelphia: University of Pennsylvania Press, 1961.

Buchan, John. *Sir Walter Scott*. New York: Coward-McCann, 1932.

Butkuviene, Gerda. "Book Review: Myths of Mayerling; *Crime at Mayerling. The Life and Death of Mary Vetsera*, by Georg Markus; *The Hapsburgs' Tragedy*, by Leo Belmonto." *The Vienna Review*, March 11, 2012.

Butterfield, Ardis. *The Familiar Enemy: Chaucer, Language and Nation in the Hundred Years War*. Oxford: Oxford University Press, 2009.

Caenegem, R. C. van. *Royal Writs in England from the Conquest to Glanvill: Studies in the Early History of the Common Law*. Publications of the Selden Society 77. London: B. Quaritch, 1959.

Cam, Helen M. *Liberties and Communities in Medieval England: Collected Studies in Local Administration and Topography.* Cambridge: Cambridge University Press, 1944.

Camille, Michael. *Mirror in Parchment: The Luttrell Psalter and the Making of Medieval England.* Chicago: University of Chicago Press, 1998.

Carruthers, Mary. *The Book of Memory: A Study of Memory in Medieval Culture.* Cambridge: Cambridge University Press, 1990.

Cassidy-Welch, Megan. *War and Memory at the Time of the Fifth Crusade.* University Park: Pennsylvania State University Press, 2019.

Cavanaugh, Susan H. "Royal Books: King John to Richard II." *The Library* 10 (1988): 304–16.

———. "A Study of Books Privately Owned in England: 1300–1450." Unpublished PhD diss., University of Pennsylvania, 1980.

Cheney, C. R. *Hubert Walter.* London: Nelson, 1967.

Chibnall, Marjorie. "Dating the Charters of the Smaller Religious Houses in Suffolk in the Twelfth and Thirteenth Centuries." In *Dating Undated Medieval Charters,* edited by Michael Gervers, 51–60. Woodbridge: Boydell Press, 2000.

Chinca, Mark, and Christopher Young, eds. *Orality and Literacy in the Middle Ages: Essays on a Conjunction and Its Consequences in Honour of D. H. Green.* Turnhout: Brepols, 2005.

Clanchy, M. T. "The Franchise of Return of Writs." *Transactions of the Royal Historical Society* 17 (1967): 59–82.

———. *From Memory to Written Record, England 1066–1307.* 2nd ed. Oxford: Blackwell, 1993.

Cochrane, J. G., ed. *Catalogue of the Library at Abbotsford.* Edinburgh: Maitland Club, 1838.

Cohen, Jeffrey Jerome. "On Saracen Enjoyment: Some Fantasies of Race in Late Medieval France and England." *Journal of Medieval and Early Modern Studies* 31 (2001): 113–46.

Coleman, Joyce. "Aurality." In *Middle English: Oxford Twenty-First Century Approaches to Literature,* edited by Paul Strohm, 68–85. Oxford: Oxford University Press, 2007.

———. *Public Reading and the Reading Public in Late Medieval England and France.* Cambridge: Cambridge University Press, 1996.

Colker, M. L. "A Newly Discovered Manuscript Leaf of Ambroise's *L'Estoire de la Guerre Sainte.*" *Revue d'histoire des textes* 22 (1992): 159–70.

Connolly, Margaret, and A. S. G. Edwards. "Evidence for the History of the Auchinleck Manuscript." *The Library* 18 (2017): 292–304.

Constable, Giles. "Forgery and Plagiarism in the Middle Ages." *Archiv für Diplomatik, Schriftgeschichte, Siegel- und Wappenkunde* 29 (1983): 1–41.

Cooper, Helen. "The Elizabethan Havelok: William Warner's First of the English." In *Medieval Insular Romance: Translation and Innovation,* edited by Judith Weiss, Jennifer Fellows, and Morgan Dickson, 169–83. Cambridge: D. S. Brewer, 2000.

———. *The English Romance in Time: Transforming Motifs from Geoffrey of Monmouth to the Death of Shakespeare.* Oxford: Oxford University Press, 2004.

———. "Lancelot, Roger Mortimer and the Date of the Auchinleck Manuscript." In *Studies in Late Medieval and Early Renaissance Texts in Honour of John Scattergood,* edited by Anne Marie D'Arcy and Alan J. Fletcher, 91–99. Dublin: Four Courts, 2005.

———. "Romance after 1400." In *The Cambridge History of Medieval English Literature,* edited by David Wallace, 690–719. Cambridge: Cambridge University Press, 1999.

Corner, David. "The Earliest Surviving Manuscripts of Roger of Howden's 'Chronica.'" *The English Historical Review* 98 (1983): 297–310.

Coss, P. R. "Aspects of Cultural Diffusion in Medieval England: The Early Romances, Local Society, and Robin Hood." *Past and Present* 108 (1985): 35–79.

Crane, Susan. *Insular Romance: Politics, Faith, and Culture in Anglo-Norman and Middle English Literature*. Berkeley: University of California Press, 1986.

Craun, Edwin D. *Lies, Slander, and Obscenity in Medieval English Literature: Pastoral Rhetoric and the Deviant Speaker*. Cambridge: Cambridge University Press, 1997.

Crook, David. *Records of the General Eyre*. PRO Handbooks 20. London: Her Majesty's Stationary Office, 1982.

Crouch, Christian Ayne. *Nobility Lost: French and Canadian Martial Cultures, Indians, and the End of New France*. Ithaca, NY: Cornell University Press, 2014.

Davis, Norman. "Another Fragment of 'Richard Coer de Lyon.'" *Notes and Queries* 16 (1969): 447–52.

Dean, Ruth J. *Anglo-Norman Literature: A Guide to Texts and Manuscripts*. London: The Anglo-Norman Text Society, 1999.

DeAngelis, Jamie. "Reading across Languages in Medieval Britain." Unpublished PhD diss., University of California, Berkeley, 2012.

Denholm-Young, Noël. "The Tournament in the Thirteenth Century." In *Studies in Medieval History, Presented to Frederick Maurice Powicke*, edited by R. W. Hunt et al., 240–68. Oxford: Clarendon Press, 1948.

Dillon, Emma. *The Sense of Sound: Musical Meaning in France, 1260–1330*. Oxford: Oxford University Press, 2012.

Donegan, Kathleen. *Seasons of Misery: Catastrophe and Colonial Settlement in Early America*. Philadelphia: University of Pennsylvania Press, 2014.

Drimmer, Sonja. *The Art of Allusion: Illuminators and the Making of English Literature, 1406–1476*. Philadelphia: University of Pennsylvania Press, 2019.

Duffy, Eamon. *The Stripping of the Altars: Traditional Religion in England 1400–1580*. New Haven and London: Yale University Press, 1992.

Dugdale, William. *Monasticon Anglicanum*. 6 vols. London: Longman, 1817–1830.

Duggan, Joseph J. "Franco-German Conflict and the History of French Scholarship on the *Song of Roland*." In *Hermeneutics and Medieval Culture*, edited by Patrick J. Gallacher and Helen Damico, 97–106. Albany: State University of New York, 1989.

———. "La France des Plantagenêts dans le versions rimées de la *Chanson de Roland*. In *Les chansons de geste: Actes du XVI congrès international de la Société Rencesvals, pour l'étude de épopées romanes, Granada, 21–25 juillet 2003*, edited by Carlos Alvar and Juan Paredes, 205–14. Granada: Universidad de Granada, 2005.

———. "Performance and Transmission, Aural and Ocular Reception in the Twelfth- and Thirteenth-Century Vernacular Literature of France." *Romance Philology* 43 (1989): 49–58.

Dunphy, Graeme, ed. *Encyclopedia of the Medieval Chronicle*. Leiden: Brill, 2010.

Elias, Marcel. "Violence, Excess, and the Composite Emotional Rhetoric of *Richard Coeur de Lion*." *Studies in Philology* 114 (2017): 1–38.

Escobedo, Libby Karlinger. *The Milemete Treatise and Companion Secretum Secretorum: Iconography, Audience, and Patronage in Fourteenth-Century England*. Lewiston: The Edwin Mellen Press, 2011.

Ewing, Tabetha Leigh. *Rumor, Diplomacy, and War in Enlightenment Paris*. Oxford University Studies in the Enlightenment 7. Oxford: Voltaire Foundation, 2014.

Fagnen, Claude. "Essai sur quelques actes normandes de Richard Coeur de Lion." In *Positions des thèses de l'École des Chartres*, 71–75. Chartres: École des Chartres, 1971.

Fein, Susanna, ed. *The Auchinleck Manuscript: New Perspectives*. York: York Medieval Press, 2016.

———. "The Contents of Thornton's Manuscripts." In *Robert Thornton and His Books: Essays on the Lincoln and London Thornton Manuscripts*, edited by Susanna Fein and Michael Johnston, 13–65. York: York Medieval Press, 2014.

Fenster, Thelma S., and Daniel Lord Small, eds. *Fama: The Politics of Talk and Reputation in Medieval Europe*. Ithaca, NY: Cornell University Press, 2003.

Field, Rosalind. "Romance in England." In *The Cambridge History of Medieval Literature*, edited by David Wallace, 152–76. Cambridge: Cambridge University Press, 1999.

———. "Waldef and the Matter of/with England." In *Medieval Insular Romance: Translation and Innovation*, edited by Judith Weiss, Jennifer Fellows, and Morgan Dickinson, 25–39. Cambridge: D. S. Brewer, 2000.

Finlayson, John. "Legendary Ancestors and the Expansion of Romance in *Richard, Coer de Lyon*." *English Studies* 79 (1998): 299–308.

———. "*Richard Coer de Lyon:* Romance, History, or Something in Between?" *Studies in Philology* 87 (1990): 156–80.

Fisher, Matthew. "Genealogy Rewritten: Inheriting the Legendary in Insular Historiography." In *Broken Lines: Genealogical Literature in Late-Medieval Britain and France*, edited by Raluca L. Radulescu and Edward Donald Kennedy, 123–42. Turnhout: Brepols, 2008.

———. *Scribal Authorship and the Writing of History in England*. Columbus: The Ohio State University Press, 2012.

Foote, Peter. *The Pseudo-Turpin Chronicle in Iceland: A Contribution to the Study of the Karlamagnús saga*. London: London Medieval Studies, 1959.

Fuentes, Marisa J. *Dispossessed Lives: Enslaved Women, Violence, and the Archive*. Philadelphia: University of Pennsylvania Press, 2016.

Gamerschlag, Kurt. "Henry Weber: Medieval Scholar, Poet, and Secretary to Walter Scott." *Studies in Scottish Literature* 25 (1990): 202–17.

Garland, Henry, and Mary Garland. *The Oxford Companion to German Literature*. Oxford: Oxford University Press, 1997.

Gawthrop, Humphrey. "George Ellis of Ellis Caymanas: A Caribbean Link to Scott and the Brontë Sisters." *Electronic British Library Journal* (2005): 1–9.

Giancarlo, Matthew. *Parliament and Literature in Late-Medieval England*. Cambridge: Cambridge University Press, 2007.

Gillespie, Vincent. "Syon and the New Learning." In *The Religious Orders in Pre-Reformation England*, edited by James G. Clark, 75–95. Woodbridge: Boydell and Brewer, 2002.

Gillingham, John. "The Context and Purposes of Geoffrey of Monmouth's *History of the Kings of Britain*." In *Anglo Norman Studies 13: Proceedings of the Battle Conference*, edited by Marjorie Chibnall, 99–118. Woodbridge: The Boydell Press, 1990.

———. "Foundations of a Disunited Kingdom." In *Uniting the Kingdom? The Making of British History*, edited by Alexander Grant and Keith J. Stringer, 48–64. New York: Routledge, 1995.

———. "The Kidnapped King: Richard I in Germany, 1192–1194." *Bulletin of the German Historical Institute, London* 30 (2008): 5–34.

———. *Richard I*. New Haven: Yale University Press, 2002.

Goody, Jack. *The Interface between the Written and the Oral*. Cambridge: Cambridge University Press, 1987.

Goody, Jack, and Ian Watt. "The Consequences of Literacy." *Comparative Studies in Society and History* 5 (1963): 304–45.

Görlach, Manfred. *The Textual Tradition of the South English Legendary.* Leeds: The University of Leeds School of English, 1974.

Gransden, Antonia. *Historical Writing in England I, c. 550 to c. 1307.* 1974. Reprint, London: Routledge, 2000.

Graydon, Joseph S. "Defense of Criseyde." *PMLA* 44 (1929): 141–77.

Green, D. H. *Medieval Listening and Reading: The Primary Reception of German Literature, 800–1300.* Cambridge: Cambridge University Press, 1994.

———. "Orality and Reading: The State of Research in Medieval Studies." *Speculum* 65 (1990): 267–80.

Green, Richard Firth. *A Crisis of Truth: Law and Literature in Ricardian England.* Philadelphia: University of Pennsylvania Press, 2002.

Greetham, D. C. *Theories of the Text.* Oxford: Oxford University Press, 1999.

Guddat-Figge, Gisela. *Catalogue of Manuscripts Containing Middle English Romances.* Munich: Wilhelm Fink, 1976.

Haider, Siegfried. "Jans Enikel." *Neue deutsche Biographie,* edited by Otto Stolberg-Wernigerode. Vol. 10. Berlin: Duncker and Humboldt, 1974.

Halvorsen, E. F. *The Norse Version of the Chanson de Roland.* Copenhagen: Ejnar Munksgaard, 1959.

Hanna, Ralph. "Auchinleck 'Scribe 6' and Some Corollary Issues." In *The Auchinleck Manuscript: New Perspectives,* edited by Susanna Fein, 209–22. York: York Medieval Press, 2016.

———. "Contextualizing the *Siege of Jerusalem.*" *Yearbook of Langland Studies* 6 (1992): 109–21.

———. "The Growth of Robert Thornton's Books." *Studies in Bibliography* 40 (1987): 51–61.

———. *London Literature, 1300–1380.* Cambridge: Cambridge University Press, 2005.

———. "The London Thornton Manuscript: A Corrected Collation." *Studies in Bibliography* 37 (1984): 122–30.

———. "The Matter of Fulk: Romance and History in the Marches." *Journal of English and Germanic Philology* 110 (2011): 337–58.

———. "Middle English Verses from a Bodleian Binding." *Bodleian Library Record* 17 (2002): 488–92.

———. *Pursuing History: Middle English Manuscripts and Their Texts.* Stanford: Stanford University Press, 1996.

———. "Reconsidering the Auchinleck Manuscript." In *New Directions in Late Medieval Manuscript Studies,* edited by Derek Pearsall, 91–102. York: York Medieval Press, 2000.

Hanna, Ralph, and David Rundle. *A Descriptive Catalogue of the Western Manuscripts, to c. 1600, in Christ Church, Oxford.* Using materials collected by Jeremy J. Griffiths. Oxford Bibliographical Society Publications, Special Series: Manuscripts Catalogues, 2. Oxford: Oxford Bibliographical Society, 2017.

Hardie, Philip. *Rumour and Renown: Representations of Fama in Western Literature.* Cambridge: Cambridge University Press, 2012.

Hardwick, Charles, ed. *A Catalogue of Manuscripts Preserved in the Library of the University of Cambridge.* Vol. 1. Cambridge: Cambridge University Press, 1906.

Hebron, Malcolm. *The Medieval Siege: Theme and Image in Middle English Romance.* Oxford: Clarendon Press, 1997.

Heng, Geraldine. *Empire of Magic: Medieval Romance and the Politics of Cultural Fantasy.* New York: Columbia University Press, 2003.

Hiatt, Alfred. *The Making of Medieval Forgeries: False Documents in Fifteenth-Century England.* Toronto: The British Library and University of Toronto Press, 2004.

Higgins, Ann. "*Sir Tristrem*, a Few Fragments and the Northern Identity of the Auchinleck Manuscript." In *The Auchinleck Manuscript: New Perspectives,* edited by Susanna Fein, 108–27. York: York Medieval Press, 2016.

Hilmo, Maidie. "The Power of Images in Auchinleck, Vernon, Pearl, and Two *Piers Plowman* Manuscripts." In *Opening Up Middle English Manuscripts: Literary and Visual Approaches,* by Kathryn Kerby-Fulton, Maidie Hilmo, and Linda Olson, 153–205. Ithaca, NY: Cornell University Press, 2012.

Holsinger, Bruce. *Neomedievalism, Neoconservatism, and the War on Terror.* Chicago: Prickly Paradigm Press, 2007.

Holt, J. C. *Magna Carta.* 2nd ed. Cambridge: Cambridge University Press, 1992.

Horrox, Rosemary. "Richard III and All Hallows Barking by the Tower." *Ricardian* 6 (1982): 38–40.

James, M. R. *A Descriptive Catalogue of the Manuscripts in the Library of Gonville and Caius College.* 2 vols. Cambridge: Cambridge University Press, 1907–1908.

Johnston, Arthur. *Enchanted Ground: The Study of Medieval Romance in the Eighteenth Century.* London: Athlone Press, 1964.

Johnston, Michael. *Romance and the Gentry in Late Medieval England.* Oxford: Oxford University Press, 2014.

Jones, Martin H. "Richard the Lionheart in German Literature of the Middle Ages." In *Richard Coeur de Lion in History and Myth,* edited by Janet L. Nelson, 70–116. London: King's College, Centre for Late Antique and Medieval Studies, 1992.

Justice, Steven. *Writing and Rebellion: England in 1381.* Berkeley: University of California Press, 1994.

Kane, George. "*Piers Plowman*: Problems and Methods of Editing the B-Text." *Modern Language Review* 43 (1948): 1–25.

Keen, Maurice. *England in the Later Middle Ages.* 2nd ed. New York: Routledge, 2003.

Ker, N. R. *Fragments of Medieval Manuscripts Used as Pastedowns in Oxford Bindings with a Survey of Oxford Binding c. 1515–1620.* Oxford: Oxford Bibliographical Society, 2004 for 2000.

Kerby-Fulton, Kathryn, Maidie Hilmo, and Linda Olson. *Opening Up Middle English Manuscripts: Literary and Visual Approaches.* Ithaca, NY: Cornell University Press, 2012.

Kisch, Wilhelm. *Die alten Strassen und Pläetze von Wien's Vorstädten und ihre historisch und ihre interessanten Häeuser.* 2 vols. Vienna: Oskar Frank, 1888.

Knowles, C. H. "*The Disinherited, 1265–80: A Political and Social Survey of the Supporters of Simon de Montfort and the Resettlement after the Barons' War.*" Unpublished PhD thesis, University of Wales, Cardiff, 1959.

———. "The Resettlement of England after the Barons' War, 1264–67." *Transactions of the Royal Historical Society* 32 (1982): 25–41.

Koch, Johannes. "Brunner, *Der mittelenglische versroman von Richard Löwenherz.*" *Englische Studien* 49 (1915): 126–42.

Kölbing, Eugen. "Vier romanzen-handschriften." *Englische Studien* 7 (1884): 177–201.

Koziol, Herbert. "Karl Brunner." In *Almanach: Österreichische Akademie der Wissenschaften.* Vienna: Hermann Böhlaus, 1966 for 1965.

Lapsley, G. "John de Warenne and the Quo Warranto Proceedings in 1279." *Cambridge Historical Journal* 2 (1927): 110–32.

Larkin, Peter. "The Coeur-de-Lyon Romances." In *Christian-Muslim Relations: A Bibliographical History*. Edited by Alex Mallett and David Thomas. Vol. 5, *1350–1500*, edited by Jason R. Dean, 268–77. Leiden: Brill, 2013.

Leach, Henry Goddard. *Angevin Britain and Scandinavia*. Cambridge, MA: Harvard University Press, 1921.

Leeper, Alexander W. *A History of Medieval Austria*. Edited by R. W. Seton-Watson and C. A. Macartney. Oxford: Oxford University Press, 1941.

Lejeune, Rita, and Jacques Stiennon. *La légende de la Roland dans l'art du moyen âge*. 2 vols. Brussels: Arcade, 1966.

Libbon, Marisa. "Douce 228, Richard Coeur de Lion, and *The King of Tars*." *Notes and Queries* 65 (2018): 8–11.

———. "The Invention of *King Richard*." In *The Auchinleck Manuscript: New Perspectives*, edited by Susanna Fein, 127–38. York: York Medieval Press, 2016.

Lochrie, Karma. *Covert Operations: The Medieval Uses of Secrecy*. Philadelphia: University of Pennsylvania Press, 1999.

Loomis, Laura Hibbard. "The Athelstan Gift Story: Its Influence on English Chronicles and Carolingian Romances." *PMLA* 67 (1952): 521–37.

———. "The Auchinleck Manuscript and a Possible London Bookshop of 1330–1340." *PMLA* 57 (1942): 595–627.

———. "The Auchinleck *Roland and Vernagu* and the *Short Chronicle*." *Modern Language Notes* 60 (1945): 94–97.

———. *Medieval Romance in England: A Study of the Sources and Analogues of the Non-Cyclic Metrical Romances*. New York: Burt Franklin, 1960.

Loomis, Roger Sherman. "*Der mittelenglische Versroman über Richard Löwenherz*, edited by Karl Brunner; Wiener Beiträge zur Englischen Philologie, vol. XLII; 1913." *Journal of English and German Philology* 15 (1916): 455–66.

———. "Edward I, Arthurian Enthusiast." *Speculum* 28 (1953): 114–27.

———. "*Richard Coeur de Lion* and the *Pas Saladin* in Medieval Art." *PMLA* 30 (1915): 509–28.

Loth, Agnete. "Les manuscrits norrois." In *Karlamagnús saga: Branches I, III, VII, et IX*, edited by Knut Togeby et al., 358–78. Copenhagen: La Société pour l'étude de la langue et de la littérature danoises, 1980.

Lumpi, Kurt. "Bibliographie der Veröffentlichungen." In *Studies in English Language and Literature, Presented to Professor Karl Bruner on the Occasion of His Seventieth Birthday*, edited by Siegfried Korninger, 284–90. Vienna: Wilhelm Braumüller, 1957.

Lysons, David. *Counties of Herts., Essex, and Kent*. Vol. 4 of *The Environs of London*. London: Cadwell and Davies, 1796.

Machan, Tim William. *Textual Criticism and Middle English Texts*. Charlottesville: University of Virginia Press, 1994.

Maddicott, J. R. "The County Community and the Making of Public Opinion in Fourteenth-Century England." *Transactions of the Royal Historical Society* 28 (1978): 27–43.

———. "Magna Carta and the Local Community 1215–1259." *Past and Present* 102 (1984): 25–65.

———. *Simon de Montfort*. Cambridge: Cambridge University Press, 1994.

———. *Thomas of Lancaster, 1307–1322*. Oxford: Oxford University Press, 1970.

Maines, Clark. "The Charlemagne Window at Chartres Cathedral: New Considerations on Text and Image." *Speculum* 52 (1977): 801–23.

Maitland, F. W. *The Constitutional History of England.* Edited by H. A. L. Fisher. 1908. Reprint, Cambridge: Cambridge University Press, 1974.

———. *The Forms of Action at Common Law.* Edited by A. H. Chaytor and W. J. Whittaker. 1909. Reprint, Cambridge: Cambridge University Press, 1969.

Manion, Lee. *Narrating the Crusades: Loss and Recovery in Medieval and Early Modern English Literature.* Cambridge: Cambridge University Press, 2014.

Manitius, Max, and Paul Lehmann. *Geschichte der lateinischen Literatur des Mittelalters: Vom Ausbruch des Kirchenstreites bis zum Ende des zwölften Jarhunderts.* Munich: Beck, 1931.

Marcus, Leah S. "Textual Scholarship." In *Introduction to Scholarship in Modern Languages and Literatures*, 3rd ed., edited by David G. Nicholls, 143–59. New York: Modern Language Association, 2007.

———. *Unediting the Renaissance: Shakespeare, Marlowe, Milton.* New York: Routledge, 1996.

Markus, Manfred. Preface in *Historical English: On the Occasion of Karl Brunner's 100th Birthday,* Innsbrucker Beiträge zur Kulturwissenschaft Anglistiche Reihe 1, edited by Manfred Markus, vii–ix. Innsbruck: Institut für Anglistik Universität Innsbruck, 1988.

Marshall, Helen. "What's in a Paraph? A New Methodology and Its Implications for the Auchinleck Manuscript." *Journal of the Early Book Society* 13 (2010): 39–62.

Matheson, Lister M. *The Prose Brut: The Development of a Middle English Chronicle.* Binghamton, NY: Medieval and Renaissance Texts and Studies, 1998.

Matthews, David. *Writing to the King: Nation, Kingship and Literature in England, 1250–1350.* Cambridge: Cambridge University Press, 2010.

Mayer, H. E. "A Ghost Ship Called Frankenef: King Richard I's German Itinerary." *English Historical Review* 115 (2000): 134–44.

McDonald, Nicola. "Eating People and the Alimentary Logic of *Richard Coeur de Lion.*" In *Pulp Fictions of Medieval England: Essays in Popular Romance,* edited by Nicola McDonald, 124–50. Manchester: Manchester University Press, 2004.

McGann, Jerome. *A Critique of Modern Textual Criticism.* Chicago: University of Chicago Press, 1983.

McIntosh, Angus. "Is *Sir Tristrem* an English or a Scottish Poem?" In *In Other Words: Transcultural Studies in Philology, Translation, and Lexicology Presented to Hans Heinrich Meier on the Occasion of His Sixty-Fifth Birthday,* edited by J. Lachlan Mackenzie and Richard Todd, 85–95. Dordecht, Holland: Foris Publications, 1989.

McIntosh, Angus, M. L. Samuels, and M. Benskin, with the assistance of M. Laing and K. Williams. *A Linguistic Atlas of Late Medieval English.* 4 vols. Aberdeen: Aberdeen University Press, 1986.

Meale, Carole M. *Readings in Medieval English Romance.* Cambridge: D. S. Brewer, 1994.

Mehl, Dieter. *The Middle English Romances of the Thirteenth and Fourteenth Centuries.* London: Routledge and K. Paul, 1968.

Menache, Sophia. "The Crusades and Their Impact on the Development of Medieval Communication." In *Kommunikation zwischen Orient und Okzident Alltag und Sachkultur: internationaler Kongress, Krems an der Donau 6. bis 9. Oktober 1992,* edited by Helmut Hundbichler, 69–90. Vienna: Österreichischen Akademie der Wissenschaften, 1994.

Michael, M. A. "The Iconography of Kingship in the Walter of Milemete Treatise." *Journal of the Warburg and Courtauld Institutes* 57 (1994): 35–47.

———. "A Manuscript Wedding Gift from Philippa of Hainault to Edward III." *The Burlington Magazine* 127 (1985): 582, 584–99.

Miller, Jennifer. "Laȝamon's Welsh." In *Reading Laȝamon's Brut: Approaches and Explorations,* edited by Rosamund Allen, Jane Roberts, and Carole Weinberg, 589–622. New York: Rodopi, 2013.

Mitchell, Jerome. *Scott, Chaucer, and Medieval Romance: A Study in Sir Walter Scott's Indebtedness to the Literature of the Middle Ages.* Lexington: University of Kentucky Press, 1987.

Moffat, Douglas. "A Bibliographical Essay on Editing Methods." In *A Guide to Editing Middle English,* edited by Vincent McCarren and Douglas Moffat, 25–60. Ann Arbor: University of Michigan Press, 1998.

Morgan, Estelle. "Two Notes on the 'Fürstenbuch.'" *The Modern Language Review* 60 (1965): 395–99.

Mortimer, Ian. "The Death of Edward II in Berkeley Castle." *English Historical Review* 120 (2005): 1175–214.

Neilson, George. *Caudatus Anglicus: A Medieval Slander.* Edinburgh: G. P. Johnston, 1896.

Nelson, Ingrid. *Lyric Tactics: Poetry and Practice in Later Medieval England.* Philadelphia: University of Pennsylvania Press, 2016.

Norgate, Kate. *Richard the Lion Heart.* London: Macmillan and Co. Ltd., 1924.

Olsen, Donald J. *The City as a Work of Art: London, Paris, Vienna.* New Haven: Yale University Press, 1986.

Olson, Linda. "Romancing the Book: Manuscripts for 'Euerich Inglische.'" In *Opening Up Middle English Manuscripts,* by Kathryn Kerby-Fulton, Maidie Hilmo, and Linda Olson, 95–151. Ithaca, NY: Cornell University Press, 2012.

Ong, Walter J. *Orality and Literacy: The Technologizing of the World.* London: Methuen, 1982.

Ormrod, W. M. *Edward III.* Stroud, Gloucestershire: Tempus Publishing Ltd., 2005.

Pächt, Otto, and J. J. G. Alexander. *Illuminated Manuscripts in the Bodleian Library.* 3 vols. Oxford: Clarendon Press, 1973.

Page, William, ed. *The Victoria History of the County of Oxford.* Vol. 2. London: Archibald Constable and Company, Ltd., 1907.

———. *The Victoria History of the County of York.* Vol. 3. London: Archibald Constable and Company, Ltd., 1913.

Paris, Gaston. "Le Roman de Richard Coeur de Lion." *Romania* 26 (1987): 353–93.

Parkes, Malcolm B. "The Influence of the Concepts of *Ordinatio* and *Compilatio* on the Development of the Book." In *Medieval Learning and Literature: Essays Presented to William Hunt,* edited by J. J. G. Alexander and M. T. Gibson, 115–41. Oxford: Clarendon Press, 1976.

———. *Their Hands before Our Eyes: A Closer Look at Scribes.* The Lyell Lectures Delivered in the University of Oxford 1999. Aldershot: Ashgate, 2008.

Paul, Nicholas. *To Follow in Their Footsteps: The Crusades and Family Memory in the High Middle Ages.* Ithaca, NY: Cornell University Press, 2012.

Pearsall, Derek. "Forging Truth in Medieval England." In *Cultures of Forgery: Making Nations, Making Selves,* edited by Judith Ryan and Alfred Thomas, 3–13. New York: Routledge, 2003.

Pearson, David. *Provenance Research in Book History: A Handbook.* London: The British Library and Oak Knoll Press, 1988.

Peirce, Ian. "The Knight, His Arms and Armour, c. 1150–1250." In *Anglo-Norman Studies 15: Proceedings of the Battle Conference 1992,* edited by Marjorie Chibnall, 251–66. Woodbridge: The Boydell Press, 1993.

Phillips, Susan E. "Gossip and (Un)official Writing." In *Middle English: Oxford Twenty-First Century Approaches to Literature,* edited by Paul Strohm, 476–90. Oxford: Oxford University Press, 2007.

———. *Transforming Talk: The Problem with Gossip in Late Medieval England.* University Park: Pennsylvania State University Press, 2007.

Plucknett, T. F. T. *Legislation of Edward I.* Oxford: Clarendon Press, 1949.

Pollock, Frederick, and F. W. Maitland. *The History of the English Law before the Time of Edward I.* 2 vols. 1898. Reprint, Cambridge: Cambridge University Press, 1985.

Porter, Pamela. *Medieval Warfare in Manuscripts.* London: The British Library, 2000.

Powicke, F. M. "The Bull 'Miramur plurimum' and a Letter to Archbishop Stephen Langton, 5 September 1215." *English Historical Review* 44 (1929): 87–93.

———. "Edward I in Fact and Fiction." In *Fritz Saxl, 1890–1948, A Volume of Memorial Essays from His Friends in England,* edited by D. J. Gordon, 120–35. London: Nelson, 1957.

———. *The Thirteenth Century, 1216–1307.* Oxford: Clarendon Press, 1953.

Prestwich, Michael. *Armies and Warfare in the Middle Ages: The English Experience.* New Haven: Yale University Press, 1996.

———. *Edward I.* Rev. ed. New Haven: Yale University Press, 1997.

———. *The Three Edwards: War and State in England, 1272–1377.* 2nd ed. London: Routledge, 2003.

Purdie, Rhiannon. *Anglicising Romance: Tail-Rhyme and Genre in Medieval English Literature.* Cambridge: D. S. Brewer, 2008.

Raban, Sandra. *A Second Domesday? The Hundred Rolls of 1279–80.* Oxford: Oxford University Press, 2004.

Reichl, Karl, ed. *Medieval Oral Literature.* Berlin: De Gruyter, 2012.

Rejhon, Annalee C. *Cân Rolant: The Medieval Welsh Version of the Song of Roland.* Berkeley: University of California Press, 1984.

Rickard, P. *Britain in Medieval French Literature 1100–1500.* Cambridge: Cambridge University Press, 1956.

Rikhardsdottir, Sif. *Medieval Translations and Cultural Discourse: The Movement of Texts in England, France, and Scandinavia.* Cambridge: D. S. Brewer, 2012.

Robbins, Rossell Hope. "A Highly Critical Approach to the Middle English Lyric." *College English* 30 (1968): 74–75.

Robinson, P. R. "The 'Booklet': A Self-Contained Unit in Composite Manuscripts." *Codicologica* 3 (1980): 46–69.

"Roger S. Loomis of Columbia Dies." *New York Times,* October 12, 1966.

Rogers, Randall. *Latin Siege Warfare in the Twelfth Century.* Oxford: Clarendon Press, 1992.

Salter, Elizabeth. *Fourteenth-Century English Poetry: Contexts and Readings.* Oxford: Clarendon Press, 1983.

Sandler, Lucy Freeman. *Gothic Manuscripts 1285–1385.* 2 vols. Oxford: Oxford University Press, 1986.

Saul, Nigel. *The Three Richards: Richard I, Richard II, and Richard III.* London: Hambledon, 2005.

Sayers, Jane. "English Charters from the Third Crusade." In *Tradition and Change: Essays in Honor of Marjorie Chibnall, Presented by Her Friends on the Occasion of Her Seventieth Birth-*

day, edited by Diana Greenway, Christopher Holdsworth, and Jane Sayers, 195–213. Cambridge: Cambridge University Press, 1985.

Schorske, Carl E. *Fin-de-Siècle Vienna: Politics and Culture.* New York: Vintage Books, 1981.

Schwyzer, Philip. *Shakespeare and the Remains of Richard III.* Oxford: Oxford University Press, 2013.

Shaw, Frank. "The Good Old Days of the Babenberg Dukes." In *Bristol Austrian Studies,* edited by Brian Keith-Smith, 1–18. Bristol: University of Bristol Press, 1990.

Shonk, Timothy A. "A Study of the Auchinleck Manuscript: Bookmen and Bookmaking in the Early Fourteenth Century." *Speculum* 60 (1985): 71–91.

Short, Ian. "Patrons and Polyglots: French Literature in Twelfth-Century England." In *Anglo-Norman Studies 14: Proceedings of the Battle Conference,* edited by Marjorie Chibnall, 229–49. Woodbridge: The Boydell Press, 1991.

Short, Ian, and Maureen Thomas. "*Karlamagnús* and the Pre-History of the *Roland.*" *Romance Philology* 30 (1976): 210–21.

Singleton, Antony. "The Early English Text Society in the Nineteenth Century: An Organizational History." *Review of English Studies* 56 (2005): 90–118.

Skärup, Povl. "Contenu, sources, rédactions." In *Karlamagnús saga: Branches I, III, VII, et IX,* edited by Knut Togeby et al., 333–55. Copenhagen: La Société pour l'étude de la langue et de la littérature danoises, 1980.

Smithers, G. V. "Two Newly-Discovered Fragments from the Auchinleck MS." *Medium Ævum* 18 (1949): 1–11.

Smyser, H. M. "Charlemagne and Roland and the Auchinleck MS." *Speculum* 21 (1946): 275–88.

Smyth, Alfred P. *King Alfred the Great.* Oxford: Oxford University Press, 1995.

Snell, Rachel. "The Undercover King." In *Medieval Insular Romance: Translation and Innovation,* edited by Judith Weiss, Jennifer Fellows, and Morgan Dickson, 133–54. Cambridge: D. S. Brewer, 2000.

Spacks, Patricia Meyer. *Gossip.* Chicago: University of Chicago Press, 1986.

Stanbury, Sarah. "Women's Letters and Private Space in Chaucer." *Exemplaria* 6 (1994): 271–85.

Steingrímsson, Sigurgeir. "Árni Magnússon." In *The Manuscripts of Iceland,* edited by Gísli Sigurðsson and Vésteinn Ólason, 85–99. Reykjavík: Árni Magnússon Institute in Iceland, 2004.

Stock, Brian. *The Implications of Literacy: Written Language and Models of Interpretation in the Eleventh and Twelfth Centuries.* Princeton: Princeton University Press, 1983.

Street, Brian V. *Social Literacies: Critical Approaches to Literacy in Development, Ethnography and Education.* 1995. Reprint, London: Routledge, 2013.

Strohm, Paul, ed. *Middle English: Oxford Twenty-First Century Approaches to Literature.* Oxford: Oxford University Press, 2007.

A Summary Catalogue of Western Manuscripts in the Bodleian Library at Oxford. Edited by R. W. Hunt, Falconer Madan, and P. D. Record. 7 vols. Oxford: Clarendon Press, 1895–1953.

Sutherland, Donald W. *Quo Warranto Proceedings in the Reign of Edward I, 1278–1294.* Oxford: Clarendon Press, 1963.

Symes, Carol. "Popular Literacies and the First Historians of the First Crusade." *Past and Present* 235 (2017): 37–67.

Tanselle, G. Thomas. "Textual Instability and Editorial Idealism." *Studies in Bibliography* 49 (1996): 1–60.

Taylor, Andrew. "The Myth of the Minstrel Manuscript." *Speculum* 66 (1991): 43–73.

——. *Textual Situations: Three Medieval Manuscripts and Their Readers*. Philadelphia: University of Pennsylvania Press, 2002.

Taylor, John. "Guisborough [Hemingford, Hemingburgh], Walter of (fl. c. 1290–c. 1305), Chronicler and Augustinian Canon." In *Oxford Dictionary of National Biography*. Article published September 23, 2004. Accessed June 29, 2020. https://www-oxforddnb-com.ezprox.bard.edu/view/10.1093/ref:odnb/9780198614128.001.0001/odnb-9780198614128-e-12892.

——. "Review of *The Chronicle of Walter of Guisborough*, edited by Harry Rothwell." *Scottish Historical Review* 38 (1959): 61–63.

Tétrel, Hélène. *La Chanson des Saxons et sa réception norroise: avatars de la matière épique*. Orléans: Éditions Paradigme, 2006.

Thomas, Hugh M. *The English and the Normans: Ethnic Hostility, Assimilation, and Identity, 1066–c. 1220*. Oxford: Oxford University Press, 2003.

Thompson, John J. *Robert Thornton and the London Thornton Manuscript: British Library MS Additional 31042*. Cambridge: D. S. Brewer, 1987.

Thompson, Stith. *Motif Index of Folk Literature*. Bloomington: Indiana University Press, 1955.

Timpanaro, Sebastian. *The Genesis of Lachmann's Method*. Edited and translated by Glenn W. Most. Chicago: University of Chicago Press, 2005.

Torpey, Sarah Beth. "Of Cannibals and Kings: The (Monstrous) Nature of Crusading in *Richard Coer de Lyon*." *Medieval Perspectives* 23 (2008 [2011]): 105–18.

Tout, T. F. *Collected Papers of Thomas Frederick Tout*. 3 vols. Manchester: Manchester University Press, 1933–1934.

——. "Medieval Forgers and Forgeries." *Bulletin of the John Rylands Library* 5 (1918–20): 208–34.

Tristram, E. W. *English Medieval Wall Painting: The Thirteenth Century*. With a catalogue compiled in collaboration with Monica Bardswell. 2 vols. New York: Oxford University Press, 1950.

Trouillot, Michel-Rolph. *Silencing the Past: Power and the Production of History*. Boston: Beacon Press, 1995.

Tuohy, William. "1889 Hapsburg Tragedy at Mayerling: 'Love Deaths' Remain Fascinating." *Los Angeles Times*, March 19, 1989.

Turville-Petre, Thorlac. *England the Nation: Language, Literature, and National Identity, 1290–1340*. Oxford: Clarendon Press, 1996.

——. "Some Medieval Manuscripts in the North-East Midlands." In *Manuscripts and Readers in Fifteenth-Century England: The Literary Implications of Manuscript Study*, edited by Derek Pearsall, 125-41. Cambridge: D. S. Brewer, 1983.

Tyerman, Christopher. *England and the Crusades, 1095–1588*. Chicago: University of Chicago Press, 1988.

——. *God's War: A New History of the Crusades*. Cambridge, MA: The Belknap Press, 2006.

Vale, Juliet. *Edward III and Chivalry: Chivalric Society and Its Context 1270–1350*. Woodbridge: The Boydell Press, 1982.

Veeder, Van Vechten. "The History and Theory of the Law of Defamation." *Columbia Law Review* 3 (1903): 546–73.

Wallace, David, ed. *The Cambridge History of Medieval English Literature*. Cambridge: Cambridge University Press, 1999.

Walpole, Roland N. "The Source MS of *Charlemagne and Roland* and the Auchinleck Bookshop." *Modern Language Notes* 60 (1945): 22–26.

Ward, H. L. D., and J. A. Herbert. *Catalogue of the Romances in the Department of Manuscripts in the British Museum*. 3 vols. London: British Museum, 1883–1910.

Warton, Thomas. *The History of English Poetry, from the Close of the Eleventh Century to the Commencement of the Eighteenth Century.* 2nd ed. 3 vols. London: Thomas Tegg, 1840.

Warren, W. L. *Henry II.* Berkeley: University of California Press, 1973.

Watson, Andrew G. *The Manuscripts of Henry Savile of Banke.* London: The Bibliographical Society, 1969.

Weiss, Judith, Jennifer Fellows, and Morgan Dickson, eds. *Medieval Insular Romance: Translation and Innovation.* Cambridge: D. S. Brewer, 2000.

Wiggins, Alison. "Are Auchinleck Manuscript Scribes 1 and 6 the Same Scribe? The Advantages of Whole-Data Analysis and Electronic Texts." *Medium Ævum* 73 (2004): 10–26.

Wilson, R. M. *The Lost Literature of Medieval England.* London: Metheun & Co. Ltd., 1952.

Zumthor, Paul, and Marilyn C. Engelhardt. "The Text and the Voice." *New Literary History* 16 (1984): 67–92.

INDEX

Aachen casket, 169

Acre, 13, 25, 39–41, 40n89, 101, 103–4, 122–23, 122n45, 123n47, 126–27, 136–38, 142, 145–47, 146n25, 157–58, 171–73, 175, 180–81, 184, 189, 194, 196–200, 205, 213. See also Third Crusade

Aebischer, Paul, 156n59

Albert of Ramsey, 97

Alexander the Great, 115, 119–20

Alexander, J. J. G., 128n66

All Hallows, London, 104–5

Allport, Gordon W., 10n20

"Almayne episode," 33–34, 36–38, 46, 49, 56–57, 193, 209. See also *Richard Löwenherz*

Ambrisco, Alan S., 32n53

Ambroise, 123–24, 133–34

ancestral history, 70–71, 81–82

Angleterre, Thomas d,' 154

Anglo-Norman language and texts, 15, 30–31, 31n46, 31n49, 70, 79, 83n64, 116n18, 120, 123–24, 123n48, 134, 152–57, 152n44, 154n50, 156n59, 157n61–62, 159, 164, 166–67, 178n13, 191n43. See also individual titles

Annales de Wintonia, 68n21

Anne of Geierstein (Scott), 26

Anonymous Short English Metrical Chronicle, 139n1, 146–47, 153, 157–58, 160–62, 162n87, 163, 178n11, 178n13, 185n26

Ansbert, 41, 41n96, 42

Antioch, siege of, 120–22, 129, 129n67. See also First Crusade

Appleby, John T., 172n116

Aristotle, 115–16, 116n24, 119n34

Arthur, legendary king of Britain, 102–3, 162

Auchinleck manuscript. *See* Edinburgh, National Library of Scotland, MS Advocates 19.2.1

aural transmission, 165n94

aurality, 6

Baker, Geoffrey, 163, 163n88

Barking Abbey, 105

Bartlett, Robert, 104n143

Beaufort fragment. *See* Gloucester, Gloucestershire Archives, MS D2700/V/I No.8

Becket, Thomas, 185n26, 195

• 237 •

Bédier, Joseph, 209, 209n96
bees, as siege weapons, 108–9, 109n7, 110 fig. 1a, 111 fig. 1b, 122n45, 137, 146–47, 158, 181, 198
Bennett, J. A. W., 167n101
Berwick, John, 95–96, 95n104
Beuve de Hantone, 154
Bevis of Hampton, 154n52, 159
Binski, Paul, 128n66
Blashill, Thomas, 53–54
Bliss, A. J., 177, 177n10
Bodel, Jean, 157, 157n61, 161n82
book history, 8–9, 13, 143, 180–81, 190, 213
Boswell, Alexander, 140–41
Boun, John de, 131n71
Boynton, Susan, 5n9
Bracton, Henry de, 62n4, 73n31
Brand, Paul, 73, 73n32, 80n54, 81
Brasseur, Annette, 161n82
Brunner, Karl, 22–23, 28–30, 29n39, 30–39, 32n53, 36n74, 48–52, 50n142, 57–59, 177n10, 190–91. See also *Richard Löwenherz*
Brussels, Bibliothèque royale de Belgique, MS 9961–62, 193
Burnley-Wiggins, Alison, 176n2
Bury, Richard de, 119n34

Caius. See Cambridge, Gonville and Caius College, MS 175/96
Cam, Helen M., 103n140
Cambridge, Corpus Christi College, MS 339, 132–33, 132n75
Cambridge, Gonville and Caius College, MS 175/96, 15–16, 24, 24n24, 25, 28, 30–31, 31n50, 31n52, 37n82, 38–39, 38n85, 56–57, 186, 191–93, 202, 202n76–202n77, 204–5, 207
Cambridge, Harvard Law School Library, MS 12, 115n18
Cambridge, Trinity College, MS O.4.32, 123n48
Cambridge, Trinity College, MS O.9.34, 120n37
Cambridge, University Library, MS Dd. 2.5, 67n17

Camille, Michael, 131n71
cannibalism, 15–16, 18, 25–27, 186n30, 192–95, 204–5, 205n85, 206n89
Carpenter, William, 114n13
Cassodorien, 36–37, 37n82, 201–4
catchwords, 175–77, 176n5, 180
Caxton, William, 167
Celestine III, Pope, 45, 46n129
Chanson d'Aspremont, 155
Chanson de Roland, La, 23n19, 153, 155, 164–65, 165n94–165n95, 169
Chanson des Saisnes, 157, 157n61, 161n82
Chanson des Saxons, La, 157n61
Chanson d'Otinel, 155
Charlemagne, 153–57, 156n59, 157–60, 159n70, 163–65, 169–70
"Charlemagne Window," 160n106, 169–70, 169n107
charters, 80, 87–88, 95–96, 101
Chaucer, Geoffrey, 3–5, 3n2, 210
Chertsey Tiles, 128, 128n66, 130
Cheta, Omar Y., 26n32
Chevalerie Ogier de Danemarche, 154–55
"Choruses from 'The Rock'" (Eliot), 1, 13, 13n22
Chronica Magistri (Roger of Howden), 123, 123n48
Chronica majora (Matthew Paris), 48
Chronicle (Walter of Guisborough), 66, 66n16, 67–69, 77n42
Chronicle of Walter of Guisborough (Rothwell), 68–69
Chroust, Anton, 41n97
Clanchy, Michael, 63–65, 64n14, 74n35
Coleman, Joyce, 6n12, 64n12
Comnenos, Isaac, emperor of Cyprus, 42, 126
completeness, 18, 31–32, 56, 190
Compromise of 1867, 52n149
Connolly, Margaret, 179, 179n16
Conrad of Montferrat, 42
Cooper, Helen, 162, 162n87, 163n88, 201n72
Copenhagen, University of Copenhagen, MS AM 180a fol, 155n55

Copenhagen, University of Copenhagen, MS AM 180c fol, 155n55
Copenhagen, University of Copenhagen, MS AM 180d fol, 155n55
Copenhagen, University of Copenhagen, MS AM 180e fol, 155n55
Copenhagen, University of Copenhagen, MS AM 531, 155n55
Cressingham, Hugh de, 77, 87–89
Crusade and Death of Richard I, The, 123n48
Crusade of Frederick, 42n100
cultural recovery, 2, 7n16, 13, 32, 210n96, 212–13

Davis, Norman, 32n53, 59n177, 59n183, 197n56, 199, 199n68
DeAngelis, Jamie, 178n13
Douce, Francis, 24n24
Duggan, Joseph J., 159n70, 169n107
Dunphy, Graeme, 44n116
Durham, Cathedral Library, MS C.IV.27B, 120n37

"Earl Warenne story," 63–71, 64n14, 84–85, 97
Early English Text Society (EETS), 23–24, 23n20, 35, 49
Edinburgh, Edinburgh University Library, MS 218, 29, 175n1, 188n33, 199–200, 200n69
Edinburgh, National Library of Scotland, MS 873, 25n26, 26n30, 27n35, 28n36
Edinburgh, National Library of Scotland, MS Advocates 19.2.1, 11, 16n2, 19n6, 21, 24n24, 29, 33n61, 59, 120, 136n86, 138, 139n1, 140–54, 157, 160–62, 162n87, 163–64, 170–71, 173, 175, 175n1, 176n2, 176n5, 177n10, 179, 179n16, 184–85, 196–97
Edinburgh, National Library of Scotland, MS Advocates 33.5.3, 68n22
Edinburgh fragments. *See* Edinburgh, Edinburgh University Library, MS 218
Edmund of Woodstock, 131n71
Edward I, king of England, 61–62, 67n17, 76–77, 89–90, 99–100, 102–5, 114, 120, 138, 183
Edward II, king of England, 107, 114, 117–18, 118n29, 127, 130–31, 184

Edward III, king of England, 107, 114–18, 120–22, 126–27, 129, 131, 138, 149, 151, 161n82, 163, 170
Edward IV, king of England, 105
Edwards, A. S. G., 179, 179n16
EETS. *See* Early English Text Society (EETS)
Eleanor of Aquitaine, 131–32, 201, 201n72
Eliot, T. S., 1, 13, 13n22
Ellis, George, 21, 24–28, 24n22, 24n24, 28n36, 30n46, 32–33, 56n169, 139, 141–42
Enikel, Jans, 42–46, 54
Érec et Enide (de Troyes), 154
Estoire de la Guerre Sainte (Ambroise), 123–24, 133–34
excision, 9, 84, 143–44, 181, 190, 198
exemplars, 8, 32n55, 33, 37n82, 51, 56–57, 118, 145, 149n29, 154, 154n50, 156, 159–60, 203
eyre visitations, 77, 77n41, 89–93, 90n86

Faidit, Gaucelm, 134
Fauconberge, Walter de, 93
Finlayson, John, 56n169, 193n47
First Barons' War, 99, 149
First Crusade, 120–22, 122n45
Fischer, Rudolf, 29, 50n142
Fisher, Matthew, 149n29
Floire et Blancheflour, 154
Flores Historiarum, 68n21
Floris and Blancheflour, 154n52
forgery, 88
forms of action, 73–74, 73n31, 74n34–36, 76, 76n40, 81, 81n55, 84n67
Fouke le Fitz Waryn, 21n14
fragmentation, 9, 18, 134–35, 143–44, 148, 180–81, 190, 196–97, 196n55, 199–200, 203, 206
France, Marie de, 154
franchises, 61–62, 61n1, 74n35, 75–76, 87, 95, 99n117
Franz Ferdinand, archduke of Austria, 58
Franz Joseph I, emperor of Austria, 51–53, 52n149, 58
Frederick Barbarossa, 39n89

Friedjung, Heinrich, 55
From Memory to Written Record (Clanchy), 63–64, 64n14, 74n35
Furnivall, F. J., 23n20
Fürstenbuch (Book of Princes) (Enikel), 42–46, 43n104

Gallagher, Eric James, 91–92, 91n87
Geoffrey of Monmouth, 102, 160
Geoffrey of Vinsauf, 79n49
George, Saint, 120–21, 121n41, 122, 130
Gerald of Wales, 202n73
Gesta Regis Henrici Secundi (Roger of Howden), 123
Gesta Regum Anglorum (William of Malmesbury), 121n41
Giancarlo, Matthew, 64n14
Gilbert of Clare, 68, 76n40
Gilbert, Robert, 104
Giles, Saint, 166–70
Gillingham, John, 40n92, 42, 46n126
Gloucester, Gloucestershire Archives, MS D2700/V/I No.8, 58–59, 191–92, 197–200, 199n68
gossip, 5, 10, 28n36, 40
Gray, Thomas, 163n88
Graz, Steiermärkisches Landesarchiv, cod. 89, 42n100
Green, R. F., 64n14
Grey, Reginald de, 101n132
Grierson, Herbert, 25n25, 139n1
Guinevere, legendary queen of Britain, 102, 162–63
Guy of Warwick, 178n13

Haider, Siegfried, 44n112
Hákon Hákonarson IV, 154, 154n51
Hanna, Ralph, 21n14, 113n12, 116n20, 136n86, 138, 140n6, 146n23–146n24, 159, 176n5
"Harleian MS," 24n24
Hearne, Thomas, 114n13, 126n60
Hebron, Malcolm, 109n7
Hegham, Roger, 88–89
Heng, Geraldine, 142–43

Hengist, 160–62, 161n82, 170
Henry I, king of England, 73, 73n32, 85, 90, 99–100
Henry II, king of England, 75, 77n41, 90, 97, 101, 123–25, 132, 201
Henry III, king of England, 75, 76n40, 85–86, 88, 90, 90n86, 98, 120, 128, 128n66, 145, 154
Henry VI, Holy Roman emperor, 33, 46n124, 47
Higgins, Ann, 159
Historia de Expeditione Frederici Imperatoris (attrib. Ansbert), 41
Historia regum Britanniae (Geoffrey of Monmouth), 160
historical fidelity, 33
historical narrative, 27–28, 69
History of English Poetry, The (Warton), 25–26
Holt, J. C., 87n73
Horn, Andrew, 78n45
Horwood, Alfred J., 95n104
House of Fame (Chaucer), 4
Hundred Years' War, 151, 171

Implications of Literacy, The (Stock), 6–7
inheritance, 82–84, 136
Isabella of France, 117, 119n34, 131, 162
Itinerarium peregrinorum, 124–26
Ivanhoe (Scott), 26

James, M. R., 108n4, 193
John, king of England, 98, 102, 135, 185n27
John of Gaunt, 199n68
John of Hessle, 123n47

Karl Magnu Krønike, 155n55, 156n58
Karlamagnús saga (Klm), 153–59, 155n55, 156n58, 161, 165
Kent, Thomas de, 120
Ker, Neil, 59, 141
Kew, The National Archives, CP 40/14, 97
Kew, The National Archives, JUST I/302, 95n104

INDEX

Kew, The National Archives, JUST I/303, 95n104

Kew, The National Archives, JUST I/1050, 82

Kew, The National Archives, JUST I/1076, 85

Kew, The National Archives, JUST I/1093, 87–88, 94

King Richard, 24–25, 59, 141–59, 142n11, 162, 170–71, 173, 175–85, 175n1, 176n5, 177n10, 196–97

Kisch, Wilhelm, 55

knowing readers, 8, 12, 33–34, 39, 114, 129, 144, 160–64, 165n95, 207

Knowles, C. H., 99n118

Koch, Johannes, 35

Kyng Alisaunder, 120, 141

Lachmann, Karl, 209, 209n96

Lacroix, Daniel, 155n55

Laing, David, 30n41, 141

Lancelot, 162–63

Lanercost Chronicle. *See* London, British Library, MS Cotton Claudius D.vii

Langtoft, Peter, 48

Larkin, Peter, 32n55

Lay le Freine, 154n52

legal fictions, 71, 82, 84, 86, 94–97

legal innovations, 100

legal memory, 63, 71, 74n35, 78–82, 84, 84n67, 97–100, 106

Legenda aurea, 167, 167n101, 169

Leopold V, duke of Austria, 39–41, 40n92, 41–46, 46n129, 54

Lincoln, Lincoln Cathedral, MS 91, 27n34

literacy, 5–6, 13, 64

literary criticism, 8, 13, 18, 213

Lloyd, James, 30n42

local literature, 7

local talk, 3, 7–9, 21–22, 29, 33–34, 45, 49, 54, 56, 67–69, 92–94, 143–44, 149, 162–63, 181, 196

London, British Library, MS Additional 31042, 30–31, 31n50–31n51, 39n87, 109n9, 114n13, 192–95, 204–5, 205n85

London, British Library, MS Additional 47680, 109n9, 114n13, 115–16, 118

London, British Library, MS Cotton Claudius D.vii, 68n22

London, British Library, MS Cotton Domitian A.xiii, 133n75

London, British Library, MS Cotton Faustina B.vi, 150n35

London, British Library, MS Cotton Julius D.ix, 168n103

London, British Library, MS Egerton 2862, 19n5, 30, 33n61, 191–92, 196–98, 197n56–197n59, 198n62–198n63, 204

London, British Library, MS Harley 978, 150n53

London, British Library, MS Harley 2253, 150n33, 182, 203

London, British Library, MS Harley 2277, 168

London, British Library, MS Harley 4690, 30, 57, 191–94, 204

London, British Library, MS Lansdowne 239, 67–68. See also *Chronicle* (Walter of Guisborough)

London, British Library, MS Royal 12 C.xii, 160n75

London, College of Arms, MS Arundel 58, 30, 30n42, 57, 186, 191–95, 203–4

London Thornton. *See* London, British Library, MS Additional 31042

London, University of London, Senate House Library, MS 593, 141n9

Loomis, Laura Hibbard, 153n47, 159, 178n13, 193n47

Loomis, Roger Sherman, 31n46, 34–35, 37n79, 49–50, 58, 193, 210

Loud, G. A., 41n97

Lydgate, John, 206n89

Lysons, David, 105n47

Maddicott, J. R. 150n35

Magna Carta, 98–99, 149

Magnus of Reichersberg, 42

Magnússon, Árni, 156

Maines, Clark, 170

Maitland, F. W., 73n31

Mannying, Robert, 48, 59, 145, 146n23

Marcus, Leah S., 210n96
Markus, Manfred, 50n142
Matthew Paris, 48, 83n65, 130n69
Matthews, David, 182n23
Medieval Oral Literature (Reichl), 7n15
Merlin, 160–61
Merton, Statute of, 72, 74, 82
Metrical Romances of the Thirteenth, Fourteenth, and Fifteenth Centuries (Weber), 25, 49
Michael, M. A., 115n18
Milemete, Walter de, 114, 116, 116n20, 118, 119n32, 119n34
Miller, Jennifer, 196n55
Mittelenglische Versroman über Richard Löwenherz, Der. See *Richard Löwenherz*
modularity, 67–68, 134–35, 143–44, 169, 194–96, 202n77, 203–4, 206, 209
Moinage Guillaume, 155
Monastery, The (Scott), 26
Montfort, Simon de, 99, 149, 149n32, 150n33–150n34, 183
Montrose (Scott), 26
Mortimer, Roger, 117, 162–63
Multon, Lambert de, 193n47

narrations of descent, 78–80, 81n55, 82n61, 83, 83n64, 84–87, 89, 95, 98, 102, 104, 132
New York, The Morgan Library, MA 426.16, 25n25, 26n30, 139n1, 202n72
Norman Conquest, 62n4, 71, 84, 97, 97n111

Of Arthur and of Merlin, 161
Olsen, Donald J., 54
Ong, Walter J., 5n10
oral transmission, 165n94, 192
orality, 5–7, 13, 64–65
Order of the Garter, 121
Oslo, Norsk Riksarkivet, MS 61, 155n55
Oslo, Norsk Riksarkivet, MS 62, 155n55
Oslo, Norsk Riksarkivet, MS 63, 155n55
Osney-Abingdon compilations, 67
Otuel, A Knight, 159, 176n5
Oxford, Bodleian Library, MS Ashmole 43, 168

Oxford, Bodleian Library, MS Digby 23, 153, 164
Oxford, Bodleian Library, MS Digby 168, 67n17
Oxford, Bodleian Library, MS Digby 170, 67n17
Oxford, Bodleian Library, MS Douce 228, 25n27, 30, 57, 191, 192–95, 203–4
Oxford, Bodleian Library, MS Fairfax 10, 123n48
Oxford, Bodleian Library, MS Laud Misc. 108, 167n102
Oxford, Bodleian Library, MS Laud Misc. 463, 168n103
Oxford, Bodleian Library, MS Rawlinson B.180, 126n60
Oxford, Christ Church, MS 92, 107–32, 109n5, 110 fig. 1a, 111 fig. 1b, 112 fig. 2, 114n13, 136–38, 145–47, 181

Paris, Bibliothèque de l'Arsenal, MS 3142, 157n61
Paris, Bibliothèque nationale, MS fr. 571, 115, 115n18, 118, 119n34
Parkes, Malcolm B., 176n5
Parry, Andrew, 198n65
Paston, John, II, 59
Pèlerinage de Charlemagne, 155
Perceval (de Troyes), 154
Philip Augustus of France, 125–26, 131–32, 135, 146
Philippa of Hainault, 115, 117, 119n34, 131n72
plea rolls and records, 63, 65, 71, 81, 83n64–65, 84, 86, 89, 91–93, 91n87, 100
Poetria nova, 79n49
Political Songs (Wright), 182
Polonius, Martinus, 63n6
Postman, Leo, 10n20
Powicke, F. M., 105–6, 105n146, 150n38
Prague, Strahov Monastery Library, MS DF III 1/4, 41n96
Prestwich, Michael, 61n2, 62n4, 122n45
proleptic reading, 144, 177
Pseudo-Turpin, 155
Purfoote, Thomas, 21

Quit-Claim of Canterbury, 103
quo warranto, 61–64, 61n1, 62n4, 64–82, 85–94, 99, 104, 106, 129–30, 134

Ralph of Coggeshall, 87n74
Reading, abbot of, 92, 95–96
Reichl, Karl, 7n15
Rejhon, Annalee C., 155n54
remembering: as term, 81n57
representative texts, 9, 13, 18, 181, 207
retrospective inheritance, 82–83
retrospective texts, 12, 18, 22, 28–29, 34, 132, 134, 143, 148–49, 165, 173, 180–81, 189–90, 195–96, 208, 210
Richard Coeur de Lion: "collective authoring" of, 142–43; copies of, 29–31, 33, 143, 157, 180–81, 190–96; fragmentation and, 196–99; history of, 21–22; as marginalized, 22–24; and modular form, 194–96; and Oxford, Christ Church, MS 92, 113, 136, 136n86; as retrospective text, 18, 195–96; rumor and, 16–20, 181, 185, 187, 189–90, 194, 208–9; title of, 20–21. See also *King Richard*; *Richard Löwenherz*; *individual shelfmarks of manuscript copies*
Richard I, king of England: arrest and imprisonment of, 10, 33, 33n59, 39–40, 39n87, 40n92, 41–48, 46n124, 51, 55, 135, 172; in Chertsey Tiles, 128–29; choice of, as focus, 10, 12; in Christ Church 92, 136–38; Christ Church 92 and, 122–23; Edward I and, 103–4; Edward II and, 127–28; in *Itinerarium peregrinorum*, 125–26; in *King Richard*, 147–48, 158–59; *quo warranto* and, 71, 75, 75n38, 78–80, 85–89; in *Richard Coeur de Lion*, 18–21; in *Richard Löwenherz*, 38–45, 46n124, 47–48, 54–55; in Third Crusade, 122–23; in *Vita Edwardi Secundi*, 126–27
Richard Löwenherz, 28–40, 32n53, 36n74, 38n85, 48–52, 56–59, 142n111, 178, 187n31, 187n33, 188–90, 210
Richard of Cornwall, 183–84
Richard of Devizes, 132–33, 133n76, 134–35, 195
Ritson, Joseph, 28n36
Robert of Gloucester, 59, 68n21, 134–35, 134n80, 135–36, 145, 172, 173n118, 195, 203
Rock, The (Eliot), 13n22

Roger le Bigod, 85
Roger of Howden, 47–48, 87n74, 123, 123n47–123n48, 134n80, 136, 200
Rogers, Randall, 122n45
Roland and Vernagu, 159, 176n5
Rolls Series, 23, 23n19
Roman de toute chevalrie, Le (de Kent), 120, 120n37
Roman de Tristan, 154
Rothwell, Harry, 68–69
rumor, 71; calcification of, 26–27; Charlemagne, 164–65; conditions for, 10n20; "core," 180–81, 185–90, 192–94, 206; Edward II and, 117–18; eyre visitation and, 91–92; history writing and, 26–28, 133–34; identity and, 186–88; inheritance and, 83; *King Richard* and, 147–48; and *Richard Coeur de Lion*, 181–82, 185; *Richard Coeur de Lion* and, 16–18; Richard I as, 10, 104; *Richard Löwenherz* and, 48–49, 51, 54, 56, 58; Richard of Devizes and, 133–34; Roger of Howden and, 47–48; text as, 20–21; text-makers and, 195–96; Third Crusade and, 79–80

Saladin, Yusuf ibn Ayyub, sultan of Egypt and Syria, 40, 79, 103, 123–24, 128–29, 128n66, 194, 205–6, 211
Sandler, Lucy Freeman, 108n4, 116n20
Saracen: as term, 16n1
Sayers, Jane, 101n131
Scalacronica (Gray), 163n88
Scattergood, John, 182n23
Schellekens, Philida M. T. A., 56n168, 180n19, 193n47
scholarly editions, 9, 18, 22, 34, 56, 209–10, 209n96
Schorske, Carl, 53
Schottenkloster (Vienna), 44, 44n114
Scott, Walter, 21, 24–27, 24n22, 33, 56, 139–42, 139n1
Scribe 1 (Auchinleck manuscript), 149, 149n29, 153, 159–63, 175n2, 176–78, 176n5, 177n7–8, 184
Second Barons' War, 62n5, 68n21, 98, 103, 121, 149n33, 150–51, 150n34, 183
Secretum secretorum (Aristotle), 115–16, 115n17, 119, 119n34

Selby, abbot of, 94
Short, Ian, 165n95
Short Chronicle. See *Anonymous Short English Metrical Chronicle*
Siege of Jerusalem, 27n34
Simonie, The, 175–76, 175n2, 176n5, 178, 184–85
Sir Tristrem, 154n52, 159
Smithers, G. V., 136n86, 141, 149n29
"Song Against the King of Almaigne, The," 149n33, 150n33, 182
South English Legendary (SEL), 167–69, 167n102, 168n103, 195
Specimens of Early English Metrical Romances (Ellis), 24n22, 25–28, 30n46
St. Andrews fragments. *See* St. Andrews, University Library *entries*
St. Andrews, University Library, MS PR2065 A.15, 141, 141n9, 175n1, 200
St. Andrews, University Library, MS PR 2065 R.4, 59, 141, 141n9, 175n1, 200
Stephen, king of England, 99–100
Stock, Brian, 6–7
Stubbs, William, 123n48
Sutherland, Donald, 84, 84n67, 90n85

Tageno, 41n97
Talisman, The (Scott), 26
talk: as exemplar and gloss, 8, 145; as field of study, 5; generation of, by texts, 163–64; and historical periodization, 2–3, 9–10; history and, 68–69; identity and, 185; and image, 8, 79, 113–14, 145–47, 147n26; local, 3, 7–9, 21–22, 29, 33–34, 45, 49, 54, 56, 67–69, 92–94, 143–44, 149, 162–63, 181, 196; ongoing, 9–10, 20; public, 11, 65, 71, 89, 91, 113, 132, 191; sound and, 4; and sound studies, 5, 5n8; suppression of, 168–69; text and, interplay between, 19–20; textual production and, 34
Tancred of Sicily, 19–20, 126, 203n77
Taylor, John, 69n25
text: and images, 113–14, 128, 136–38, 141, 145–47, 203n79; representative, 9, 13, 18, 181, 207; retrospective, 12, 18, 22, 28–29, 34, 132, 134, 143, 148–49, 165, 173, 180–81, 189–90, 195–96, 208, 210; as rumor, 20–21; sound and, 5–6; talk and,

interplay between, 19–20; theoretical, 21, 142n11
text-maker: as term, 18–19
Third Crusade, 10, 13, 39, 79–80, 99, 103, 121–24, 129, 132–35, 138, 145, 171–72, 185n26, 196, 200
Thomas of Lancaster, 184
Thomas of Lydell, 131n71
Thornton, abbot of, 87–89
Thornton, Robert, 27n34, 30, 192
Tiptoft, John, 105
Tokyo, Keio University, MS 170.X.9.11, 123n50
Tristram, E. W., 121n41
Troilus and Criseyde (Chaucer), 3–5, 3n2, 210
Trouillot, Michel-Rolph, 212
Troyes, Chrétien de, 154
Turville-Petre, Thorlac, 161n82, 162n87, 186n30
Tyerman, Christopher, 124, 171, 171n113

Unger, C. R., 155n55

Vale, Juliet, 102–3
variants, 30–31, 56, 67–70, 210
Vatican City, Biblioteca Apostolica Vaticana, MS Reg. lat. 1659, 123n50, 134
Vie de Charlemagne, 154
Vie de saint Gilles, 167, 167n100
Vienna, 21, 28–29, 33–34, 39, 40–45, 49, 51–53, 52n149, 53–54, 53n153, 54–55, 54n162, 55–56, 55n164, 58–60, 104, 143
Vita Aegidii, 167
Vita Edwardi Secundi, 126–27, 126n60, 127n61–127n62
Voragine, Jacobus de, 167
Vortigern, 160–61

Wagner, Otto, 53n153
Wake, Baldwin, 85–86
Wallace, William, 62n5
wall paintings, 79n50, 103, 120n38, 121n41, 128–29
Walpole, Ronald, 159
Walter, Hubert, 100–102

Walter of Coutances, 47n133
Walter of Guisborough, 62, 63n6, 66, 66n16, 67–69, 77n42
Warenne, John de, 62–65, 62n5, 68–69, 68n21, 75, 81, 183
War on Terror, 211–12
Warton, Thomas, 25–26
Weber, Henry, 25, 49
Westminster, Statute of, 71–72, 82, 98, 183
William I, king of England, 62n4, 85, 130n69, 161
William of Longchamp, 125
William of Malmesbury, 121n41
William of Newburgh, 63n6, 125n55, 172n116
windmills, 108–9, 110 fig. 1a, 111 fig. 1b, 146–47, 146n23, 158, 181, 183–84
Worde, Wynkyn de, 16n2, 24n24, 31; 1509 edition of, 24n24, 29, 31, 31n52, 37n82, 38–39, 56–57, 202, 202n76
Wright, Thomas, 134n80, 182
Wright, William Aldis, 134n80

Yvain (de Troyes), 154

Zettl, Ewald, 146n19–20, 149n29
Zouche, Alan de, 68n21

INTERVENTIONS: NEW STUDIES IN MEDIEVAL CULTURE
Ethan Knapp, Series Editor

Interventions: New Studies in Medieval Culture publishes theoretically informed work in medieval literary and cultural studies. We are interested both in studies of medieval culture and in work on the continuing importance of medieval tropes and topics in contemporary intellectual life.

Talk and Textual Production in Medieval England
    MARISA LIBBON

Scripting the Nation: Court Poetry and the Authority of History in Late Medieval Scotland
    KATHERINE H. TERRELL

Medieval Things: Agency, Materiality, and Narratives of Objects in Medieval German Literature and Beyond
    BETTINA BILDHAUER

Death and the Pearl Maiden: Plague, Poetry, England
    DAVID K. COLEY

Political Appetites: Food in Medieval English Romance
    AARON HOSTETTER

Invention and Authorship in Medieval England
    ROBERT R. EDWARDS

Challenging Communion: The Eucharist and Middle English Literature
    JENNIFER GARRISON

Chaucer on Screen: Absence, Presence, and Adapting the Canterbury Tales
    EDITED BY KATHLEEN COYNE KELLY AND TISON PUGH

Chaucer, Gower, and the Affect of Invention
    STEELE NOWLIN

Fragments for a History of a Vanishing Humanism
    EDITED BY MYRA SEAMAN AND EILEEN A. JOY

The Medieval Risk-Reward Society: Courts, Adventure, and Love in the European Middle Ages
    WILL HASTY

The Politics of Ecology: Land, Life, and Law in Medieval Britain
    EDITED BY RANDY P. SCHIFF AND JOSEPH TAYLOR

The Art of Vision: Ekphrasis in Medieval Literature and Culture
    EDITED BY ANDREW JAMES JOHNSTON, ETHAN KNAPP, AND MARGITTA ROUSE

Desire in the Canterbury Tales
    ELIZABETH SCALA

Imagining the Parish in Late Medieval England
    ELLEN K. RENTZ

Truth and Tales: Cultural Mobility and Medieval Media
　EDITED BY FIONA SOMERSET AND NICHOLAS WATSON

Eschatological Subjects: Divine and Literary Judgment in Fourteenth-Century French Poetry
　J. M. MOREAU

Chaucer's (Anti-)Eroticisms and the Queer Middle Ages
　TISON PUGH

Trading Tongues: Merchants, Multilingualism, and Medieval Literature
　JONATHAN HSY

Translating Troy: Provincial Politics in Alliterative Romance
　ALEX MUELLER

Fictions of Evidence: Witnessing, Literature, and Community in the Late Middle Ages
　JAMIE K. TAYLOR

Answerable Style: The Idea of the Literary in Medieval England
　EDITED BY FRANK GRADY AND ANDREW GALLOWAY

Scribal Authorship and the Writing of History in Medieval England
　MATTHEW FISHER

Fashioning Change: The Trope of Clothing in High- and Late-Medieval England
　ANDREA DENNY-BROWN

Form and Reform: Reading across the Fifteenth Century
　EDITED BY SHANNON GAYK AND KATHLEEN TONRY

How to Make a Human: Animals and Violence in the Middle Ages
　KARL STEEL

Revivalist Fantasy: Alliterative Verse and Nationalist Literary History
　RANDY P. SCHIFF

Inventing Womanhood: Gender and Language in Later Middle English Writing
　TARA WILLIAMS

Body Against Soul: Gender and Sowlehele *in Middle English Allegory*
　MASHA RASKOLNIKOV

www.ingramcontent.com/pod-product-compliance
Lightning Source LLC
Chambersburg PA
CBHW030109010526
44116CB00005B/170